DUST IN A DARK CONTINENT

By the same author:-

The Benefits Racket
Down Among the Dossers
The Decline of an English Village
The Hunter and the Hunted
Weather-forecasting the Country Way
Cures and Remedies the Country Way
Animal Cures the Country Way
Weeds the Country Way
The Journal of a Country Parish
Journeys into Britain
The Country Way of Love
The Wildlife of the Royal Estates
A Fox's Tale
The Fox and the Orchid.

Children's Books

How the Fox got its Pointed Nose
How the Heron got Long Legs

DUST IN A DARK CONTINENT

by

Robin Page

The Claridge Press
London and Lexington

All rights reserved. No part of this publication may be reproduced or transmitted in any form or by an means, including photocopying and recording, without the written permission of the copyright holder, application for which should be addressed to the Publishers. Such written permission must also be obtained before any part of this publication is stored in a retrieval system of any nature.

First published in Great Britain 1989

by The Claridge Press
43 Queen's Gardens
London W2
and Box 420
Lexington
Georgia 30648

Copyright © Robin Page 1989

Typeset by
Wordsmiths Typesetting Ltd
London N1
and printed by
Short Run Press
Exeter, Devon

ISBN 1-870626-90-7

Page, Robin: *Dust in a Dark Continent*

1. Travel

To my Father, for his example, his humour,
his eccentricity and his friendship; as
well as for giving me some of his vision
of Africa.

Also to Elspeth Huxley and Sir Laurens
van der Post with gratitude – and to the
memory of George Adamson.

Apart from people such as George Adamson and Michaela Denis – the names of most of the characters in this book have been made up. Any similarity between them and anybody in Africa with the same name and occupation is entirely coincidental.

Contents

The Africa of Others	11
Introduction	15
1. Sowing the Seed	19
2. Dutch and English	45
3. Sweet and Sour	63
4. Home and Away	81
5. Bush War	89
6. The Convoy	121
7. Desert Interlude	147
8. Leopard and Lion	167
9. Warnings of Drought	201
10. The Booze Cruise	221
11. Waiting for Madagafufu	237
12. Arrival in Wonderland	269
13. The Great Dictator	293
14. The New King	311
15. The Last Laager	319
Reflections	339
Final Thoughts	345
Acknowledgements	347

The Africa of Others

Journeys into Africa is how you want to see Africa; never come and live here.

Anon

Looking back on a sojourn in the African highlands, you are struck by your feeling of having lived for a time up in the air. The sky was rarely more than pale blue or violet, with a profusion of mighty, weightless, ever-changing clouds towering up and sailing on it, but it had a blue vigour in it, and at short distance it painted the ranges of hills and the woods afresh deep blue. In the middle of the day the air was alive over the land, like a flame burning; it scintillated, waved and shone like running water, mirrored and doubled all objects, and created great Fata Morgana. Up in this high air you breathed easily, drawing in a vital assurance and lightness of heart. In the highlands you woke up in the morning and thought: Here I am, where I ought to be.

Karen Blixen, Out of Africa 1937

All day long we saw game of many different kinds. The animals were still there in unsuspecting millions, they did not know that they were doomed. Tommies with their broad black insignia wagged their tails as if the world belonged to them, giraffe bent their patchwork necks towards the small spearing acacias. No one has ever seen a thin zebra, although they are stuffed with parasites; these were no exception. They looked like highly varnished animated toys. It would be tedious to list all the kinds of animals we passed.

Elspeth Huxley, The Flame Trees of Thika 1959

Even since I can remember I have been struck by the profound quality of melancholy which lies at the heart of the physical scene in

Southern Africa. I recollect clearly asking my father once: 'Why do the vlaktes and koppies always look so sad?' He replied with unexpected feeling: 'The sadness is not in the plains and hills but in ourselves.'

> Laurens van der Post, *The Lost World of the Kalahari* 1958

On my first evening, when a port official had led me to the edge of the desert, and asked me to look at it, I asked him what lay above, below, and out beyond us. 'Nothing!' he said, with a note of hysteria in his voice. 'It's just miles, and miles, and miles – and MILES! – of Sweet Fanny Adams!'

> Negley Farson, *Behind God's Back* 1940

For Llewelyn (Powys), Africa was 'a country frequented by clawed creatures with striped and gilded pelts, where nettles sting like wasps and even moles are large as water-rats.' Worse than that it was a continent where 'the sun, naked as when it was born, sucks out one's life blood, and nourishes savagery long since made dormant by the pious lives of ones ancestors.' 'Kill! Kill! Kill! is the mandate of Africa.'

> Quoted by Elspeth Huxley, in *Out in the Midday Sun – My Kenya* 1985

Introduction

Of all the books that I have written, this one has undoubtedly been the hardest to write. The problems have not simply arisen out of travelling from one continent to another; or from the need to be at home on the farm during springtime and harvest, so necessitating several visits to Africa, instead of one long journey. They have been far deeper, for in facing the great beauties, contradictions and frustrations of Africa, I have inevitably become involved personally – emotionally, intellectually and even spiritually – with what I saw and felt. The problems of Africa are age-old and will not be solved in my lifetime; yet, despite the endemic violence, conflict, struggle and despair, its landscape, peoples and wildlife have always had a deep fascination for the European mind, and this too will go on for as long as man continues to inhabit the planet.

Dust in a Dark Continent is not an historical or political assessment of post-colonial Africa, for numerous such books have already been written, some completely re-writing history for the sake of convenience or fashion. Neither is it an effort to climb on to any bandwagons to combat famine, or the conflicts of race, for my journeys into Africa were started before Africa became the sudden focus of world attention and popular efforts of aid. It is a personal view of Africa, based on a number of visits that followed years of interest and a period in my early life when the whole family almost moved to pre-independent Kenya.

My 'journeys' depended on time and opportunity, with the old colonial countries of East and Central Africa being my main aim, although my first visit was to Zaire in 1974, followed by Rhodesia and South Africa in 1976 and 1979. It was only after those initial trips that I decided to write a book. But history in Africa is moving more rapidly than ever before, and since those early visits Rhodesia, then an 'illegal regime' at the height of its bush war, has become the independent black state of Zimbabwe and the full storm has moved further south. Consequently, although my original intention was to write about Africa since 1980, I have included those earlier visits, for they help to put later events and attitudes into perspective.

Because of the number of journeys, I have telescoped some into one visit, for the sake of the narrative and to avoid repetition. However, the events, conversations and observations have not been changed. I have altered several minor details, as well as the names of most of the people, simply to protect their identities. Sadly, most of Africa does not permit the same freedoms of speech, thought and action that we still enjoy in Britain: identification could therefore put them in real physical danger, either now or in the future.

The rest remains as I experienced it, recounted as accurately as possible. Unfortunately 'truth' is not always appreciated when applied to race and Africa, and sadly, if the political climate at the time of writing persists beyond publication, *Dust in a Dark Continent* may well be banned in several places north and south of the Limpopo River. It could make it unpopular, as well as unfashionable, in the West too; if that is the price I have to pay for attempting to be honest, then I will just have to pay it.

1. Sowing the Seed

It is difficult to remember when precisely the seeds for these journeys were sown; all that I know for certain is that they germinated early and their roots go back deep into my childhood. Wild animals in picture books were often associated with Africa or India, and many favourite stories also focused on one continent or the other. Little Black Sambo outwitted tigers and so was said to be Indian, while I always placed Little Black Quibba, possibly quite wrongly, firmly in Africa, where he encountered an evil green snake in a mango tree. Both books gave me much pleasure, with their simple plots and happy endings made real by illustrations that even now retain their charm.

The small tattered volumes are still in the bookcase of our farmhouse, but it is an indication of how fashions and interpretations have changed that in many homes and schools these tales, that once fed an interest in distant lands, have now been branded 'racist'. As a consequence, some children are denied part of the innocence of childhood, in which all races and colours are part of the same extended human family.

Another book that I loved, and which my mother would sometimes read to me on cold winter evenings, was Rudyard Kipling's *The Just So Stories*, my favourite being *The Elephant's Child*, or *How The Elephant Got Its Trunk* – a drama that took place 'on the banks of the great grey-green, greasy Limpopo River'. It gave me a view of the African 'jungle' that even then I wanted to turn into reality during later life. A degree of reality came on Sunday School outings to Whipsnade Zoo; there in the flesh were the animals of the African plains, rivers and mud-holes – zebra, giraffe, lion, monkey, crocodile and hippopotamus.

The 'natives' were another part of the early attraction and I was fascinated by the first black men I met. They were two West Indian airmen who, immediately after the Second World War, worked in an RAF bomb store, 'the dump', just outside my home parish. Often they would attend the small Baptist chapel in the High Street on Sunday afternoons, and afterwards come into the farmhouse for tea. They always struck me as being unusually happy, laughing people and I would sit on the lap of Mr James and run my fingers through his short fuzzy hair, which to me was quite extraordinary. Even then we heard how the ancestors of Mr James had been taken as slaves from Africa to the West Indies and America, to harvest sugar cane and cotton.

Stories of slavery, discovery and adventure were continued in the classroom of the village school, where the predominant colour in my atlas was red – depicting the countries of the British Empire. We heard of the great explorers – Livingstone and Stanley – and learnt where cocoa beans and bananas came from, as well as how they were grown. Whenever the King and Queen visited their dominions, we would follow their journeys, which for Africa would mean scrapbooks gradually filling with pictures of mud huts, coconuts, wild animals and the spectacular tribal gatherings that welcomed the head of the Empire.

We learnt still more in the chapel, and every year a real live missionary would visit. Invariably those from Africa had stories to tell of witch doctors, lepers, snakes, and crocodiles. One, a medical doctor, was an authority on the 'talking' drums of the Congo, while another who had been a school friend of my father worked in Angola. After the service he spoke at length about the great natural beauty and wealth of the Portuguese colony and, as if to confirm his story, he produced postage stamps, bearing the pictures of exotic animals and birds.

The missionaries were not simply 'spreading the word of God', they were teaching, running hospitals and clinics, and encouraging the native peoples to produce food more efficiently; they were continuing the work started by Moffatt and Livingstone, whose lives and example were symbolised by Albert Schweitzer, still working as a doctor in the depths of the West African 'jungle'. Books on Livingstone's journeys were in the bookcase of the farmhouse as well as other books on the pioneers of old Africa, such as 'Mackay of Uganda', and 'C.T. Studd', the cricketer turned missionary.

The books that really fired my imagination were about 'The Jungle Doctor', an Australian medical missionary, Paul White, working in Africa. There, he was in constant peril: he was attacked by lions, harassed by witch doctors and confronted by snakes, all while coping with a constant stream of requests for 'Bwana' to attend one crisis after another. I received my first 'Jungle Doctor' book, *Jungle Doctor on Safari*, at the age of nine as a Sunday School prize for 'good attendance'. Shortly afterwards a programme called *On Safari* appeared on television, introduced by an astonishing couple, Armand and Michaela Denis. They became household names and each week I would eagerly wait for the words, 'And now, on Safari with Armand and Michaela Denis', which heralded their arrival on to the screen of our small nine-inch black and white television set. He was tall, moustached, with a heavy continental accent; while she was a sophisticated blonde with a cultured voice of indeterminate origin. In retrospect their programmes, full of fierce looking tribesmen, impenetrable jungles, and herds of stampeding animals were contrived; but at that time, they took the 'real Africa' into millions of homes for the first time. They aroused in many a sense of adventure and the desire to travel, and they were among the pioneers of wildlife on television.

At this time too I saw a genuine jungle doctor, for Albert Schweitzer visited Cambridge to become an Honorary Doctor of Law. My mother took me and my younger sister Rachael to the University Senate House to see the great man on 22nd October 1955. From the gallery we had a fine view of the old, white-haired missionary, with his matching moustache. Although he was 80 years old, he still returned to his hospital at Lambarene in Gabon, to work and to die. The whole ceremony was in Latin and I did not understand a word, but I felt a deep sense of privilege to see a man who really had become a legend in his own lifetime.

So, by the age of 12, Africa had become firmly implanted in my imagination; I saw it as an ancient continent of vast open spaces where animals and Man still roamed free. It was a place too for travellers and adventurers, as well as for missionaries, dedicated men and women who gave up the comforts and security of Europe to fight disease and superstition under the hot African sun.

The following year dreams promised to become a reality, for father suddenly announced that he was going to Kenya for three months, and if he liked it we would all be leaving our small Cambridgeshire farm for a larger one in the White Highlands of Kenya. The news came as a complete surprise, but it was entirely in keeping with Father, that he should decide to fulfil a long-held ambition just at a time when it was unfashionable to become a 'white settler', and the words 'colonialist' and 'empire' had already become disreputable. To make things worse the Mau Mau rebellion was not completely over; it had started among the Kikuyu in 1952, and in 1956 when he decided to visit, the army had only just withdrawn from active operations.

At home he was buying the farm, struggling with both the unyielding soil and a bank overdraft, and so when he saw the advertisement in *The Farmer and Stockbreeder* placed by the European Agricultural Settlement Board wanting settlers with £5,000, it was an opportunity too good to miss. By selling the farm he would receive enough money to go to Kenya, wipe out his overdraft, and have some to spare. It would get him away from the cold, damp English winters, as well as the heavy clay. He could start again with a large farm, and, as he saw it, not only would he be farming but he would be helping to teach the natives how to improve their land, while my mother, a teacher, would be running her own farm school for their children. It was hardly a vision of 'exploitation' – making quick and easy money out of the Africans, which is the caricature of the 'White Settler' often taught today.

From the outset I did not want to go – the Africa of my imagination was fine, but the reality of Kenya, Mau Mau, and all held little appeal. My world had become one in which the most important thing was cricket – playing it, watching it and discussing it; it seemed to me that cricket in Kenya would be second-rate and my mind was made up. I wanted to remain at home with my friends and, more importantly, my cricket bat. I did not want to see Father go either and it was a sad day, at the end of May, when we took him to the London Air Terminal, where he caught a BOAC (The British Overseas Airways Corporation) bus to 'London Airport' – Heathrow.

The first generation of settlers to Kenya, including Elspeth Huxley, travelled by boat, train and ox-wagon. The second generation, including Father, travelled by plane, which was still quite an experience. Father's flight was in a four-engined Argonaught and by today's standards he hedge-hopped his way to Kenya, stopping at Rome, Cairo, Khartoum, Entebbe and finally Nairobi. It took more than a day – much faster than his return journey with the Air Work Company; then he travelled in a twin-engined plane that flew low along the great valleys of the Sahara, stopping for whole nights at Wadi Halfa and Malta.

He was away for three months, and although he sold some of the dairy cows to raise money for his trip, there was still much work to be done in his absence. The farm was run by Mother, with my brother John milking the cattle before and after school, and various uncles dropping in to offer help and advice. We eagerly awaited letters and I sent long epistles about cricket – almost ball by ball commentaries on the England v Australia Test Matches.

On his return it was immediately obvious that the reality of Kenya was even more attractive to him than his original vision and his mind was made up; we would be moving to Kenya. His stories were of large fertile farms, the friendliness of the Kikuyu and the Masai, the mountains, plains and clear air, as well as Lake Nakuru, pink with flamingos. He spent long periods of time talking quietly with Mother and then the day I feared finally arrived; a 'For Sale' notice was put on the field gate, announcing our departure. It was a traumatic time; people in the village were continually asking when we intended to go and did I really want to leave? A trickle of potential buyers also arrived, prying behind every nook and cranny, some seemingly criticising, others admiring. When a baldheaded sculptor and his wife appeared at the door, the end was obviously near; he was not interested in the land or the animals, but was attracted by the house, its thatch and antiquity; a wall could be knocked out here, a window added there, and 'that would make a fine place for my studio'. He made an offer which Father accepted, leaving only the contract to be signed.

I was devastated; I would be leaving more than cricket after all – the fields I loved to roam, the small brook, the dogs who were my constant companions and the whole village which was my home. Mother, too, clearly had worries about severing her long local roots and for the first and only time during my childhood the farmhouse held an atmosphere of tension, misery and doubt.

The climax came on a warm, sunny morning; I was, as usual, playing cricket on the lawn with a friend, before briefly going into the house. Mother and Father were in each others arms crying – crying over Africa: Father because he wanted to live there, Mother because she did not. For the sake of his family Father cancelled the sale, the notice was taken down, and we were to stay.

Things did not return immediately to normal, for Father's dreams had been shattered. For months there was a deep sadness about him, and even in later years he was sure that he had made the wrong decision. His despondency was compounded by hardship, for in anticipation of our move he had allowed the farm to run down and the overdraft to grow. As a result several years followed of hard physical work with little financial reward.

But although it was a disturbing time for me, as well as for the rest of the family, it reinforced my interest in Africa and, ironically, once we had decided not to go, I was more curious to see the country that had affected my father so deeply. The experience also allowed me to feel for the first time the real emotional ties of land and farm, as well as family; the same feelings that many 'settlers' were soon to feel as 'the wind of change' swept independence into most African countries, forcing the Europeans, often with much bitterness and financial loss, to move elsewhere.

* * * * * * *

My first opportunity to visit Africa came in 1974, when my sister Rachael went to work in a mission hospital, deep in the equatorial rain forest of Zaire, and I decided to visit her. It was a country where the 'wind of change' had arrived suddenly, in the early sixties, fanning the fires of prejudice and injustice into an orgy of bloodshed and death. With little warning, the Belgians withdrew from their huge Congo colony, leaving a vacuum filled by violence. Civil war, mercenary action, abduction and murder followed, on a grand scale. The mission station that Rachael joined had been abandoned and over-run, as that part of Africa reverted to its primitive past, with the help of sophisticated modern weapons of destruction from the 'civilized' West. Eventually an army officer seized control, to become President Mobutu Sese Seko; the country was renamed Zaire, the River Congo became the Zaire, and the currency was based on the Zaire. By the time I arrived, Zaire, the country, 900,000 square miles of it, had returned to peace. The missionaries, too, had gone back to resume their work of helping and 'saving' the people.

As always my journey was tense, for I hate flying, and each year still more flights make it no easier. My condition was not helped at Brussels airport where the Boeing 707 was parked outside the departure lounge for five hours after the scheduled time of take-off. Engineers had one engine in pieces and it seemed to me that they could not remember how to put it back together again. Eventually the engine was reassembled and, 17 years after Africa had first appeared on the horizon as a possible, but unwanted destination, I was travelling to see it for myself with a sense of eager anticipation.

The initial feel and smell of Africa was everything I had expected; on reaching the aircraft's steps I was embraced by warmth, with humid air holding the pungent, sweet but bitter smell that seems to pervade the whole continent – it contains heat and dust, storm and rain, fire, wind, mystery, and scented flowers. Floodlights lit the electric night and large bats followed the dizzy flight of countless dazzled insects.

Once in the airport buildings I encountered something else that I have now come to expect from Africa – a slow-moving queue to a desk, where a bored, reclining official, wearing a uniform that gave him power, was looking at passports. With some he found fault – questioning and considering at a pace that showed time to be an irrelevance – at others he simply gazed imperiously and waved the owners through. He looked at mine carefully and thoughtfully, turning over every page with an air of bureaucratic power, before handing it back and allowing me to pass; he had been studying it upside down.

The only thing the throng of arguing taxi-drivers were interested in was money, with hands clutching at bags and urgent requests, in French, for custom. The fare being demanded in Zaires was excessive – airport taxi-drivers are the same the world over – but my appalling French took the urgency out of the situation by giving the false impression of casual indifference. Eventually I isolated one driver, laughed at his exhorbitant fare and in return offered him £3 sterling – apparently a highly illegal transaction. He readily agreed and soon we were rattling into Kinshasa in his clapped out Triumph. How a car could rattle along a road so smooth I could not work out in the darkness for, as is customary in the Third World, the road from the airport to the capital was impressive. It was a rich twentieth-century artery, pushing life and wealth through poverty, the inevitable sprawl of townships and squatter camps at Kinshasa's edge. An overcrowded jumble of mud walls, thatch and corrugated iron were divided by litter-strewn dirt roads and paths where rural Africans of the timeless Third World had been sucked into the great throbbing city, reaching for the First World; they had dreamed of streets paved not with gold but transistor radios and office jobs, the artefacts of modern status and success. Instead, most had found poverty, exchanging rural subsistence, freedom and dignity, for urban slums, overcrowding and squalor.

Once through the outer ring came the city's centre of lights, flats, construction sites and office blocks, before moving on to a suburb of old colonial houses with gardens and palm trees, where the missionary society had its headquarters in a large compound. This was the residential area of colonial Leopoldville, before its reincarnation as Kinshasa, where the Belgian civil servants had lived in elegance, comfort and heat. Dawn was breaking with a crimson glow in the eastern sky and the liquid notes of tropical birds welcomed the return of day. The taxi-driver opened my door – he was astonished: '£3 – you not understand – £3 and 20 Zaires.' I did understand, and gave him £3; he sat sullenly in his car for an hour before driving off into the waking city.

It was a fascinating time to be in Zaire, for President Mobutu's drive for African 'authenticity' was in full swing. He had outlawed the Western kiss; Christmas holidays were banned and every woman had to wear an 'authentic' cotton 'limputa'; a dress made from lengths of imported printed cloth, which is extremely attractive but which for working women in a hot climate seemed most impractical. No woman was allowed to wear trousers, but the President had cancelled his edict banning brassières on medical grounds. One European cynic was not impressed: 'He should let them wear trousers too, it would be much simpler, then, once they've had children, instead of wearing brassières, they could simply tuck their breasts into their trousers'.

Being a patriarchal society, the men claimed 'authenticity' when wearing Western shoes, shirts and trousers, just so long as they never wore a tie, which in the heat and humidity of Zaire would have been most uncomfortable anyway. In Kinshasa a new form of independent African authenticity had also started, for none of the traffic lights worked and most of the buses were not running because of minor faults that through 'Africanisation', made them beyond repair – consequently each working day the city became chaotic, with lines of revving, hooting cars and their gesticulating drivers.

The suburb in daylight was a pleasant place – exotic trees, bougainvillaeas and palms overlooking the river, in which clumps of water hyacinth (the world's fastest growing weed) were being swept seawards by the strongly flowing current. Nearby were rapids –

spectacular waves and walls of white-topped water that prevented navigation to the sea. I had to spend several days in Kinshasa, trying to get out; the river boat was fully booked, so were the planes, and I had time to kill. 'Don't go out at night,' I was told, 'you will get attacked and robbed. It's not safe after dark.' There were the bustling ivory and food markets to visit. At one, an old man carrying a bag of cement on his head was suddenly forced up against a wall and beaten with clubs by two policemen; for some it was not even safe during the hours of daylight. A restaurant offered frogs' legs and pâté de foie gras, more echoes of Kinshasa's colonial past, while a hospital reminded of the present: it was large and impressive, built with American money and run by American doctors and nurses for the top echelons of Zairois society. Television was less inspiring – World Cup football, featuring Zaire's national team as Africa's representative; as soon as a goal was scored, in the Zaire net, the live satellite broadcast ceased. Every evening's viewing started in the same way, with speeded up clouds scudding over the vast African bush. A small dot then appeared in the top right-hand corner, gradually increasing in size until the President's face filled the whole screen. The possibility of 'upward social mobility' is said to be one of the advantages of living in Western society. 'Upward financial mobility' is obviously one of the advantages of leading a Third World country, for it was being claimed that President Mobutu had risen to the rank of seventh richest man in the world and was still rising.

One evening I joined a missionary family to meet a new arrival at the airport. As we passed through a township, where small groups of children were busy doing homework beneath the occasional floodlight, a car suddenly cut in front of us, forcing us to stop. Armed men ordered us out, pointing their automatic weapons at our stomachs; they claimed to be policemen looking for bandits who had been active in the area. I cannot tell the difference between legal and illegal gun barrels, but they were soon satisfied and let us continue on our way.

Some of the traffic-policemen had developed the art of combining both careers, that of bandit and law officer. They would deliberately stop any Europeans in an obvious hurry and then slowly go through the formalities of checking licences, passports and work permits, before threatening prosecution for a minor traffic offence, until bribed to go away.

* * * * * * *

At last a seat on a flight was possible and I was able to continue my journey, a trip of 450 miles up river to Mbandaka, over dense forest. There were few signs of life below us, just occasional wisps of smoke curling through the foliage as the plane bumped and bounced in the thermals of equatorial air. The black stewardesses were unconcerned by the turbulence, noisily chewing gum, or nuts, except one who was spread-eagled, asleep, over empty seats. The river appeared huge and never ending, being up to 20 miles wide in places, and the whine of the jet engines seemed to be the only intrusion into the old Africa of Livingstone and Stanley.

Mbandaka was a small town on a bend in the river, where the current was so fast that, swimming furiously against it, I just managed to stay in one place. Indian and African tailors worked with their ancient Singer sewing machines on their verandahs and an old lady was selling large white, wriggling maggots from an enamel bowl – a delicacy, eaten raw and alive. She was better stocked than most of the food shops, for 'Africanisation' had recently replaced Asian ownership with African. The almost empty shelves of the new owners were universal, for instead of spending their money from sales on new stock they had spent it like water on themselves, discovering too late the simple mechanics of shop-keeping. Those who did still have supplies had a few sacks of Chinese rice, together with tins of South African pilchards and Rhodesian beef. I was baffled, for the climate was ideal for home-grown rice, and I had been under the impression that Black African countries refused to trade with 'racist' Southern Africa. The largest, most modern industry was the brewery, while along the road stood the barracks, guarded by one soldier, leaning against a wall with his right hand over the end of his rifle barrel – a crow-scarer thrown with precision would have created havoc.

The local mission school was run by Americans. It is strange, how it is always pleasant and amusing to meet someone living as a complete English gentleman, in the middle of a desert or a jungle – as it is to eat cucumber sandwiches and drink afternoon tea with an Asian or African anglophile. But the Americans were living as Americans; friendly, but noisy, brash and alien, making few concessions to the tempo of Africa. As night came fireflies filled the air with brilliant flashes of white light and the chorus of crickets and cicadas built up to a crescendo. We ate frogs' legs, the bones of which were put in the 'trash can' by the houseboy.

The village where Rachael worked was 80 miles south-east of Mbandaka along a single-track dirt road, winding through swamp and forest. In dry weather the occasional vehicle threw up clouds of choking red dust into the air, but after rain it was virtually awash. The villages along the way were small, and whenever we stopped, to deliver letters, children wearing only shirts, shorts or nothing, ran out smiling, waving and shouting: 'Mondele, mondele' (white man, white man).

The village itself was typical of those in the area, with huts of mud and thatch, dusty roads, violent and spectacular electric storms, heat, humidity and children, who seemed to swarm from every doorway. Forest crowded in on three sides with a lake the size of Sussex on the fourth.

The national movement for authenticity was not really needed in the village, for the work and ways of the people were largely unchanged and genuinely 'authentic'. Most of the villagers lived in the traditional square or oblong huts, with walls made from bricks of sun-baked mud and roofs of palm thatch called 'ndele'. The cooking fires were open, burning inside some of the huts, and as smoke seeped through the thatch the deposit of soot acted as a waterproofing agent.

I was immediately made at home, with a group of smiling Africans laying fruit – mangoes, paw paw and bananas – on the grass as a sign of friendship and welcome. Most days I would spend several hours wandering around the village; nearly all the men classified themselves as hunters or fishermen, but there were also craftsmen for, apart from the need for fuel oil, beer, cloth and oddments, the village was almost self-sufficient, with a lorry arriving from the outside world only every other day, filled to overflowing (in both directions) with passengers, and goods for sale.

There were tailors, potters, thatchers, carpenters, bakers, a chairmaker and men who collected palm wine from the top of the palm nut trees (it was wine the colour of milk which in three days was potent). Some also worked as tree-fellers and boatmakers; they went deep into the forest looking for workable wood. It was a strange experience to be walking in the darkness and dampness of the forest suddenly to come across fresh chippings and a skylight in the forest foliage where a tree had fallen. Work proceeded on the spot, with the tree cut into beams and boards, or dug out into a canoe, before being hauled several miles back to the village.

But for many of the men life was easy, as most followed the manly pursuits of fishing, hunting and sitting under trees. The fishermen would go out with lines, spears or more usually nets, made from bamboo or reeds; they would try to trap fish in a large circle of net that would gradually be drawn in and the small victims scooped out with baskets. Fish traps were also used, made out of a framework of pliable woods; they were very similar to the traditional eel traps of the English fens. It was remarkable to me that two cultures, separated by so much in both distance and history, should produce something so similar. But the trap was the only similarity. The fishermen used dug-out canoes for their work which they paddled or punted; sails and wind-power had still not reached that part of the continent.

The lake was over-fished, just as the forest had been over-hunted and there was little left to hunt. A few hunters had shot-guns, but most had bows and arrows, metal-tipped arrows for antelope and civet, and wooden ones dipped in poison for monkeys. The poison was obtained from the sap of a special creeper, its strength being judged by taste and its effect neutralised by sucking sugar-cane. When a monkey was hit it took a quarter of an hour for it to become drowsy and fall out of its tree. A few of the hunters used the traditional hunting dogs of the area – the Basenji, also known as the Congo Bush dog – small silent dogs, that never bark, with tightly curled-up tails.

For the women life was different, leaving the village at dawn with empty baskets on their backs; the trails of bare footprints along the numerous sandy tracks, wandering between trees and termite mounds, would show where they had gone. Often they would walk miles each day to work in the gardens on which each family depended for most of its food. Indeed, that is still the most common sight in rural Africa – people walking miles from anywhere through apparent emptiness.

Every garden was about a quarter of an acre in size; the men cleared the forest, then it was up to the women to cultivate, plant, weed and harvest. Two or three crops were usually grown on the same piece of ground in quick succession, before moving on to a freshly cleared plot, leaving the old ground to be reclaimed by the jungle. The main crop was manioc, with each plant grown from a stick stuck into a small mound of earth; in addition maize, sweet potatoes, pineapples, tomatoes and groundnuts were all planted.

From mid-morning to mid-day the homeward trek began, with the women, equatorial Africa's only beasts of burden, loaded up with firewood and food. The young girls in their early teens thrived on the physical work, being upright and attractive with straight necks, broad shoulders, rounded well-developed biceps and generous firm breasts – everything in posture and development that the average urban typist in the West fails to achieve.

Deportment was not attained by balancing books on their heads at finishing schools, but by carrying baskets loaded with wood strapped to their foreheads, and buckets of water carried on their heads. Sadly, the physical work inevitably took its tool, and after a lifetime of toil and bearing a succession of children, the old women were left bowed, wizened and shuffling, but still working without complaint.

Once home, the work of cooking and preparing manioc would begin. The preparation of manioc seemed as tedious as its cultivation: the leaves were heated in water to make them tender and the softening process was then continued by repeatedly rubbing them over a rough piece of wood and chopping them with a knife; they were then boiled, laced with red peppers and served as 'pondu' (it tasted like hot, watery spinach). The large tubular roots of the plant were also eaten, but first they had to be taken to the 'kwanga pools' to soak. The pools were dark, damp places, where creepers hung down from the trees and the leaves shut out the light; the water in the pools was black and stagnant, a breeding ground for mosquitoes and dragonflies, and things that crept and slithered could be heard moving over fallen leaves and through the grass.

The water and ooze was knee-deep and the women had to wade in to leave their baskets of roots to soak. Unfortunately they could do no other, for the manioc root contains hydrocyanic acid which is highly poisonous, but which the water washes away. After a week the pools were entered again and the roots peeled, before being dried and pounded into flour from which balls of 'fu-fu' were made, or they were simply cut up, boiled and eaten as 'kwanga'. Both helped form the staple diet of the people, but provided little of sustenance, only carbohydrate; to Western palates kwanga tastes like dry boiled potatoes, mixed with a stiff, starchy glue.

The women of the village worked their gardens and kwanga pools six days a week, unlike those in some of the smaller surrounding villages who worked only five; they refused to go into the forest on Tuesdays as that was the day when phantoms and evil spirits were said to be loose. The only time the men condescended to visit the kwanga pools was when they went to collect yard-long worms to use as fish bait.

One woman exempt from work was the 'walekele', a young girl with her first baby, who had returned home for two years, until the child was weaned. Then, with great ceremony, dancing, drinking and playing the drums, her husband would arrive to re-claim her. All she wore was a loin cloth, together with brass bangles on her wrists and ankles, although on some days she was also covered with red clay.

Sunday was the only day when most of the women could rest – to join the menfolk sitting listlessly under trees or attending the long church services with their happy singing and clapping. The young girls would spend hours braiding their hair in complicated patterns; the most beautiful girl was a 'mulatto' – where Portuguese and African blood had mixed to create a most attractive girl with a pale skin, sparkling eyes and a ready smile. Her hair was tied in long spikes and her light colour was said to be of great appeal to the men and youths of the village. One shopkeeper had already let it be known that he wanted her for his fifth wife.

In many ways the children had the best of village life, and at first they watched me wide-eyed – how could anybody be that white? Then, as I swam among them every day in the lake, they would giggle, splash and stare at my patchwork-quilt of sunburn, in the same way that years before I had marvelled at Mr James's black skin and fuzzy hair. After a fortnight I made an even more amusing sight – brown legs and arms, red back and lily-white feet.

They still had the freedom, open spaces and access to nature, so often absent in modern Western childhoods. Once out of school they could chase the village goats, try to catch bats as they spilled out from underneath the church roof at dusk, swim naked and unselfconsciously in the lake, and 'scrump' mangoes, breadfruit, paw-paw, grapefruit and numerous other edible fruits, including my favourite, known only as 'coeur de bouef', which they could eat or sell to the missionaries. The start of the mango season was nearly always heralded by the bruises and even breakages of careless small urchins falling from the trees.

The children also enjoyed more organised games; the boys played marbles and bare-footed football, which when I joined them made me steam with sweat. Individually they had great skill, but the wish to do back-heels and spectacular scissor-kicks seemed greater than their desire to win and play as a team. The girls amused themselves with 'nzango', a game of laughter, clapping and jumping, and 'dada', a sort of double dancing hopscotch. Those old enough for school started each day with half an hour of singing, chanting and shouting slogans, as the drums pounded, in praise of President Mobutu; these were greeted with the same enthusiasm as the games.

But there was another side to the village as well: mothers with obviously malnourished children; sick, elderly people racked by malaria, but only receiving 'native medicine'; and the underlying presence of superstition and fear. Consequently, although at first glance the village and its setting seemed to be on the edge of paradise, beneath the surface the illusion of peace and tranquillity gave way to the hard realities of forest life, in which death, disease and fever were always present. Because of this most villagers seemed to have developed no appreciation of beauty, as have more sheltered Western eyes, for the needs and realities of everyday life were too pressing. Hence a fiery sunset over the lake, seen through a fringe of palm trees, was simply night falling; a rain storm meant more water at the spring and a wild animal was meat on four legs. The local word for animal was 'nyama', which also means 'meat' in much of Africa, and to most villagers the concept of watching animals and birds for pleasure was totally incomprehensible.

There was a passive acceptance of the inevitability of suffering and discomfort; as a result pain often seemed to go unrecognised. It was demonstrated most clearly by an old African pastor. He was a quiet, gentle person, who during the week worked among his flock, helping, advising and counselling, and on Sundays he would preach. With grey hair, kind eyes and a matching smile, he fitted the short but accurate description of a 'good man'. One day, much to my surprise, he asked me if I would like to go hunting with him in the forest, as he had a 12-bore shot-gun and cartridges filled with buckshot. During our 'hunt' he shot two hornbills, large birds with horn-like bills. Both were badly wounded, one with shattered ribs, gasping for breath and in obvious pain. The pastor did not see the suffering; he simply carried the stricken birds for more than an hour, without killing them to bring relief. It showed a darker side to life that I have seen several times since. It is almost an endemic indifference to pain, even cruelty, which seems to be as much a part of the continent as desert, lake and forest.

'Prejudice' was another presence which surprised me, for early on in my stay I noticed a fence marking the end of the Ntumba huts, the main tribe of the village, behind which were the smaller huts of the Batwa tribe, a pygmoid race of mixed ancestry. The Ntumba traditionally and literally looked down on the Batwa, and even some of the local Christians believed that they were animals and would not go to Heaven. The Batwa worked in the main as servants and odd-job men, but again the Ntumba would not let them touch food as they would make it unclean. It was in every sense 'apartheid', for tribal differences and dominances were an integral part of Africa long before the arrival of the white man. The Batwa seemed to accept their lot quite happily. Their huts were full of smoke and children, and several had filed, pointed teeth – either as a cosmetic aid, or as an indication of earlier dietary preferences, for in some areas it is said that filed teeth went hand in hand, if that is the right expression, with cannibalism. Because of the prejudice against all the pygmy peoples, President Mobutu had actually started an original civil-rights movement – to encourage the Bantu tribes to treat 'pygmies as people'.

One African, Mompongo, already treated them with dignity, setting an example too by letting his Batwa houseboy prepare food – including ice-cream, made in a paraffin-fired refrigerator. He was one of the most remarkable men in the village and its natural leader. He went to the local mission school, but ended his education with a degree at Washington State University in the USA. Unlike many educated Zairois, instead of moving to Mbandaka or Kinshasa, where he could have enjoyed a comfortable life-style with an inflated salary, he wanted to remain in his village, to live, work and improve the lives of his people.

The fact that he had no wish to move was itself important, as the power of the big cities to suck both the educated and illiterate to their rich suburbs, or shantytowns, remains one of Africa's greatest problems. Ambitious schoolboys leave their villages with shiny leather shoes and briefcases, hoping for success, and others straight out of the forest expect to find work – most find nothing, apart from hardship. Some had left the village by the lake earlier, as migrant workers, leaving their families, to return just once a year, while others had gone with wife, or wives, and children too. Zaire's population increase, coupled with growing urban population, is frightening. In 1960 the population was 17,755,000; in 1980 28,532,000, and the projected total for the year 2,000 is 54,410,000. The percentage of those living in towns has grown even more; in 1960 it was 22.3 per cent; 1980 – 33.5 per cent, and in the year 2,000 it is expected to have climbed to 56.3 per cent.

Mompongo designed, raised the money, and did manual work for the village secondary school. He built his own bungalow of bricks, was building another one for his father, and had started school projects in agriculture and the manufacture of bricks; he regularly preached in the local church and sang in its choir. During a short dry spell when the flow of the spring reduced to a trickle he organised the making of a small dam so that the water would not run to waste, and he fitted a simple tap from a length of rubber pipe to make things easier and cleaner. For generations, during the frequent rains, the women had slipped and slithered up and down a muddy bank to get their water; no doubt when steps are eventually cut into the slope, he will be the driving force behind that too. He was an outstanding, unambitious man, with ability and vision which had won for him the nickname from some of the villagers of 'the black white-man', said as a compliment, not as an insult.

His father demonstrated the distance his son had travelled in just one generation, for the old man still had his traditional tribal feathers and furs, complete with spears, which he would occasionally wear to impress, as well as frighten. His thrusting spear for combat was lethal: 'How are you supposed to get it out of a victim?' I asked. He smiled: 'The quickest way is to push it right through and out the other side.'

* * * * * * *

The missionaries were trying to encourage others to make Mompongo's journey, offering them education, health, better food, and, of course, God. Rachael, and Mary another English nurse from Sussex, lived in a large brick house with a corrugated iron roof. Next door was an agricultural missionary from the Midlands, with his wife and two small children, as well as Peter, a farmer's son from Suffolk out for two years to help with the agricultural project.

Every day the nurses would work at the hospital, while relatives of the patients sat cooking or talking outside. Today there is much fashionable criticism of missionaries, arguing that they should have stayed away from Africa and not interfered. A visit to the hospital showed one of the reasons why those early travellers, with Bibles and medicine chests, heard their 'call' – compassion.

It is a moving sight to see the sick and suffering, who with Western medicines, administered with dedication and care, can easily be cured. The hospital, its primitive wards and clinic, dealt with the common ailments of the forest – 'fever', malaria, worms, anaemia, bronchitis and epidemics of measles that periodically devastated the children. Malnutrition could also be a problem with the young – not through lack of food, but from being given the wrong food. Most of the conditions, if left to native medicine, would simply have lingered on, or even led to death. Burns too were commonplace and horrific, with children stumbling into hut fires. There was no doctor and so the nurses had to act as surgeons, gynaecologists, general practitioners and midwives. Trained African nurses helped them and they were supervised by the hospital administrator, a post recently 'Africanised', and held by a man with little knowledge of administration and no laces in his shoes.

Not only was a doctor absent, but drugs were also in short supply, with many urgently needed medicines being pilfered on the way up from Kinshasa. Sometimes there were more difficult diseases to treat, such as leprosy, and others that defied diagnosis and were attributed to 'the evil eye', when a normally healthy person would simply give up and die, without responding to any form of treatment. Curses were blamed, but the villagers would not talk about the problem or the perpetrators. It showed yet another side of life in the forest, still beyond the understanding of Western man.

One evening as we sat quietly in the house, enjoying the gentle light of the oil lamps, with lizards and rats scuttling in the rafters, an urgent call for help came from the hospital. Rachael ran down the dirt road to find that a teenage girl had received a cut eye after her father had thrown a beer bottle at her. In candle light, with thread and needle, she sewed up the ugly gash, without any local anaesthetic, which had failed to arrive from Kinshasa. The blunt needle, coupled with the tough skin – black skin is harder to sew than white – made me wince every time a new stitch was inserted. But with no tears or flinching, the girl sat without any emotion, or reaction, accepting her lot.

John, the agricultural missionary, had various schemes in progress: to improve hen and egg production; to make manure from washed-up water hyacinth; to breed rabbits. He was meeting with mixed success, and local interest varied from enthusiasm to total indifference. I could never understand why he did not include the local goats in his venture, for the villagers often needed milk, having to buy milk powder to satisfy their requirements, yet the goats went unmilked, through superstition, and the missionaries failed to set a new example.

Peter, from Suffolk, was coming to the end of his stay and one day had to go to a village along the lake to get his work permit extended until the time of his departure. We went along the forest track on a motorbike, again with naked children running out to wave to us, passing through a rubber plantation where a Belgian was still in overall control. The permit office was in a wooden building, with an official sitting at an empty desk listening to the radio. He studied the passport and the permit, and decided he had to make a phone call; but where was the telephone directory? He searched through drawers and looked on another desk, before remembering – it was under the cushion of his chair. After a short conversation he placed an old typewriter on his desk, returned the directory to his seat, to make him the right height for typing, and slowly typed out a form, using one finger.

That village had a convent, with a school and hospital, where the nuns taught and nursed. In theory they also had an African doctor, but he rarely attended. With their white habits and pale complexions the nuns went about their duties with an air of serenity; I could not help but admire them, having turned their backs on the affluence of Europe to live lives of obedience, simplicity and service in one of the most inhospitable climates in the world.

Peter was soon to return to his Suffolk farm, but before he left, the village held a party for him, as he had fitted in well and had quickly learnt the local language, Lingala. The host was a man who had energetically followed the agricultural advice given to him, and healthy hens from English stock scrapped around his huts and supplied good eggs – a marked contrast to most of the scrawny local fowl. Tables were set up outside, with assorted cutlery, china and enamel; there was kwanga, fufu, pondu, small fish – cooked whole like whitebait – large fish, goat meat and fruit, all washed down with cold water poured grandly from a teapot. It was a warm, happy affair, with speeches, as well as tears, and the host trying hard to give his departing friend what he imagined to be a reminder of home; the fact that he failed, as such a meal and setting would never be seen in Suffolk, was irrelevant.

The only other Europeans in the area were from the American Peace Corps, some of whom appeared to be hippies on an African sabbatical. Two were living with young African girls and several had to be treated at the hospital for syphilis. An earlier volunteer had actually married a local girl and taken her back with him to New York. It was a remarkable proposition for a young wife from a mud hut in the equatorial rain forest, living the life of an earlier age, to be transported to an urban metropolis of the twentieth-century. I often wonder which she found to be the most hostile jungle.

Some of the Americans smoked 'dope' – cannabis – and one, with accuracy, could only be described as a dope. He wore his hair long, tied with a ribbon, hardly the most suitable style for the heat and humidity of Zaire, and when I met him he was in the middle of a great oration in praise of Africa: 'And the people are marvellous. Back home they are said to be backward, but in reality they are so highly developed. Have you heard the way they play the drums?' It was the first time I had heard development equated with an ability to play the drums, and the bags of Chinese rice and the tins of Rhodesian beef immediately came to mind.

'You think playing the drums is more important than being able to feed yourself properly?' I queried. Silence followed and he did not speak to me again.

* * * * * * *

It was entirely in keeping with the American image that the Peace Corps should have a boat. Not a workhorse, with a reliable in-board motor to transport people and goods, a boat badly needed, but a speedboat with an out-board motor and a wash that almost tipped over the local canoes. Despite this, the nurses borrowed it one day to take themselves and their drugs to a village on the other side of the lake. Once loaded up they said goodbye to Louis, their Batwa houseboy, giving him instructions for work in the house during their absence, and prepared to leave. When all was ready the out-board failed to start. A mechanic was called, whose philosophy seemed to

Sowing the Seed

be, 'if it's got a nut on it, or a wire coming from it, hit it with a spanner'. The engine remained dead and we returned to the house – it was empty – Louis had already forsaken his instructions and gone home.

Eventually Louis was found and returned; finally the engine started and we departed. I had thought that the mission village was backward, but Nkoso gave the words 'under-developed' new meaning. There was no brick or sheet of corrugated iron and no internal combustion engine had ever travelled up the village street. We were greeted with enthusiasm by the villagers, including a thin golden labrador, who treated us like long lost friends. He had been left behind when his former Belgian owners had returned home and his new owners treated him like any other local dog – giving him the occasional scrap, and little else. His tail wagged, he licked us and whined, clearly thinking that his luck had changed.

We were put in a mud hut, sleeping on the floor, with a roofed toilet, 'a long drop', behind. The two nurses started their work almost immediately; they had no option, as a long queue formed before they had even unpacked their drugs and equipment. For the rest of the day they worked, treating malaria, sores, coughs and worms. They took blood samples to test for anaemia and filaires (a type of worm living in the blood stream) and checked recently born babies. There was a help-yourself service too – a large box of old spectacles, donated by English Baptists who had been asked to give up their unwanted glasses. Old men and women with failing eye-sight would sort through the box, testing and looking through the lenses with squinting eyes, until a suitable pair was found. Success would bring smiles and a look of sophistication as they walked away proudly wearing a pair of smart horn-rims, or National Health specials. Much of the nurses' equipment had been donated in this way, including many of their syringes and hypodermic needles – discarded after one jab in a British hospital or surgery, but used repeatedly until totally blunt in the jungle clinic short of supplies.

Very early on it was clear that other medical practices were also being carried out in the village, for there were women with white clay daubed on their heads and arms, and one had bells hanging from the basket on her back, to keep the evil spirits away as she went into the forest. She had lifeless, staring eyes and a small tiara on her head, made from mosses and feathers. Her tinkling bells could be heard long before she appeared.

Late in the afternoon Rachael and Mary were summoned urgently to the other end of the village where an elderly lady was said to be dying. The inside of her hut was dark and stifling; a fire was burning, hens scrapped between low bamboo beds and the wizened old woman was lying on her side wheezing and coughing. Numerous faces looked on as her temperature was taken and the stethoscope used. She had a bout of 'fever', with a temperature of 105°F.

The men were told that the old lady needed urgent quinine at the clinic, and she should attend as soon as possible. We expected the men to carry her to our hut on her bed – one at each corner. Instead they made her walk by herself. Fortunately the quinine worked quickly and the following morning she had almost completely recovered.

At the end of the long day a schoolteacher, with a smattering of English, wanted to talk to me and show me various features of the forest. He could not understand why I wanted to help the nurses wash up their instruments and coffee mugs: 'That's women's work,' he said, with contempt.

During the night a build-up of black, towering clouds shut out the starlight, but soon the forest lit up and shook to a spectacular electric storm, without a drop of rain. Sheet and forked lightning cascaded down as bolts of thunder obliterated the normal noises of the night. Shadows danced and the forest flickered in and out of focus in blinding bursts of light. In such a setting the storm became an awesome demonstration of natural power.

The following night there was an even stranger demonstration of unknown power. The nurses had again had a long day of constant work, and we were sitting quietly in candle-light listening to the night. Suddenly, at the far end of the village, drums started, and it became obvious that our part of the village was empty – no fires or lights and an absence of people talking.

As we walked along the dark, deserted track, the drumming grew louder and more frenetic, until we came to a great throng of people outside a hut with a roaring bonfire. There were two drums and in the bright light, with moving shadows, there was a mystical, eerie atmosphere. The crowd was waiting expectantly and the excitement and anticipation could be felt in the air. An old lady came out of the hut wearing a long, flowing limputa and began to speak in French.

Sowing the Seed

She came over to us and shook our hands and as she did so her voice developed a peculiar affectation. Her ramblings and exhortations then drifted into pure mumbo-jumbo, as if the drumming and the tense, vibrant night had driven her into a trance.

As the drums played on, another old woman began to dance with stamping feet, shouting out as the onlookers sang and clapped. She then began to wave a feather whisk and wooden rattle, and people filed out in front of her and gave her money. She was joined by a large man wearing a skirt, a shirt and a green hat, who danced with a more frenzied concentration; he was a visiting exorcist. Earlier travellers would have described him as a 'witch-doctor', and the crowd chanted with him to get rid of evil spirits from several clay-daubed women, who were left writhing on the dusty ground. The whole atmosphere was seething with the presence of unknown forces. There was a thickness in the air, a darkness that could be felt and almost touched. Mary had never seen anything like it before in more than 20 years of work in Zaire; she looked anxious and said she felt the presence of evil.

It was a remarkable, exhausting experience and its effect did not remain in the small lakeside village. In Zaire I took more than 200 transparencies, most of which were good quality, and some were later published. With his permission, I took two of the exorcist at work, but they were the only slides to come out completely blank. The flash worked, the shutter functioned and the camera was pointed at the fire, but the slides were totally dark, without any definition or intrusion of light.

The easy explanations are that the camera did not function, or I set it wrongly. But I do not believe either of them, for others too have had peculiar experiences. When Laurens van der Post was filming his outstanding documentary *The Lost World of the Kalahari*, he promised his guide there would be no killing as the expedition approached the sacred hills of the bushmen. One of the group did not know of the undertaking and shot an antelope for food – then, once at the hills, the camera broke down for no apparent reason. It went to Johannesburg for repairs and a thorough check, but as soon as it was returned it broke down again, as did the sound recording equipment.

In India, Jim Corbett, the old hunter of man-eating tigers, and pioneer of Indian conservation, usually an accurate and reliable recorder of events, witnessed another strange occurrence. He was hunting a tiger near a shrine, said to protect life, where shooting was not allowed. He found the troublesome animal close by, walking towards him along a track when, for no obvious reason, three young, healthy trees fell across the path. The tiger turned and walked back into the forest, and Jim Corbett quite inexplicably lost the chance of his shot.

There are many people who will pour scorn on such incidents, explaining the unknown in terms of chance or imagination. I believe that these happenings go much deeper and, although Western man considers himself to be the sophisticated master of his own destiny, there are powers within ourselves, and beyond, that we do not recognize or understand.

Despite the fact that the exorcist was claiming to cure others, he obviously had problems of his own, for next day he attended the nurses' clinic and bought 140 indigestion tablets. Later one of his helpers held an afternoon session and, with the aid of beer, a rattle, his hands and the repeated order to the spirits of: 'Come here, come here,' he too appeared to remove a number of 'spirits'. He seemed to be using a form of hypnosis to reduce his customers to a state of rolling eyes and trembling limbs. This, it was said, was the evil spirit leaving its victim, encouraged by the beer which was spilt on the ground to help lure it out.

The performance of the exorcist was rooted in superstition, but it is also true that his elementary psychology did appear to help a number of apparently neurotic women – disturbed, or even suffering from 'post-natal depression'. There was another peculiar aspect as well, for in some ways the performance varied little from 'the speaking in tongues' and the 'laying on of hands' practised in some evangelical branches of the Christian church.

Mompongo did not rule out all aspects of native medicine, pointing out that broken bones often healed faster when given a traditional poultice containing certain forest leaves, than those set in plaster of Paris. But there was also little doubt that much native medicine was bad, based mainly on fear. On our last night at Nkoso the drums were silent, yet I have another memory that lives with me, of a mother sitting forlornly outside the exorcist's hut, wearing the signs of native medicine, with her small baby crying continuously. It was crying from hunger, as the mother's flow of milk had dried up. The nurses could have treated her and given milk powder for the child, but the woman was one of the few who would not attend the clinic or accept Western medicine, and so the baby was doomed to die.

* * * * * * *

It was well before dawn that I had to leave the main lakeside village in the mission Land Rover for Mbandaka, to catch the plane out. The reason was simple: although some airlines run late, Air Zaire sometimes flies early, and one plane had once left three hours before a scheduled take-off. It all depended, so it was said, on whether the President needed an aircraft. Without warning the Land Rover lurched as we bounced over a wooden bridge; on one side there was a large unmarked hole that John swerved to avoid. At greater speed or with less care we would have plunged through to the river bed below, with certain injury.

On the plane an English businessman in a lightweight suit, but still sweating, was airing his thoughts: 'What a dump,' he said, 'I'll be glad to get away from this place. The plane's overloaded you know – they'd never be allowed to take off like this in England – we'll end up in the river with the crocs and hippos – have you seen them. They're monsters.' 'I've been in a village by the lake.' I butted in. 'I liked the people and got on well with them – the young girls there were very attractive.' 'Really? You must be in a state – how long have you been out of England?'

I was thinking of the village: an American missionary wanted to start a new building programme – would he turn a traditional African village into a township? Recently too, a boat had been seen on the lake, where it had stayed for several days. It had not been searching for fish or water hyacinths, but looking for oil. If oil came, then the friendly people of the lakeside would be stampeded into a new urban world; it seemed that they would lose far more than they would gain.

2. Dutch and English

Zaire, it seemed to me, was the typical face of the new Black-Africa – proud, independent and chaotic, stretching out to reach for the material possessions of the First World, but with its feet firmly planted in the Third. In one hand its leaders held out begging bowls for international aid, while in the other they juggled with private bank accounts and the keys to their new Mercedes saloons. Away from the seat of government old Africa remained virtually unchanged, as it had for hundreds of years: T-shirts, tin-cans, new brief-cases and the occasional lorry or Japanese pick-up truck being the main reminders that the world outside had changed and was still changing. If aid was suddenly cut off and those who administered it went home, then the jungle would again assert its authority, with the foliage closing in high above, shutting out the shafts of new light.

To see under-developed West Africa in its true perspective, there could be only one destination for my next journey, for South Africa is still the only region on the continent that can in any real sense be described as 'developed'. After Zaire, South Africa and Rhodesia had one other advantage – English is widely spoken and I could forget my inadequate French. But the main disadvantage was equally obvious: Rhodesia was caught up in a vicious 'bush war'.

For me there was one other unavoidable drawback – the flight; it would be even longer than the one to Kinshasa, a real handicap with my aversion to flying. It was my first time on a Boeing 747 'Jumbo' – an accurate description, for it was so large that simply to fall down the steps while it was stationary at the airport could have been fatal – let alone tumbling from 40,000 feet. My nerves were not helped by the Welshman sitting next to me: 'I work on these things', he said, 'as a British Airways engineer. For safety's sake I never fly on any of the planes I've worked on, so you should be all right'. Did those who had worked on this plane have the same philosophy, I wondered? He went on to explain how Jumbo engines had their various systems constructed in triplicate so that a complete mechanical failure was 'almost' impossible. He sounded convincing, but I did hear the word 'almost' quite clearly.

Flying to Africa gradually becomes routine – with plastic-tasting food, piped music, and tedious films, all supplied to help pass the time. Occasionally a city appears far below, like a giant illuminated snowflake with crystals and reflections fused together in white light, then for hours – nothing.

I'll never forget my first East African dawn: a long red glow cutting into the darkness, a brightening and concentrating flame like the bright red rim of an angry eye, until suddenly the sun exploded above the horizon with blinding light. Below, a vast, barren lunar landscape began to change until small lakes, glinting like glass beads, signalled the start of our descent to Nairobi. Bush, earth roads, farms and the outline of Mount Kenya all came into focus, then as we flew low to land, the Africa of my imagination briefly appeared: grassland scorched brown by the sun, with giraffe and a small group of wildebeeste; herdsmen with native cattle; small shanties and Africans walking along a dusty track – touchdown again linked the old with the new.

A group of Japanese tourists and a few Europeans got on, under the watchful eye of an African soldier in a long great-coat, clutching a Sten gun. I hoped it would not be too long before I would also be setting foot on Kenyan soil, to see if my Father's earlier odyssey had been right or wrong. It was peculiar travelling to Johannesburg, via Nairobi: another of those strange African double-standards for, although most of the world's airlines fly over Africa while heading south, South African Airlines fly virtually the whole journey over the sea, as only Namibia and Botswana allow it airspace. The other airlines could be full of business men going to trade with South Africa, and even Africans seeking Pretoria's financial or technical assistance – that is allowable; but to undertake the same journey, for the same reasons, in a South African plane is considered to be a heinous crime.

Soon we were in the air again, and climbing, to gain an unforgettable view of one of the most extraordinary birthday presents ever given – Mount Kilimanjaro, which Queen Victoria gave to her nephew Kaiser Wilhelm II. Her generosity was a great shame as far as the modern traveller is concerned, for access and availability would have been far simpler if left to the Kenyans, rather than the Tanzanians. But time and ownership make no difference to its impact, for with its high, snow-topped dome rising from the dry, dusty plains it is one of the sights of Africa and I could only marvel at it. From the air the rest of Tanzania appeared to fit the famous phrase heard by Negley Farson: 'Miles, and miles, and miles – and Miles! – of Sweet Fanny Adams!' Barren, arid bush country – hot, harsh and virtually empty.

Gradually, far below, change came; roads increased and farms and field patterns painted the landscape where wilderness had been transformed into rolling farmland. The Third World had been replaced by the First; poverty by wealth; black faces by white rule. Division too could be seen: a haze of mist and smoke over the large African townships and the gem-like blue of countless swimming pools mapping out the areas of European homes. From the air one of South Africa's sources of wealth was marked too, for the spoil tips of Johannesburg's gold mines shone yellow in the sun. As we banked sharply one bore a message in large letters that seemed appropriate –'Awake Jesus Cometh'; fortunately he did not and we landed safely.

Jan Smuts Airport was a pool of dry heat and dazzling light, as different from my Kinshasa landing as it was possible to be. Inside the terminal building the differences were even more marked. The queue through immigration moved smoothly and quickly, with smartly dressed officials in white socks, shorts and shirts, checking and stamping passports efficiently and the correct way up.

For many years various individuals and organisations have tried to persuade people not to visit South Africa, and in some cases persuasion has even turned into threats. I was glad to have made the journey, for one of my illusions was immediately dispelled: instead of hearing English, as I had expected, all I could hear was Afrikaans – even less intelligible to me than French. It was written over the entrance to the toilets as well, although there its meaning was clear – 'Whites Only'. But there were blacks walking and working with whites, and black policemen with guns; I had expected all the guns to be pointing at them.

The contrasts with Zaire continued as Afrikaner friends drove me towards Pretoria; traffic lights (robots) were working, buses were running and there was more than one road with a good surface. Pretoria, apart from being the capital of the Republic of South Africa, is the very heart of Afrikaner tradition and culture. It is in the centre of what was once the independent Boer republic of the

Transvaal, which together with the Orange Free State was the Dutch settlers' answer to the British-dominated regions of Natal and the Cape. Lieb had studied in England and knew how most people in Britain viewed South Africa from 8,000 miles away: 'Rrobin', he said in an accent containing a prrreponderrance of Afrikaner rrrrrs, 'before you get on with your own travels, I will show you Prretoria; it will help you to understand South Africa's problems more clearly.'

The city had the air of a booming, bustling metropolis – with high-rise flats, administrative office blocks and wide, tree-lined streets. In the spring (our autumn) the trees become a mass of blue-mauve blossom giving Pretoria the additional name of Jacaranda City. It has an estimated 70,000 trees that give a seasonal haze of colour, with flowers in the air and petals underfoot. The Jacaranda has been used to brighten many of the cities of central and southern Africa, but it is not a native of the continent, having been imported into South Africa from Argentina in 1888.

Several quite ancient buildings also show that Pretoria's roots go back deep into the last century. The longest street is Church Street, more than 25 miles long, and it was there that Lieb took me to Paul Kruger's house, a modest bungalow with a corrugated iron roof. Inside, it remains largely as it was when Kruger was President of the South African Republic, a man who vowed never to bow to the British flag. Despite defeat in the Boer war and exile, he has been elevated to the position of Afrikaner saint, and there, in almost holy silence, visitors were looking reverently at the austere surroundings: his desk, his chair, his bed. All around, Kruger was gazing back from numerous photographs, severe and unsmiling, with his sideboards meeting under his chin in a strip of white beard – it is an Afrikaner fashion still popular today, and almost as distinctive as the beard of a Jew or Sikh. Mrs Kruger too gazed down sternly; they must have been a formidable pair – what they lacked in looks, history shows they made up for in resolution.

History also reveals that during Kruger's stand against the British, the Boers enjoyed much support from various parts of Europe. Evidence of this is on display in the bungalow as well, with glass cases full of letters from Russia, France, Switzerland and Germany, all offering moral and material help. Boer relief funds were set up selling pipes and mugs in Kruger's distinctive nasal image, to raise money, and they too have warranted display, on historical not artistic grounds. The Germans seemed particularly eager to help, showing that Afrikaner links with Germany go back long before the rise of the Third Reich, a fact that some modern-day historians and commentators conveniently forget.

Kruger was a 'Voortrekker', one of those Boers who trekked into the interior, away from the British, which means that his ox-wagon is another possession to have attained the status of holy relic, to be displayed and revered. It is large, sturdily constructed, and must have required many 'spans' of oxen to pull it over the rough terrain. By the time Kruger had risen from Voortrekker to independent, obstinate President, so his means of transport had improved to luxury railway carriage – also now parked in the Kruger garden.

Church Street has other reminders of Pretoria's past: the Dutch Reformed Church where Kruger worshipped and strengthened his fundamentalist faith, and Church Square where the great man's statue stands looking towards the Palace of Justice. Nearby are the Union Buildings, designed in 1910 by Sir Herbert Baker as South Africa's main administrative building of government; its domes and pillars of sandstone, set on a hilltop above terraced gardens, make it one of the most attractive and impressive colonial buildings ever constructed. Later Baker went on to work with Sir Edwin Lutyens in New Delhi. But even at the Union Buildings, Boer pride surfaces in the form of a fine statue of General Louis Botha on horseback, an Afrikaner hero of the First World War.

Finally Lieb took me to the Voortrekker Monument, a huge stone building on a hilltop that has been erected as the Afrikaners' most sacred shrine. It was built not only as a monument to those Voortrekkers who died as they moved north, but as a symbol of the Afrikaners' 'civilizing' influence on South Africa, an influence which, like the building, is intended to be permanent. There is no doubt that the Boer sees his role in history as bearing civilization to Africa – giving light to the dark continent. Even now, official information pamphlets state: 'Western civilization was brought to South Africa by the Dutch who settled at the Cape in 1652.' With the French Huguenots, who joined them later on in that century, they still consider themselves as great luminaries – a status undermined by the arrival of the British who were more liberal, commercially minded and morally suspect.

The huge building is surrounded by a large wall, on which a circle of wagons and Voortrekkers is carved, in the form of a 'laager'. At

the entrance of the shrine itself is the bronze figure of a mother with two children clutching her skirt; it depicts both fortitude and trust. On the walls of the building the story is told of the Voortrekkers' great journey to the promised land – a drama involving Zulu treachery and violent death, before salvation on 16 December 1838 with victory at the Battle of Blood River. In the high roof is a small hole and at noon on the anniversary of the battle, a shaft of sunlight, 18 inches across, falls on a block of polished granite bearing the simple inscription:-
ONS
VIR JOU
SUIDAFRIKA
It means: 'We for thee South Africa'. Close by there is an ever-burning oil lamp and another inscription – '1938 Torch Flame, Symbol of Light of Civilization Carried Forth by the Voortrekker Movement'.

Leaving the Monument I could already see South Africa differently, for I was not visiting a country of simple conflict, white against black, but a country in which the white population was also deeply divided – nationally, culturally and historically. To the Afrikaner, the Voortrekker Monument was more than a memorial, it was a temple on holy ground. But to those from an English background it was of less significance, almost an act of Afrikaner self-indulgence, to emphasize the Boers' independence and nationalism – they were still fighting the Boer War, and winning.

But where did the Africans fit in to all this, and did they still need 'civilizing'? As we drove back we passed an African township of small shacks, dusty paths and, inevitably, children. Some of the more affluent residents were playing golf on a course that in England would have been regarded as waste ground, with long grass, bumps and ruts, and putting-greens of bare soil – a golf-ball manufacturers' dream. At a group of shops we stopped, one was a 'muti' shop, where Africans could get 'native medicine' – roots, leaves, monkey-skins, bones and pieces of dried crocodile. There were bags, bottles, lotions and potions – one was labelled 'Flesh Restorer' – it was a different world, but in the same country.

The European homes in the suburbs were luxurious, most with large gardens and swimming pools, but Lieb lived in the middle of the city in a flat. It could have been anywhere in the Western world, apart from the black servant working during the day. He and his wife were unusual for Afrikaners – they were 'liberals'; they thought that the African, particularly the urban African, had received a raw deal. Lieb did not go as far as 'one man one vote', for he retained the Afrikaner fear of being dominated by another race, whether English or Zulu. He hoped that some federal system of government would develop to allow the Afrikaners to control their own destiny, but at the same time he wanted rapid and radical changes. He considered the Pass Laws to be harsh, as they limited the movement of black Africans and required them to carry a 'pass'. He despised the Immorality Act which legislated against two people of different colours falling in love; he objected to the Group Areas Act that required each race to be confined to its own special living area; and he thought it was wrong that 'job reservation' should protect jobs for whites, even if there were blacks more able and better qualified to do them. Most employers got over the last hurdle anyway. If no whites could be found to take a 'white job', the black 'assistants' usually did the same work just as well.

Much of the white fear was based on the belief that if Africans received more money and better employment, there would be inflation and unemployment. As an economist, Lieb disagreed, considering that it would stimulate the consumer market and create the ideal of most western economists – an 'economic boom'. The added advantage would be that a sizeable and influential black middle class would be formed to whom the politics of revolution and Marxism would be an anathema. Already he saw the race conflict being turned into a political battle, where lack of opportunity and black poverty was being turned into Marxist opportunity and the politics of revolution. The answers then became easy and were obtained through the barrel of a gun. The proof of such a theory was easy to see further north, over the border in Rhodesia.

The political grievances came from the fact that white education was free, whereas blacks had to pay (based on the fact that most whites paid tax and most blacks did not) and fourth generation urban blacks were being told that the towns in which they lived were not 'home' – their actual 'homes' being in the 'homelands' – distant rural areas that some had never seen. To Lieb, the third and fourth generation urban black had just as much right to consider himself South African as the third or fourth generation white. He went even further, for he considered that most urban Africans had almost completely lost their rural outlook and were in fact new Africans.

They had been moulded in the city by boredom, overcrowding and violence – all exaggerated by race. Such Africans needed help and recognition, not separation and legislation.

In the afternoon a different view was put by a university lecturer, who would occasionally break off his conversation in Afrikaans to profer me a few words of wisdom in English. Just as President Mobutu had been searching for Zairian authenticity, so Jan considered himself to be the voice of the authentic Afrikaner. 'And remember', he said, 'Afrikaner means son of Africa. Don't be misled, our problem is one of race – South Africa must have separate development. If the argument is changed to the class struggle, there will only be one winner – we will be swamped. We will only accept that if people are talked into false feelings of guilt; that would lead to a decline – like you in Britain. There must be no compromises.'

Two days later a shiver went through the whole of white South Africa, for on 12th February 1979, a second Viscount aircraft was shot down by terrorists in Rhodesia, using a heat-seeking Sam missile. The shock waves were made worse by Joshua Nkomo, one of the leaders of the Patriotic Front, laughing at the carnage during a television interview from Lusaka.

All during our conversation, more violence was occurring on the television screen, for a rugby match was in progress. To many Afrikaners rugby is an even greater God than Paul Kruger, and to the English a visit to a rugby test match is certainly more important than visiting the Voortrekker Monument.

Although serious political conversations are an inevitable part of visiting South Africa, many of the people have a fine sense of humour too, laughing at their own predicament, just as much as they laugh at others. They see the humour in their love of rugby as well. One joke was particularly apt: 'Do you know what they call a queer in the Free State? Somebody who prefers women to rugby.'

Even in Pretoria the evening was a pleasant time, with crickets and cicadas starting their night-time chorus. A football stadium was bathed in light, and there I had another surprise. After hearing of the reasons for separate development there, at the football ground, black, white and khaki were all training and playing together in harmony. In the lounge of a large hotel I saw an African with his wife and children eating chips and beans. He was a social worker and he was the personnel officer of a large firm; both were friendly, intelligent and articulate. Would one man one vote come in his life-time I asked? He laughed: 'God only gave us three score years and ten you know.'

The bar contained nearly all Europeans, as alcohol seems to play an important part in the life of the white man in Africa. An Afrikaner was obviously the worse for drink, much to the amusement of a young Englishman from Durban: 'You should visit Durban, there's more English there, not these ignorant Slopies,' he informed, pointing at the drunk.

'Slopies?' I queried.

'That's right, Slopies, or Slopes. Your forehead goes straight down; an Afrikaner's slopes backwards, like stone-age man. If you get an African and an Afrikaner's skull side by side, you can't tell the difference. We also call the Dutchmen ropes – they are thick, hairy and twisted. The really thick ones are called van der Merwe [pronounced Merver]. That drunk is a typical van der Merwe.'

He then introduced me to another South African delight, the van der Merwe joke. They are all about a not very bright Afrikaner called van der Merwe, and are the equivalent of the 'Irish jokes' told in Britain, with Van replacing Paddy and Murphy. Many are funny, some are basic, and others are just insulting, but I enjoyed them. The Englishman then went through his repetoire.

Van der Merwe walked into a bar with an odd-looking monkey on his head. 'Where did you find that strange thing?' the barman asked. 'In the middle of the Free State,' piped up the monkey.

One that has become my favourite involves van der Merwe and two friends driving over the Kalahari desert on their way to Windhoek for a holiday, when their car breaks down. It was a dangerous position to be in, miles from anywhere, in the scorching dry heat, so they decided to walk to Windhoek, after first drawing lots to take something of use from the car to help them survive. Koos was first: 'I'll take the radiator,' he announced.

Van was puzzled: 'What! Why the radiator man?'

To Koos it was simple: 'Then when the sun gets really hot, I can have a drink of water.'

Peiter was next. He thought carefully, then said: 'I'll take a hub-cap.'

This again puzzled Van: 'Och man, why the hub-cap?'

'Oh Van, use your intelligence man. When the sun gets really hot, I'll put the hub-cap on my head and it will reflect the sun's rays back

into the sky.'
Van was not impressed: 'It's my turn now. I'll take the front door.'
The other two were now baffled: 'Why do you want to carry the front door Van?'
'That's simple. Then when the sun gets really hot, I can wind the window down.'

By this time, without the bar counter in front of him the alcohol-guzzling Afrikaner would have been paralytic. A black barman stood by him, conveniently adding up an order in biro on his white palms. The white man seized his tray and angrily put a one rand coin on it and waived the waiter away. 'What did you do that for?' I enquired.
'To get him to piss off,' came the charming reply.

* * * * * *

The train pulled out of Johannesburg almost empty, with a quiet clerk being the only other passenger in my compartment. We almost immediately passed through an African township – huge and smokey: 'Don't be surprised,' he commented, seeing my interest, 'an African is not happy unless he's surrounded by smoke, with a three-legged pot.' Some of the shacks had small gardens – while most had boulders on their roofs to keep the sheets of corrugated iron down. The stations for Africans were crowded – centres of noise, dust and litter.

At the next European stop, two more men entered our carriage – a swearing Afrikaner railway driver, going home, and an old, bald-headed man who seemed irritated: 'Where are you going?' he asked me.
'Durban.'
'It would be a nice city, but it's full of kaffirs and coolies – the thieving lazy bastards.' He then accelerated into an enthusiastic anti-African tirade, with the driver nodding in complete agreement; the clerk quietly read on, in a world of his own. The bald man had a captive audience, and I was a prisoner: 'Look at the bloody kaffir states that have got independence. They've even eaten all their maggots and worms and come knocking on our door to feed them. And what do they know about war? One bomb and they would be a hundred miles away hanging in the trees like monkeys. They go over the border into Rhodesia and murder an old woman and are

described as heroes by the rest of the world, when all they are is murderers. They say it's about democracy – if a black man had a farm and had a hundred baboons on it with him, would he grant majority rule?'

The train stopped, the driver got out, but the old man went on: 'I'm over 70 you know, but I still work – as a groundsman.' Evidently sport, too, left much to be desired. By the time the train was travelling at speed and the clerk had gone to bed, I was hearing how the Second World War had been won single-handed; complete with a striptease interlude to show me his scars.

Dawn came and his wisdom poured out again, as soon as he awoke. He was agitated, tapping his feet – but there was not long to go before Durban. By now we were passing through the planned homeland of Kwazulu – rolling hillsides with scattered shacks and Zulu huts. Some Zulu women were working at the side of the railway and one was breast feeding her baby. 'Look at that,' he growled, in a state of even greater agitation, 'they're a dirty lot of sods.' He started coughing and on clearing his throat he spat. Phlegm spattered over the window: 'Oh,' he said, trying to clean up the glass with a dirty handkerchief, 'I thought the window was open.' I wondered what the breast-feeding Zulu woman would have thought of that.

* * * * * * *

It was a relief to be off the train, away from the confinement, the hectoring and the lecturing, and into the fresh air. Tinged with the scent of herbs and spices, the atmosphere was warm and damp, smelling of the Indian Ocean. At first glance Durban seemed like a mixture of high-rise wonderland, port and colonial country town; but on second glance, that was far too simple. There were many white faces, speaking English. But among the white faces there were also brown and black: Indians – Hindus, Muslims and Sikhs – as well as Africans. There were Afrikaners too and the place seemed a complete jumble of styles, cultures and backgrounds; colour, creed and language. A mixture of England and the Orient – Worthing and Calcutta, with a few touches of African township, old Afrikaner residence and twentieth-century tower-block thrown in for good measure.

Durban started its life as a trading outpost and grew into an administrative centre, gaining its name on the 23rd June 1835 from the Governor of the Cape, Sir Benjamin D'Urban. Its early history was turbulent, being on the edge of Zulu country, with black and white, Dutch and English, all taking part in the action and with each group being opposed to the other two. The divisions and mistrust were given another dimension with the arrival of a large Indian contingent, brought in during the nineteenth-century to work on the sugar plantations to the north.

With such a background and such an assortment, everthing and everybody seemed surprisingly relaxed. A Zulu rickshaw owner posed for a photograph in his gaudy garments and headgear, while outside the City Hall – a great domed replica of the City Hall in Belfast – an African came and sat next to me. My pale skin from an English winter made formalities unnecessary. 'You come from England?' he enquired, with a perfect English accent. 'You will like our country. Although we've got problems.' With little prompting he gave me his articulate evaluation of South Africa's condition – one I had not expected. 'If you are black like me you feel frustrated and restricted, but majority rule would be a disaster. The people in the country are not ready for it – they are not in the townships either, where the tsotsis roam.'

'Tsotsis?'

'They are criminals – young men who fight, steal and intimidate.' He paused: 'I know nothing about mechanics and couldn't repair a car. In the same way my people do not know enough about politics and democracy to run the country. Giving one man one vote would be like giving a horse to somebody who cannot ride.' I could not believe what I was hearing; after hours of listening to an ignorant old white man, who had the vote, but seemed incapable of using it properly, I was now talking to an intelligent black man who had no vote and apparently did not want it. 'Don't get me wrong,' he went on, 'I'm not typical – many of the young blacks are getting very militant. There is a place for whites in South Africa, if they are men of goodwill; everybody can work together. Unfortunately the Dutchmen are so arrogant and want everybody to call them sir.'

Although the beach was segregated, the waiters were Indian, and the food was good – octopus, salad and chips. The sea food of the Natal coast is rich and tasty. Unfortunately the food-chain is not all one way and a shark protection net has to be placed out to sea to prevent swimmers and surfers from becoming warm shark-snacks.

The aquarium showed exactly why the net was needed, with a variety of sharks. The aptly-named ragged-toothed shark looked particularly menacing.

Nightfall had many things to offer: expensive restaurants; a 'bioscope' (film show) at the YMCA; Spike Milligan at the theatre. There were Wimpey bars, as well as those selling Col. Saunders Fried Chicken – complete with an advert on television in Afrikaans. An attractive Asian girl was selling other, more traditional wares – her profession was immediately obvious to two young African boys: 'Fucking cash-cunt,' one spat out at her as he passed; he could have been only 11 or 12. Her pimp, a suave Indian wearing high-heeled cowboy boots, emerged from the shadows and after a brief conversation she moved off to try her luck elsewhere.

The real world seemed so chaotic, that I settled for an evening watching Spike Milligan. He was his normal self – extrovert, amusing and entertaining. The audience was totally integrated and they enjoyed his performance, including his jokes about the Boers. Black, white and khaki all sat, laughed and applauded together. There are those in Britain who condemn actors and entertainers who visit South Africa. Presumably they would prefer South African whites to entertain only whites, and blacks to perform only to other blacks; to my simple country mind it seems that such people actually encourage apartheid.

In the morning, I was due to be met by a member of South Africa's infamous Information Department. Infamous in Britain for its misinformation and activities seen as 'whitewashing Pretoria's racist regime.' It had also been deeply involved in the establishment of *The Citizen* newspaper – ostensibly an independent daily paper, but in reality a newspaper set up by the government, to support the government.

Again, some people who view the complexities of Africa so expertly from an ocean's width away in London or New York, would never deal with the South African Information Department. I have always believed that in order to see a problem clearly, it is essential to see all sides of an argument – official and unofficial – in focus and out. One of the few things of use I ever learnt at school came from a wise but cynical geography master. 'Some people tell you to listen to both sides of an argument,' he would say, 'they are wrong. There are three sides to every argument. Your side, their side and the truth.' When dealing with Africa – north, south and centre – there are probably more than three sides.

As I waited in the foyer of a new tourist hotel, full of Argentinians, I read a newspaper – not *The Citizen*. It helped to create another puzzle, for although South Africa is often called a 'police state' it has the most open and articulate press in Africa. Every day there are articles criticizing the government, condemning apartheid and urging reform. There was an article by Alan Paton, the long-standing opponent of racial separation and author of *Cry, the Beloved Country*. While in the Reader's Digest, Laurens van der Post, another outspoken critic of division based on colour, had also written an article; he was the first man to write a book portraying the evils of apartheid, *In a Province*, published in 1934. As an Afrikaner, writing in English, the book made him many enemies.

A journalist, working on the *Durban Daily News*, began to chat. Surprisingly, he claimed to have few problems writing, although he was opposed to the government: 'The so-called censorship laws are not all that suppressive,' he said, 'although they are very hot on anything to do with the military. Even if a military car crashes into a lamp post there are problems reporting it.'

My name was called; the Information Officer had arrived. I was expecting a smartly dressed Afrikaner with a suit and tie, continually calling me Mr Page. Instead, to my astonishment, I was confronted by a bra-less blonde with green-blue eyes calling me Robin. Mary was most attractive – a farmer's daughter, a graduate and a divorced mother of one. Was this the soft side of the Ministry of Information? If it was, it would not remain soft for long, as she wanted to leave. She disliked bureaucracy; she disagreed with many of the country's policies; and, to round things off nicely, she found most of the official visitors objectionable. A large number were British and German 'guests', considered to be 'opinion-makers' in their own countries, who were shown the 'real South Africa'. 'Most are unbearable – self-opinionated politicians, journalists and local councillors. They think they know all the answers before they get here – all they want to do is eat and drink at our expense. They are just a load of over-fed and over-weight free-loaders.'

The arrangement was simple – she would take me to wherever I wanted to go. I was very interested in the Asian element of the racial jig-saw and so we went to see something of the Indian community and the industry which attracted it to Natal in the first place – sugar.

An Indian Primary School was astonishing. It was run like a sun-tanned English junior school of 20 or 30 years ago. It had smart, orderly classes, and teachers who apparently took a pride in their school and their teaching. One also took a pride in himself: 'Oh Mr Page, where do you hail from?' he asked. He had every affectation of an upper-class Englishman and would not have been out of place teaching Latin at Eton. 'My brother studied in a white class in the UK once. He found many of the questions unanswerable as they all related to Western culture. Consequently I consider single race teaching has considerable advantages.' This was the pure gospel of apartheid being preached by an Indian. It is a strange gospel that is preached in several forms. In some parts of England – in London, Birmingham, Bradford and Leicester – it has a following of assorted, leftward leaning 'community workers', educationists and social workers. They do not refer to it as 'apartheid' of course, they call it 'combatting racism'. It is said that opposites are often remarkably similar: peace marches and riots, democracy and dictatorship, socialism and fascism. In the same way the philosophies of Afrikaner fundamentalism and black activism seem to spring from the same root.

Durban harbour was full of large boats; despite South Africa's isolation it is still one of the most important and attractive ports in the world. Mary wished we could go beyond the harbour – surfing. It would have been difficult, for the large official black car, an enormous Ford Fairlane 500, with tinted windows, would have been rather out of place on the beach. Instead we went to the South African Sugar Terminal, where huge mounds of cane sugar were stored prior to export. The manager was a jovial Englishman. 'We have no trouble selling it. South African sugar is among the purest in the world; it is in great demand, especially in Japan and the USA. We used to sell it in bags from Pakistan, via Holland to avoid embarrassment for the Pakistanis. Now we have direct dealings with Pakistan and the bags have no markings on them to show their place of origin.'

He found all the racial tension and differences tedious. 'This petty apartheid nonsense should be scrapped immediately. At one time we had toilets and washing facilities for blacks, whites and Indians. But I refused to continue the practice. I didn't like it and nor did visitors. When a factory inspector came round and pointed out the lack of signs for each colour, I told him to go ahead and do whatever he liked. If the signs returned I would refuse to allow visitors. He never mentioned the missing signs in his report.

'The sugar-cane comes from the surrounding area, and most of the workers are Indian. That's why the coolies were brought in, in the first place. Some are still backward and we employ a teacher to help the illiterate ones.' Outside Durban the sugar-cane seemed to cover whole hills, thousands of acres – obviously important in providing jobs and, more importantly, foreign currency.

Many Asians live in the Pheonix Indian residential area, just north of Durban – a variety of smart new houses, from small terraces to large, opulent bungalows. Several gardens had Hindu flags flying on poles and there were plenty of cars showing, as always in Asian communities, affluence as well as poverty. It would have been impressive but for one small fact: many of the families had been moved there against their wishes. Their old houses had been knocked down to enlarge and improve an area reserved for whites.

Some of the house interiors had a peculiar atmosphere – Indian, mixed with the traditional trappings of an English living room. It was a reminder of the continuing, everyday influence of Empire and how many Indians were attracted to the alien ways of the 'British'. It is odd seeing a print of Constable's 'The Hay Wain' hanging over an English sideboard, among Hindu pictures, and Indian smells – in Africa. On the opposite wall was one of the strangest calendars I have ever seen: it was advertising the Durban Funeral Services.

Among the Indian population there are Hindus and Muslims, and Durban's Grey Street mosque, in the Asian quarter of the city, is said to be the largest in the Southern hemisphere. The whole area smells and sounds of India, with numerous African additions. Close to the mosque among shops selling curios and spices was another muti shop, well-stocked with roots, monkey skins, shark fins, chopped bark and a variety of highly coloured liquids and powders. The old white-haired shop-keeper claimed that traditional medicine continued to be popular although he had some worries: 'I am still asked for some substances that I am no longer allowed to prescribe.' He showed me balls of limestone, taken by women to prevent conception and to treat stomach complaints, and shark fins that could be burnt to keep away evil spirits.

More orthodox spiritual efforts were taking place in the mosque, with two Muslims facing Mecca and praying and bowing with such enthusiasm that it seemed they would eventually perform headstands. More bare-footed people came in, but the atmosphere seemed far from holy with people talking and children playing in the entrance hall. It was cool inside, like a great marble cave. Chandeliers hung from the ceiling and a large carpet, marked in squares, showed where the faithful should worship – facing a plain wall. Those wanting to pray, washed their feet first in a pool containing carp and goldfish.

As I put my shoes back on, more potential worshippers removed their sandals and walked in. An old Englishman scowled with contempt: 'Look at them,' he said scornfully, 'they're a thieving bunch of sods. They'll pray five times a day and then pinch anything they can get their hands on.'

With a tight schedule and my flight to Rhodesia booked, my time in Durban was already at an end. Not wanting to fly, or risk another train journey, I decided to hitch-hike to Johannesburg. On a hot, clear morning the large black Ford picked me up at 6.30, and Mary dropped me on the outskirts of the city. She smiled, wished me well in Rhodesia and hoped I would be back, before returning to England. I kissed her goodbye. It was the first time I had ever kissed an Information Officer.

* * * * * * *

Like everything in Africa, the early morning traffic was peculiar. Bus loads of Africans were being driven into the city, while cars, mainly with white drivers, were heading out of the city. Soweto – Johannesburg's most notorious township – was evidently not the only African area with problems, for the black bus-drivers were protected in their cabs by heavy wire mesh.

Almost immediately I was picked up by a middle-aged Scottish woman driving a Volkswagen 'beetle'. In England the main topic of conversation seems to be the weather – 'warm fronts', 'dry spells' and 'wet,windy conditions'. In South Africa, the introspection is of rather more consequence, with the internal state of the country dominating all – 'levels of violence', 'sanctions' and 'coming to an accommodation with the blacks'. She talked incessantly about South Africa: how its image was far worse than its reality and how there were wrongs that would soon be righted.

Her answer to the whole of South Africa's problems was simple – 'Christ': 'The Holy Spirit is going to sweep over this nation like a tidal wave.' She claimed to 'speak in tongues' and to be part of the 'charismatic movement', meeting with people of all denominations and colour. Then, as if to confuse the whole issue, she stated that she was a Roman Catholic. I had never heard of a charismatic Catholic before, and had assumed her to be a Baptist or Pentecostalist. 'Oh no', she said triumphantly, 'I am a Catholic,and we are getting stronger all the time. The reason is simple – Christ changes lives. My daughter was a junky; now she is free. My house boy smoked cannabis and roamed with the Tsotsis; he has been transformed. That is how you behave when the Holy Spirit baptizes you. He was zapped by the Holy Spirit.' Again I had not been involved in a conversation, but subjected to a discourse, not uninteresting or uneducated on this occasion, but still non-stop.

The dual-carriageway outside Pietermaritzburg was not a good place to stop. White drivers sped past, not wanting to slow down for anything or anybody. Blacks chugged by driving a variety of old vehicles, bursting at the seams with people, and Asian vans swayed past over-flowing with fruit and vegetables. Eventually a young, quiet English-speaking white offered to take me all the way to Johannesburg.

Before Pietermaritzburg, the countryside had been hilly. Beyond, were vast undulating areas of grassland, scorched brown by the sun and broken only occasionally by large rocky outcrops – 'kopjes' (koppies). There were ranches with black cowboys and occasional clusters of traditional African huts. Birds of prey showed that all South Africa's wildlife had not disappeared with settlement and farming. Briefly, a small herd of antelope was clearly silhouetted on the horizon – a fleeting glimpse of the old plains of Africa that I had still not properly seen. My day-dreams stopped suddenly as the car braked hard, some small black children were driving a herd of long-horned cattle over the road to new pasture. Somehow there was still an atmosphere of frontier living – but where and what was the frontier?

3. Sweet and Sour

Just when it seemed that Johannesburg would never arrive, it appeared in the distance – a cluster of skyscrapers in a haze of industrial pollution. Johannesburg during rush hour is the same as any other great city: noise, heat and turmoil as the streets respond to the twice daily ebb and flow of people.

Johannesburg has always been a city in a rush; the first happened in the 1880s when gold was discovered. A prospector found an outcrop of the main gold-bearing reef of the Witwatersrand in 1886, and by 1889 Johannesburg had become the largest town in southern Africa. Today the city still has a remarkable feeling of energy and vitality and it has grown into a vast conurbation, almost 60 miles across, from east to west. Like most of the old colonial centres of Africa it is not a jumble of streets and haphazard development – the roads are wide, straight and parallel, allowing even rush hour to have an element of order in its chaos.

Gold continues to be vital to the South African economy and it still lies close to Johannesburg's heart. It is mined by black workers in the main, far underground, with white overseers. It is another of Africa's many bitter twists that racial division and job reservation – the seeds of apartheid, were sown in the mines, with white working class miners, mainly from England, wanting to remain socially and financially above the blacks, who were pouring in for work and a new economic way of life.

Today the working class white still feels threatened by African advancement. Whereas the British trade union movement vociferously condemns racial discrimination – as most of its members feel no threat – the South African working class of European origin makes up apartheid's staunchest supporter. Not only does it feel under threat – it is under siege.

Gold was being discussed in crystal-clear, cut-glass English accents in the Carlton Hotel, where a group of immaculately dressed women were considering necklaces and earrings of 22-carat gold. Kruger rands, each an ounce of solid gold, were also causing travellers cheques to change hands. The Carlton certainly had a different class of person from the YMCA in Durban, at 5 rands a night.

Out on the streets more jewellry was for sale – young well-dressed African youths were offering 'diamond' and 'gold' rings for a mere 15 rand. 'That's cheap,' I commented naively. 'Oh no Baas, it is very good quality and very good value. It is worth nearly all the money – I make very little.' I sympathised but regretted the rings were not for me – so one persistent salesman tried a new tack, hoping to appeal to my liberal foreign nature: 'We are kept down by the Boers you know – they won't let us earn much – Vorster is a dog.' I failed to respond; presumably I too became a dog.

What a contrast with the empty shelves of Zaire: the Johannesburg shops were full, from basic commodities to every conceivable luxury – home-produced and grown, as well as imported from as far away as Italy, Denmark and China. They were available to members of all races able and willing to pay the price.

Gradually the number of trains leaving the large station lessened; they were jam-packed with Africans going back to their township homes. The townships are a number of large satellite cities surrounding Johannesburg, where its black workforce eats, sleeps and breeds. Two young white drunks approached me unsuccessfully for money – I was a dog again – and on a grassy bank a 'down and out' who would not have been out of place on London's Embankment was oblivious to the world. An equally ragged African was in a similar condition – they at least were in a multiracial state of alcoholic bliss.

Nearby, more alcohol was being consumed in a bar closely resembling a British pub, and from somewhere came the un-African sound of bagpipes. A middle-aged electrician, Bruce, was drinking beer. I asked him about the rings. 'Steer clear of them', he warned, 'they buy them for about two rand and they immediately call them 18-rand 'wedding rings' and 'engagement rings'. That's 16 rand profit each – it's good money'. He was born in South Africa, but was depressed. 'The whole world's against us, so this place must go up in smoke. If it comes to violence I will happily die, but I will take as many blacks with me as possible. The problem is that most of the blacks are alright. I was brought up with them; I know them and speak their language. It's the minority who cause the trouble.

Compared to the rest of Africa they live like kings, and under Vorster things improved considerably. We are the ones who should be moaning. Over the last two years my wages have gone up 10 per cent, black wages have increased from between 25 – 40 per cent.

'We try to help the blacks, but with many of them it's impossible. In the townships most can afford to go on to electricity but they prefer their smokey fires and oil lamps. I know some who had toilets, but they still went out and squatted outside. It's terrible – they go anywhere – what can we do? All they seem interested in is getting children. It's true what they say about black men – I saw enough of them in the mines. They can get both hands on their old man when its just dangling. It's a pity God gave them so much down there and not more up top.'

Johannesburg is in the Northern Transvaal, 35 miles from Pretoria. Consequently it is not only the industrial and business centre of South Africa, but its high-rise tower blocks also represent Afrikaner defiance: a laager based on bricks, mortar and commerce. The city itself was named after two Afrikaners – Johannes Rissick and Christian Johannes Joubert – commissioners appointed to bring some sort of order to the gold rush.

Because of the Afrikaner influence (even dominance) it seemed peculiar to be walking the streets on a warm evening – sharing the pavements with all races. A billiard hall was completely multiracial, as was the J G Strijdom tower – the Post Office Tower. From its top – more than 880 feet from the ground – Johannesburg spread out like a huge star-spangled diamond. Pop music throbbed out as people danced and drank, while some, after furtive glances and whispered conversations, exchanged money and packages, as what I assumed to be cannabis changed hands. Again the activities were multiracial – legal and illegal. On the door of the bar was a notice: 'Rights of Admission Reserved'; even so an African with a large floppy hat, gold earing and as 'high' as a kite on drugs had found access no problem. Neither had a heavily made-up prostitute; somehow her bright red lips and perspiring ebony skin did not make her the greatest beauty I had ever seen. 'Hallo sweetie,' she said with a gum-revealing smile, 'what hotel are you in?'

'The Carlton,' I replied innocently.

'What room number?'

Warning lights flashed: '42', I replied convincingly – an inaccuracy of at least 250.

'See you later then.' She left with a wink and a blown, toothless kiss. I could not understand it – the whole scene was simply as unrepresentative of apartheid as it was possible to be. I had not seen anything like it shown in or on the British media.

I returned to my room for a good night's sleep. I felt sorry for the occupant of Room 42.

* * * * * * *

Post breakfast time in hotels is a time of waiting for people and meeting others in similar circumstances. I was due to meet another Information Officer; I hoped she would be as pleasant as the last. While I was waiting I began talking to a Swede, a Swede who actually liked living in South Africa. I had assumed that such a species would be as rare as the Dodo. Since then I have met Scandinavians living in many African countries, not involved in aid projects but commercial enterprises, almost as an act of rebellion against the socialism and inflated social consciences of their homelands.

A small, smart African with a bell and my name on a board walked by; the Information Officer had arrived. Mr Trichardt was a smartly dressed, upright Afrikaner with oiled, well groomed hair, combed back. He was as I had imagined every Information Officer ought to be: 'Yes Mr Page,' 'No Mr Page,' 'Certainly Mr Page,' 'You must understand the nature of our problem Mr Page,' 'Whatever you want to do Mr Page we will do it.' I wanted to meet people in business, private and public. Consequently I was introduced to leading men in commerce, the mines and the South African Broadcasting Corporation. They all seemed to be tall, tanned, well-groomed Afrikaners with names such as Le Roux, du Toit, Struik, Steyn, Swanapoel, van der Walt, and of course a real, live van der Merwe. They were all polite and precise – expressing a mixture of concern, confidence and hope for the future. They also showed how completely the Afrikaners had really won the Boer War – socially, economically and politically.

The image given of Soweto throughout the world is of a vast African slum; a shanty town where white South Africans condescend to allow their black brothers to exist in squalor. Some people even assume that the name Soweto itself is an African word for 'despair'. In fact Soweto means South Western Townships.

Believing, like most other people, that the whites just let the blacks get on with their lives I suggested to Mr Trichardt that he showed me some of the schemes that the South African government had carried out for the Africans. It was a sign of my naivety and ignorance, for white South Africa pours in hundreds of millions of rands every year into the black townships and homelands. Whereas a 'third world' black dictatorship can benefit from huge amounts of aid from the West to help provide hospitals, schools, houses and clinics, South Africa, as an international outcast, has to provide most of the money itself. But like the rest of black Africa, South Africa has a never ending problem caused by its high African birth-rate, sucking up resources almost as fast, and sometimes even faster, than the rate of economic growth.

Although the air conditioning of the large black Chevrolet was on full blast, Mr Trichardt was perspiring and touched down his hair as we approached the outskirts of Soweto. First stop was the huge Baragwanath hospital, again not an African word – it was named after a Cornishman. The hospital covered 180 acres, with 2,600 beds and 6,800 staff including 480 doctors, of whom 80 were black, coloured and Asian. In 1977 Baragwanath cost 28 million rand to run each year, with only 1.3 million rand coming from patients. That statistic pleased Mr Trichardt: 'You see Mr Page the rest of the money comes from taxation, so the white section of the population already thinks it is paying its share to help the blacks – a fact the world forgets.' It was an impressive place. The maternity ward dealt with 70 new arrivals a day, with all the most modern equipment to deal with emergencies. A black sister was proud of the unit: 'The family planning message is gradually getting across. The men don't like it, they think it is an affront to their manhood and some get violent if their wives want the pill. But about 10 per cent of the women are now practising family planning. As the young people become better educated the percentage will quickly increase.'

There was an intensive care unit where two girls had just had open heart surgery, as well as a special paraplegic centre; it was badly needed, as each year the hospital has to deal with numerous knife wound cases, many resulting from stabbings in the back. In addition the hospital was the only one in the Transvaal to have a complete body-scanner. Because of this, whites requiring a body scan also had to attend the black hospital.

Close by too was the St John's Eye Hospital, a sister hospital to the one of the same name in Jerusalem. Again a white doctor and sister were working in harmony with black colleagues. There are a number of smaller hospitals and clinics scattered throughout Soweto, to cater for its one million inhabitants. In Johannesburg there is another hospital for blacks, to cater for accidents and emergencies in the capital itself.

The first thing that struck me about the township, was how much better it was than the sprawling suburbs of Kinshasa. The most common house was a small, box-like bungalow, with a garden, built for unskilled workers to rent. They reminded me of the 'prefabs' built in Britain shortly after the Second World War to provide mass, cheap temporary housing. Some of that 'temporary' housing is still being used in England today. But there were other larger houses, built by the more affluent on plots they had been able to purchase. Some bungalows were luxurious, complete with houseboys and gardeners, showing the emergence of an affluent black middle class. Outside one such house a cow was tethered, grazing on the grass verge – old roots die hard. Like all cities, many of the small houses were spotless, comfortable and smelling of polish, while others were dishevelled and in disrepair, almost as if the residents regarded them as nothing more than shelters – rural shelters built in the city. In the older part of the town the straight dusty roads, the litter and the mature banana trees gave it the unmistakable stamp of black Africa.

Soweto started out as a squatter settlement, when rural Africans were sucked towards Johannesburg to work in its war industries. It is the old, old story of people with rural roots gazing in wonder and hope at the city and its riches. Thousands decided to aim for what they saw as a better life; they uprooted themselves and trekked to the city of gold. Some found work and a new affluence; most found subsistence urban living in small over-crowded conditions and some experienced hopelessness, hardship and disease.

Today, simple country people continue to be drawn to Soweto, to live among truly urbanised Africans who have known no other way of life. That too creates problems with the newcomers often being preyed on by the petty criminals and Tsotsis of the city.

New houses are still being built, together with shops, sports grounds, churches, schools and play areas. One new football ground we passed would have been the envy of most footballers in Britain. But somehow even a new shopping centre managed to look seedy; a mixture of dust, litter and mothers with shoals of small children. Mr Trichardt was not impressed. 'Everything we do seems to make no difference. All the African seems good at is spawning. A lot of our troubles have been caused by Christians getting involved with the Africans – they should let the Africans get on with their own affairs.' I could not really see how an illiterate black rural African placed in the middle of Soweto could deal with illness, education and housing without help from outside. Nor could the South African government from the millions of rands that had obviously been poured into Soweto. Perhaps the Information Officer should have been given more information.

My own rural background still shows itself by the fact that I call the mid-day meal 'dinner' – but Mr Trichardt wanted to stop for 'lunch'. The African-run Diepkloof Hotel was near a shop bearing the slogan 'Don't smile at it, Buy it, You'll like it.' Dinner made me smile; I did not buy it and I did not like it. The lethargic waiter produced one menu which circulated slowly then, without taking orders, he served the food. It was the standard lunch, not on the menu. Mr Trichardt kept a stiff Afrikaner upper-lip: 'I didn't really expect anything else, they simply do not understand,' he muttered. Our black companions did not seem to mind; they were already well into the Information Department's free drinks. Daniel, from the Education Department, was on gin, and George, a member of the local Community Council, from a protestant, Congregational background had already swigged a double whisky and had started on the wine.

Thin soup was followed by beef, complete with splinters of bone. As I drank my first glass of wine, George was emptying the second bottle, praising the homeland system as he did so. 'I was born in Soweto,' he said, 'but I don't feel part of it – I feel much more attached to my Homeland.' He smiled at Mr Trichardt. Mr Trichardt failed to say a word, his face said it all: 'I want to go home – I don't want to stay here and listen to this.'

Daniel was quieter and did not take the same official line: 'We Africans have a lot more time for the Afrikaner than for you British,' he said to Mr Trichardt's satisfaction. 'When the British had power they treated the Afrikaner as a second-class illiterate. Now that the Afrikaner has been educated he runs the country. The African can learn from his example. We are treated as second-class citizens, but with education we will one day run the country.' Mr

Trichardt winced, patted his hair, and joined George in another large brandy.

Fortunately the still laughing George had a driver, while Mr Trichardt took me on a tour of schools. For the size of the problem, with the high black birth rate in urban surroundings it was impressive – although it failed to impress Mr Trichardt. 'What a place Mr Page. It's not as bad as it used to be. The best thing that ever happened to Soweto was the riots in '76. Do you know Mr Page, when those blacks were shot, the crime-rate plummetted. Those involved in the rioting were not concerned with politics, they were Tsotsis and criminals. They had nearly all got police records for theft or violence.'

Back in Johannesburg my guide claimed to be leaving me with great regret: 'I'm sorry Mr Page but I can't join you at the mines tomorrow, but I am sure you will enjoy your visit.' He seemed relieved to be back in his city among his own kind. I did not kiss him good-bye.

* * * * * * *

Although I could never recommend the food of the Diepkloof Hotel on the evidence of my one visit, I would never decline an invitation to dine at the Three Ships Restaurant at the Carlton Hotel. It has soft light, softer music and good food. Each guest also gets a box of matches with his or her name embossed on the side. The other astonishing fact is that it has a menu with a wide choice of food and the waiters actually give customers what they order.

My companion, an adviser to the Chamber of Mines, ordered oysters followed by steak. I had the same; I needed a good meal. White South Africans eat enormous quantities of steak, and during the course of my trip I ate so much that it effectively put me off all beef. South African wines are another matter; they are excellent and to me the best in the world.

Mr Kloof was an Afrikaner with the manners and bearing of an English public schoolboy, but he knew his subject: 'Gold is vital to our economy; it's also important to many of our black neighbours. Fifty per cent of our miners are migrant workers from Lesotho, Swaziland, Transkei and Malawi. The rest come from South Africa, including the homelands. We don't make them come, they come because they want to. The number dropped from Malawi for a time, that was when Dr Banda had an Africanization programme going. It led to a plane crash killing 70 miners. Africans were getting the jobs at the airport and a black filled a prop plane with jet fuel. The engines just cut out – it's what we call the K-factor – the kaffir factor. The average unskilled worker gets about 135 rand a month, when in some parts of Africa and India the average income is only 40 rand a year. Sixty per cent of the cost of mining comes from labour. Because of this, over the next few years we will invest in excess of 150 million rand researching less labour-intensive methods of mining. You must remember too that our mining is probably the most advanced in the world; already we are sinking shafts for your National Coal Board.'

* * * * * * *

The Western Area mine was such a large complex that the tourist bus had to be met by a guide. There were piles of pit props, great buildings where rock was crushed and a smelter, where the ore was transformed into heavy gold ingots. 'But first,' we were told, 'we will visit the training area for new recruits. Because they all come from different countries with different languages, we teach them a new language – Franakolo – a mixture of Afrikaans, English, Zulu and Xhosa – and here we have four illiterate blacks learning it.' Our semi-literate working-class Afrikaner had learnt his script well, but he sounded bored. We saw lessons for scooping rocks, winding trollies and shovelling stones. Then on to the black living quarters – very basic dormitories, 16 men to a room in bunk beds, complete with an old tortoise stove. 'The men are divided ethnically, with each black separated according to tribe, language and tradition. If not they knock the shit out of each other.'

Men not on shift were sitting in harmony on the grass, with their washing around them drying in the sun. Nearby were the kitchens and the brewery for African 'mealie beer': 'They love beer, and the bar in the workers' compound has a turnover of 2 million rand a year. The company takes 4 per cent of the profit and the rest is sent to the homelands.' The gold the miners produce is sent and sold all over the world; it is strange having a 'sophisticated' international economy still based on shiny lumps of refined rock.

* * * * * * *

The *Reader's Digest Illustrated Guide of Southern Africa* (fourth edition) has no mention of Soweto in its index. It mentions Sandton however, a small, rich dormitory of Johannesburg. It makes up the 'mink and manure' belt of the city; mink as in fur coats, and manure as in horses. There are some very large, luxury houses with extensive gardens in Sandton. The garden I found myself in was a mere 12 acres: Peter McIlroy lived there with his wife, four dogs, two cats, five children and a houseboy who stayed in a small brick hut at the bottom of the garden. He had moved to South Africa from Northern Ireland 20 years before and had interests in shipping and insurance: 'We are happy, we work hard and we create employment for whites and blacks, so I have nothing on my conscience. And remember too,' he said with emphasis, 'when you look at my house and my houseboy's – we come from totally different cultures and backgrounds. Dealing with ordinary Africans you can have problems; one of my men worked very well. I was so pleased I gave him a large rise. Instead of being pleased or grateful he lost his temper and left. He said that if he was really worth his new wage, he should have been paid it a year ago – that was the last I saw of him.'

Like many Irishmen Peter loved horses and suggested we went for a ride; as we rode through trees and over grass, dust and grasshoppers flew. He was fond of information of unknown accuracy: 'Over there's a prison with a lot of political prisoners in it from Robben Island; they say Nelson Mandela is there at the moment.' Some of the grassland over which we rode had been used, with the help of clever camera angles, as the vast rolling veldt in a feature film involving Zulus: 'That is another thing about the African, when he is wound up nothing will stop him. The Zulus became so worked up during the battle scene that they started knocking hell out of each other – it took hundreds of police to break them up.'

At mid-day several horsey people arrived for a barbeque lunch – a 'brai' – served in the garden. One was a former English show-jumper who had married a South African. Recently she had been invited to take part in a televised show-jumping competition in London. She had wanted to jump as a South African, as that was now her home, but if she had, the Labour Minister of Sport would have withdrawn a large grant for equestrian sports. So she had reverted to being English: 'It's pathetic,' she complained, 'don't

British politicians realise that there are good things going on here as well as bad?'

As evening drew on, Peter began talking without his usual bursts of laughter: 'Robin, you must be careful in Rhodesia – that's turning into a really nasty war. Don't take risks. If you need any help I have friends in the Grey's Scouts. They are a tough bunch who hunt terrs [terrorists] on horseback. The whole thing's getting dirty and even the black soldiers are as keen on killing terrs as anybody else. A year or two ago some businessmen tried to start a campaign based on the word 'harmony', for a multiracial society. It fell apart; at the sound of 'harmony', the troopies [soldiers] just changed it to 'Ha-many – ha-many terrs have you slotted to today' (how many terrorists have you killed today). The authorities here are not stupid. They can see what's going on; they've been taking thousands of blacks into the police force for months.'

Peter drove me back to the Carlton in his Mercedes. Ephraim was at the entrance door of the hotel, and Thomas gave me my key. 'I love African names,' Peter observed, 'they use every name in the Bible. Many of the old African place names, which we have adopted, are vulgar. Once a Zulu chief arrived at a pool in a river where young girls were bathing naked. He said: "Look at those nice fannies." In Zulu it is still called "nice fannies". The Dutch Reformed Church is very puritanical – they would be shocked if they realised what they were saying.'

My plans for the journey were proving to be a mistake; the schedule was far too tight. I was forever packing and un-packing my bag and I had no time to see an impressive Anglican clergyman in Johannesburg called Tutu. As I packed my bag yet again, the television was on. It was a rigidly controlled television service to ensure that programmes in English and Afrikaans were exactly matched. Consequently the cricket from the Cape was in English, while that from Johannesburg was in Afrikaans. Boxing from London had the referee's orders in English and ring-side comments in Afrikaans. Even Anglia television's outstanding natural history programme *Survival*, produced in London, had its English commentary erased. It seemed to emphasize how the Afrikaners are also determined to survive.

* * * * * * *

Another plane, another place, another strange conversation and another man smelling of alcohol first thing in the morning. Today is Monday – it must be the flight to Cape Town. The conversation on the Airbus was not surprising: 'Roll on Cape Town. It's wonderful; it's got the best tits in the world. Each year they get better and the bikinis get smaller.' My neighbour was a grey-haired, distinguished looking man in his late fifties – the last person I would have expected to start a conversation about 'tits', with a complete stranger. 'What do you do for a living?' I asked.
'Oh, I'm a doctor,' he replied casually, 'I have an interest in a practice in Cape Town as well as Johannesburg.' His bearing and black bag seemed to confirm the information. I was grateful that I was not an attractive woman suffering from bronchitis. It seemed to me that without drink and sex, the lives of a large number of South Africans would be empty, even emptier than the lives of many Britons and Americans.

* * * * * * *

Cape Town was fine and clear with magnificent views of Table Mountain, that great flat-topped chunk of sandstone which told early travellers they had reached the very end of Africa. Cape Town's roots go back to 1652 and the arrival of Jan van Riebeeck who set up a trading station for the Dutch East India Company. Before him Sir Francis Drake rounded the Cape in the Golden Hind as long ago as 1580. He too was impressed by its beauty and wrote: 'This Cape is the most stately thing and the fairest Cape we saw in the whole circumference of the earth.'

There are high cliffs, low dunes, small bays cut into rock, birds, flowers and a deep blue, white-flecked sea. Once more I wanted to see and feel the old Africa – the one that drew people to it and held them, before luring them into the interior. But I was whisked away again to see the jig-saw of South Africa's present, with one slight concession to what was considered to be my eccentricity.

'Can I see your penguins?' I had asked. 'It has always been one of my ambitions.'
'Penguins, Mr Page? We have lions at the Kruger Park, but penguins?' Mr Voight was totally bewildered by my request: 'Shall I find out if Cape Town has a zoo?' To appease me I was put on a tourist boat for a choppy trip around an island – there were plenty of

fur seals and cormorants, but no penguins. 'Penguins! I have never been asked about penguins before, Mr Page.'

Although penguins were not on the agenda, politics were, including the position of the Cape coloureds – yet another section of the complicated South African racial jig-saw. The Cape Coloureds are not black, not white, but coloured. They are people of mixed race, resulting from early settlers and native women – often Hottentots – not having the same racial inhibitions as those living today under apartheid. The South African Official Year Book has an interesting phrase for the process of white and black producing brown – it calls it 'a biogenetic contact situation'. By coincidence a local paper revealed that biogentic contact situations were still occurring in South Africa. During 1978, 404 people were prosecuted under the Immorality Act and 265 had been found guilty.

The Cape Malays also form part of the coloured community; they were brought in from the East by The Dutch East India Company – Indians, Chinese, Indonesians and various others. More than 80 per cent of the country's coloured population lives in Cape Province and it is increasing at a rate of nearly 3 per cent a year, one of the highest birth rates in the world. In simple arithmetic, if population growth is greater than the rate of economic growth the people can become poorer, as still more money has to be found for schools, houses and hospitals. In Britain we absurdly criticise our own 'lack of services', although our population is virtually static and we have a standard of living and affluence that most people in the Third World only dream about.

Around Cape Town are several coloured townships which Mr Voight thought I should see. Athlone was large and sprawling. One school showed how racial views were polarising. It did not play sport against white schools, in case it was 'blacked' by other coloured schools. Nearby, built among sand dunes, was the huge new town of Mitchell's Plain. Again it was impressive, with more character than Milton Keynes, except that most of its coloured residents had not wished to be moved there in the first place. At my request the squatter slum of Crossroads was also on the agenda – a shanty town of open sewers, corrugated iron and ragged children.

Then we visited the English answer to the Voortrekker monument – the Newlands Rugby Ground; it was very grand, as was the Mount Nelson Hotel – an opulent reminder of colonial days. The Mount Nelson stands as if Empire had never faded away; the people too seemed from another age. The QE2 had berthed and several passengers had come ashore for a few days. Elegant, rich English women were buying jewellry; two elderly ladies discussed the merits of putting on their 'terrace dresses' and a sour-faced man in an absurd new safari suit was being irritable: 'Waiter, can't you get anything right? Get this ice out of my whisky.' A group nearby were neighing and braying in caricature upper-class fashion – some public schools have a lot to answer for. There was a young Yorkshireman too, with his wife and two small children. He would have been just as happy at Skegness, but the stickers on his suitcase would not have been so impressive.

The Cape Polo and Hunt Club was another part of the old empire. It could have been a well-to-do horsey event in Britain – cucumber sandwiches and 'Oh darling, how lovely to see you. Where's Nigel?' Many had dogs, large and small, that also seemed to appreciate apartheid – wagging their tails at whites and barking at blacks. Two ugly, panting Pekinese erupted every time an African syce (stableboy) went by with a horse. Polo was the order of the day, and included some visiting Argentinian players and their horses. One 65-year-old ex-brigadier flew from his horse at speed, as the horse itself did a spectacular roll, but fortunately both were unhurt. The brigadier simply brushed himself down, smiled, smoothed his moustache and remounted.

There were politicians to meet in Cape Town too, including a Progressive member of parliament who considered himself to be a liberal. I wondered what members of the Afrikaners' United Party would be like, as he resembled a hunting, shooting, fishing right wing Tory, complete with upper-class English accent.

One coloured leader was perceptive and amusing. His main aim was to get a fairer society by scrapping race classification, the Group Areas Act and the Immorality Act. 'People have a strange view of South Africa,' he said, 'even me, a coloured, gets black-balled, if you'll excuse the expression, for being a South African. Foreigners must get off our backs; if there is to be a revolution here, I will blow the whistle, not a bloody loud-mouthed politician in Britain or America. I went on a trip to Germany recently. They looked at me in amazement as if I should have gone wearing a monkey skin, not a shirt, and a ball and chain round my neck instead of a tie. I was even asked if I liked walking on the pavements in Germany. I couldn't believe it.' As he drove off, I noticed a large sticker in the rear window of his car: 'Meg Wet – Apartheid must Go.'

Almost inevitably and confusingly, the most impressive politician was an English speaking nationalist from a Cape Town constituency. He sat in a deep armchair at the Mount Nelson and ordered me coffee; he had 'rooibos – red bush tea'. He was quite adamant that South Africa was not on the verge of revolution: 'In England they've been prophesying immediate doom since 1950, so they've been wrong for 30 years; why should they be right now? We have fewer police per capita than Britain. The whole of our police force is smaller than that for New York City – some revolution.'

'The entire South African story is one of change and struggle: the Boer War – rebellion – the First World War, in which we lost a higher percentage than Britain – a flu epidemic – riots – the great depression – drought – the Second World War – the Berlin Airlift – Korea, and then a short period of peace before Sharpville, Soweto and Angola – so trouble is not new.'

'Despite this, people are still voting with their feet; we have 60,000 workers here from the socialist paradise of Mozambique; we could have 300,000 if we wanted. We have the best conditions for Africans in Africa; we have an annual food surplus, we have industrial growth and the best ports and roads of the underdeveloped world – and we are part of that world. We need help and encouragement, not repeated kicks up the backside.'

'The homelands are not as bad as people say either. Why shouldn't the Africans be allowed to do what they want to do in their own land? Forget the propaganda, they have some of the best land with a lot of potential; and why should they have more land just because their birth rate is so high? Does that mean India, or even Belgium, should be given more land?'

'The rest of Africa is going backwards; Kenya is the only pool of partial light. Did you know that despite the rhetoric we are dealing with 49 other African countries? If ever sanctions are applied the blacks will be the first and the worst to suffer and the economies of the West and Asia will be badly hit. Russia will be the only country to benefit. The Soviets are the real redcoats of 1979, but they don't have the humanity of other empires. Russia has brought disease and guns to Africa, not tractors and doctors. Dealing with Russia is dealing with a regime that does not stick to the rules. You can't play cricket with people who use a lead ball and bowl at your head. The Russians are not interested in people, only power.'

He finished his tea; he was almost the first person I had met not drinking alcohol. I asked him how he got his Christian name 'Kent' – he laughed: 'My mother used to live in Kent.' I smiled too; it was lucky she had not come from Middlesex.

* * * * * * *

The whole area of the Cape is beautiful. Passing a bay of surf and white sand I wanted to stop, but Mr Voight refused. He was not being awkward; it was because of apartheid. 'That's the strange thing about it all, Mr Page. That is a coloured beach and we can't go there, even if we want to. You see apartheid works in more than one way. The rest of the world sees it as a device to prevent blacks from doing what they want; but it prevents whites from doing what they want too.'

We drove inland to an area of mountains with rocky peaks and green, fertile valleys, full of vineyards, orchards and woodland. The air was clear and fresh, with a wide blue sky; we were in South Africa's wine-lands. There were farmsteads, impressive white, thatched, Cape-Dutch houses, that had a look of permanency.

At one we stopped; it belonged to a Mr Myburgh, a large, white-haired Afrikaner of almost Biblical appearance, with a Kruger-like beard. His ancestors arrived in South Africa in 1756 from the Dutch-German border and they had been there for eight generations. At one time the farm was 150 miles across and took an ox cart eight days to get from one side to the other; but with each generation land division had occurred leaving just 1,000 acres of grapes for red wine, and sheep.

The house was started in 1693, with a tightly thatched roof and thick stone walls. The sea could just be glimpsed from the house, giving it the name of *Meerlust – Sea View*. Inside, the high ceilings gave summer coolness and the stout wooden beams lent an air of antiquity. Copper pots, an open fireplace and an old grandfather clock added to the feeling of permanence – the house and its occupiers were rooted to their part of South Africa.

'My family has been here a long time,' Nico Myburgh mused, 'we have a family graveyard out there and that is where I want to be buried and my children after me. When we arrived here it was an empty land; in fact the Africans did not arrive in the area until just after the last war, apart from those working on my farm. A lot of the

Africans do not impress me. If you pay them too much they just stop coming to work and if you pay them too little you are said to be exploiting them. Do you know, I once had a coloured woman who could pick 23 bushels of grapes in the time it took some Africans to pick one? It is a pity, but we can't pick by piece-work as the quality suffers too much. If ever the blacks took over I don't know how my farm people would manage. I have 80 families here – 300 people in all. I have built them a school, given them a church hall and soccer field.'

His wife had just returned from Salisbury and she had worries: 'I have just been up to Rhodesia. I went for the funeral of an uncle who died of cancer. I ended up by going to six more, all victims of the war. While I was there news came through of the Viscount being shot down – there were blacks singing and dancing in celebration in the streets of Salisbury. When my plane left to fly back here it seemed to climb almost vertically to get out of missile range as soon as possible; the whole thing is simply frightening.'

If there was fear or mistrust of Africans, it was difficult to detect that evening in Cape Town. Streams of people were drifting along the pavements to the Cape of Good Hope Centre, a large new building where the Woodstock Rock Festival was taking place. I joined them for a few hours of enthusiastic rock music. It was a totally integrated audience of several thousand with blacks outnumbering whites by about 10 to one. The music was vibrant and throbbing – primitive rhythms brought into the 20th century with electronic technology. There were black groups such as the Radio Rats, the Minerals from Soweto, complete with miners' helmets, shovels and the clenched fist of Black Power, Bloodshed, a coloured group from Cape Town and two white groups. It was an evening of happiness with no racial inhibitions – but there was no mention of it in the British press.

In every sense it was a high note on which to be leaving South Africa. But was I really leaving? I was not quite sure.

4. Home or Away

I did not know whether the next stage of my Southern African journey could really be regarded as leaving South Africa, for I was going to the Ciskei, a Xhosa homeland about to get its independence in the same way as the Transkei. Although South Africa regards homelands as totally independent countries, the rest of the world still sees them as parts of South Africa, controlled by black puppet governments.

To fly to the Ciskei is difficult as it has no international airport and few people want to visit. Consequently I had to fly from Cape Town to East London, on the Eastern Cape.

Shortly after take-off the pilot thought he was doing us a favour by dipping his wings to give a view of Table Mountain. I would have preferred the view without the terror. Table Mountain was wearing its 'table cloth', a tightly hugging white cloud, sweeping down the side, like a smart, white table cloth.

The journey to East London, another important South African port, was short. As Mr Bakker from the town's Department of Information office drove me out we passed through a run-down white area, complete with old cars, unkempt gardens and a feeling of lethargy. It was yet one more piece of the jig-saw, for they were not simply members of the white working class, but at the very bottom rung of their particular racial ladder. As a group they would be near the bottom of any ladder – white, black, or multiracial.

We drove on to King William's Town – still not in the Ciskei, but an enclave of about 12,000 whites almost surrounded by blacks. Logically, if the Ciskei was to have credibility, then King William's Town should have been its capital – its administrative and economic centre. But white sensitivities had prevailed. Apparently coloureds could be moved from Cape Town to Mitchell's Plain, and Indians from Durban to the Pheonix residential area, to make apartheid more acceptable and logical, but whites could not be moved in a similar fashion from King William's Town to East London.

King William's Town was founded in 1835 by Sir Benjamin D'Urban on the site of an old mission station built in 1826. The town became capital of what was then known as British Kaffraria. It has old stone buildings, and others with tin roofs and verandahs over the pavement. It was a garrison town for many years and still has a feeling of being perched on a border, fearing retreat and with a sullen, suspicious atmosphere.

The military atmosphere continued in the Central Hotel, with a sergeant-major-like landlady ordering her black waitresses and cleaners about with a mixture of sarcasm and rudeness: 'Don't keep the customers waiting.' 'Get the sugar.' 'Won't you ever learn – the fork goes on the left.' I had already come to accept that if an establishment was black – run, or badly run,there would be no sugar and the cutlery would be laid out in a variety of original combinations, but a courteous request soon put things right. Some of the waitresses actually needed commending: it seemed remarkable how such large ladies could get between the tables. Xhosa women are not the most beautiful in the world, at least not to the Western eye. With age their posteriors seem to expand; their breasts respond to gravity and they waddle when they walk, rather like ducks.

Coffee had taken half an hour – the sugar and tea spoons had been found; we were now ready for the Ciskei. There was no border post, passport check or notice of welcome. One second we were in South Africa, the next in the homeland of Ciskei. The further in we travelled the more like Black Africa it became. The pace of life slowed from industrial to pastoral – from European to African – from tar roads to dirt. Children were herding cattle and old women sat outside their thatched huts, with scraggy hens scrapping around them. Some had spots of white and orange clay on their faces and children had complicated wire toys – cars and men on bicycles, all with working wheels. 'They copy them from white children,' Mr Bakker informed me. He was wrong, there were no white children to copy. It was a skill I had noticed miles from anywhere in Zaire too. In fact all over Africa many small black children seem to have the same ability with wire. The mystery is, that as they get older so their creativity seems to decline.

At one traditional group of huts we stopped. They were owned by a large, middle-aged lady with several children. One hut was for cooking, another was her bedroom, then came those for her children and one for storing food. Her husband worked in Cape Town and returned home just three or four times a year.

At a large African township, Dimbaza, Mr Bakker was keen to show me the Microsteel Bicycle factory. It had been established to try to bring industry and employment to the Ciskei. It employed many blacks, but was actually run by 15 whites, producing sturdy bikes, ideal for long, bumpy, dusty roads. The factory did not make bikes, but assembled them with a variety of components imported from Taiwan, West Germany and Czechoslovakia. I had always been under the impression that countries from the communist block did not trade with South Africa and its homelands – I was wrong again.

The African workers were earning about £20 per week and it was an attempt to introduce rural Africans to a cash economy and industrial work. That seems to be one of the aims of 'development' and 'aid' throughout Africa, but it is a movement that raises many questions, for is it really desirable to change simple, pastoral people into urban, industrial workers? It must surely be better to herd your own cattle or goats, in your own time, than to perform monotonous, repetitive work in a stuffy factory. Many of the factory jobs could have been mechanised, but then another problem – less employment; the Microsteel factory would have been accused of holding back the blacks, by denying them work. For me the factory visit sowed seeds of doubt, but for Mr Bakker it was a shining beacon of success – 'progress'.

An agricultural project left me with reservations too. It was run by a former colonial civil servant, John Brown, who had worked for the British government in Zambia and Rhodesia. He radiated gloom and despondency. Since independence he had seen Zambia's once flourishing agriculture go backwards and the war in Rhodesia had allowed the tsetse fly to re-colonise many of its old areas. Now he was being asked to set up a new scheme in the Ciskei and he assumed that as soon as independence was granted and he left, the whole thing would crumble. 'The problem is that in a European context they are not farmers, although they have been in contact with whites since 1700. If we do get somebody who works hard for a year, as soon as he gets money he is so happy that he stops work until he has spent it all and his plot has reverted to wasteland.' The project's aim was to create ten acre plots, with gardens and a house. The occupants could then lease cows and use a communal tractor to produce milk and maize. It seemed to be working, but John Brown was not convinced: 'For this to work the Africans need self-discipline and that's exactly what they haven't got.'

The rolling hills of the Ciskei with trees and grassland extend down to the sea. With agriculture and tourism it could succeed in Western economic terms, but it was obvious that its future would still depend on South African aid and expertise for many years to come. The quality of the local black leadership would also be important.

That evening I met the Chief Minister of the Ciskei, the Hon. Chief L. L. Sebe. There was a stir; the hotel staff woke from their slumbers and a big, well-dressed man marched in, followed by three even bigger men, his body-guards, also in dark suits. The Hon. Chief Sebe did not look as if he needed another meal – but he ate a large dinner with great enthusiasm. As we ate, his three henchmen sat in the shadows; they had bulges in their jackets, suggesting pistols, and two wore sunglasses: whether this indicated very good eye-sight or very bad glasses, I was not sure.

The Chief was quite definite that he wanted total independence from South Africa: 'We will do very well – and why shouldn't we have independence – Britain gave it to Swaziland and Lesotho.' Like the rest of Africa, Ciskei has an exploding population, but he did not think birth control was important: 'If a man has two children he needs one loaf of bread. If he has more, then they eat less and he has to earn more, so they learn by experience.' I did not fully understand his logic – nor, it seemed to me, would those with just one loaf of bread.

He had few fears about the future: 'I will manage. I am a great admirer of Winston Churchill and have read all his books on history, war and government.' Briefly things became tense – was he a good democrat like Churchill, I asked, and how did he regard any opposition parties? He stiffened: 'I have been elected by the people,' he said sternly, 'therefore if anybody opposes me, that is subversion.' He rolled his eyes as if to emphasize his point; briefly, he reminded me of Idi Amin.

* * * * * * *

There was something depressing about the Ciskei, hard to explain or to identify, and I was glad to get away. My final destination before Rhodesia was another homeland of a sort, a homeland for the remnants of South Africa's wildlife – the Kruger National Park.

The Kruger Park was one of the first game reserves in Africa and had grown into one of the largest. It lies along South Africa's north-east border, next to Mozambique. The original 'Sabie Game Reserve' covered 840,000 acres; today it has grown to 4,676,467 – between the Crocodile River in the south and the great, grey-green greasy Limpopo River in the north, along the Zimbabwe border. Its wildlife includes an estimated 450 species of birds, more than 200 trees, 138 mammals, 115 reptiles, 50 fish, 33 types of frog and countless flowers, butterflies and insects.

The aircraft from Johannesburg to Skukuza was a small two-engined Douglas DC3 – a Dakota, once the most widely used transport plane in the world. Although rather like travelling in a mechanical sardine-tin, it is strange how I am always more relaxed in small planes. Perhaps it is the totally false psychology of seeing the propellers go round – the means of support is visible. They also fly lower than large planes and so the ground's features can be identified. To me, quite ludicrously, this always means survival – through any emergency.

We flew at first over the farms and fields of the 'high veldt': the land then suddenly dropped away, with cliffs and rugged stream valleys plunging down into the hot 'low veldt'. The small plane bucked and bounced in the turbulence caused by heat, and below, farms gave way to bush.

At Skukuza, developed white Africa, fragmented black Africa and political jig-saws seemed unimportant. I had reached what I regarded as the real Africa – the world of *On Safari*, where the spirit and wildlife of old Africa still lived. Again it was a quaint view, for man has been part of the African scene for millions of years – yet in national parks 'man' the game-warden, the researcher and the tourist (the provider of foreign currency) is permitted, while 'man' the native, the natural inhabitant and neighbour of wildlife, is moved on or kept out. It is something that occurs in all parts of the world.

For me, simply arriving at Skukuza was to enter the old pioneering age of Africa. The name Skukuza was a nickname given to Major James Stevenson-Hamilton, who worked as chief game-warden from 1902 to 1946. Not only was he regarded as 'the father' of the Kruger Park, but also as the father of conservation in Africa.

Because of his anti-poaching enthusiasm he was nicknamed 'sikukhuza' – a local Shangan word for 'he who sweeps clean'.

Several days followed of Land Rovers, heat, dust and wildlife. As soon as I arrived at the camp there was a stir – a lioness attacked a group of drinking impala, one of the most common and beautiful antelope in the park. She had missed her kill, just as I had missed the entire drama, as I had been locked in conversation. It was disappointing: I had always wanted to see a hunting lion and a successful kill; life and death at all levels, it seemed to me, was the essence of Africa.

Bruce Bryden, a wildlife ranger, had a superb job. 'I'm doing what I've always wanted to do; my work is my hobby. It makes me feel semi-retired already. My father recently asked me what my ambition was; I haven't got one, I'm perfectly happy.' He worked on anti-poaching operations, conservation schemes and coping with tourists.

He took me to see a large enclosure where white rhinos were being kept in captivity for re-introduction. Both the white and black rhino had earlier been wiped out by white hunters and black poachers. Black rhinos from Kariba, in Rhodesia, had already been successfully re-introduced. He did not regard rhinos, buffalos or lions as the Kruger's most dangerous animals: 'Hippos are the worst – they don't bite you in two – but three. Their mouths are so big, your body stays in the mouth – your head and legs fall out the sides.'

No part of Africa is free from the influence of man and so no wildlife population can be called truly natural; 'natural balances' cannot therefore occur. Artificial water-holes in the Kruger mean that the park can hold more animals than it once could, and fences prevent the annual migrations. Consequently the populations are controlled by the wardens, to prevent imbalances and damage being done through overgrazing. The park has its own abattoir; on one occasion a load of dead hippos fell from their tarpaulin-covered lorry, in front of shocked tourists. The authorities try to keep visitors and the realities of culling well separated.

The elephant fence and tar road close to the Mozambique border seemed to be far more than aids for controlling elephants. There is a military presence in the park and it was clear that the animal sanctuary was also seen as a buffer zone between South Africa and Marxist infiltrators from Mozambique.

* * * * * * *

After the main Skukuza camp I joined a group of Americans at the Sabie Game Lodge one of the several exclusive, private game parks along the western edge of the Kruger. The Americans were happy; the imitation African huts were air conditioned and there was an ample supply of ice for their continuous stream of whisky and gin. In camp they never stopped talking and on excursions into the bush, in the Land Rover, they were no better. They were all dressed in safari suits and wide-brimmed hats: 'When are we going to see the pussy cats?'; 'We have bigger cows than those buffalo in Texas;' and 'Don't worry honey; have any tourists been eaten around here?'

The camp did walking safaris too, when in theory a ranger, armed to the teeth, walked a group in single file through the bush to hear the birds and smell the wild, aromatic scents. All I could smell was the woman in front of me – a walking advertisement for Elizabeth Arden perfumes and cosmetics, complete with lacquered hair, red fingernails and high-heeled shoes that sank into the sand.

On our arrival at the river a large hippo summed up his feelings well: he relieved himself in spectacular fashion. When hippos answer the call of nature they wag their short tails rapidly; it has the same effect on their droppings as a farmyard muck-spreader. According to a local Shangan story this developed through a confrontation with the local crocodiles. At one time hippos and crocodiles were enemies. The crocodiles attacked baby hippos, and the hippos fouled the water, making no effort to keep their home clean. Things became so bad that a meeting was called; it was agreed that if the crocodiles spared the young hippos, the large hippos would stop relieving themselves in the water. The pact has lasted ever since, but the hippos have cheated – they still foul the water, but they chop it up and spread it with their tails quickly, so the crocs don't notice.

* * * * * * *

It is strange how in films the ordinary hero is sitting alone on a plane when a beautiful girl walks on board and despite the many empty seats, she sits next to him. I must be an 'anti-hero'; on my return trip to Johannesburg a beautiful girl in jeans and jumper appeared. With brown, shoulder-length hair, vivid blue eyes, outdoor tan and good figure, she turned heads as she walked. By her general manner she also conveyed the impression of good taste and wealth. She took one look at me and walked on, to sit by herself. Slowly the plane began to fill; a large perspiring Afrikaner wheezed by and sat next to Anne-Marie. She took one look at him, picked up her hand-luggage and excused herself. Then, despite other empty seats, she sat next to me.

Her father owned a large ranch that had been made into part of a private nature reserve catering for wealthy Americans, most of whom she found as tedious as I did. She talked happily and laughed infectiously – she stopped only when the Dakota hit an air-pocket and fell like a stone. Although the fall must have lasted just a second, or two, it seemed like an age and two women in the seat immediately behind screamed. So much for my theory of small planes being safe and comfortable.

Anne-Marie called herself a progressive liberal, wanting a common voters' role and a relaxation of apartheid: 'There are problems though,' she said, 'I like being friendly towards Africans, but I sometimes wonder if it's worth it. I went to Botswana recently; every black man I spoke to tried to proposition me – all they wanted to do was lay me. It almost made me a racist.' Not only had she been to Botswana, but also to Britain, America and Rhodesia. That evening she had a party in Johannesburg – would I like to go with her, it would be fun? Our encounter would have made a good film script – a farce, for my connecting flight to Rhodesia was due to leave immediately we landed.

She wished me a safe trip to Rhodesia, hoped she would see me again and gave me her address and telephone number. I was met by an agitated airline official; we were late, and I had missed my Air Rhodesia flight to Salisbury: I would have to stay the night at his expense in Johannesburg. While checking in at the hotel I lost Anne-Marie's address. That evening, instead of arriving in Rhodesia, or going to a party, I sat eating pancakes and strawberries and cream, with a bottle of wine. I had lobster soup and ostrich steaks too; on reflection it was rather an inappropriate menu with which to finish my first wildlife safari.

5. Bush War

I expected Rhodesia to be a country of danger and depression, on the verge of collapse. Indeed I had misgivings as I boarded the plane, simply about the flight. I would be flying into what could only be described as a war zone, where two civilian airliners had already been shot down by Russian-made Sam, ground-to-air missiles.

With every piece of turbulence and change of engine pitch, my heart leapt. Flying during daylight made it worse; instead of being cocooned in darkness, hiding our height and position, I could see clearly how high we were from the ground. My only slight consolation was a 'fact', that I found hard to believe: apparently we were out of range of heat-seeking missiles, except when coming in to land.

Before leaving for Africa I had consulted my doctor about my flying phobia. He had offered me valium, but admitted that his in-flight tranquilliser was whisky. As soon as we were airborn I followed his example by ordering a large gin and tonic – a 'sundowner' with the sun still high in the sky.

Since the shooting down of the second Viscount all planes taking-off and landing in Rhodesia varied their routine. To land, some arrived very low, while others descended rapidly from a great height, and the direction of the final approach varied with every flight. We came in low, almost hedge-hopping for several miles, over what seemed to me like terrorist-infested bush. With long grass and boulders I imagined a Sam missile to be behind every tree and in every shadow.

Passing through customs I wondered why I had been worried. The atmosphere seemed totally relaxed, with no hint of civil war, terrorists, freedom-fighters or bloodshed. Black and white mingled easily, relatives were welcomed back and there was much smiling and laughter. A large notice informed 'Rhodesia is Super', and another even greeted new immigrants: 'Welcome to your new home – Rhodesia. The Ministry of Information, Immigration and Tourism welcomes you.'

Driving into the city was almost like driving into a botanical garden, past bungalows with large gardens full of flowering trees and shrubs. Cars and lorries were numerous: Africans were everywhere and the Europeans seemed to be going about their normal business – how could this be a country under siege?

The bus to the town centre was half empty and I sat next to a bronzed, middle-aged farmer in shorts and an open-neck shirt. Brian was returning from a business trip to South Africa. He farmed 55 miles north of Salisbury near Umvukwes. Although many farms in Rhodesia covered thousands of acres his was just 500 – a 'plot' – of which 100 were arable, growing seed maize. The rest had beef and dairy cattle. 'I employ 43 blacks,' he told me, 'pay them and feed them. They all have their families and various relatives with them too. If we Europeans were to pull out, it would be tragic; our farm would revert to bush and our Africans would go hungry.'

'Do you know – after a lifetime out here I still do not fully understand the African; yet British politicians become experts on the subject without leaving their country. Terrorism is getting worse but I've been lucky so far. Terrs have been through the farm and stayed with my workers. When they were there they came across a native reserve policeman and cut both his feet off with an axe and just left him.'

He invited me to Meickle's – Salisbury's oldest and most famous hotel, dating back to the days of 'the pioneers' and 'Fort Salisbury.' There, overlooking Cecil Square, we ate cucumber sandwiches and drank tea, as did several other whites, including two elderly ladies who would not have been out of place taking tea in Cheltenham during the 1940s.

Salisbury was how I had imagined it to be: an old style colonial administrative centre, spacious and spotlessly clean, without the bustle and industrial urgency of Johannesburg. Most of the wide, long, straight streets, called 'avenues', were named after those remarkable people who had helped to shape the country: Rhodes, Jameson, Livingstone, Baines, Baker, Stanley, Selous and Speke. Pioneer Street also linked past with present, but the origin of Rotten Row was not obvious.

The Court House, Parliament Buildings and the Cathedral were fragments of Victorian England erected on the plains of Africa. A large statue paid tribute to Cecil Rhodes, the founder of modern

Rhodesia and in Cecil Square a bronze flag-pole marked the spot where the Union Jack was hoisted for the first time, on 13 September 1890. Cecil Square contained many Jacaranda trees, that in the spring would have looked stunning. It had a fountain too, built in 1950 to mark the city's Diamond Jubilee.

As well as the old and colonial, Salisbury had new, high-rise hotels, offices and department stores. Despite 'economic sanctions' the shops were full, and on the surface at least, racial tensions and discrimination appeared far less than in South Africa, and I had considered South Africa to be reasonably relaxed.

An election was approaching, and the sparring of party politics seemed more obvious than the real violence of war. Seeing that their position was unwinnable the whites under Ian Smith had come to an 'internal settlement' with a number of black leaders, the most popular of whom was Bishop Abel Muzorewa, leader of the United African National Council. He was an unassuming, almost timid Methodist minister, but had also been an African nationalist for many years, including several out of the country, and had genuine and large-scale support among the African population. He had plenty of financial support and a massive advertising campaign was under way; his slogan was simple (and, as it turned out, accurate): 'Vote for the Winners – UANC.' He promised black rule, sensible rule and peace. This last promise he could not keep, as the Patriot Front of Robert Mugabe and Joshua Nkomo intended to keep fighting. At that time, an election and black rule were not an attractive proposition to the Patriotic Front, as in all probability they would have lost. Others destined to lose were members of Zupo – the Zimbabwe United People's Organisation – a group of traditionalists and tribal chiefs. To them economics and foreign policy seemed unimportant. There was even one election leaflet all about dress: 'Do not vote for those who have humiliated you in public by removing wigs from your heads, cutting your trousers at the markets – refusing you to exercise the freedom of dress. They will never change. They will be worse if they have the power. Freedom of dress – VOTE ZUPO.'

Most whites seemed bored with the election; they were certain that 'the Bishop', a moderate, would be elected. Things would not change much and they hoped that sanctions would be lifted and international recognition would follow. To a large crowd on a Sunday afternoon, cricket was the only activity of importance – a game between Rhodesia and Western Province (South Africa) in the Currie Cup. With shirt sleeves and summer dresses it was like a sunny summer afternoon in England.

Western Province had a coloured spin bowler in their team, as well as Garth Le Roux, who later played for Sussex in the English County Championship. He was regarded as the new white thunderbolt – fast and belligerent, in the same mould as Fred Trueman and Denis Lilley.

People were picnicing, talking, laughing and appreciating the match. Above the cricket ground white-bellied storks were circling in thermals of warm air, as were yellow-billed kites; was this a country at war? The main war seemed to be on the pitch, where Garth Le Roux was bowling bouncers: 'Wouldn't it be sad if you were shot down on the way back,' someone shouted, amid cheers and raucous laughter.

On looking more closely there were signs of tension: shoppers, black and white, had their bags searched on entering the department stores and books and newspapers were printed on coarse, discoloured paper, reminding me of my own storybooks just after the Second World War. Printed T-shirts proclaimed messages of pride and defiance: 'Come to Umtali and get Bombed' was an invitation to visit a small town on the Eastern border that was regularly mortared from Mozambique. Others included: 'I'm an endangered species – Melsetter Farmer' and 'I'm Proud to be Rhodesian.' There were others, beyond the realms of defiance or acceptable taste. One showed a skull with a bullet hole through the temple above a simple greeting – 'Hallo Gook' – Gook being an Americanism for 'terrorist.'

Beyond the bravado, the deeper, tragic effects of the war could also be seen – in the Intercession Book at the Cathedral of St Mary and All Saints, where defiance had turned to sorrow and grief;

'We came here today for my dear brother's birthday and his dear wife – Hunyani Viscount victims.'

'For Exiles from Rhodesia; Air disaster – Sue Morgan and her parents. Goodbye Sue.'

'Please pray for my Dad who is dying in hospital after his testicles were blown off in a land mine.'

'Please pray for peace in Rhodesia, and the end of terrorism, that all may live peacefully in this wonderful land.'

On the streets the military side of the war could also be glimpsed:

police reservists in pairs after dark, armed with FN rifles, and army lorries, usually travelling at speed, full of soldiers in combat gear. One load of African soldiers, members of the Rhodesian African Rifles, were singing an African song. It was a chilling contradiction – soldiers, heavily armed with modern weapons, singing ancient songs of war.

In one of Salisbury's adjoining townships the rhythms of war had become too real. A large squatter camp had sprung up next to the market; the residents were rural Africans who had fled from the violence of the countryside. During daylight the security forces ruled, but during darkness 'the boys' or 'the comrades' took over. The ordinary African going about his normal life in the villages was trapped in the middle, harassed and threatened by both sides and sometimes caught in the cross-fire.

Those in the squatter camp had decided that Salisbury offered them sanctuary. Their shelters were made of wood, tin and polythene, held in place by stones, logs and loose bricks, offering them only enough room to sleep on the ground in rags. Smokey fires cooked maize meal and some of the squatters had started growing maize and bananas between their hovels. In hot sun the camp became an oven of dust and flies, while rain turned it into a quagmire; but to the residents, life had improved.

* * * * * * *

The Rhodesian countryside was beautiful – vast open landscapes and huge skies, rolling plains, kopjes, farms and bush. Yet travelling north to visit Brian the realities of the war were clear to see, with white farmhouses surrounded by high-security fences and floodlights, and Land Rovers transformed into bomb and bullet-proof boxes on wheels. The army too had various vehicles with long wheel-bases, thick steel, and gun-slits, for resisting attack and hitting back.

But there was still an unexpected feeling of normality, with the farmers' wives stocking-up in the small towns and the farmers themselves supervising their farms – ploughing, or harvesting maize by hand – with an FN or machine-pistol close by.

At Mazoe dam both blacks and whites were fishing and the great citrus plantations were loaded with ripening oranges. Brian's farm was miles from anywhere, approached by dirt roads – ideal for mines and ambushes. On the surface he was unconcerned: 'When your number's up, your number's up, and there's nothing you can do about it.' There were no fences around his bungalow and the only concession he had made to terrorists was wire mesh over his windows, to prevent grenades or bombs being thrown in. 'Three terrs held up a tractor driver for money yesterday, so they're in the area, but I'm not worried, I have my FN, a wireless transmitter and my dogs. The terrs round here are mostly Shona; they are mediocre – cowards. If they get shot at, some just throw their guns away and run. The Matabele are a different kettle of fish; they come from warrior stock; they are brave and proud.

'Some Shona attacked a farmhouse recently with rockets from 25 yards. Only one hit and that did hardly any damage. They ambushed a car too: they had four hits from 200 rounds and again no real damage was done.' Although he appeared brave and confident, he had left his wife in South Africa with friends on his recent trip. As we sat on his verandah drinking tea he said sadly: 'How could I leave this?' The birds were singing, a slight breeze rustled the leaves; it was one man's personal paradise.

A neighbour, ten miles away on a large farm, was a third generation Rhodesian: 'One grandfather arrived here with the Moody Trek in 1892 and the other came with the British South Africa police in 1903.' The farmhouse was like a fortress, with a high wire fence and floodlights: 'We farmers are in the front-line – we are the soft targets, the terrs see us as easy pickings. Fortunately they are useless buggers. If they had been the IRA we'd have been finished long ago.'

* * * * * * *

Ken Mew had been fighting his own war in Salisbury for years – not against African nationalism, but against white intransigence and prejudice. He was an English Methodist; he had opposed Rhodesia's Unilateral Declaration of Independence (UDI) and had wanted the country to develop into a genuine multiracial society. He was also in constant trouble with those members of the ruling Rhodesian Front who wanted Rhodesia to become a little South Africa, with rigid apartheid and separation of the races. He roused their anger simply by running Ranche House College in Rotten Row, a multiracial college of further education.

As I approached the college shortly after dark, Rotten Row was certainly living up to its name. Already black prostitutes were plying their trade; it seemed that prostitution had become Rhodesia's fastest growing war-industry, and as a result the area was out of bounds to troops of all races. One exceptionally beautiful coloured girl came out of the shadows as if to speak. She was wearing a flimsy, light-weight summer dress that clung to her body as she walked. Suddenly, without warning, she flung her arms around me, pulling me tightly to her and moving her hips rhythmically as she did so. As I struggled to get away her sales technique became even more direct as one of her hands groped deep into my trouser pocket.

I pushed her off and she smiled, with a remarkably misplaced look of innocence: 'Oh come on in and play,' she purred. 'Where are you going?' Thanks to my sheltered Baptist upbringing I was in a state of complete shock: 'I'm going to a meeting, I can't stop,' I stuttered, holding on to my trousers in case of renewed attack.

'We'll still be here waiting when your meeting's over,' a fat, black tart, wearing a mini-skirt assured me, with a disgusting gesture; she was as ugly as her associate had been attractive. I went back to the city centre another way.

* * * * * * *

Ranche House College was set behind trees and I was ushered into Ken Mew's book-lined study. He was short, amiable and grey-haired with a lingering northern English accent. As he laughed and joked it was hard to see how he had been threatened with imprisonment: 'Oh it's true,' he said with a shrug, 'I'm not popular because I try to be honest. The sooner majority rule comes the better. There was a chance for gradual change, a common electoral role and franchise qualifications, but that has all been lost. One of the problems is Ian Smith – he's as thick as an oak plank, but when all the trouble is over the European will still have a place and a function in the new Zimbabwe. At the moment if there was a common franchise based on money then discrimination would be used subtly; the wages of the blacks would be kept down below the level.

'The tragic thing is that discrimination is not all one way. When a catholic Bishop talks about security force brutality the world is horrified, but what the soldiers do is mild compared with the atrocities of the terrorists. Then some blacks who are not very bright get grants for education abroad, from Britain and America, simply because they know the right people, whereas whites with proper qualifications get ignored; it's racial prejudice in reverse.

'Smith has changed his position 180 per cent and done virtually everything Britain asked him to, yet Britain gets more intransigent. In fact David Owen [the then Labour Foreign Secretary] does not seem to understand the situation. When he first visited Salisbury he was asked what would happen if the Patriotic Front, Mugabe and Nkomo, refused terms for a settlement – he said:"Too bloody bad." That has now happened and all he wants to do is pacify the Patriotic Front. He was so arrogant when he was here, he seemed to do more harm than good.'

'Another Labour minister came out here, with a secretary like a block of Siberian ice. He complained that no one was talking to the blacks in Meickles hotel – does he just go up and talk to every black he sees in an English hotel? He was asked if he wanted to change hotels and go to an African hotel in Highfields, that was too much for the multiracial traveller.

* * * * * * *

I borrowed a car to visit the Highfields township on the outskirts of Salisbury, just before dusk. It was seething with people; workers returning home, school children playing in the streets and mothers doing late shopping. I was directed to a small, box-like house with a garden full of bougainvillaeas belonging to Mr Marufa, an elder of the Methodist church and supporter of Bishop Muzorewa. He greeted me with a smile and a handshake. His home was simple and spotless. He showed me into a back room where a daughter brought us orange squash on a tray. He was happy with events. The nationalist struggle was bearing fruit – it would bring peace and freedom: 'The guerilla fighters are doing the right thing and have brought change. After the elections we Africans must be given more land – family planning is not important, our country is so vast. We want the good Europeans to stay on, but we don't want the guerillas in the police force, they are too young and inexperienced, with too many weapons. The war has put brother against brother. Even in the church there have been problems - some support Bishop Muzorewa, some Nkomo and some of our white congregations have many Smith men. It has led to division and bitterness. It is not just white against black, but it is black against black as much as anything, and it could get worse.'

Outside in the darkness the streets had almost emptied. A youth was hitch-hiking to Salisbury, and as I stopped for him three others ran from the shadows and piled in. They were going to a 'disco' and were excited at the prospect. How did prejudice affect them, I asked. The most voluble replied: 'If you pissed outside the police station you would get away with it because you are white. If I did it, I would get arrested.'

I told him that it was not my normal habit to relieve myself in the street, but if he wanted to put his claim to the test, I would oblige. He declined the challenge.

* * * * * * *

'You've been to Highfields after dark? You must be mad, the place is crawling with terrs, man.' A troopie could not believe what he regarded as stupidity: 'Without a gun too – I would never do that.' Meickles always seemed to have groups of soldiers and farmers drinking tea or beer: there was an electrician who had just done his stint at the 'sharp end'; a middle-aged farmer who had left Kenya and Mau Mau to get away from violence, and another middle-aged farmer who looked white and drawn – he had recently learnt that both his teenage sons had been killed in separate incidents while serving in the army.

The troopie was a young Jew, with the unlikely Jewish name of Bruce; from his fighting talk his occupation was appropriate – he was a butcher. 'I've lost count of the terrs I've slotted [killed],' he informed me, 'I feel no guilt or sorrow – they are nothing but murderers and bullies. If you'd seen what I've seen you would feel nothing for them either. Tomorrow, if you like, I'll introduce you to a Viscount survivor; his story will make your hair stand on end, but it will show you what the gooks are like.'

'They don't fight a war with weapons, head on, they bully and terrorise their own people. What they do to loyal Africans is beyond belief. They pull their lips off with pliers. They cut their ears, noses and balls off and make their wives cook them and eat them. Then they beat people to death slowly, or cut them up slowly – what villager is going to argue with them, or resist them? It makes some of us go hard; there's a bounty hunter in Matabeleland who is slotting wanted terrs for money – he collects the ears and scalps of all his victims.' He seemed to be on 'a high' caused by war and like many blacks and whites he had adopted much American vocabulary from the Vietnam war.

His friend, a 'stick leader', was quieter. They had both just come back from the bush where they had experienced several 'contacts' ['firefights' – clashes with terrorists]. In the bush they travelled light, wearing only 'takkies' [sports shoes] without socks, shorts, shirt and cap, together with a rucksack with 90lbs of equipment and a rifle. A 'stick' normally contained between 7-15 men and carried out surveillance, follow-up, ambush and patrol. They would be out in the bush for several days, entirely self-sufficient and sleeping on the ground. There was no doubt that many of the 'Rhodies' were brave, tough and dedicated young men. It was slightly disquieting too: at an age when in England their contemporaries would be sitting school exams or rioting at football matches, they were being asked to fight a dirty war.

Neither troopie was worried about the future: 'There may be a bullet with my name on it,' Bruce smiled, 'I don't know and don't want to know. I've been fired on out in the open, from 100 yards, on automatic. The bullets have been so close they've kicked dust into my eyes – but they've always missed. Yet some people have copped it from a random shot. Who can tell why, or how?'

The shop at Meickles had turned into a souvenir shop for the litter of war – cartridge and shell cases, highly polished and made into a variety of knick-knacks, from pens and paper-knives to large brass vases, nearly all proudly stamped with the word 'Rhodesia'. The girl behind the counter was not complaining: 'The war's good business and we are sending a lot of stuff to America. Service medals are already big money and some troopies are selling their medals for a hundred dollars or more.'

At every turn, it seemed, sanctions could be broken: maize, tobacco and medals were flowing out, while petrol, the mainstay of the Rhodesian war effort, was flowing in. For virtually everything else Rhodesia had become self-sufficient, from diesel locomotives to machine-pistols.

Television however, was an exception. Yet within two or three days of being broadcast in Britain, British programmes were appearing on Rhodesian television, from wildlife to 'Top of the

Pops' and football. Records, too, from the British and American 'hit parades' were on sale; unfortunately some had a slight time-lag, with the updated Christmas song *Mary's Boy Child* becoming a best-seller at Easter.

* * * * * * *

I had arranged to meet Bruce and the Viscount survivor at a hotel in Fife Avenue, late one afternoon. 'Fife Avenue please,' I asked the taxi driver.
'Fifth boss, no problem.' 'No problem' is a favourite African expression. It was a problem however, and I repeated: 'Fife Avenue please – Fife.'
'Yes boss, Fifth, I heard.' Sure enough, we arrived at Fifth Street and the taxi stopped. 'We are here,' Moses grinned.
'No we are not, I want Fife Avenue.'
'Yes Fifth.'
'Fife, this is Fifth STREET, not Fife AVENUE.'
'No problem.'
Eventually we found Fife Avenue, with Moses periodically stopping to ask pedestrians the way. It was the first time I had been totally lost in a taxi.
Bruce considered the episode to be very educational: 'There you are, you've discovered the K-factor.' He had again been drinking heavily, as had an old farmer in long green shorts at a nearby table. On trying to stand he toppled over backwards and cracked his head on the concrete; amazingly he did not seem to notice. He simply stood up and staggered drunkenly towards his car.

There were several troopies drinking beer with Bruce by the swimming pool. Some attractive girls with them were sipping gin and tonics; one was a typist from Bradford with a broad Yorkshire accent who had been in Salisbury for three years. 'There's no way I'll ever go back to England unless something catastrophic happens,' she said aggressively. 'They are real people here – back home they are all becoming the same, looking alike and thinking alike. The British media is disgraceful the way it distorts the truth. You wouldn't recognise this place as the same one written about in England.'

Paul arrived, looking cool in shorts and an open-necked shirt; he was one of the few survivors of the first Viscount disaster. His whole trip had started badly as he had lied to his wife; he had told her that he was going to Kariba on business; in fact he went with a girlfriend. 'I had a premonition about the return flight,' he mused, 'and as there was no seat allocation I was first on the plane and went to the back. My girlfriend wanted to go to the front but I persuaded her to go to the back as I had read somewhere that the back was the safest place. I was always a little apprehensive as my brother had been killed when piloting a military helicopter in 1970.

'Suddenly there was a hell of an explosion that shook the plane when we were about 5,000 feet above the ground. It made the air hostess who was taking drinks stagger. Two of the engines were on fire and the plane was going like a blow torch, with bits falling off the wing and then all you could see out of the windows was flame. I thought we were going one way – I thought for sure this was it. A lot of people stood up screaming and shouting in panic. The pilot put it into a steep dive and the air hostesses managed to get them back into their seats, heads between their knees holding their ankles. I had no great fear, just acceptance that there was no hope of survival.

'I kept looking down to see how high we were and I thought the wing was coming off. Then the pilot said: 'Brace yourselves for impact.' It was like being thrown into a concrete mixer going twice the usual speed, filled with gravel. I felt it hit the tree tops and then one wing must have touched and we dived into a ditch. The front exploded in a ball of fire and the tail broke off and rolled through the fire and out the other side.

'It was suddenly still and I thought, shit, I'm still alive. The fire was still burning and I could see a small hole. I tried to move, but couldn't and remembered my seat belt. I undid it and crawled over the seat and squeezed through. The hole was about 4 feet high and 18 inches across – but I managed to get out. The two air hostesses were badly injured: one had broken arms and the other had a badly cut forehead and a broken leg. The blaze burnt out, but the survivors moved about 100 yards away into a little gully. I noticed that some people had disappeared but I couldn't find them. I asked the hostess if there had been any guns on board as I was worried about terrs, but they had been up front with the captain, and everything was burnt, including the soil.

'I went back to the rest of the survivors and one bloke went to a nearby kraal to try to get some water to treat the injured. On his return he said that it did not look good as the villagers weren't helpful and locked themselves in their huts. He went off again to find some water and I went back to the plane to look for suitcases, for bandages as the two hostesses in particular were so badly injured. I was expecting rescue soon as I thought that they must know where we were.

'Another couple had just reached the plane before me and suddenly bullets were flying all over the place. They were tracers, making lines through the air. I decided that there was no future in staying there so I ran in a zig-zagged line. They fired at me, but after a hundred yards I went over a ridge and down into a gulley. I thought they would be on my heels and crouched down, thinking that I could take one and get his gun. I had been there five minutes when I heard a terrific burst of firing. When I heard them firing I went 200 yards further on in tall grass, close to where a fire was still burning from the plane, moving slowly in front of it as it advanced, thinking that they wouldn't look there.

'I lay there praying for it to get dark. I lay there two hours and heard noises twice and heard a plane in the distance after dark. After the two hours I crawled back in a hell of a state of shock. There was no-one still alive so I went round in a circle again and hid in the grass. I had thrown away my shirt earlier and so all I had on was a pair of tattered shorts. I got cold and didn't sleep all night. As the sun came up I dozed a little and I could see the wreckage from where I was. At 10.30 a Dakota came over and I rushed out and waved. It circled for about half an hour and then about 20 parachutists jumped out. When I walked back to the plane I found another couple still alive. Helicopters then came in; eight of us had survived.

'I felt great anger and horror afterwards as the buggers had been so brutal. All those shot had been women and children, except for a one-armed man. One mother was sheltering her child with her arms; they had been bayonetted too, but they had not been raped. What a load of cowards.

'I was a liberal; I never voted for the Rhodesian Front. But I've had enough now, I want to get out. I think we should offer the place to the highest bidder while we are still in control – to America, or Russia; if not we should wreck the place and get out. After all, we built the place up, so why not knock it all down. It's funny, when we were building it up the rest of the world, including Britain, said wonderful. Then all of a sudden, when political fashions changed, we became racist pigs overnight. In many ways Britain got us into this, but they show no interest in getting us out, and all the time black and white are getting ironed out. I knew two of the last Viscount victims very well, and four others vaguely; I was luckier than they were, poor sods.'

* * * * * * *

As we had been speaking the pool had emptied and darkness fallen. Bruce and friends were still drinking heavily. I could not see how they could physically manage it and had given up all thoughts of keeping up, having turned to orange juice. Peter, another troopie, had also turned off alcohol. 'We want to start a new Olympic games,' he laughed, 'the beer-drinking Olympics. We Rhodies would win easily.' From an inside bar it sounded as if training for the beer-drinking olympics was becoming even more enthusiastic and boisterous, with singing, shouting and the occasional sound of breaking glass.

Paul got up to go: 'They're bush happy in there man; drunk on alcohol and the war. I want to abstain from them both.'

Peter stayed on. He was just 22; tall, quiet, muscular and, much to my surprise, an Afrikaner. Since arriving in Rhodesia, nearly all the whites I had met had been from British stock. 'I don't feel Afrikaner,' he said quietly, 'I'm Rhodesian and I'm going to stay here. The only way they'll get me out is feet first. They've tried that already. I even had a note from the terrs saying that they intend to cull me – but let them try.' When he was not serving in the Rhodesian Light Infantry he was running the family farm, north of Karoi, well on the way to Lake Kariba. He lived with his elderly parents: 'It's tough. It's one of the 'hottest' parts of the country. It's where the war really started and terrs are coming through all the time. I'm going home now for a week. Come up and stay, I could do with some company. Few people want to visit.' He sounded depressed so I promised to visit him during his holiday.

I was on the verge of leaving, with Bruce still drinking, when four police cars screeched to a halt. Fourteen British South African Policemen of assorted colours spilled out, each wearing a flat khaki cap, tunic and shorts; they seemed very young and apprehensive. An officer and two constables immediately marched to the cocktail bar, closely followed by me and Bruce. Inside it was a formidable sight: ten large, young whites, each with long hair and beards, looking as hard as nails, were drinking; the table in front of them was solid with empty glasses and bottles. 'This should be fun,' Bruce grinned, 'they're pissed Selous Scouts, the real tough nuts of the army. They are named after Selous, the old hunter.'

The officer looked uncomfortable and told them to finish their drink: 'Hurry up and get out, you've been making too much noise.' The Scouts jeered and cheered. The officer turned to the barman and, amid booing, ordered him to close the bar. Immediately he had gone a Scout went up to the bar: 'I want another beer Amos.' Amos was frightened and became totally absorbed in the task of wiping a glass. 'Amos – another beer'; still Amos wiped. The Scout suddenly sprang on to the counter and down the other side, knocking bottles and glasses to the floor as he did so. 'Excuse me Amos,' he said politely and placed a crate of beer on the bar. A colleague accepted the gift gratefully and the party resumed.

The singing became louder. When one wanted to relieve himself, he simply stood up and aimed at an empty pint mug on the floor, amid great cheers and with astonishing accuracy. Again the bar was raided and the fridge plundered.

Six more police cars arrived with lights flashing and sirens wailing. Then came military policemen followed by dog-handlers and their dogs, but they kept their distance: 'Come and get us if you want taking out,' one of the Scouts taunted. The assorted police kept well back. Another car drew up, driven by a single middle-aged white officer. He walked straight into the bar quite unafraid; the Scouts fell silent. He called one over to a corner and spoke to him briefly and quietly, before leaving immediately. 'Come on lads, time to go,' the Scout informed his friends. They picked up their guns, left their bottles and filed out, to be directed into the waiting vehicles. As the drunks were driven off into the night they wound down the rear windows of the police-cars to make loud imitation siren noises.

* * * * * *

The Quill Club always seemed a strange place to me. It was a club for members of the Press. It was usually full of the same faces, of assorted colours, staring into glasses, mugs or bottles of alcohol. There they waited patiently, and alcoholically for news of press-

releases and interviews: 'Smith is giving an interview in the morning – are you going?'
'No, I'm going to Karoi.'
'Whose giving an interview there?'
'Nobody; people just live there.'
'Oh, is that all.'

They seemed oblivious to the dramas taking place beyond the four walls of the bar or Information Department. Jim, a young American reporter was astonished: 'Is this how all the great reporters work,' he said, 'writing stories from press releases and alcoholic conversations with other reporters? No wonder there's so much crap written about this place. When I came here I was very much anti-white. Now I'm amazed. How have they been able to survive for so long with the whole world against them and hostile borders on three sides? Boy have they got guts.' He told me that he had heard of a press trip leaving from Karoi in three days time, to visit Tribal Trust Land, in terrorist country. We agreed to meet in Karoi on the morning of the visit.

Back in the street I did a strange thing, on impulse. I decided to celebrate a safe return from Karoi with a trip to Kariba; then, with no hesitation, I walked into the Air Rhodesia office and bought a ticket to the lake – by Viscount. 'Can I have a window seat?' I asked as usual.
'Oh we don't allocate seats,' the girl smiled, with an instant, automatic smile, 'there will be plenty available.'

* * * * * * *

Not many people seemed to be travelling to Karoi. Eventually I was offered a ride all the way by a laughing African, but I was unsure whether or not to take it. His ancient Morris Traveller seemed to be a museum piece; it was overtaken by even the slowest lorries and each of the four wheels appeared to be travelling in different directions at the same time. It swayed and rattled, and to open the passenger door Harry had to pull the inside handle, then the outside, then hit and kick the door until it opened. His own door had to be lifted before he could get in or out; it was on one hinge and as soon as it opened, it dropped six inches.

I had to get to Karoi however, and so I accepted his offer. He was entertaining company, but a journey that should have taken two or

three hours took all day. The car rattled in places that I thought had
no moving parts or joins, and between my feet the road could be
seen clearly through a large hole in the floor. The warm day
gave Harry a thirst, which meant that after every few miles he
stopped for a beer, or a Coca Cola, which in turn led to other stops.
Everything about him seemed to be over-active. He claimed to be
married, with a wife and children in Salisbury, yet he waved
vigorously to every teenage girl we passed, screeching to a halt in
front of one cyclist, forcing her to stop. She was chubby, with
enormous, uplifted breasts, and she was clearly flattered by his
attention. He asked for her name, her address and what she liked
doing. He arranged to see her on his way back later in the week.
'Would you like to come with me Lobin,' he beamed, 'she might
have a sister.' I got used to being called Lobin, as many Africans
have trouble with their R's; I declined his kind offer on the grounds
that the exact day of my return was unknown.

At Sinoia, we stopped again, this time in the middle of an African
township where he had a 'girlfriend' – she was out, only her children
and mother were at home. That too became a call for the return
journey.

As we travelled through the countryside, his imagination seemed
to wander almost as much as his car. At the beginning of the drive
he claimed to be working for a transport company; by the time we
were approaching Karoi he had become a farmer with more then
1000 acres. He boasted too that he was still working for the Special
Branch, after leaving the Rhodesian African Rifles several years
before. He also said that he had once been wounded in the head by
a bullet, and suffered slight brain damage – at last I had heard
something easy to believe.

Still more stops followed, to show me pieces of volcanic rock:
'You get semi-precious stones round here Lobin. If you trust me and
pay me £2,000, I will give you stones that will make you over
£20,000 when you get back to London. I do it for clients all the time;
you take them back in your underpants. If customs worry you, then
just before you land you go into the toilet and swallow them, or
better still push them up your arse – it's not all that uncomfortable.
As soon as you're out in Heathrow, find a toilet. It will make you
rich and I've made a lot of people rich.' Again I declined his kind
offer – I did not know one piece of volcanic rock from another and I
could not see why, if he was making so much money, he had a car

that was literally held together with string and pieces of wire.

We arrived at Karoi at dusk, and Harry dropped me at the Karoi Hotel. He was in a hurry: 'Goodbye Lobin, I have to go and see a girlfriend.' Not surprisingly the hotel had only a handful of guests, and the cocktail bar held just three locals having a night-cap. It also had a display of gem-stones, all of which the manageress claimed were genuine: 'There are a lot in this area. The Africans are clever; they know what the Europeans want and go off into the Tribal Trust Lands to find them. There's a lot of illicit dealing going on. If you know what you are doing you can make a lot of money; if you don't you'll be fleeced.'

As I went to my room, several army trucks roared by, then peace returned. The crickets and cicadas seemed extra loud, but soothing; I fell asleep quickly.

* * * * * *

I awoke with a start at first light; someone was knocking on my door. It was the receptionist, with a note – would I visit room 14. I was puzzled as I had not yet phoned Peter to tell him of my arrival.

I should not really have been surprised: 'Come in,' boomed a familiar, joyful voice. It was Harry; male and female clothing was strewn over the floor, and next to him in bed a young black girl peeped coyly from beneath the sheets.

* * * * * *

Peter arrived at nine in an ordinary Land Rover, without any armour plating and with his FN rifle by his side. He was pleased to see me: 'I didn't think you'd come – the place is crawling with terrs at the moment.' As he spoke his sentences were littered with typical Rhodesian phrases 'What a pleasure'; 'It's a pleasure'; 'To be sure' and 'Just now.' Anybody he liked was 'really switched on.' Bruce was 'really switched on, to be sure.' Before heading for the farm he had some groceries to buy, as well as a bag of 'mealie meal' for his houseboy: 'I'll be back just now.'

He returned quickly and we headed North towards Kariba, before branching off along dirt roads. 'Don't you worry about land mines?' I asked, not being too impressed with the Land Rover.

'It's all right if you keep your eyes open,' he replied reassuringly, 'disturbed soil is the give-away. Ambushes are the worst. The terrs can hear you coming and see the trail of dust as you approach.' We had clouds of dust and sand billowing in our wake as we passed isolated farms, ranches, and groups of African huts.

The farm buildings stood next to quite a large flat-topped kopje. The farmhouse, a bungalow, was like a miniature fortress, with a high wire security fence and floodlights. Once inside the garden a terrorist would have encountered trip wires and Adam's grenades, as well as five dogs. Wire mesh covered the windows and sand bags were piled up to the window sills. The final line of defence was a bunker-cum-command post in the middle of the house. There the agri-alert radio could be switched on to inform neighbours and the army of attack and various switches could be flicked to detonate the grenades in the garden. The bungalow was on a slight hilltop giving good all-round vision, apart from the kopje which looked rather menacing.

'Why do you want floodlights?' I asked, 'Doesn't that make it easy for the terrorists to pick you off at night.'

'They don't. We keep the lights low in the house and you need to see what you are firing at when you are under attack.'

'In that case why don't they shoot the lights out?'

'They haven't thought of that, that's why we're winning-against the odds – they don't think.'

'Are they still gunning for you?'

'No, my workers had a message the other day to say I'm no longer on their cull list – big deal.'

Peter's parents were old and frail. His father Daniel, was over 70 – he had arthritis and did little work, yet his lined face was the colour of leather after a life out in the wind and the sun. He carried a pistol: 'You can't trust these Africans – I'm not leaving for them.' The old couple had moved to Rhodesia from South Africa 30 years before; they still spoke Afrikaans as their first language; a Bible in Afrikaans was on the sideboard and every meal was preceded by grace, again in Afrikaans.

* * * * * *

Peter had a busy day ahead. He started by taking some stock down to the farm store: 'It was set on fire by the terrs last autumn, but we quickly repaired and opened it – the secret is not to let them get a foot in. All the workers were driven off too, except for five or six, but they've gradually returned. We've got guards now.' The guards did not look too terrifying or efficient, but they apparently acted as a deterrent. Two were riding 'shotgun' on a trailer, taking workers to pick tobacco; they wore navy overalls and carried old Second World War .303 rifles.

The farm covered more than 2,000 acres, with 500 down to maize and tobacco, the rest was used for ranching cattle. He showed me his beef cattle with pride-a mixture of Afrikander, Brahman and Herefords, with a few milking Jerseys thrown in for good measure. He was pleased with his maize too and we walked to a large field along a farm track. To the east the land fell away gently, where farm fields stopped and a dirt road vanished into bush. It was hot and peaceful, and a Bateleur eagle cruised effortlessly overhead. In the distance we could hear engines slowly approaching. Suddenly there was a loud explosion, followed by two more – they were deep booms that echoed through the trees and off the kopje. Automatic rifle fire followed, immediately answered by more bursts on automatic. Peter slipped the safety catch on his FN; being unarmed I had a feeling of total helplessness. There was silence. Then another burst of gunfire. Peter was surveying the bush about a mile away with no fear but urgency in his eyes, like a hunter looking for his prey. 'It's a contact,' he whispered, 'they were RPG's we heard first [hand-held armour piercing rockets of Russian origin] – then the AK 47's of the terrs – then the FN's or G3's of the security forces as they responded. The last burst was an FN, fired at the terrs running. That's it, a normal contact, all over in a minute – hit and run; you have to respond straight away or you'll never see them in thick bush. They'll sort out any casualties and start a follow-up. The terrs will be gapping it to Tribal Trust land, or hiding-up. I doubt if we'll see any movement from here, but we may be in trouble tonight.'

Two armour-plated vehicles emerged from the bush. They had obviously been ambushed, and drove off towards a nearby police camp. Almost immediately two helicopters homed in on the area of the contact; one went in to land and the other circled before it too landed: 'A helicopter gunship and a Casvac – casualty evacuation – they've taken casualties.'

* * * * * * *

That evening we sat in the bungalow, away from the windows, talking. Outside the floodlights blazed, attracting clouds of dizzily flying moths. 'It's at times like this Robin, that I worry. When I'm away from here and my father and mother are alone, with terrs just outside.' Peter had seen a lot of action: 'I've been in the Rhodesia Regiment's "fireforce"; that's responding to trouble. I've lost count of the number of contacts and ambushes I've had. In the first ambush it took several seconds for the penny to drop. Now I react automatically – you have to, else you are dead. I don't feel fear; everybody reacts differently. One guy had a nervous breakdown in an ambush – he had to be taken out by helicopter. I've seen blokes walking about for hours without knowing what they were doing, after land-mine explosions.'

Like most of his contemporaries, Peter had killed: 'It's either a case of kill, or be killed. My first was amazing: a gook with a gun came out of a hut 800 yards away, without seeing us. I quietly put my sights on maximum, layed down and shot. It hit him in the temple and killed him stone dead. What a pleasure man, we'd been after him for some time.

'I've been pinned down in gulleys where we've got out by lifting our hats above rocks to draw their fire, so that someone else can move. We've ambushed gooks too; we got some by lobbing phosphorous grenades into the cave where they were holed-up. After an ambush we follow-up, but when dusk comes we always circle back on our tracks to set up an ambush, cum camp, in case we're being followed. I make sure I keep fit, it helps you to survive.'

For a farm on the 'bundu' (bush) we had a late night, retiring to bed at ten. Inevitably Peter slept with his FN at his side. I awoke with the sun already blazing; I had slept like a log. Peter had heard more gunfire shortly after midnight and had been out of bed four times in response to unfamiliar noises. Sleeping out in the bush, often in danger, meant that any new sound had the same effect on him as an alarm-clock. My less well-tuned senses slept on.

* * * * * * *

An insurance agent arrived shortly after breakfast, wearing a pistol in a holster, like a cowboy from a Western film set. A lot of insurance was being sold in Rhodesia at the time, but premiums were high. Business was brief and Peter began talking about the war and the power of the FN: 'What a weapon – do you know you can even slot a terr sheltering behind a tree, the bullet will go straight through it, no problem.'

'It does better than that,' Alf responded. 'With only a medium-sized tree it could go through a whole row of gooks. The tree would start the bullet tumbling; it would make a very big hole – what a mess.'

* * * * * * *

Alf got me to Karoi by ten, where members of the 'Press Trip' were immediately offered the chance of seeing more 'big holes.' An immaculately dressed army officer, complete with peaked cap, cravat and upper-class English accent was saying: 'Before we get going chaps, you ought to go across the road to see the floppies.' Several dead terrorists had been brought in and laid out on the grass in a small, sun-filled compound.

There were eight or nine floppies in their tattered T-shirts and trousers, together with a collection of weapons – AK 47's, rocket launchers, grenades, landmines and rounds of ammunition. The officer would not say where they were from and I was never able to find out if they had come from the contact near the farm.

On television war takes on a romantic, heroic aspect, where bravery triumphs and bullets seem to inflict only minor wounds. Out in the African bush the reality was brought home in pain, finality and futility. There were no simple flesh wounds; where high velocity bullets had hit, legs and arms had been ripped off, leaving torn flesh and splintered bones. Where a bullet had entered, the wound was small; where it had left was a fist-sized hole. One young 'terrorist' was minus both legs and an arm, and another, shot in the back of the head, had three-quarters of his face blown away. Black or white, terr or Selous Scout, it seemed such a waste.

A German photo-journalist was in his element, photographing the contortions of death – close up and from every angle. In the sun the bodies were already beginning to smell, but he was quite unconcerned. Journalists of several nationalities were present, except those from the British dailies, who were presumably still at the Quill Club waiting for press releases and refilled glasses.

We travelled in four 'crocodiles' – long, armour-plated but roofless troop-carriers, with flaps at the sides which could be opened to allow firing from inside the lorry. Two of the vehicles were full of assorted journalists, officials and members of the Central Intelligence Office, while the remaining two were spilling over with soldiers from the First Battalion of the Rhodesian African Rifles to 'protect' us in the event of trouble. A Land Rover tagged along behind containing more special branch men with pistols and machine pistols.

Instead of turning right, off the main Kariba road, the convoy turned left towards the Urungwe Tribal Trust Land. The lorries stirred up dust as we travelled at speed along dirt roads, at first through fields of maize and then undulating bush of long grass, acacias and large rocks. We arrived at a bush camp with tents heavily camouflaged, vehicles spread out and groups of 'auxiliaries' – some drilling, others dismantling and assembling guns, and others in a simulated 'contact'. They had new G3 rifles, a NATO gun, and looked well-trained and disciplined. Their uniforms were simple – floppy bush hats, combat trousers, boots and brown T-shirts bearing the slogan 'Pfumo re Vanhu', meaning 'Spear of the People.' They were the military auxiliaries of Bishop Muzorewa.

The suave officer explained the scheme of things: 'These auxiliaries are the men who could win the war. When the terrs started they used one of Chairman Mao's concepts, that revolutionary warfare succeeds best when its forces are 'like fish in the sea and swim with the people.' The auxiliaries are now being introduced as cells in the villages; they are the ones now swimming with the people. There, they get information about the terrs and the gooks find they get their food cut off and they have become fish out of water.

'It is the terr policy to close down schools and clinics by burning them out and ransacking them. Eight schools and two clinics have now reopened. The problems around Urungwe started in 1977 and intensified in 1978, with rapes, murders and disciplinary killings. In that one year more than 100 such murders took place, so the locals had to support the terrs. Now the balance is tipping the other way. In the last three weeks there have been 30 contacts; food stocks and arms caches have been taken, and the terrs are now concentrated in the extreme north and south west – about 400 of them.'

In view of the 30 recent contacts, someone asked the number of kills: 'Only one terr has been actually slotted by the auxiliaries so far. It works out at about 10,000 rounds a kill. That's not too bad, in the Second World War it was 100,000.' He claimed that 10 per cent of the auxillaries were 'turned terrs' – terrorists who had come 'on side.' 'They kept their old uniforms and weapons – in the early days some were culled by mistake, as terrs, but now we've got it all sorted out.' As we left the camp the auxiliaries were singing in Shona: 'The war has arrived and we are happy with the troops.'

We stopped at a village where a large school had been reopened, and at another where a village meeting was in progress. The village chief had recently been 'rescued' from the terrs by the security forces; he now claimed that the spirits had led the soldiers to the terrorists and the same spirits were instructing him to join the government fight. He was forecasting victory amid much dancing, singing and ululating. The sock worn over his head was said to be a sign of his spiritual position.

Nearby some 'turned terrs' were watching the proceedings; they looked terrifying, heavily armed, with bandeliers of bullets around their necks. One sported reflective sun glasses and another was dancing with a group of teenage girls – he was enjoying the rewards of war, and was high on 'dope.'

The Land Rover joined us, driven by a hard-looking special branch man in shorts, sports shoes, cravat, and armed only with a pistol. Kevin's vehicle was mine-proofed underneath, but it had open sides. It also sported a name plate – 'Apollo 2', as well as a rhyme:
'Winkle Winkle little rectum
 You hear the bangs
 When you least expect them.'
Another white, special branch man, with machine pistol slung over a shoulder, was following on a motorbike.

Kevin was pleased with what was going on: 'Don't tell the boss, but we should have started this years ago – it's too late now because of the number of terrs and international pressure; but here it works a treat.' He called an auxiliary over: 'Commander – this guy's really switched on.'

Luke held an AK 47 and looked ferocious; he was a young school teacher and despite his appearance he spoke quietly and well, with little trace of the normal African accent: 'I became an auxiliary after the terrorists closed down my school. Why interfere with the children's education in pursuit of a political goal? I want to protect the people so they can vote freely and things can get back to normal. Some people are not fighting the war of the people, they are just getting enjoyment from killing the people.'

Kevin then shouted to another commander – 'Never Mind' – 'He's not so articulate, but he's a rough diamond – he's good news.' At first glance Never Mind was like a walking arsenal, with bandeliers of bullets, a revolver and an automatic rifle. 'Why are you called Never Mind?' I asked.

He smiled: 'Because if I die – Never Mind. I don't mind dying, whether it is in one second or ten seconds – Never Mind. All I want to do is clear out the bloody shits. I want peace, not bloodshed, we are killing each other for nothing, so we've got to clear out the shits.'

Kevin stayed behind, talking to his commanders and the convoy headed back towards Karoi. As we passed some small, waving children at the roadside, dust engulfed them. Others sat fishing on the banks of a muddy stream; there were kraals, children herding cattle and bee-eaters and rollers flying, with the sun catching their brilliant wing feathers. It seemed too beautiful for war, until two helicopter gun-ships passed low overhead to remind of reality.

The commander was pleased with his day: 'There you are – all back safely and no gook in sight. By the way, did anybody not see the floppies this morning?' The German photographer scuttled away again, cameras at the ready.

* * * * * * *

Peter was up three times during the night after hearing 'noises', but again I slept through them. We went to the barns where tobacco was drying, straight after breakfast, and I was surprised by the number of small children running about. 'It's the terrs,' Peter complained, 'they've shut the clinic and the school and we can't get them open again – it's too dicey for the Africans involved. Two children have died with measles just now, because of it, the terrs hit their own people much worse than us; they're totally intimidated.'

At mid-day Peter dropped me off on the main road in Karoi. 'Sorry to see you go Robin. I won't see a soul now until I get back to Salisbury. I hope you get there quickly.'

At four pm I was still waiting. Few cars seemed to be going past, and those that did showed no interest in stopping. What made it worse was the fact that travel along the main road was not recommended after four o'clock because of the increased chances of ambush.

At last a bus came along and I waved it down. The black driver smiled: 'Yes boss, we're going to Salisbury.' I climbed aboard; it was half full – the passengers were all Africans, except for five hens with their legs tied together. A large lady in the seat in front was eating peanuts, throwing the shells on the floor and out of the window. Pieces of sweet corn debris and egg shells littered the floor and empty beer bottles rolled noisily about at every corner, as did five drunks on the back seat.

I had thought we were heading straight for Salisbury. I was wrong. We turned right, to hit dirt roads – long, straight dusty roads, with occasional Africans walking and more passengers waiting outside small wayside stores. There were many stories of bus hold-ups for money, but I was not unduly worried by the circular tour of Tribal Trust Land, although one white face in a sea of black was the subject of much interest to the locals.

The bus filled – almost emptied, and by the time we were back on tar at last, heading directly for Salisbury, it was full again. I had no idea where we were when the driver stopped: 'We are in Salisbury now boss. You get out here, we're going on to the townships.'

I was not sure whether I was glad to be back in Salisbury. The brief trip to Karoi had flashed by, with no time to worry about anything. I now had two nights and a day to think about the flight to Kariba. I switched on the television in my room at the Oasis – a troopies' hotel, I hit the adverts – a warning, urging the populous not to 'spread rumours', and an advert for a double long-playing record featuring a troopie with a guitar. It was called *Rhodesia the Brave and the Beautiful*; already nostalgia had set in for the war.

* * * * * * *

I had felt no fear at Karoi, but arriving at Salisbury Airport I was tense and apprehensive. Even now I cannot really explain why I decided to do something that I knew would terrify me. It was almost as if I wanted to find out how I would face fear.

The Viscount had been painted brown, in an attempt to reduce its heat retention, which in theory would reduce the effectiveness of any heat-seeking missiles fired at it. It seemed a psychological manoeuvre to me, rather than a serious military innovation. After all, in many wars, planes and helicopters had been painted brown, yet it had not stopped them being hit by missiles.

There were just 19 passengers on board – more than I had expected; but the Air Rhodesia girl had been right, finding a window-seat was no problem. The engine whine turned into a roar and we accelerated along the runway. Once airborne the pilot spiralled up, almost vertically, directly over the centre of Salisbury. The stewardess offering drinks was blunt: 'We do this to get out of range of the terrs, and we assume there are none in Salisbury – at least none with missiles.' Once at an altitude considered safe, the flight continued normally. I sat stiffly by my window for the full duration of the flight, scouring the bush for a tell-tale flash and swigging gin and tonic. Suddenly, the great ribbon of Kariba was below us, and again we descended rapidly in a series of tight circles, this time over the lake, before making a low-level dash for the airfield.

I was the only passenger going to the Cutty Sark Hotel, and had a combie to myself. As we approached the town I was rather alarmed: the telephone wires were down and being so close to Zambia and several terrorist infiltration routes, I assumed it was the work of terrorists. 'Don't worry Sir,' another smiling Amos assured me, 'it's elephants, not terrs. They have been coming into the town every night for a week.'

The hotel was virtually deserted and my every move was watched by many pairs of eyes. In the dining room, bored waiters almost fell over themselves in their desire to actually do something, and at the pool, as soon as the ice hit the bottom of my glass, a race was on to see if I wanted a refill. Some of the neighbouring hotels had closed through lack of custom, but others hung on doggedly.

It was wonderful being in a deserted, exotic hotel – deserted that was, apart from a solitary Irish vet called Dermot. He had only arrived in Rhodesia three years before, from Dublin: 'War can't be a bad thing, can it, if it frightens people away from a place like this.' Another beer arrived to interrupt his sun-bathing. He had been drafted into the Grey's Scouts: 'I'm a Captain already; I suppose it's only because I'm a vet. The Scouts are very effective as they cover so much ground through the bush. The horses help too, as the hotes [another slang word for the Africans] are frightened by them. Even so a lot of the horses get killed and wounded. The Africans on our side are good blokes, but the ordinary Af in the street is only interested in telling you what he thinks you want to hear. My houseboy, Finneous, is the same. I love the way they start a sentence with ah-eeee – I think it's to buy time while they think what to say.'

We swam, ate, drank and water-skied; were there really Sam missiles in the neighbourhood? Another guest arrived early one morning: 'Oh my God,' Dermot observed, 'he's either bush happy, or else he's cracking up after being revved.' He seemed hyperactive, with wide staring eyes which always avoided making contact during conversations. His conversations with me were always the same: 'You must come tiger fishing, it's brilliant, you'll enjoy it. I don't want to go by myself.' Dermot made it clear that he was not interested, but eventually I succumbed, simply to provide him with company.

It was pleasant cruising about on the lake. Close inshore among lush grasses and reeds was a large herd of elephants, with cattle egrets stalking the disturbed insects. Some of the animals were large old tuskers, and the sun on their ivory matched the brilliant white plumage of the birds. An island had its own herd of impala, and from time to time the evocative calls of fish eagles floated through the still, airless heat. As Nick fished, other fishermen joined him – cormorants and darters, and there were terns too, seabirds who obviously regarded Kariba as a real sea. I fished briefly and caught two or three tiger fish, weighing about seven pounds each; with stripes and interlocking, needle-sharp teeth, their ferocity seemed to epitomise Africa. It had been a relaxing, but unexciting afternoon.

At times that evening, it seemed as if Nick had spent the afternoon somewhere quite different: 'Dermot, you missed a great time – at times the lake boiled with the action, you must come tomorrow.' The reason for the fever pitch of excitement became obvious when Nick handed me what I thought was a note – it was a bill for a 'fishing trip, with guide and inboard bar'.

'You must be joking,' I said, believing it to be a rather tame joke, 'I hate fishing, if that's the best in the world, what's the worst like?' His actual reply was a highly concentrated cocktail of abuse and obscenities. Dermot was amused: 'You should have seen that coming, shouldn't you. With eyes like that he's probably been blown up by a land mine and his brain is still out there in the bush somewhere – scrambled. 'I paid him for two cans of Coke and told him to go away and look for his brain.

* * * * * * *

The final evening turned into a water-born riot. Several times each week at 'sundowner' time the 'Booze Cruise' got underway. It was a large luxury launch, full of drink. The sales patter was simple: 'Buy your ticket here, and drink as much as you like, or can.' Again Dermot and me were the only tourists – but the boat quickly filled with off-duty 'troopies.' It was a beautiful sun-set, with the sun firing the clouds of the entire sky, which in turn streaked the surface of the lake with dying flame. As darkness fell the lakeside lights flickered, and fishing boats took to the water. The Zambian shore seemed close; it was remarkable to be in a war-zone, within a stone's throw of a hostile country and guerrilla guns, yet all those on board were totally unconcerned. 'It's amazing,' Dermot mused, 'all this water – but they've got it all covered with radar, you know – no end of terrs have been slotted trying to sneak across.' Soon there was singing, shouting, staggering and urinating over the side: –
'Come on you terrs, where are you?'
'Let's raid Zambia.'
As it got darker the lights of the fishing boats shone above the water, attracting the fish. Dermot shook his head:'That shows why Africa needs Europeans. They are fishing for "kapenta" – small fish, like whitebait at home. They were introduced on the Zambian side to create a small fishing industry for food and employment. The fish increased throughout the lake, so the Rhodies have set up a successful fishing industry and the Zambians are still sitting on their backsides pleading poverty and hunger, and asking for aid. Kaunda must be one of the biggest comedians in Africa.'

Comedy was much nearer home, for the troopies had reached the swimming stage – plunging in from the top deck. Rifles and clothing littered the floor; raucous laughter and shouting filled the air. Why none of them drowned still remains a mystery.

* * * * * * *

Flying out of Kariba was again terrifying – tight circles upwards, over the lake. It was a relief to land at the Victoria Falls, another 'hot' zone, with occasional mortar bombs and rockets falling from Zambia.

The Victoria Falls Hotel was in the best colonial style – comfortable, relaxed and still with tourists, mainly British and Rhodesian, including servicemen on leave. The terrace was peaceful, looking out on to bush and an old iron bridge over the gorge of the Zambezi. The cicadas were in full harmony and the distant roar of water plunging on to rock made a background of soothing sound. Suddenly a shrill whistle intruded: soon it came again and an old memory stirred: 'What, a steam train? What's going on?' I asked. A soldier was sitting with me: 'It always comes at this time – on the dot.'

Sure enough, trucks came into view, together with an engine pushing them. Once on the bridge the train stopped and the engine was unhitched. A Zambian engine arrived from the other side and pulled the trucks into Zambia.

'But I thought there were sanctions in operation,' I observed, genuinely puzzled.

'You must be joking – Kaunda is. He's never stopped dealing with Rhodesia. Zambia would be even more broke if it did. There's at least two trains a day – KK's the biggest con-man in Africa, he always has been. The only thing he's good at is crying; he can turn tears on and off whenever he likes – like a woman. He goes on British television, bursts into tears, and everybody thinks he's a wonderful sincere man with deep feelings.'

'But at home they all say how wonderful and intelligent Kaunda is.'

'Intelligent – an intelligent Zambian – oh man. Now wait a minute – oh yes, I did hear of two once. Kaunda had them both arrested. He doesn't like intelligent blacks and he's certainly not one himself.'

Ian was coloured, in army uniform and agreed with Paul. He was in the psychological unit working on propaganda to get the terrorists to change sides: 'It's a good scheme – Paul works on the terrs' bodies – I'm after their minds; a lot are switching at the moment. Nkomo's support is falling away all the time; he's a depleted force – a psychopath, like Hitler. Why can't people in Britain see that?'

The situation at the bridge fascinated me. The whistles of the Zambian train could still be heard, as the Rhodesian engine had reversed back along the track in a cloud of steam and smoke. I walked down to get a better look. The bridge was an impressive monument to the early engineers of empire. It was built in 1905, spanning the gorge of the Zambezi and the rapids far below. As I approached I could see Zambian soldiers watching me through binoculars from the far side. When I raised my camera with its telephoto lense they began shouting and unslinging their rifles from their shoulders; I beat a hasty, but dignified, retreat.

The rain-forest by the falls was luxuriant – jungle, bathed in a permanent drizzle of mist. The Falls themselves were spectacular; I was quite unprepared for their size and grandeur. The water thundered over rock into a gigantic chasm of foam, spray and angry water, above which two perfectly formed rainbows reflected the colours of the brilliant sunlight. There were several cascades and cataracts of water and I stood in awe and wonder. Nearby, dressed in a flowing cotton dress of many colours, an African woman began singing softly, and beautifully, with tears in her eyes, shaking her head slowly from side to side, almost in disbelief. I could understand her feelings. I tried to understand how Livingstone had felt too, after his long journey along the Zambezi valley, to suddenly come across such a sight – the first European eyes to gaze on something truly wonderful. Those early European explorers, missionaries and adventurers were remarkable, and Livingstone's view of the Victoria Falls must have made all the discomforts and hardships completely worthwhile.

Somehow the Zambezi 'booze cruise' above the falls, seemed inappropriate in such a place. The crocodiles kept revellers in the boat on this occasion and a speedboat with a machine gun at its front kept any terrorists on the Zambian bank, out of sight. I promised myself that I would return to see the Falls again, preferably in peace time.

* * * * * * *

Like Kariba, the Wankie Game Reserve's 3.5 million acres on the edge of the Kalahari, was almost totally without tourists, although teeming with wildlife. A ranger thought the war was a good thing: 'It's strange, the wildlife is thriving – there is less poaching and the terrs seem frightened of wild animals.' It was a good way to see wildlife, driving with an African ranger, James, along deserted park roads, deserted apart from giraffe, wildebeeste, wart-hog, zebra, white rhino and elephant. The elephants had much shorter tusks than usual; James claimed it was because they wore them down, digging into the sand for water during the long dry seasons.

Wankie, now Hwange, is one of the best areas for wildlife in

Africa, being a mixture of forest, bush, pan and semi-desert. Its soils are poor and it would make useless farmland, consequently its future should be secure.

Tribal Trust Land bordered the Park, and illustrated one of Africa's age-old problems. In the national park, despite the land being arid, there was vegetation cover. In the Tribal Trust Land, there was over-grazing caused by cattle, sheep and goats, leaving much bare soil and areas of soil erosion.

A nearby village was hot and dusty, with thatched mud huts built close to a large Baobab tree, and food stores built on legs to combat rats and dampness. Women were pounding maize and a little girl was carrying a young goat; she gave me a Baobab pod as a present. The only brick-built house was a small classroom outside which sat an African teacher and a European Methodist missionary. The teacher wore a smart suit with shiny leather shoes and seemed to think they gave him sophistication. It was a false impression; he wanted to get married but could not afford the lobolo (dowry). He had no cows to pay for his bride and so was having to save up £200, which would take him several months.

He wanted us to stay, but the missionary was becoming agitated. There had been a lot of terrorist activity on the Tribal Trust Land recently and he wanted to be away before dusk and the curfew. It seemed that after dark the terrorists ruled. Back in the park a lion roared. All over Rhodesia fear and power arrived with the night.

6. The Convoy

Dermot the Irish vet had given me another contact – Bill: 'You'll like him,' he said, 'he's got aristocratic blood in his veins – somewhere; but quite which side of the bed sheet it got in, nobody is sure. He's got contacts at Melsetter, right on the Mozambique border – the "hottest" part of the country. I'm sure he'll get you there if you want to go. Oh, and don't lend him any money, you'll never get it back – he's always in debt.'

For someone with a cash-flow problem Bill lived well and was extremely generous. Although his home was 50 miles away, he invited me to 'lunch' at the Salisbury Club: wall-to-wall carpeting, deep leather armchairs and a good line in Yorkshire pudding, roast beef and horseradish sauce. More importantly for those sharing Bill's table, it also had an ample supply of sherry, wine and port.

They were a mixed group – Bill, Julian a friend of the family out from England, Edward a local farmer, and an English officer in the Rhodesian African Rifles, just about to leave to join the Hong Kong police force; to some he would have been regarded as a mercenary, although he saw his service in Rhodesia as an extension to his ordinary army career, fighting for a cause in which he believed: 'This is a good place, although the Rhodesian Army is not as hot as it thinks it is – there are too many part-timers. There are some good soldiers in the black units, loyal too. They are the ones I feel sorry for; if the extremists take over, they have nowhere to go. They are still loyal to Britain and cannot understand why the British government is so hostile, or why the Queen does not come over to sort it out.

'There would be no place for me in any new Zimbabwe under a black government, that's why I'm going. My wife likes it here, but we'll probably end up in Australia or back home in Britain. Britain would be a better place if it had a Prime Minister like Ian Smith.'

The last comment pleased Edward, who thought Ian Smith was indispensable. His support had so far cost him the loss of one son killed in an ambush and another son at risk in the police force: 'My son did not die in vain; this place will be all right. I'm not running any more. We came from Kenya, after Mau Mau, and I don't want to leave here. It's these terrs who are the problem – the trouble is, a lot of them wear overalls. It's easy to hide an AK 47 under them – you can't tell who is a worker and who is a terr.'

Julian had all the airs and graces of an ex-public schoolboy: 'Father sent me out to Rhodesia to get a bit of experience of life. As the terrs are still in season, I thought I would come over and cull a few.' It was impressive talk from someone who had seen no action and who, I found out later, had failed his Commission in the British army. Bill was not impressed: 'I can understand the Africans fighting; they get treated abysmally. I have had workers wounded at roadblocks, for no reason.'

'If the West continues to do nothing, then the Patriotic Front will win. Nkmomo has no chance, he is a fool and has been since 1961.' We all laughed at Bill's political naivety. Like most of the Europeans in Rhodesia (and British politicians and civil servants) we knew that the Patriotic Front had no chance of ever winning an election, and if they did, then Nkomo would be the leader. 'You can laugh,' he responded, 'we shall see.'

I did not understand why he was fighting if he thought Mugabe would win and the Africans had a case – for like the other Europeans he did his military service: 'It's not a contradiction, for there have been advances under Smith. So I'm fighting for a state where there are freedoms for the individual. After all, Communism in Africa is a pseudonym for Russian colonialism. I'm a social democrat – I'm fighting the van der Merwe mentality, just as much as I'm fighting the Patriotic Front.'

By the time the port had been reached, both Bill and Edward had stopped telling us how they were determined to stay in Rhodesia. The conversation had turned to ways of getting their money out of the country – from semi-precious stones in the car boot, to an airborne dash to South Africa.

* * * * * * *

Fortunately, the temptation to 'gap it' was not immediate, and Dermot had been right, Bill was going to Melsetter, and we arranged to meet at Umtali, to catch the convoy. With a few days to fill, more friends of Dermot came up with a bizarre invitation: 'You must come with us Robin, we are just going to the hunting, shooting, fishing competition at Inyanga – you'll never believe it.' Hayden was right; for a country at war the sporting weekend was astonishing.

We stayed at the Brondesbury Park Hotel on the edge of Inyanga – mountains and forests with streams and fast-flowing water, reminding me of the Lake District in England. The signs inside the hotel bore no resemblance to England, however: 'Emergency Procedure – These instructions are issued purely as a Precautionary Measure. So as to avoid panic in the unlikely event of an attack....
If an attack occurs while guests are in the public rooms please move away from the windows and lie on the floor. Guests with firearms are requested not to use them indiscriminantly and only to fire in retaliation in the direction of the attack. The all clear will be issued by the Management. We thank you for your co-operation.'

The weekend's competitions started with drink, on the Friday evening – drinking yards of ale, which meant two pints of beer inside 30 seconds. The time limit was much too high, with the average time being only about 18 seconds – for the women, it was half a yard inside 40 seconds; again it proved no competition – the capacity of the Rhodesians to down alcohol seemed to have no limits. Then, after beer, they turned to whisky and, despite 'sanctions', the Hotel claimed to have the greatest selection of genuine Scottish 'scotch-whisky' in Rhodesia – malt and blended.

For the actual 'Hunting, Shooting, Fishing' competition, there were a number of teams, each with three members riding, clay-pigeon shooting and fly-fishing. The name of each team summed up the seriousness of the competition: The Bootleggers, the Unspeakables, the Scrubbers, Brown's Marauders and various others. The rules were simple: – '1) The competition is only open to ladies and gentlemen of fine quality and breeding and anyone else. 2) The judges, whose decisions are final, are to be treated with respect and copious drinks.'

The first event was the cross-country, and again it started with alcohol – an enormous stirrup-cup of brandy and red wine. The first rider summed up its effect simply: 'It made me feel as sick as a pig, before I even got to the first jump.'

Those taking part were a mixture of recent immigrants and second and third generation Rhodesians. At one end of the social scale was 'Farmer Brown' – a young, over-weight farmer-cum-clay-pigeon shooter, whose stomach hung over his belt as a tribute to the Rhodesian brewing industry. All day long he refreshed himself with bottles of 'Lion' and he seemed to be enjoying the war almost as much as his clay-pigeon shooting. At the other end was Elizabeth Warren-Codrington, the country's leading horsewoman, who had moved to Rhodesia from Bedford in 1940. She spoke like someone from the English shires, and ran an equestrian centre near Salisbury: 'We had to hold the competition this year, to keep the morale up of the Inyanga people – you don't drop everything when you are threatened – no fear.' Of her equestrian centre she was equally positive: 'It's a horse hotel and horse hospital – I'm host for horsey happenings and happy hacking. The curfew area comes right up to the edge of my farm, but we manage – we've got to show that we can make this multi-racial business work. The trouble is that Britain does not really know enough about Central Africa; I am afraid the indigenous people are not really capable of coping on their own in a modern world.'

* * * * * * *

On the Saturday night the indigenous people, the waiters, had a remarkable view of the modern world. It started towards the end of the meal when the decorative flowers from one table, were thrown at the occupants of another. Pieces of bread followed, until mayhem broke out – sticks of celery, globules of butter and great tablespoonfuls of trifle went hurtling through the air, accompanied by the contents of wine glasses and beer bottles.

By Sunday afternoon the fun was over – the curtains of the dining room were being washed and the competitors were returning to their homes. The hotel was suddenly deserted, apart from Ted, a retired farmer from just outside Salisbury; Nigel, a photographer from the Information Department; and Denis, the 'bright light' – a 49-year-old banker. Despite his age he still had to undertake 70 days army servive a year – mobile patrols, reaction sticks, sweeps through the bush, convoys and guarding hotels.

With his hotel virtually empty, Den, the hotelier, decided to enjoy his normal Sunday afternoon activity – a visit to the casino, at a neighbouring hotel, the Montclair. The fact that, a few weeks earlier, terrorists had burst in at mid-day, shooting indiscriminately, killing and wounding several of those enjoying Sunday dinner, was no deterrent.

Guns were leant against tables and walls, as a variety of games were in progress – black jack, pontoon and roulette. The customers were a mixture of hoteliers, farmers and coffee-growers from the Eastern border – hard, tanned, beer-drinking, laughing men and their rather dumpy, over-made-up, blue-rinse wives.

A large, fat, elderly woman swept in. She was an extraordinary sight, with a long black flowing dress, strings of pearls and dripping with jewellry. Her hair was heavily lacquered and her face, a pale mask of creams and do-it-yourself artwork. To call her mutton done up as lamb would have been rather unfair to all sheep. She looked like an elderly eccentric duchess, but was loud and coarse. With a cigarette in a holder hanging from her mouth and a glass of whisky, she first played the fruit machines, before sweeping to the roulette table: 'Make room for me Den, you uncouth bugger – you're the perfect gentleman until you start stretching all over the bloody roulette table.' It was a remarkable scene; the complete picture of First World decadence. One of the reasons given by the Europeans for fighting the war was to maintain Christian standards and values; on this particular Sunday afternoon God must have taken a holiday.

* * * * * * *

The next day Tsanga Lodge made a refreshing contrast to the casino. It was reached along dirt roads which wound into a beautiful forested valley. The air smelt of mountains and pine needles – it was clear and cool, and very close to the Mozambique border.

The Lodge was run by Dick Padgett, a Yorkshiremen who had arrived in Rhodesia in 1954 aged 21. Wearing shorts and a T-shirt he looked fit, and much younger than his 46 years. It was a rehabilitation centre, started and run by Dick for those injured in the war. He could take just 16 at a time: 'The idea is to have a family atmosphere – to give them security and motivation – for everybody who comes here has suffered the most terrible injuries. Europeans are the easiest to motivate – then come the Africans, and finally, surprisingly, the coloureds. If we get a chap who limps, and who limps just as badly when he leaves the Lodge but has a smile on his face, then we have succeeded. I had one hopeless case who had lost a leg. He made such a good recovery that he went into the bar at

Meickles – attached a saline drip to counteract the alcohol, took off his artificial leg, blocked the holes with toilet paper and passed it round full of booze.'

When we arrived Dick was working with a young coloured soldier, who had been blown-up by a land-mine. He was getting him to lift his left leg up, to kick his hand. 'Come on,' Dick urged, 'you've got the chance you've always wanted, you can kick a honkey.'

'But I like this honkey,' came the immediate reply.

Nearby an African was sitting in a wheel-chair: 'Esiah was shot in the back. He had a raw deal. He laid for over a year – all twisted up with no proper medical treatment – the African nurses called him a "sell-out". We've now got his legs straight and he can almost stand.'

One of the medical orderlies was an example of the success of Dick's work. He had been an ex-patient, with badly broken legs; he could now walk and run almost normally. Although he had recovered he was angry: 'The West calls the terrs 'freedom-fighters.' They are not, they are a bunch of bandits – holding up trucks and buses and murdering innocent Africans. I know of a kraal headman who refused to feed them – he had both his arms chopped off before he was killed. They show no mercy and are completely without discipline. Do the politicians in London call the IRA freedom fighters or terrorists?'

Tsanga Lodge showed the positive side of war, where the human spirit emerged intact through pain, trauma and despair. Sitting on the verandah in the sun, the only reminder of the violence came from the digging of bunkers in case of mortar attacks: 'The terrs are very active here, but we can handle them.'

As we drank coffee, a small Lynx spotter plane flew over, high. It was followed, suddenly, by two vampires flying low, hugging the mountains into Mozambique. Shortly after, came the muffled sound of explosions.

* * * * * * *

On leaving the Lodge, we stopped at a small garage as soon as we hit the tar road. Bullet holes showed where it had been shot up twice within recent weeks. The whole place seemed ideal for ambushes, especially as it was so close to the guerillas' supply lines and camps in Mozambique.

In a green valley with a trout stream and pine trees, the Troutbeck Hotel could almost have been 6,000 miles away at the other Troutbeck. In the bar the illusion was carried still further, with prints of British steeple-chasing hanging on the walls, together with a picture of an old countryman ploughing with shire-horses. Several old locals were drinking whisky and gin. An ex-squadron-leader came straight out of Biggles. 'Leaving? Certainly not – this bunch of comedians won't move me. We haven't even got a security fence – we don't need one – they know what they'll get if they come near me. My wife doesn't carry a hand-bag, she carries a sten gun.'

As we spoke a Dakota, with its parachute door open, and two helicopter gun-ships swept low down the valley, from Mozambique. It was obviously connected with the spotter plane and vampires. 'Mmmm,' Nigel pondered, 'it looks as if it's been a full scene; they've probably taken out a terrorist camp.' On returning to Salisbury I could get no information on the raid and no reports of it appeared in the English Press. I could get no information on the 'contact' at Karoi either. I still wonder if the true scale of the fighting and the number of casualties in the Rhodesian War is actually known.

* * * * * * *

Back at the Brondesbury Park, the sun was beginning to sink in the western sky, when Ellen, the owner's wife, suggested a round of golf. It is a game that I do not normally play, but using a range of cricket strokes as golf shots, I can manage without losing too many balls. It was a relaxing way to end the day, sharing one set of clubs, and a caddy called Johannes. In the middle of one of the fairways thousands of winged ants were bubbling out of the ground and spiralling upwards where half a dozen small falcons and a larger yellow-billed kite circled, feeding on them.

The sunset was going to be another of Africa's specialities. We seemed to be on top of the world with a huge, clear landscape of ridges, rocks and forest. Above, the vast expanse of open sky glowed with reds, pinks and mauves, fired into a sea of fading blue.

As shadows lengthened we missed out some of the holes; it was still, and warm, with the cicadas and frogs in full chorus. Suddenly we heard an African voice – Ellen froze, her eyes full of fear. Johannes looked frightened too and whispered 'gandangas' – the Shona word for terrorists. My throat went dry, and for the first time fear hit me in the pit of the stomach. We were totally exposed and unarmed – all I had was a golf club and the hotel was a good half a mile away. 'Fancy coming all this way and ending up being shot on a golf course,' I thought. An African came out of the trees, wearing a floppy hat; both Ellen and Johannes greeted him with 'Andrew, it is you.' They breathed audible sighs of relief. 'We'd better go back,' Ellen whispered, 'we were daft coming all this way without a gun.' We went straight to the bar where I had a quadruple gin and tonic.

* * * * * * *

At 2.15 am I awoke with a start. The night chorus was in full voice and a dog was barking. Suddenly the barking stopped; there was an eerie, still atmosphere with the stars and moon bright. Shivers went up and down my spine. Somehow I felt an unwelcome presence close by in a clump of trees. There was now only Nigel in my wing of the hotel and I expected to get 'revved' at any moment.

At breakfast, with no prompting, Nigel made a confession: 'That was a strange night. I woke at 2.15, for no reason, and felt uneasy. I could not get back to sleep for half an hour and felt certain we were going to be hit. I moved my machine pistol on to my bed.' Who knows what, if anything, was going on outside. It was said that much witchcraft was taking place in the border areas, with the terrorists using spirit mediums to help them. A fortnight later the hotel was 'revved'. Strangely, the terrorists opened fire just as all the lights were put out. Many windows were shattered, but there was no other damage; as soon as the fire was returned the 'terrs' fled.

* * * * * * *

Ted volunteered to make a detour to Umtali on his way back to Salisbury, to drop me off, and taking Nigel with him. We crushed into the front, as he filled the back with 'nannies' – buxom African women, also wanting to go to Umtali. 'Look at that,' Nigel observed, 'it proves we are multiracial doesn't it. Yet nobody believes us. Even St Peter thought we were a bunch of racists. Three members of the security forces got shot the other day and ended up outside the pearly gates. There was an Englishman, a Rhodie and an African. St Peter was very pleased to see them all getting on so well. 'There's no racism in heaven, everybody is welcome, you just have to pass a simple spelling test. He turned to the Rhodie and asked: "How do you spell cat?" "C A T." "Good, you can go to cloud 92." He turned to the Englishman: "How do you spell mat?" "M A T." "Go to cloud 47." He then looked at the African – "How do you spell chrysanthemum?"' The van swayed with laughter.

* * * * * * *

The approaches to Umtali were beautiful; great kopjes grew into mountains, and euphorbias, like giant cacti, were everywhere seemingly rooted in solid rock. The town itself was quiet and peaceful, although there was an obvious military presence – white and black. One white policeman made his presence felt soon after Ted had left for Salisbury. I was taking a photograph using a telephoto lense, of a white policeman and a black policeman looking under the bonnet of their police car. The white policeman decided that he did not like being photographed: 'What are you doing, are you a journalist? Come with me.' He spoke slowly, with a broad South African accent. From his bearing and manner I thought his name was perfect – Constable Kloppers.

In the police station I was confronted by questions: Who was I? What was I doing? Why, when and where? Eventually a young Irish officer gave me coffee and told me I could go, camera intact: 'We have to be so careful. People are trying to knock us all the time.' It seemed strange for an an Irishman to be in a hot-zone by choice: 'Why? I feel safer here in Umtali than Belfast.'

With a day to fill before finding Bill again, I hired a car. A young African completed the required paper-work efficiently. 'It's strange,' I told him, 'in England, Umtali is reckoned to be under constant threat, with terrorists everywhere, but it looks totally relaxed.' He smiled: 'That's right, you are white, racism does not appear on the surface, but for those of us who are black and who live here it is like a number of pin pricks. At first you do not notice them, but you can only take so many, and then they hurt. Some of my brothers have decided they are in pain; it will all be all right again one day.'

Vumba is a great granite ridge close to Umtali, known to the local people as 'mubvumbi' – 'the mountains of drizzle'. It still has damp areas of dense, primeval forest, with great musasa trees, as well as warm valley sides ideal for plantations of tea and coffee. Again it had an isolated, widely spaced community of Europeans who showed remarkable confidence – even those actually overlooking Mozambique.'

At the very bottom of one valley was a farm totally exposed, run by a middle-aged woman living by herself. Her husband was away, her daughters were in South Africa at university and she was running the farm alone. The bungalow was like a fortress, including a barricade to stop grenades being thrown from the valley side. She was happy and optimistic: 'Change will come. It is bound to. Life will be difficult as the Africans adjust to power, but it will be OK. We must make sure that the Africans who have been fighting with us get their proper rewards however. Remember too, that in general the European has been good to the African. Rhodesia really only started 80 years ago when the Africans were in rags. What we have achieved, we have got from the sweat of our brows and the sweat of the Africans' brows. It has been a joint venture. Rhodesia is going to be a great place and lead the world. Come back here after independence and see – I'll still be here.'

* * * * * * *

Much to my amazement Bill was on time for the convoy, with Julian at his side. A Portuguese looked hard at the old Land Rover: 'Are you going to Melsetter in that? You must be mad.' The body of his Land Rover was unrecognisable. It looked more like a miniature tank, with double back wheels. The only unprotected spot was a small strip of canvas in the roof: 'That's to prevent your eardrums being shattered by blast if you hit a land-mine.' That was one consolation – our eardrums would be all right.

With five minutes to go before departure, Bill remembered that he was almost out of petrol. We got back just as the convoy was moving off. This was far different from the relaxed convoy of the hunting, shooting fishing competition. At the head and rear were two Dad's Army pick-up trucks, each carrying a Browning machine gun in the back, complete with swivel and shield. 'Whatever happens,' an old soldier shouted, 'if we get hit, keep driving like hell or else you will cop it. If there's any trouble, let us sort it out.'

Much of the journey was through Tribal Trust Land and most of the roadside stores were closed, some had been burnt out, showing that terrorists were active. The maize and cattle were in poor condition – the people had both drought and war to contend with. A bridge had been blown up and repaired with girders and scaffolding, and a heavily armed bunker of sand bags protected the new building-work.

Gradually we headed into the mountains again, with steep gradients and cliffs overlooking the road; with forest too, there were several likely ambush points in every mile. Each vehicle in the convoy bristled with weapons. Bill had his FN by the dash board. Julian clutched his machine pistol and I had a .303 and a small pistol. 'It's a good thing these terrs shoot across the road in an ambush,' Bill mused, 'that's why they miss so often. If they shot up it we would all be dead.'

* * * * * * *

Melsetter was a tranquil, attractive little village, tucked away in the mountains – surrounded by bush, forest and high ridges and ranges that extended on into Mozambique. The bungalows, nearly all with security fences, had large, well-manicured gardens with exotic flowers, where sun birds fed on the nectar of extravagant blooms.

Bill's friends were titled, a Lord and Lady – genuine members of the British aristocracy. Although they were liked by some of the local Europeans, by others they were regarded as 'kafferboeties' – an Afrikaner word for 'kaffir-lovers' or, more accurately, 'little brothers of the kaffir'. Just as earlier, in South Africa, some Afrikaners had exaggerated what they saw as the faults of the Africans, her ladyship, especially, seemed to elevate their favourable qualities almost to the point of beatification.

It was ironic that with such opinions the titled pair were having to live in a bungalow within the village itself. Normally they lived in their farmhouse some way down a quiet valley but, despite their views, it had been burned down while they had been away. Her ladyship claimed that the security forces had lit the match, because of her association with, and love for, the Africans. 'The Zimbabweans would only have done such a thing under coercion,' she claimed; 'coercion by an armed fanatic.' The police had a more simple view: 'The terrs did it – 40 of them.' As we chatted, a jogger trotted by with ginger hair and bright pink, sun-scorched skin.

Tea was brought out and demonstrated another peculiar irony. Although the couple were totally behind the 'Zimbabwean' cause, it was the first house I had visited where the servant girls were in uniform – brown hats and skirts, with white blouses. Her ladyship gave the intructions for tea sternly. It seemed, on the surface at least, to be the complete master-servant relationship – liberal vision hiding the conservative reality.

* * * * * * *

As I expected, I was the only guest at the Chimanimani Hotel. It was hardly surprising, as there had been 16 terrorist incidents in and around the village during the previous fortnight, and the road to Umtali had been mined the day before.

I was made to feel welcome and safe, but told to read the notice in my room carefully:

'A CALM HEAD IN TIMES OF STRESS IS A NEED INDEED.

1) Please read and acquaint yourself with your SAFE AREA which from here is No 3.

2) In the event of an attack on the Hotel proceed quickly and quietly to your safe area.

3) If you have time take with you a blanket and a pillow.

4) At your Safe Area wait until your Hotel Warden arrives and takes charge.

5) Try not to panic or get involved.

6) Finally – only in the event of an Internal or CLOSE attack will residents get involved with or in the attack. Arrangements have been made by the local Security Forces and Village Defence Sections for the external retaliation. Any inconvenience is regretted.'

* * * * * * *

Down in the bar was another conspicuous notice: 'We know you know all the answers, but telling everybody is killing us. You may be the next – Belt Up.' Two men in camouflage, combat clothes were drinking, disregarding the notice completely. They were working as private security agents in the surrounding forests. One was Dean, an

American Vietnam war veteran, and the other, a former street trader from Portsmouth. As they were talking about their work, two young constables of the British South Africa Police came in and sat drinking beer; one was the runner with ginger hair and bright pink skin.

Dave, the English mercenary, liked the war: 'It's all action – the gooks are getting better all the time.' They spoke about contacts and ambushes and then asked: 'Would you like to join us one night; we are called out after terrs most nights?' It seemed like an interesting idea and we agreed to meet at the same time in the same place the following evening.

As I sat in my room writing my diary, the sun was streaming down on to the great solid block of the Chimanimani mountains; it was going to be another spactacular highland dusk. A knock came on my door, but before I had time to move, it was kicked open; the two young policemen from the bar burst in, their automatic weapons pointing at my stomach. They were aggressive. The ginger-haired runner was a Scot, still with a broad Scottish accent. Again it was – what was I? Who was I? What was I doing in Melsetter? Who had given me permission? How did I know his lordship? What was her ladyship saying to me that afternoon? and, had I taken notes of the conversation? I was gradually getting angry: 'I don't have to write things down; I record everything in my brain. What are you going to do about that – take it out and try to read it?'

'Don't get clever with us Mr Page – you're in enough trouble already. Don't leave your room – we have to phone headquarters about you.' They left, taking my camera with them. After five minutes I decided to leave, to phone the Information Office in Salisbury, to ask them to tell the jumpy little policemen to leave me alone. I also phoned her ladyship, to let her know that I was in trouble; it seemed that my main crime had been speaking to her.

'Where are you going, Mr Page?' a Scottish voice called as I reached the bottom of the stairs. 'You're not going anywhere – you are coming with us.' I asked the receptionist to let his lordship know of my predicament as they pushed me through the door. They ordered me into their Land Rover and drove me to the heavily guarded police headquarters where the gates were unlocked by a black soldier.

The Inspector was rude and aggressive – I put his condition down to altitude. Once more I heard the same questions: Who was I? Why was I there? Where was my document from Combined Operations giving me permission to be in Melsetter? He then started mixing questions with comments: 'We've had people like you here before – causing trouble. I can have you put in the cells, thrown out of the country, or whatever I like.' Voices came from the 'reception'; Bill and Julian had arrived.

When I was a boy I had the misfortune of having an uncontrollable temper, but over the years I have managed to control it, most of the time. Due to the Inspector's attitude however, I could feel anger, of the old style, gradually welling up. 'What pictures did you take?' the officer asked.
'Of an African watchmaker,' I replied, 'I expect he was making time bombs.'
'You people are all the same,' he sneered, 'you're asking for trouble.'
Something in my brain clicked into automatic: 'If I'm the same as the others, you are certainly different,' I shouted. 'You are the first person I have ever met in a position of authority to have shit between his ears instead of A BRAIN.' For good measure I banged my fist on the table. The two young policemen looked startled, and a still small voice in my head whispered: 'Robin, you shouldn't have done that.' I had surprised myself, as I don't like using bad language; the Inspector looked surprised too. He scowled: 'Thank you Mr Page. You can go now. Don't leave your hotel – we will be sending you away from here in the morning.' I was still angry; her ladyship was fuming and said she would phone round her contacts in Salisbury. I went back to the hotel.

The following morning started in a now familiar fashion. I was still in bed when there was a knock on my door and one of the youthful policemen barged in: 'Get up Mr Page. You are going to Chipinga – you are having a free lift and you have no choice.' At the hotel reception, the woman presented me with a bill: 'You must be joking,' I said angrily, 'I booked in for the weekend – not for being bundled out on the first day.'
'Pay up,' Mr Page, the policeman ordered, 'don't be so immature.' I was losing control again: 'You had better not talk to me about maturity until you are old enough to shave – and mind your gun doesn't go off, you might frighten yourself.'

He phoned through to the Inspector for more instructions: 'He's being difficult and won't pay his bill.' The answer was very short:

'The Inspector wants to see you again Mr Page. Before you get kicked out.'

I had visions of another slanging match, or even a prison cell, so I was taken aback by the Inspector's abrupt greeting: 'I've changed my mind Mr Page. You can stay – get out of my office.' There was no explanation – no apology – I was just returned to the hotel and left at the front door.

* * * * * * *

Melsetter was most attractive in the warm sun; on the village green was a brick and stone monument to the members of the Moodie Trek, who founded the settlement in 1892. With the rocks and mountains, it must have been an incredible journey, travelling on horseback and in ox-wagons. The small church with its square, stone tower could have been from a small English village and on the Sunday morning its elderly congregation of Europeans sang to the accompaniment of an ancient foot-pedalled harmonium.

Some children were playing and were excited at seeing a new face. 'Come and see these bullet holes from last week,' they clamoured. A brick wall had been pock-marked by bullets, and astonishingly three had gone straight through. 'Any one of the Africans here could be gooks,' a fair-haired boy of about eight informed me. 'The whole village is surrounded by bombs fixed to trip-wires.' 'My Dad's been ambushed lots of times,' another chimed in. The fair-haired lad was not to be outdone. 'My Dad's been ambushed 14 times in one day.' I didn't believe him, nor did the others. At one time the most popular game in the village had been cowboys and Indians; now it was 'security forces and terrs'; the only problem was that nobody wanted to be a terr.

'The kids don't really understand what it's all about,' the local butcher told me. 'The other day we had a very rare event – a bus load of tourists was expected – my youngest misheard. When is the bus load of terrorists coming Dad, he asked me, I want to see you shoot them.'

The milkman – or more accurately the milk-lady – was remarkable. She still lived outside the village – approaching her farm along an isolated dirt road. Her neighbours had been murdered, but she refused to budge. She had a pistol, a rifle, three African members of the guard force, a 'Bright Light' and two dogs – a great Dane and a bull terrier. 'They'll stop the milk round over my dead body,' she told me defiantly. 'They haven't managed it yet. I like the ordinary munts (slang for Africans); I sell them milk and get on well with them – but the terrs are a bunch of cowards. Unfortunately, dairy farmers like me are particularly vulnerable. At Chipinga recently three were slotted because of their regular habits. My immediate neighbours were killed – so were the ones over the hill, as well as his guard force. In the worst month we had eight people killed around here, but they know if they want me, they've got a fight on their hands.'

In 1976 there had been 225 European families in the area. By 1979 the number had fallen to 105. Thirty Europeans, mainly men, had been killed, but the casualties included a family with two children, and an elderly couple who had been murdered and set on fire.

* * * * * * *

Later his Lordship drove me to see his burnt-out farmhouse – along dirt roads, with forest right up to the roadside in places. The view of mountains made it an ideal site – now holding just a charred, roofless shell. Again her ladyship repeated the view that the dastardly deed had not been done by the 'Zimbabweans': 'You speak to my garden boy, he will confirm it.'

On his own the garden boy would confirm nothing: 'I don't know who did it – I was not here when it was done.' He was quite open about other things however: 'The people are fed up with war. At night the boys threaten us – then in the day the security forces come. I have been threatened and hit by them. It is the Afrikaner who is the trouble – they treat us like rubbish. Why doesn't Britain do something? When I was at school I was taught that Britain was the motherland – now she does nothing.' I asked him about the election, believing like almost everybody else that Bishop Muzorewa would win: 'I am not voting – it is not worth it. There will be no peace in this country until the Patriotic Front wins. The boys tell us every night that the war goes on until Mugabe is the winner. We have to call them comrades and they lecture us – anybody who disagrees is beaten up.'

* * * * * * *

Back at the bar of the hotel the two mercenaries arrived: 'Ah Robin, we are glad you're here – you've got to come tonight, we had a hell of a scene last night.'

Dave was excited, wearing only a shirt, shorts and sports shoes, with his FN in his hand. 'We were revved when we were called out to the woodmill. After an exchange of fire the gooks gapped it – two of our hotes legged it too when the bullets were flying. Dean had to beat them up. We had no choice – you've got to teach them a lesson; if they run, it's our lives they put up for grabs – the no good mother-fuckers.' I thought he had been watching too many American films, or had been listening to Dean for too long.

Grabbing my pillow and a blanket I left with them and six of their black soldiers, in a 'Kudu'. It was noisy inside, but reassuring to know that we were surrounded by a layer of thick steel – again with a hole in the top to allow for 'blast'. Inside were two bench seats, complete with straps, to reduce injuries in the event of an explosion.

We drove along the main road: it was already dark and the curfew at sun set meant that it was deserted. At the sawmill we turned on to a narrow dirt road and drove deep into the forest. Dave took up a firing position in case of trouble. Pines and long grass grew to the edge of the track, which was only wide enough for one vehicle. Dean was scanning for any sign of disturbed earth or movement. The headlights briefly caught the dizzy flight of moths before fading into a wall of darkness. It was an ideal place for trouble.

The forestry guards' headquarters was at an isolated bungalow, inside a security fence, with fir trees almost up to the perimeter. Floodlights blazed and an African, in a boiler suit and armed with a .303 rifle opened the gate and let us in. The entire force consisted of just the two whites and nine Africans.

We sat in the open garage, with the lights still full on. Again I could not understand why we were not picked off. Dave shrugged his shoulders: 'It would make little difference if there were gooks out there, whether we were in the light or dark.' Various insects of the night were in full song and the night air was sweet with the cool scent of mountain pines and fresh dew.

Dave was an odd, but likeable individual; he was big and brawny and first impressions were of aggressive brashness, yet he often spoke quietly and at times seemed to have an air of great sadness. He claimed to have been to public school but had turned down the chance of going to Southampton University. Instead he had joined the navy, before leaving and working as a 'barrow-boy' on the edge of the law. He became disillusioned and depressed with England and so moved to Rhodesia where he joined the Rhodesian Light Infantry. After a term in prison for selling army weapons to farmers, he was discharged; now, in the forest, he felt settled for the time being. 'I am a mercenary – I'm fighting for money. But I'm fighting for what I believe in. I would never just fight for the sake of fighting – for something against my principles.'

Dean, at 35, was three years older. To him fighting had almost become a drug: 'I got blown up and wounded in Nam – then joined the Jordanian army, and have been here eight years. It's a great country, but my wife can't take war any more – the tension and the uncertainty. She's just left me and gone back to the States with the children. It's too bad, I'm staying to see this lot out.'

One of the Africans lit a fire in a wheelbarrow and was boiling a kettle on an upturned milk-crate for tea. 'You're not doing what you did last night then Jacob? He was cooking a rat on a stick – we call rats African sausages – they love them. They catch them by suspending mealies over water – so the rats over-stretch and drown.' Another was smoking 'dagga'. That did not seem like a good idea if we were expecting to be called out, but Dave also took a long draw: 'It's good – it soothes your nerves.'

Two other African soldiers and a sergeant joined us. They were filing down the ends of their .303 bullets, making 'dum dums', complete with a filed cross on the end to gain maximum expansion and damage on impact. One of them laughed: 'Gooks don't like meeting these.'

Dave was talking to the sergeant about witchcraft and he agreed to get a witch doctor to the bungalow: 'He would put things round the fence so that if a gook saw them he would just freeze and would not be able to move. Native medicine is very strong.'

Both whites claimed to have seen Africans killed by witchcraft – men who had been told that they would die and who had just sat down and slowly faded away. The sergeant had other good news: 'The witchdoctor can stop men sleeping with your woman too. He can make the lover die – or he can make them stick together like dogs until you come home and find them.'

Another African arrived, with a radio, which Dean commandeered: 'Listen to this Robin – real good stuff. He tuned in to Radio Maputo.' It was the regular evening broadcast of the Patriotic Front to Rhodesia. It was spine-chilling – about the 'terrorist Smith'; 'the quizzling Muzorewa'; 'the collaborator Sithole'; 'the white racists' and 'the running dogs of capitalism'. It told listeners that the country would soon be in the hands of 'the people'; that the land stolen by the 'racists' would be returned to the 'masses' and the rivers would be red with the blood of the Europeans. 'That's nothing,' Dean smiled, 'very moderate tonight.'

Sometime after Rhodesia had become Zimbabwe, I read an article by the late Lord Soames, an upper-class 'expert' who was the last white governor of Rhodesia. In it he criticised the white Rhodesians for hanging on so long. If he had ever listened to Radio Maputo, he would have known the reason; it gave the Europeans only one option – to fight on.

* * * * * * *

'We had better turn in,' Dean suggested at 10.30, 'we are bound to get called out again and we ought to get some sleep. If we go Robin, it's entirely up to you whether you join us. You can come with us, or stay here. I'll get you a gun.' Instead of an FN or even a .303 he returned with a single barrel shot gun and a handful of buck-shot cartridges. 'I'm sorry we've got nothing else.' The sergeant laughed: 'That's for shooting guinea fowl man, not bloody gooks.'

I slept in Dave's room. Just before climbing into bed he lodged a piece of wood against the door, so that it would crash down at the slightest touch. The generator was turned off and the lights faded. The crickets and cicadas were joined by the occasional nightjar; there was no moon, but the stars were bright. Instead of sleeping, Dave lit a cigarette.

* * * * * * *

I woke with a start; it was only 12.15 and the telephone was ringing. Dave leapt out of bed and after a brief talk, he shouted: 'Move – the sawmill's being attacked again.' I was apprehensive, but dressed quickly; a single barrel shot-gun was not all that reassuring. Five of the Africans joined us in the Kudu, the other four had to guard the bungalow. The floodlights burst into brilliance and we roared out of the compound. 'It's exactly like last night,' Dean whispered, 'it must be an ambush, to take us out with a biscuit-tin bomb [a TMH 46] or with an RPG 7; they've got them now and they're armour piercing.' He was scouring the edges of light for movement, but fortunately the terrorists were not thinking along the same lines.

With trees hemming us in it was like travelling in a long, dark corridor, with dust swirling behind us and finding its way into the body of the vehicle. I had expected to feel fear; instead, with the adrenalin flowing, I felt a strange sense of anticipation – my senses seemed sharper – every sound, every depression in the uneven track and every tree seemed clearly defined. With the engine roaring it was a bumpy, dusty ride; we halted at the gates of the sawmill – the guards had fled. The back doors burst open and everyone, except Dean and me, tumbled into the grass covering 360 degrees in a defensive formation.

Dave shot the lock off the gates with two rounds and I found myself running with them into the compound, expecting a barrage of gunfire at every stride. Nothing happened; the sawmill appeared to be deserted. Finally a guard emerged, then three more, together with a European and his guard, Corporal George.

The terrorist attack had been simple – the European had rolled his Land Rover after having too much to drink, so he and Corporal George had decided to walk the five miles home. On passing the sawmill the guards had seen movement and opened fire, assuming them to be terrorists. Over 40 shots had been loosed off, but again every one had been high. The two men had circled the sawmill and crept in under the fence, behind the guards, to stop them shooting. It was fortunate that the terrorists had never used the same tactics. It was while the shooting was going on that a guard had phoned, saying they were under attack, when in reality they had been the ones doing the attacking.

'It's about par for the course,' Dave muttered, 'they should let me train their guys.'

We drove up the hill to make sure the Land Rover was not blocking the main road and then on to a roadside clinic, again fenced, as Corporal George had a badly cut eye. The moon had risen, giving everything an eerie quality; all was quiet in the compound and there was no sign of life.

'Tune them,' Dave instructed the sergeant.

'Police – police,' he called. Nothing happened so he tried a different tack. 'Sisters, sisters, we need help,' he followed it with something in Shona.

'OK,' Dave nodded. His men scaled the fence easily; with their dark overalls, floppy hats and guns, they looked exactly like terrorists. We followed; I had not realised that 'security' fences were so insecure. The nurses and a doctor were roused. They claimed that they had not answered the calls as they thought we were terrorists; initially they had certainly appeared to be extremely frightened. Corporal George was quickly stitched up, showing no sign of fear or discomfort, and we returned to the bungalow for one and a half hours of sleep.

As I left big and burly Dave to join the convoy, he surprised me: 'Robin, when you get back, contact my mother. Tell her I'm all right and there's no need to worry. I think of her a lot. I've had this premonition that I'm going to die in Rhodesia.' I never did discover what happened to Dave.

* * * * * * *

Bill was going back to his farm on his own, in a Mercedes, leaving Julian at his lordship's. There were three pick-up trucks with mounted Brownings for the return trip – one at each end and another in the middle: 'Notice how they shoot through wire – that's to tumble the bullets to cause as much damage as possible,' Bill observed. The convoy sped through the wild landscape, again with no dramas.

* * * * * * *

It seemed entirely in keeping with Bill that once we left the main road to drive to the farm over dirt, his speed increased to over 70mph, leaving a great trail of dust and flying stones in our wake, with the tyres struggling for grip on the bends. In the gathering gloom the farmhouse seemed enormous; a great sprawling bungalow in which each bedroom had its own adjoining bathroom.

He was greeted with a happy smile by his young black housekeeper, Lucy. It was not the servant/master relationship of his lordship's house, but more easy-going and relaxed. She called him Bill and his arrival did not modify the decibel level of the Abba record blasting from the record player. Before my first meeting with Bill a farmer had said: 'Oh him – he loves blacks – quite literally – that's not good news in our present situation.' What Bill's situation was exactly, was not clear. Lucy served us with dinner; she was happy, pretty and at one stage burst into song. She wore no uniform but a flowery cotton dress with a white collar. Following dinner she disappeared and after a quick whisky so did Bill, claiming fatigue.

* * * * * * *

The garden looked beautiful bathed in the sunlight of early morning; birds were singing, a grey lourie – the 'go-away bird' – was shouting 'Go away, go away' and brilliantly coloured sunbirds were sucking the nectar from clumps of lillies. A white arched wall, covered with trailing shrubs, gave the scene a peculiarly Spanish air.

Bill was proud of his farm, but it was obvious that he did very little farming: 'There's too much hassle in farming. But I still claim my full farming fuel allowance – you'll see tonight.' He showed me an impressive new school he had opened for African children on his farm, and a workshop where mechanics were working on a tractor and a car. It seemed that he was getting his income not from farming, but from engine repairs. 'They are good men these. I trained them myself.'

One of his mechanics told him of an African who had been shot after drinking in a nearby village. 'You have to expect this sort of thing in a war. They say they don't know who did it.' He had to break the news to the man's sister, at a nearby kraal for workers and their families. The hut was dark, smelling of woodsmoke and African bodies. There were two women inside, sitting on the floor, one with a small child. He broke the news to them in Shona as gently as he could; heart-rending wailing broke out immediately and he left them to their grief.

* * * * * * *

Although I wanted to get back to Salisbury, Bill was reluctant to leave. Each time I suggested setting out, he remembered another job to do. Just before dusk he filled the boot of his Mercedes with cans of petrol. 'OK Robin, we're ready now.' Close to the tar road was an armoured car and soldiers with dogs, but he stopped only to give two black soldiers a lift. Close to Salisbury a road block was stopping African cars and buses; all bags and baggages were being searched for weapons. Bill, with his white face, was waved through, despite his special cargo.

By the time we reached Salisbury and dropped the soldiers off it was dark: 'We are going to Seki township,' Bill told me at last. 'I sell them all my spare petrol on the black market – well above the odds. I make a lot of money.' We were slightly early for his appointment and stopped outside an African bar. Again there was a different feeling being in a 'black' town, hard to pin-point, but definite – more noise, everything slightly more dishevelled and an impression that order was only just ahead of chaos.

'Let's have a drink,' Bill suggested. Judging from the reaction of the customers we were obviously the first white faces to have been in the bar for months. Eyes stared and lips smiled. One drunk on a stool at the bar shouted: 'Come here boss; I want to talk to you and buy you a beer.' Much to his amusement I had a carton of Chibuku – 'The Peoples' Beer' – mass-produced alcoholic porridge. It was also known as 'Shake, shake' – a reminder to mix up the sediment with the liquid. Bill may have liked Africans, but his regard did not stretch to their beer. The African was drinking orthodox Castle lager. 'What's your name,' he slurred.
'Robin.'
'Lobin – beer is wonderful. I like Europeans, they have given us bars and beer, which means I don't have to stay at home with my wife.'

* * * * * * *

Bill drove to a large grocery shop and general store, full of the smell of dust, Africans and carbolic soap. It was a strange building - its walls appeared to be crumbling, but it had a brand new ceiling – a peculiar combination. Customers ordered their supplies at a long counter – tea, maize meal, Kariba fish and saucepans. Older Africans smiled and said 'Hallo', but many of the younger males had the surly, sour look that can be seen in the adolescent urban black anywhere. It appears to be a condition produced by city living, for the young rural African invariably seems happy and more content.

The shop owner was pleased to see Bill: 'Oh good, Mr Bill. We were wondering when you were coming. The petrol is all spoken for already.' He was very black, smartly dressed in a dark, western suit. From his reaction it seemed to me that he would literally be smiling all the way to the bank.

As we spoke I noticed a tall well-dressed man call the security guard. He was talking urgently, looking at us. Soon he was joined by two more. 'Don't worry,' the shop owner assured us, 'they are the Bishop's auxiliaries. The terrorists moved in and demanded money from us shop-keepers. Now the auxiliaries give us protection, but they need paying too. I'm in a very vulnerable position and there is a lot of trouble in the township between the Bishop's men and the Patriotic Front.'

Although affable and polite, his political analysis was a surprise; yet another view which suggested that I, the British and American Press, and the West in general, had got it wrong. 'The new constitiution is a fraud. It is only designed to keep the whites in power for another ten years. I want Mugabe in power, that is the only way forward.'

I was puzzled as he was obviously a capitalist and Mugabe was a self-declared Marxist: 'That's no problem,' he laughed, 'he has to say all that rubbish to satisfy his backers. When he returns to this country he'll change.'

'But what about all that revolutionary stuff on Radio Maputo – driving the whites out and giving their land to the people?' I asked naively.

'Don't take any notice of that, he doesn't mean it. He's playing to the gallery, like a man on a stage.'

Bill's car was unloaded, he stuffed a large wad of notes into his wallet and we drove out through a mass of black faces. Bill felt uneasy: 'We should have come earlier Robin – here, have my pistol just in case.'

* * * * * * *

In many ways I was sorry to be going from Rhodesia. I had found both blacks and whites friendly and the atmosphere was totally different from that portrayed in the British media. I had also been surprised by the pride, resolution and feeling of camaraderie that existed among the Europeans, something I had never experienced in Britain. In fact travelling in Africa helps bring into focus just how pessimistic and self-deprecating the average Englishman is. Black and white Africans all seem to love their countries, although their vision and purpose are often diametrically opposed. In the same way, others travelling through Africa – Americans, Australians,

Swedes, New Zealanders and even the rather dour Swiss - all seem to speak of their countries with pride. Yet the average English traveller, whether journalist, tourist or businessman, is full of gloom, doom and petty complaints about their homeland. The areas of complaint become so magnified that any good elements of English life become completely obliterated, as do the differences between the First World and the Third, the rich and the poor, the well-fed and the hungry. It is a strange condition to be in.

* * * * * * *

As I left, Rhodesia was a tragedy gradually drawing to its close.

7. Desert Interlude.

By the time I had decided to visit another major troublespot of Southern Africa – Namibia – Rhodesia had at last found peace, as Zimbabwe. The election of 1979 had been won by Bishop Muzorewa, but the war had continued until Britain intervened. Then in 1980 fresh, British-supervised elections were held. The result confounded me, as well as 'the experts' – the British and American Press, and the British Foreign Office; Bill, his petrol buyer and the gardener at Melsetter had been right. ZANU, of the Patriotic Front, had won convincingly and Robert Mugabe 'terr', became Robert Mugabe 'Prime Minister'.

After such an upheaval the attention of many people turned to Namibia, that area of baking desert in south-west Africa administered by South Africa – a 'mandated territory' passed on to South Africa by the old League of Nations on 17th December 1920. With South African government, a system of apartheid had developed and for years law suits and motions at the United Nations had tried to remove the South African presence. For their part the South Africans maintained that they had no intention of leaving until South West Africa was stable and advanced enough to manage its own affairs responsibly – they said they were not going to make the same mistakes as Britain, France and Belgium, by leaving too early. At the time of my visit the South Africans claimed to have dismantled apartheid and were anxious to give Namibia its independence, under a properly elected government. Given the politics of the rest of Africa, and the United Nations, such a proposition could not be accepted by 'the world' – any Namibian settlement, it was said, had to involve the South West Africa Peoples' Organisation – SWAPO – who had been waging a guerrilla war in Northern Namibia for some years. SWAPO had already made it clear that it would not participate in South African-supervised elections. So, in the war of words there was stalemate – South Africa was keen to show that the Namibian situation bore no resemblance to Rhodesia, SWAPO insisted that the position was identical and victory would soon be theirs.

With this background, when an invitation arrived from the SW Africa/Namibia Information Department to go on a 'fact finding' visit, I had no hesitation in accepting. The reason for my acceptance was simple: in terms of African turmoil and change Namibia was at an interesting stage, but it also had other attractions which I considered to be even more important than the politics – Etosha Pans, one of the most significant areas for wildlife in Southern Africa: 'Skeleton Coast', a coastline of astonishing ominous beauty; and 'Bushmansland', the last home of the Bushmen, those small wandering people whose way of life, spirituality and plight had been made so real to millions through the writings of Laurens van der Post. Consequently when the Information Department asked me who or what I wanted to see it must have received a shock, for high on my list were not politicians, but lions, Bushmen and inevitably penguins.

Some people with unlimited resources take a high moral view concerning the evils of accepting free trips abroad, arguing that any such visit must result in a tinted, partial view. I have never had such a problem. I have always managed to see everything I wanted and have written as I have found, seen and heard; to me, the invitation to Namibia represented possibly my only opportunity of seeing that great tract of dust and desert.

In one way the invitation was strange, however: it came from a Public Relations company representing the Namibian Information Office, run by a former secretary of Harold Wilson who was knighted by the ex-Prime Minister for services rendered. One minute Namibia must have been a favourite focus of Socialist hatred, the next, a welcome business opportunity.

I enjoyed arriving at Heathrow on a sunny April day to check in at the First Class desk of South African Airways. Gone was the herding, the crowds and the discomfort of tourist class; instead I was ushered into the Executive Lounge of British Airways. It was small but plush, with 'executives' taking liberal helpings of 'free' drink. I joined them for a double dose of my flying-phobia antidote.

The flight was comfortable, with a lounge, room to stretch legs, champagne, a nine-course meal and free wine. The only reminders of the normal discomforts of flying were the canned music and the dreadful 'in-flight entertainment' – a film, it seemed, designed to induce sleep.

Once in South Africa, flights to Windhoek, Namibia's capital, leave from Johannesburg. The plane was full and the seat next to me was actually overflowing. It held a most enormous, smiling African woman. When she pulled the tray down in front of her for coffee, it acted as a corset, completely trapping her in the seat: 'I'm so happy to be going back,' she beamed, 'Namibia is beautiful, I hate to leave it.' For the whole flight she read a small paperback *Love me for Ever* by Barbara Cartland; there was certainly a lot of her to love. I read the local Namibian morning paper to see how the world news was shaking Windhoek; the front-page headline was revealing – 'Kudu Scares Windhoek Family'.

The small airport was modern and the officials friendly: 'Do you want your passport stamped Mr Page, or your visa?' He stamped my visa as I had several visits to make to 'Black Africa' and I did not really want South West Africa stamped all over my passport – I wanted to keep potential problems to a minimum.

The drive from the airport was through wild, rugged country, with hills and outcrops of rock. There were flowers too, mainly yellow, responding to unseasonal rain; the whole desert was beginning to flower. There were ranches with Old Cape Dutch farmhouses, and one large bungalow had a flag-pole at its gate, where the dry wind proudly blew the old Rhodesian flag.

Windhoek is an unusual city; its German name means 'windy corner' and its German past has added to the problems of the present and future. Much of the architecture is German; German is still heard in the streets and the country is popular with German tourists. Consequently, unlike Rhodesia with just one white tribe, Namibia had three – English, Afrikaner and German, encompassing the whole political spectrum from liberal to neo-nazi and from those hoping for a multiracial future to those wanting to become part of the Republic of South Africa.

The tribal differences among the Africans of South West Africa were also more pronounced than those of Zimbabwe. In Zimbabwe the two main groupings were the Shona and the Matabele, but Namibia had many distinct tribes, each with their own traditions and claims: the Nama, Damara, Ovambo, Herero, Bushman and the Rehoboth Basters – another coloured group, showing that in Namibia too the early trekkers had managed to get themselves into a 'biogenetic contact situation'.

In Windhoek the Herero women were conspicuous, still wearing brightly coloured, full-length cotton dresses, introduced by nineteenth-century German missionaries. Wearing shawls and bright, elaborately tied head-cloths, they looked incongruous travelling up a shopping-centre escalator or getting into a new Mercedes car. The women were black reminders of nineteenth-century Northern Europe, yet they were living in a modern twentieth-century city, surrounded by semi-desert.

The internal politics of the country seemed simple and based on the one aim of preventing Namibia from following the path taken by Rhodesia. As a result a multiracial alliance had been formed to give all racial groupings and tribes an interest in government. This was seen as the most positive way of countering the influence of SWAPO. Most of SWAPO's incursions were said to come from bases in Angola affecting, in the main, the Ovambo people in the North of the country. The Ovambos made up Namibia's largest tribal group, accounting for 46 per cent of the country's one million population.

Among Namibia's black and coloured leadership, most seemed to have belonged to SWAPO at one time or another, and all spoke as contemptuously about the external nationalist leadership as they did the extreme Afrikaners. In fact several even claimed to have been among the actual founders of SWAPO. Their stories were remarkably similar: in an effort to oppose apartheid they had left the country to form a more positive and coherent opposition. Once out, the leadership had fragmented, and at various times they had all been put in prison – not by whites but by SWAPO in Zambia. There, they had suffered 'torture' and 'brutality', with the Zambian authorities unable, or unwilling, to intervene. Freedom and safety had come only with escape and a return to Namibia, where they considered that they had been partially successful in dismantling apartheid and helping to create a society based on racial freedom and tolerance. They all claimed huge popular support for their particular parties, which if true would have given Namibia a population of at least five million.

Several viewed Britain with suspicion and wanted to avoid South West Africa being handed on a plate to SWAPO by the United Nations or 'the Front Line States'. One white politician was particularly scathing about Dr Owen during his time as British Foreign Secretary: 'He was a disgrace. He preached democracy, yet when he was out here he acted like a complete autocrat. In Rhodesia his political ambition allowed him to walk over all the bodies he had created without even putting a handkerchief over his nose.'

An amusing coloured woman, again ex-SWAPO, blamed the Afrikaners for Namibia's problems: 'There is a tremendous base for harmony and co-operation in Namibia, but the Boers are so hostile and suspicious of all change. It's best demonstrated by a crude van der Merwe joke. Van had got two tickets for a rugby test match in Cape Town. Unfortunately, as he was driving down there, he had a car accident and ended up in hospital. When he came round an English doctor was standing over him: "Mr van der Merwe, you've had a tremendous knock – for your own good I'm afraid we'll have to take your testicles away from you." Van was horrified: "No way man. I'm never parting with them. I demand another doctor." An Afrikaner doctor was summoned who carried out another examination: "Van, look here, things are very bad – you must give us permission to remove your balls." Van smiled radiantly, he was so relieved: "Oh, is that all man, go ahead, I thought you wanted my test-tickets."'

She laughed gustily, obviously enjoying her much told joke: 'That sums it up – tunnel vision – replace Van's test-tickets with Afrikaner nationalism – their so-called identity. If they see it threatened they won't budge an inch; they would rather see the whole of South Africa go up in flames.

Against all popular conceptions, one of the most pleasant and articulate men with a view on Namibia's political situation was the South African military commander in South West Africa, Major General J. J. Geldenhuys; a relaxed, affable man, with a small moustache and clear blue eyes. 'I don't see this place as another Rhodesia. The various groups have been trying to come to a political settlement among themselves – but apparently that is what the rest of the world doesn't want. SWAPO is not banned; why don't they all come back and fight an election?

'South Africa doesn't want to stay here and we have plans for a withdrawal worked out already. But we will not allow SWAPO to have military bases in South West Africa. I cannot see any independent arbitrator stopping SWAPO's violent activities.

'If terrorism continues it has to be countered, for power commands respect. Without us here any sort of proper elections would be impossible; only one of the political parties has an army and that is SWAPO. Their leader has said that the United Nations will chase out the old Boers and then SWAPO will clear out the black Boers – in other words, anybody who disagrees with them.'

He considered that terrorism was under control, with a kill ratio of 37 terrorists for every member of the security forces. The anti-terrorist work was carried out by the local multiracial defence force as well as South African soldiers – many of them national servicemen. 'The national servicemen are good – very fit and aggressive – very good in a shooting war. They have to be watched however, because they are not too diplomatic. If they are checking a village near the border they'll steal chickens for the pot if they get the chance, which can undo all the good work that has been done with the locals.'

* * * * * * *

Although Windhoek was a pleasant town, complete with an assortment of German and Boer generals carved in stone, I was glad to get away from its over-political atmosphere. Like all capitals it seemed to dominate the country, a country of nearly 320,000 square miles – almost four times as large as Britain – stretching from the Orange River in the south, to the Angolan border in the north.

I was offered a circular tour of the country in a small single-engined plane. It seemed a good idea. My travelling companions would be Simon, a diplomat from the Department of Inter-State Relations, who always carried a brief case with a small heavy bulge at the bottom; the pilot, Hans, a dour Afrikaner who had managed to turn boredom into an art form; and Paul, a young Namibian photographer – he was a Polish Jew from Windhoek, whose father boasted of having travelled from Poland to Polo in one generation.

First stop was Luderitz, a small fishing town to the south, in diamond country. How a pilot could seem bored flying over such spectacular country I did not understand. We passed over miles of barren wilderness: areas of shattered rock, baked and burnt by the sun, great chasms and kopjes sculptured by wind, water and sand, and miles of dunes, shimmering and deserted. Flying over land so parched and hot it was peculiar to have rain freeze against the windscreen from a small solitary cloud.

Hans looked slightly more interested as he landed. It was like landing in an oven; the temperature was unrelenting – burning and intense as the whole landscape of sand and rock appeared to glow with heat. Such a climate must affect the lives of the people too, and as a result Luderitz itself seemed locked in lethargy. It was tired and dying – old houses with cracking, peeling paint looked peculiar with no gutters and Bavarian snow roofs, ideal for allowing the run-off of wind-blown sand. It was how I imagined those seedy run-down towns on the West Coast of America to be, described so vividly by John Steinbeck.

From a record shop came the sound of Pink Floyd's *Another Brick in the Wall*, a record banned in South Africa because of its adoption by nationalist groups. 'You must meet a friend of mine, Robin,' Simon informed as he turned and entered a small bottle store. 'It's run by Andy, he's a grandson of Baden Powell.' A grandson of Baden Powell running a bottle store at such an isolated, almost forgotten place? It was bizarre. Andy was quite a sad figure. He had arrived in Luderitz to write a novel, but seven years later it was still unwritten; in fact it had not even been started. His life seemed to have fallen into one of inconsequential routine. Both he and his wife wanted to get away, but how do you sell a bottle store in a forgotten town? He had not even intended to stay in Luderitz in the first instance, but he had put a local German girl in the family way and so had stayed on and married her – marooned on the edge of the desert – on the edge of a continent. If only he had remembered his grandfather's famous motto – 'be prepared'.

Andy had helped to form a local organisation to 'save Luderitzbucht' and part of his plans included turning Luderitz into the main deepwater port in South West Africa. It would be linked to a trans-Kalahari railway to serve those countries of Southern and Central Africa that did not wish to rely on South Africa. It seemed an idea that matched the dreamlike atmosphere of the town. The ethereal mood was emphasized as a Cape gannet drifted over, brilliant white against the dazzling sky; it came so close that I could see the colour of its clear blue eyes.

Inland from the town the desert sweltered – a wasteland of sculptured rock, wind, glare and heat. But where the land hit the Atlantic it was suddenly cold from the rush of cool air sucked in from the green cold sea. The sea felt like freshly melted ice; it was the Benguela current, flowing directly from Antartica. Where the iced water and scorched air met it was a fusion of surf, mist, heat and cold. Great white-topped emerald rollers pounded on to the jagged rocks of small offshore islands, and there through the mist, were unfamiliar birds. They stood in the cold, like contemplative old men, hundreds of them: 'There you are,' Simon sighed with relief, as I recognised rockhopper penguins. 'I have had visitors ask for women before, black, white and brown, but never penguins,' Hans was not impressed.

Further along the coast it was like visiting a graveyard – a deserted whaling station of tangled, twisted metal – pipes, boilers and an old harpoon. I shivered: my thoughts of death and the many hundreds of whales hauled bleeding and dying out of their element, were made colder by the wind from the sea. We stopped on a cold headland of waves and spray. There was a memorial – a stone cross, a replica of the one erected by the Portuguese explorer Bartholomew Dias in 1487. How did those early navigators survive such a hostile sea in their small wooden boats, so long ago?

In the evening the local members of the 'Save Luderitzbucht Action Committee' held a party. It seemed another excuse for alcohol to be consumed in large quantities. At first the members and their wives were quite formal and reserved, but gradually the liquor loosened their tongues until there was much raucous laughter and story telling. 'It's not much like a desert here,' I told Andy, 'there's enough liquid in this room to turn the desert into fields of wheat. The trouble is, it's all in bottles.' He laughed: 'That is about the only place we get it. We had an Englishman come once who loved facts and figures. When he asked about rainfall he was told quite accurately that some years we don't have any. He kept saying things like: "But you must have a measurable quantity." His host eventually got fed up. "You are right," he said, "we can measure our rainfall. You remember when Noah built his ark and most of the world was flooded? Well, Luderitz had three inches."'

If I lived in Luderitz I would be slightly worried, for close by is the town of Kolmanskop, in the heart of diamond country. It is deserted, a ghost town – a monument to those who were once lured into the desert by the thought of money. Doors were off hinges, windows had broken and sand had returned. Some houses were half hidden by dunes, while others were still almost habitable. 'Be careful,' Simon informed with a laugh, 'you can be arrested if you bend down in this place – it's still a restricted diamond area.'

Despite the high hopes of the Luderitz committee, I had visions of Luderitz eventually going the same way as Kolmanskop under the twin onslaught of sand and sea.

The whole coastline was incredible – an unrecognised 'wonder of the world' – a mixture of beauty and hostility, a surging cold sea, wind and boiling desert. Hans had seen it all before and maintained his indifference as we flew north. We flew over true wilderness; for as far as the eye could sea a land of perpetual drought, with shimmering dunes and slowly shifting canyons of sand, stretching and winding away into the heat. Where the dunes met the sea, sheer sand cliffs plunged into the mist and waves. African fishermen in small boats and wearing red sou'westers were buffeted by wind and water. There were the skeletal remains of long lost ships and a lagoon filled with thousands of pink flamingoes – it was like flying through a dream. In one sandy waste by the sea, a solitary jackel stood, and further inland were the straight sandy tracks of a herd of larger animals – possibly oryx, appearing from nowhere and disappearing into infinity.

Hans was so pleased to arrive at Swakopmund that we bounced along the airstrip in a kangaroo landing. He had been there many times before, even when he was not working, as it was a popular coastal holiday town for those living in Windhoek. He quickly disappeared, seeking further opportunities to sleep or drink.

It was another strange place, again like a small market town in Germany except for the heat, sand, palm trees and black faces. There was a railway station, that could have been in a backwater of rural Bavaria, and a fine Lutheran church dating back to German colonial times. Just outside there was even an old steam engine, perfectly preserved but left where it had become stuck in the sand. It was called Martin Luther, after his famous pronouncement: 'Here I stand: God help me, I cannot do otherwise.'

Modern hotels were built close to the sea, full of Afrikaners and Germans on holiday, as well as South African soldiers on leave. Tourist brochures claimed that: 'The water is cold, but the beaches are spacious.' The description was not strictly true: under such a hot sun, the sea, quite remarkably, felt so cold that it numbed arms and legs almost immediately. Consequently small, glistening groups of white people seldom swam; instead they collapsed on to the sand nearest their hotels, worshipping the sun. Further away from the hotels, the 'spacious' beach emptied and it was difficult to see where beach became desert – perhaps it was all the largest beach in the world.

Walvis Bay is another oddity. It is an important South African enclave, inherited from the British Empire, just 20 miles from Swakopmund. It possesses the most important, developed deep-water harbour in South West Africa and as a result a journey that once took ox-wagons all day, through drifting dunes, now takes just 20 minutes along a straight tar road.

The port is vital for many reasons. Its strategic importance to South Africa was shown by the large number of South African soldiers present; while its importance to black Africa was demonstrated by a Liberian registered boat being loaded with salt, destined for Zaire. Walvis Bay has also become one of the pilchard and anchovy centres of the world, so spreading its impact beyond Africa and into Europe. There were several trawlers tied up from Spain and Greece, and there were two Russian boats, bristling with aerials, suggesting that they were trawling for far more than fish.

With its bays, pools and pans, Walvis Bay has spectacular birds, such as pink flamingos, bright against the brilliant blue of sky and water. Pelicans were resting in floating rafts, while at the edges of some of the pools black-winged stilts and avocets fed. In a continent obsessed with colour, it is interesting to realise that the iris of the male avocet is red, while that of the female is brown.

We drove back through the dunes as dusk was creating great parabolas of light and shade and the sun was turning the sand from yellow, to gold, with a deep orange glow. The high ridges had an almost architectural precision and after every footprint each dune vibrated as its sand readjusted, almost as if it had life. As the sun dropped lower, the wind increased and cooled, blowing a mist of fine sand over the summits and ridges of the dunes, giving them movement in an ever-changing desolate landscape. Every dune in its individual way seemed a wonder of continuing creation – a creation that, as the Namib desert, rolled away towards the setting sun for as far as the eye could see.

* * * * * * *

Etosha National Park is separated from the coast by more spectacular wilderness. There were the yellows and browns of the desert, streaked with the diluted tints of copper and iron. Then the

Desert Interlude

Brandburg range of mountains – high sculptured peaks and canyons of heat- and wind-shattered granite, like a giant spectacular tombstone to the memory of the Bushmen, whose ancient paintings it still held.

Gradually drought-land gave way to scrubby bush, which in turn changed to grass and green leaves, showing the presence of fresh water. Hans buzzed the white, stoney airstrip to clear it of springbok and zebra, and made a perfect landing.

Etosha is one of the most important National Parks in Southern Africa, a huge low lying area of scrub, bush, plains and pans, covering well over 8,000 square miles. Etosha means 'the big white place', for the local Africans were intrigued by the great pan of clay and salt that gives the park its name. Usually it is hot and dusty, a place of white heat and mirages, but after the rains it fills with water, forming a huge, shallow inland lake that can be as large as 45 miles wide and 80 miles long.

The drive to Fort Namantoni was brief; it had once been a real fort, and painted white, with battlements, it looked like something out of the French Foreign Legion.

Several tourists were at Namantoni, including Afrikaners, Germans, and two English girls, on holiday from working as nannies in Windhoek. Even at midday one looked as if she would have been more at home at a disco. She was noisy, laughing and drinking, wearing high-heeled shoes and with eyes almost hidden by eye-shadow. Her mannerisms were strangely reptilian to me – I kept expecting her tongue to flick out, but it never did.

A Dutchman, from Holland, gave us a game-drive. It was a wonderful place, rich in animals, birds, insects and flowers. Artificial water-holes had been created, to ensure an increase in wild animal populations. They also gave the best opportunities to see the larger animals as they went to drink: zebra, hartebeest, springbok, impala, gemsbok, kudu, giraffe and elephant.

The springbok were attractive, graceful little antelopes; they get their name from their strange habit of 'pronking' – bouncing, stiff-legged, with their backs arched. When several do it at the same time it looks like a contagious form of animal insanity. Although they stand less than three feet high at the shoulder, when they pronk they can bounce up to ten feet in the air. The gemsbok is much larger, standing four feet high and weighing up to 450 pounds. It is one of the most striking members of the oryx family, with impressive straight, pointed horns of up to four feet long.

The most magnificent animals going to drink were the greater kudu. The males stand over five feet high – slate blue-grey with vertical white stripes, giving them excellent camouflage when in bush country. Their horns are the most spectacular in Africa; again they can be over four feet long, but with two or three corkscrew twists. The hornless females are more slender and graceful, with their large dish-like ears having an attractive pinkish tinge. Somewhere in Africa there must be a story of 'how the kudu got its horns', but so far it has eluded me.

The kudu played an important part in the life of one of twentieth-century Africa's most remarkable men – Laurens van der Post. After years of fighting and captivity in the Second World War he returned to South Africa, and before even visiting his mother, who believed him to be dead, he collected a tent and provisions and went into the bush: 'I could not face human beings. I felt that I couldn't face this destructive and impossible species, so I went to live in the bush alone. I remember the first evening in the wild, seeing the first kudu bull as I made camp on the Pafuri river. He came out of the river where he had been drinking, sniffing the air between him and me. He threw that lovely head of his back, and I looked at him with a tremendous feeling of relief. I thought, "My God, I'm back home! I'm back at the moment when humanity came in."'

I was keen to see members of Etosha's thriving lion population. Some scientists had recently concluded that the population was thriving too well and were experimenting with the pill, to try to reduce numbers. Unfortunately we were unable to track down either lions or scientists.

Elephants also thrive at Etosha and like those at Wankie, they had quite short tusks. With a change in location the reason for the stunted ivory had changed too, from 'wear caused by digging', to 'a mineral deficiency in the diet'. The new explanation seemed more likely.

In most of Africa the birds are spectacular, and Etosha was no exception – from ostriches at one end of the scale to sunbirds at the other. In between were vultures, hornbills, eagles and assorted birds with names to match their beauty and habits, such as the lilac-breasted roller, swallow-tailed bee-eater, black-breasted snake eagle, double-banded courser and the rufous-bellied crombec. I was particularly pleased to see the large kori bustard – a close relative of the European great bustard. Both species are claimed, by some, to be the heaviest flying bird in the world. We were lucky, too, to find a secretive crimson-breasted shrike. It was while we were trying to photograph the crimson-breasted shrike that Hans fell asleep.

As soon as we arrived back at the Fort, the pilot's enthusiasm for life returned. The English girls were drinking and laughing, and German tourists were drinking lager as if it had only just been invented. One of the camp employees in his 'macho' park uniform was also joining in the fun, telling 'jokes': 'What's green and black and crawls about on the lawn – a kaffir cutting the grass.' Klaus was revelling in being the centre of attention, until his wife arrived: 'Klaus, don't you think you had better come home now.'
'Don't you come here and talk to me like that, woman,' he retorted angrily, 'Get back home and get my meal ready – why else do you think I married you.' His wife left, humiliated. At least Klaus was being multiracial – he was obnoxious to black and white alike. 'Now your turn for a joke,' he commanded the reptile-like English girl. She had no jokes, except for a drunken party-piece. Somehow she managed to put her whole right fist into her mouth – making her look even more reptilian.

We met another entirely unfunny man at the Northern town of Oshakati, a military garrison in the heart of Ovambo land, the country's main operational area against SWAPO.

We found the local District Commissioner sitting at the bar of a hotel drinking beer. He was an Afrikaner and greeted us without enthusiasm. He was exactly how I imagined van der Merwe to be. He was pink and sweating as he took in more beer and his safari suit was light and ill-fitting, struggling to hold in his stomach and bulging mid-riff.

With all the army activity I wondered if the area was safe: 'Safe, I should think so. These blacks are the worst blacks in Africa; they are useless man. They did hit a bungalow with a mortar last year, but that's all – boy, they buried that oakey so deep that he got his breakfast in the evening. The only thing you have to worry about is the mosquitoes – but as a rule, they don't bother us with all these blacks around.' He was not too keen to leave his stool or his beer: 'You all look tired,' he said, 'we'll go and look round tomorrow.'

Van was still perspiring when he waddled in next morning. His list of priorities was surprising: our first visit was to a new African township, with small, well-built housing. I thought he was showing us how South African money was helping the African, but no: 'Now where is it. I know it's here somewhere,' he kept saying as we drove slowly along identical looking streets. At last he smiled: 'Boy, here it is.' and he stopped outside a house that looked as if its roof had been blown off. 'Now take a look at that and remember the comedian who lived there. He came home and smelt gas, so he lit a match to take a look. Oh man, did that Ovambo have a surprise. He was a flying coon and he is not coming down yet.' He shook his head in disbelief. The fact that there were hundreds of African homes with their roofs intact was beyond him. I wondered if the Information Office in London had ever invited visitors from abroad to look at all the buildings in Britain demolished by gas leaks.

We stopped at a kraal where an old, half-naked man showed us one of his huts, in which a fire smouldered. He showed us a clay kiln where he made pottery, a wooden container where his wives pounded maize and his maize patch. As the tour proceeded slowly around the kraal, Van hung back, mumbling: 'Ooh man – I don't believe this.' 'How these people live – it's disgusting.' 'These liberals can call them what they like – they're still jungle bunnies.' He had to return to the offices in the afternoon too for a local Ovambo Council Meeting: 'Oh man, is that bad news. I've got another executive committee meeting where I've got to hear those witch doctors talk shit again.' As he was listening to the 'witch doctors' once more, we were shown around the large military camp, with its collection of captured Russian-made weapons – AK 47's, land-mines and RPG 7's.

It was a relief to meet a District Commissioner who actually liked his charges, at Rundu, on the banks of the Okavango river, in the extreme north-east of the country, where the northern bank was Angolan. He was keen to help the locals, and the country. He had schemes to help them improve their cattle and maize and as we drove along the dirt road he waved to women working in their gardens and old men sitting under trees. As we passed a couple and their child he braked hard; they were smaller, lighter people, with clear Bushmen features. The woman wore a short, dirty cotton dress, with her child carried on her back. The man wore holey trousers and a T-shirt; both were smoking. The DC spoke with them for several minutes before driving off. He was pleased: 'They were not pure Bushmen, but that's as near as you'll get here. They had a lot of Bushman blood in them.'

'What did you talk about,' I asked, expecting the conversation to have been about interesting aspects of local life.

'Nothing really; most of the time they were asking me for cigarettes – Bushmen love smoking.'

The river itself was in flood. In places it was at least half a mile wide, and because of the rain the vegetation was lush and green. Women were taking great bundles of clothing down to the water's edge, on their heads, and when they had washed their clothes, they washed themselves.

It was exciting being on the banks of the Okavango, for it is one of Africa's most famous rivers. Instead of flowing westwards, taking the shortest route to the sea, it flows eastwards. Its water never reaches the Indian Ocean however, for it spreads out and disappears into the sand of the Kalahari. Consequently the Okavango swamps form an area of great wildlife wealth – it probably forms too, the largest oasis in the world.

Not all the people on the southern bank of the river were locals. For just as some Ovambos had fled northwards to become refugees in Angola, so many Angolans, both African and Portuguese, had fled southwards as refugees to Namibia. Politicians thrive on double standards and on the subject of South West Africa there were plenty. Because of the South African presence, which had a fragment of legality, the 'world' claimed to be horrified: yet the Cuban presence in Angola, with 'advisers' from Russia and East Germany supporting an unelected, unrepresentative government, invoked no sense of universal outrage. In Namibia, where the South Africans wanted to get out after holding elections, the world said it would not recognise the results, although it continued to call for 'one man one vote'. In Angola, where the government, with minority support, seized power, the world is indifferent to the need for democratic elections and 'one man one vote'. Furthermore, in Namibia, members of SWAPO, the party dedicated to the acquisition of power through terrorism, were called 'freedom fighters', while UNITA, the rebels fighting in Angola, who would probably have won a properly conducted election in the first instance, were regarded as 'South African stooges'.

A South African sergeant was not sure who controlled the bank directly opposite, UNITA or the ruling FNLA: 'It's changed hands several times, only there's not much there to change, only a couple of bombed-out buildings and bush.' 'Could we get a boat and go and see after dark?' I asked. 'Normally we could, but it's a bit dicey with the river in flood.'

He was another who liked the locals: 'But to be perfectly honest I don't know if it's right to develop any part of Africa. A few years ago there was an African sitting on the jetty out there, fishing. He was happy and content. A fisheries adviser saw him and said: "They're good fish. If you sold them you could buy another rod and catch even more fish and buy a boat, then you will be able to get the bigger fish in the middle." So it went on until he had a fleet of trawlers and a successful canning factory. The fisheries adviser was pleased. But the African, dressed in his new, expensive suit, looked at him sadly: "I'm not happy; I have never been so sad in all my life. All I ever wanted to do was sit on the jetty and fish – now I don't have time to do that any more." The worrying thing is that this story is not only true for the African, but it's true for us as well.'

* * * * * * *

The final leg of my Namibian journey was the one I had been looking forward to most – a visit to Tsumeb, a small settlement of shacks and administrative buildings, miles from anywhere: it was the capital of Bushmanland. Sadly it turned into a very brief visit, but it was also a very disturbing one, showing the positive and the negative sides of apartheid.

The positive side was simple and obvious: although part of Namibia, 'Bushmanland' had been set aside for the Bushmen, where they could live, follow their traditions and keep their ancient customs alive, in other countries, especially Angola and Botswana, the Bushman, his pride, individuality and history had been swept away. Even in Botswana, almost the only true and trouble-free democracy in Africa, the Bushman's needs and wishes had been swamped by the will and the demands of the majority tribes. It is a disturbing fact that in virtually all the practical forms of democracy, the weak gradually lose their identity and get swept aside. For although 'democracy' can be a great social good, it can also be used to excuse injustice, ignorance and even tyranny. Consequently most of the world's trouble-spots have developed from racial minorities not getting what they see as their due.

Yet although the Bushman had their land, their rights and their identity, their lot was not a happy one, for national and regional boundaries, in the form of fences, meant that they and the animals they once hunted in order to live, could not roam unhindered. Even part of Bushmanland itself had been declared a wildlife reserve, where the Bushmen could not hunt, and where the ancient bond between wild animals and man, the hunter-gatherer, had been broken. They could gather, but they could not hunt, which in turn meant that they could not feed as they ought. As a result the Bushmen had mixed lives; most no longer roamed, yet they retained many of their traditions, developed through centuries of wandering. Unfortunately when nomadic people cease to wander they find much of the ephemeral tinsel of civilisation difficult to cope with. As a direct result some of the Bushmen had problems with alcohol, smoking and general squalor in the form of discarded tin cans and assorted rubbish. Fortunately, others had come to terms with their new life and just about managed to cope with the intrusion of the twentieth-century into their lives.

One of the saddest sights I saw was a classroom of small Bushmen children; the girls in little cotton dresses and the boys in shirts and short trousers, while outside, other children were playing almost naked in the grass. In the school, they were learning Afrikaans – outside they were talking in the click language of the Bushman. Even if the children had been learning English, an infinitely more useful language in the modern world than Afrikaans, I am still not sure that such a change would have been right: I simply do not know the answer. Is it still possible to live a romantic dream? And why should a life lived close to nature be considered a romantic dream anyway?

The District Commissioner at Tsumeb was a fine, heavily bearded man who loved the people. He offered to take me into the heart of Bushmanland on horseback to look for the last few families still living their traditional lives: 'If you want to do it, Robin, you must let me know soon; they will all be gone in four or five years' time.' It remains one of my biggest regrets that I was never able to take up his offer.

The negative side of apartheid, or the Afrikaner mentality, could be seen in a courtroom drama as we arrived. The Bushman's representative on the country's Council of Ministers was being prosecuted for shooting a protected Roan antelope. The District Commissioner was embarrassed by it: 'Fancy prosecuting any

Bushman for killing an antelope which he regards simply as meat, let alone their government representative – a Minister. What humiliation. What an insult – it's absurd. If he did it, this white man's law and the need for it could have been explained to him. He's a decent, simple man; there would have been no problem. Instead they have followed the letter of the law. What do these people understand about the letter of the law?' Nearby, a half-naked Bushman woman in beads and skins was making a necklace out of an ostrich egg shell, and a small group of men, dressed in western suits for the trial, sat smoking under a tree.

Luckily, a leading advocate from Windhoek won the day for the Minister. The defence's case had been that the Minister's bodyguard had shot the antelope. The Minister got off and the guard received a warning.

The Minister seemed relieved, he was a small, shy man, dressed in a smart black suit and shiny leather shoes; the 'primitive' hunter had been 'civilised'. He smiled, but his deep brown eyes had a tired, distant look, full of relief and confusion.

Sadly, almost as soon as it had begun, the visit to Bushmanland was over. The advocate had to return to Windhoek immediately and our plane was the only transport available. Five people had to get into an aircraft designed for four. It was not the advocate who had to squeeze into the jump-seat at the back with the luggage.

Being back in Windhoek early was not good news, for with time to spare it meant back to the political round. The local Herero chief was a large, exuberant man, dressed like a banker. In the walled courtyard of his bungalow a group of Africans waited for the chance of telling him their problems. Armed guards with modern G3 rifles were also present, as the chief's predecessor had been assassinated by SWAPO.

Once in the large, comfortable sitting room of his modern home, his wife, wearing traditional Herero costume, brought us tea and biscuits on a tray; three of the cups were of best china, the remaining two were of glass. The Chief was a member of the Council of Ministers and claimed to have the support of 93 per cent of the Hereros. If he was correct, I could not see the necessity for quite so many armed guards, although he did say that he was on SWAPO's 'death list'. He was an articulate, jolly man, with a hearty laugh. 'Our campaign is to do good – SWAPO's is to do harm. I want to see people not as black and white, but as Namibian. We want people accepted on their merits. Despite having our problems in Africa, you must not judge us too harshly. Africa's wars and tribulations are no different from the problems experienced by Europe as it fought and argued its way to civilisation.'

He was a pleasant, likeable man, but that is one of the problems with politics – so was one of his opponents. Unlike Rhodesia, which banned many of its nationalists, and South Africa, where the ANC was outlawed, Namibia allowed SWAPO to operate politically inside the country, and I spoke with Daniel Tjonguerero, an active member and a worker for the Council of Churches in Namibia. He agreed that most of the apartheid in South West Africa had been dismantled by legislation, but he was still worried: 'For it is impossible to change apartheid of the heart.' In much the same way I suppose it is impossible to deflect a politician from the pursuit of power and dominance; if it were possible, there would be less trouble, confrontation and suffering in the world.

* * * * * * *

As I was driven to the airport I wondered how Namibia's view of the world had changed in eleven days. The local paper's headline gave the answer; the subject of greatest concern was still the activities of the local kudu population – 'Kudi Injures Elderly Grandmother'.

One thing had changed however: the official at passport control. He was an Afrikaner, and it seemed that God had given him a large body, but a very small brain: 'Passport,' he snarled.
'Could you stamp my visa please, like the official when I came in,' I requested politely.
'Why? You have been into this country haven't you? What are you ashamed of?'
'But I don't want a stamp, as I have to make some visits to Black Africa later.'
'You've been here, so you get the stamp. I don't care what the blacks think about it.' He brought the stamp down savagely on the fresh page of my passport. It did not seem the most intelligent way for my sponsored visit to finish.

Flying over the Kalahari desert from Johannesburg to London was unforgettable. A huge thunderstorm was emptying its heart over that parched land, and at 40,000 feet we were not completely clear of the angry anvil of black cloud. We were bounced and buffeted in the charged, unstable air. Once, I heard a Baptist minister claim in a sermon that flying over a thunderstorm was 'exhilarating'; the word that immediately sprang to my mind was 'terrifying'.

8. Leopard and Lion.

One of the disappointments in writing this book was the complete unhelpfulness of my national airline – British Airways – supposedly 'The World's Favourite Airline'. Even a slight relaxation of their normal rules, to reduce the cost of flying to Nairobi, would have been appreciated – but no. Instead, both Aeroflot, the Russian Airline, and Egypt Air offered me tickets at half the British Airways price, the catch being an eleven hour wait in Moscow, or five hours in Cairo. I chose Egypt Air and was directed to an Asian 'bucket shop' near Marble Arch in London; it was a small second floor office, manned by Indians and specialising in cheap air tickets.

The plane was three-quarters full, with a smattering of Europeans, the rest being Egyptians and Asians returning home or visiting the sub-continent via Cairo. The airworthiness of the new Airbus was helped by a copy of the Koran, fixed to the door of the flight-deck. 'Don't be fooled,' a cynic informed, 'when a plane caught fire in Saudi Arabia – the crew, – all good Muslims, were so busy saying their prayers that they didn't open the doors and several people burnt to death – quite needlessly.' That is the type of reassurance I do not need when I am flying, but Roger went on. 'Some of the African airlines are even worse, you know, they have African pilots now – non-reflectors – "this is Captain Midnight calling." Do you want to hear a perfectly true story?' I nodded. 'An African crew was recently flying to London with some black VIP's aboard. Once cruising the pilot went to talk to the guests – he was followed by the co-pilot and then the navigator, leaving the flight-deck deserted. Suddenly they hit turbulence. The cabin door slammed shut, firing all the automatic anti-terrorist locks. The plane was flying with nobody flying it. The terrified passengers then had the treat of seeing the crew hacking frantically at the door with fire axes. They got back in just as they were about to hit Libyan air space.'

At Cairo, those waiting for connections were very cosmopolitan,

wearing Indian saris, an assortment of flowing robes, Arabian head-dresses and various items of African apparel, varying in appearance from pyjamas to night-shirts. Two pale, bespectacled English women sat next to me. They worked as missionaries in London. I was amazed. 'Do they really need missionaries in London?'
'Oh they need missionaries everywhere.'

* * * * * * *

As we queued to get out of the airport building, the need for missionaries in Cairo became apparent. An attractive blonde in tight jeans was in front of me. When it came to her turn for the hand-held metal detector, the laughing little Arab in charge repeatedly passed it over a metal stud on her back pocket to make it bleep. After three repeat performances he let her through. 'Eet vos good,' he leered, 'it eez because she has a big bum.'

* * * * * * *

Helen was English, going out to Kenya to see Africa for the first time. Like Roger she was trying to play the part of an independent, hardened traveller – the difference being that he was succeeding, whereas she looked tense and lost. Her mood was not helped by a large party of Mexicans, all showing false bravado, laughing and joking with enforced jollity until the ageing Boeing 707 was airborn. As we landed the Mexicans burst into spontaneous applause; in alarm, Helen grabbed the first thing that came to hand – my knee.

It was a beautiful pale dawn, with palm trees silhouetted against the soft pink sky. The air was warm and scented and I wondered if it had been a similar dawn when my father had made his journey to Kenya, nearly 30 years before. Two other planes had recently landed and the concourse was full of mainly white visitors – businessmen and holiday-makers – some already in obviously new safari-suits, reminding me of the old song: 'It ain't what you do, it's the way that you do it.' Did they really expect to see lions on the way to Nairobi from the airport?

I shared a taxi with Helen. It was parked near flower-beds criss-crossed with barbed wire to stop people walking over them. It was a short, but puzzling drive to the city centre. How did an old taxi of unclear origin rattle so much while travelling along a smooth road? Only three doors opened, the driver having to slip over the front passenger seat in order to get to his. Daylight actually showed through one door and the floor felt flexible; I refrained from folding the old sacking carpet back in case my feet hit the road.

Towards Nairobi the verges became crowded with Africans walking into the centre from the suburbs, townships and shanty towns. The city was waking and sucking people into its alluring core. Once in the centre I was whisked away in a new Mercedes and for the rest of the day I slept.

My hosts ran a large travel company in Nairobi. He was English, with an hyphenated name, and accent to match. She was American and half his age: 'We often get mistaken for father and daughter' she laughed. Both were having problems over the renewal of work permits, although Brian had lived and worked in Kenya for many years.

Their bungalow was large and comfortable, with African carvings, shields, photographs of big-game hunting and bead necklaces, giving it the traditional 'settler in Africa' atmosphere – a feeling heightened at meal times when a small silver bell was rung. It summoned Henry, the houseboy, to bring in the next course and take away the dirty dishes. At first I was uneasy and felt embarrassed by it and my half-hearted request to help with the washing up was met with: 'Of course not – that's what he's paid for.' By the end of the trip, I had grown to quite like the service.

If the house was the domain of the houseboy, it followed that the garden was the territory of Abraham, the 'garden-boy'. It was a large garden, full of flowers, trees and birds – sunbirds, weaver birds, mousebirds with long flowing tails and even hornbills. Kites were ever-present too, searching for anything suitable on which to prey or scavenge.

'We've got fewer helpers than most,' Brian told me. 'You must remember that if we did all the domestic chores ourselves, there would simply be two unemployed Africans. They've both got families – what would they do then? Unemployment's bad enough in the city already. The middle-class Africans all have cooks, houseboys and servants – it's not just a white privilege.'

How the middle-class Africans lived, I could not tell as Brian and Clare lived in a white enclave of bungalows, large gardens, luxury cars, domestic help, guard dogs and security systems. Indeed some of the properties were like miniature fortresses in which complete sections could be shut off with iron doors, chains and bolts, even after intruders had gained access to the main house. During a robbery or break-in, radio alarms could instantly summon mobile African security men wearing helmets and swinging cudgels.

It was apartheid – not rigid, state-controlled apartheid, but voluntary apartheid, free and easy and overlapping at the edges. The whites simply liked living as a group, sharing the same interests, culture and life-styles, and the same applied to the blacks. It would even be possible for a European to visit Kenya and never meet an African, except as a driver, houseboy, or customs official. It confirmed my view that legal apartheid could be outlawed in South Africa tomorrow – it would not change how the ordinary whites or blacks actually lived, nor would it lead to great movements of population – but it would remove a great political and social irritant.

That evening, for my benefit, a drinks party was held. Various neighbours and their partners arrived, a variety of 'short-term' professionals, with contracts in engineering, accountancy or University lecturing, and various long term locals in tourism, and other commercial ventures. Those who had opted for Kenyan citizenship had few problems with work permits, while 'British citizens' had similar problems to Brian.

After a quarter of an hour of listening and nodding it became apparent that white Kenyan society had become very inward looking and incestuous, which is a polite way of saying that it loved gossip. Much of the conversation, between refills of whisky and gin, seemed to be concerned only with who was sleeping with whom, and I quickly learnt that to see a couple together did not mean they were husband and wife. They may well have been married, but not necessarily to each other. So, the old Kenyan saying of: 'Are you married, or do you live in Kenya?' still applied. With Nairobi being at 6,000 feet and the gin flowing freely, another piece of white Kenyan folklore was also confirmed: 'Kenyans live on the three A's – altitude, alcohol and adultery.'

* * * * * * *

As a city Nairobi had neither the shambles of Kinshasa, nor the pristine order of Salisbury or Pretoria. The wide streets and colonial buildings clearly showed its British past, while the high-rise office blocks and hotels revealed its belief in a mass-produced, modern future. Yet at the same time it had a somewhat seedy present for, although its centre represented modern city living, it was fading at the edges with chipped, sun-bleached paint, pot-holes in the pavement and a feeling of the Third World just around the next twentieth-century corner.

On the streets, shiny new cars competed for space with old charabancs held together by faith, hope and inexpert welding. While on the pavements smartly dressed, Westernised Africans passed beggars: the blind, the halt and the lame – including polio victims with twisted limbs, shuffling along in rags.

Tourists were plentiful, still in safari-suits and bush shirts, with strips of synthetic leopard skin around their hats. To those wanting genuine animal artefacts, elephant hair bracelets were being openly but illegally touted on street corners. An American in a stetson hat and weighed down by cameras bought one – in his own eyes he was already 'going native'.

The shoe-shine boys were offering a more practical service, as was the 'watch-doctor' and the man selling 'sliced-wood' [kindling]. Previously I had been under the impression that Jomo Kenyetta had expelled most of the Asians. If he had, then Nairobi's Asian population must have once been enormous, for much of the commerce still seemed to be in Indian hands. Religion was more evenly distributed with Hindu temples, mosques and Christian churches.

A tall African youth tagged along with me: 'Hallo – how are you?'
'I'm fine, how are you?' It was reassuring to find the natives so friendly; he was obviously practising his English.
'How is England?'
'How is your trip here?'
'How is English Education?'
'I believe that in England, education is free?' Oh no; I was disillusioned already. I could imagine the next question.
'In Kenya it is not free – it is very expensive. I come from Uganda and I want to learn. My mother has been killed in the civil war and I have no money to go to school. If ever you want to go to Uganda I will help you.'

Soon, it seemed, every other idle youth on the street corner had miraculously become a Ugandan refugee with a deep desire for education.

One other approach was also popular: 'You want to change your money on the black market – I'll give you a good rate.'
'You have dollars! Let me count your money first. I must give you your Kenya shillings in an envelope so the police don't see.' Americans abroad have a tendency to boast about their 'good deals' on the blackmarket; in Nairobi they pay large sums of money for envelopes full of newspaper.

* * * * * * *

The new arrival in Nairobi can make mistakes; mine was to visit the National Museum before I had seen anything else of the country. It was a fine museum, run by Richard Leakey, the famous anthropologist son of a famous anthropologist father, Louis Leakey. It contained numerous glimpses of Kenya's past and present and included a collection of paintings by Joy Adamson of the peoples of Kenya. It also had a section about independence and the struggle of the Mau Mau 'freedom fighters' against colonial rule. It was not really surprising that despite the museum's attention to detail, the fact that the Mau Mau killed far more of their own people than they did Europeans, or members of the security forces, was not recorded. It was an example of the growing modern tendency to rewrite history to suit current political myths. Another simple fact was also missing: if the Mau Mau uprising was seen as Kenya's war of independence, then the Mau Mau lost. In fact the 'rebellion' was virtually over by 1956: independence did not come until 1963.

My problem arose from the premises adjoining the National Museum – the Nairobi Snake Park. One of my few aversions in life, apart from flying, is snakes. I have tried to like them; but all my efforts are in vain. To me, snakes are creatures of loathing and evil, and there in the Snake Park were some of Kenya's most deadly species – spitting cobras, mambas and puff-adders – terrifying in their slothful malevolence.

Walking back to the bungalow I was seeing snakes under every leaf and lump of grass. A Salvation Army band was holding an open-air service, with much clapping and banging of drums, unaware of the potential dangers. Away from the city centre there were patches of cultivated land between houses, growing bananas, maize and manioc, over which a bird of prey circled; I hoped it was a snake eagle.

One of the first birds I saw on leaving Nairobi was an eagle, a long-crested hawk eagle perching on top of a tall sizal stem, staring intently towards the ground for signs of movement. With its crest fluttering in the wind it looked rather like a large black cockatoo. James, the African driver, was good on birds: 'Some people just call it the long-crested eagle; it eats rodents and sometimes snakes. It is a useful bird.' It was good to know that I had some anti-snake allies.

We were going on a black and white striped safari, a small group of tourists in a zebra-patterned combie being whisked from game park to game park. My travelling companions were a mixed group: Brian's wife Clare, her American friend Ginny, an elderly American Professor and his wife and a young English photographer who was endlessly dusting her lenses, and demanding to use the nearest refrigerator: 'I must use it. My films will be ruined in this heat.' Other photographers seemed to be managing without dust or ice.

We followed the main tarred road north to Thika. It seemed incredible to me that just 70 years before, as a child, Elspeth Huxley had made the same journey in an ox-cart along a dirt track. Then the bush had been so wild that she saw game virtually all the way, in countless numbers – antelope, buffalo, zebra and many more, surrounded by the sights and scents of ancient Africa. She loved the smell of Africa: 'One cannot describe a smell because there are no words to do so in the English language, apart from those that place it in a very general category, like sweet or pungent. So I cannot characterize this, nor compare it with any other, but it was the smell of travel in those days, in fact the smell of Africa – dry, peppery, yet rich and deep, with an undertone of native body smeared with fat and red ochre and giving out a ripe, partly rancid odour which nauseated some Europeans when they first encountered it but which I, for one, grew to enjoy.'

We stopped at Blue Posts after an hour – Elspeth Huxley had stopped there after two days. Then it was a genuine watering-hole for travellers; now it had become a tourist-trap, with necklaces, fly-whisks and carvings, as well as a 'viewpoint' for the spectacular waterfall. After that it was genuine safari – hard driving between lodges, where time was spent game-viewing, eating, sleeping, drinking, talking, and in the case of the photographer, searching for a refrigerator.

At each new venue all the Americans became excited about the rooms: 'Have you got a shower – ice – a fan?' If all three were present they were happy; if just one was absent they felt as if they were coping with African life at its most primitive. Their favourite time was sitting close to the bar at a game lodge, gin and tonic in hand, noisily crunching ice and watching rather lethargic animals drink or scratch. The thought that it would have been cheaper to have stayed at home to chew ice, drink gin and tonic and watch a wildlife film on television, had not occurred to them.

Once the photographer had located a 'fridge', her time was spent waiting for dawn and dusk. She was up with the sun and her camera went down with the sun: 'The light in Africa is wonderful,' she explained. For the rest of the time she had a permanently glazed look as she drifted about gradually acquiring necklaces, bracelets and a spiral of brass for her arm: 'I'll never take it off – Africa is so special.' She spent long periods too, just gazing into the bush, communing with nature and Africa. She seemed to think that she was the first white woman to fully understand the peoples and wildlife of the continent – all from a striped combie and game lodge. 'She's really freaking out,' was Ginny's comment. James the driver had a different view: 'She's suffering from culture shock; we've got the culture, she's got the shock,' and he roared with laughter. He took me to one side: 'English and American women often do this; travelling does something to them. You men seem to manage.' I was reassured.

Quite famous people have also 'freaked out' in Kenya. The most obvious being Karen Blixen. *Out of Africa* is beautifully written, but in it Karen Blixen is obviously moving into the world of dreams and mysticism, helped by the spectacular nature of her surroundings. She was 'freaking out' gently and creatively. This, I suppose, explained the photographer's extraordinary behaviour – she was Blixenating.

At the Outspan Hotel, in the Aberdare Mountains (now called the Nyandarua mountains – a name I can never remember), it was like a tourist factory: 'stop the combie – bags out – tourists out – sign here – lunch is being served over there – come and see the genuine Kikuyu dancing.' The Kikuyu dancers seemed bored as they danced, wearing faded zebra skins and daubed with brown and white clay. A German completely ignored all the other tourists with cameras. He stood in front of them, reversed on to them and barged them out of the way, all to get a better shot. Sometimes he held his camera within a foot of the dancers' expressionless faces, as his daughter followed him with a cassette recorder. Later among the sounds of dancing and singing he would have learnt many variations, in English and American, of the phrase 'go away and don't be so rude you misbehaving German gentleman'.

There was an extraordinary woman at the Mount Kenya Safari Club. I met her and an African admirer in the game viewing hide that overlooked a deserted water-hole. She claimed to be a missionary and was wearing a long black dress, black shawl and black socks. 'I was called to preach out here in Kenya for a month.' Her calling was helped by a donation from America of £4,000 – how else would she have been able to live in the expensive luxury of the Mount Kenya Safari Club? She claimed to have been preaching to the Masai in the Rift Valley and made numerous converts.

'Do you speak Masai?' I asked her.
'No, I had no need, I had an interpreter.'
'What did you preach about?'
'I warned them of the evils of drinking blood. It's mentioned in the Bible seven or eight times.'
'Is it, whereabouts? I've never read that.'
'I can't tell you now. I have all my references in my room.'

It seemed a peculiar concept, preaching to simple tribesmen, in a foreign language, condemning a traditional part of their diet – for the Masai drink milk mixed with blood. It was a uniquely American approach.

She then started to run down American negroes: 'Their "Afro" hair styles are absurd. There just are no haircuts like that in Africa.'

At dinner I was served by a small, smart waiter with very short hair: 'What tribe are you from,' I asked.
'Kikuyu – are you American?'
I shuddered; I hadn't got a new safari suit and possessed only one camera: 'No, no I'm English.'
'I'm interested in America, they have black tribes like us. We had a person from the Negro tribe the other day.'
'Really, what was his hair like?'
'Oh, like mine, but the woman, she was funny; it is a very funny tribe.'

My favourite game reserve was Samburu on the edge of the Northern Frontier District. As we drove there from the Safari Lodge, a martial eagle swooped down and stole a hen being minded by a small boy. He shouted and threw sticks as the large bird flew off to perch, with its meal, on a nearby telegraph pole. Samburu is hot, dry country of bush, kopje and plain, with rich riverine forest growing along the banks of the Ewaso Nyiro, another river that never reaches the sea; instead it flows eastwards to evaporate and filter through the sun-drenched soil. The area is hot, dry and spectacular, with 'dust devils' spiralling upwards from the plains and the kopjes giving huge views of one of the world's final great remnants of wilderness. At last it was possible to feel a part of wild, ancient Africa, even if it was from a black and white striped combie.

Some of Samburu's wildlife is unique to semi-desert: the beautiful gerenuk, a graceful, long-necked antelope that often stands on its hind legs to browse; Grevy's zebra, an increasingly rare zebra whose stripes are closer together and ears rounder than the more familiar Burchell's; the reticulated giraffe, with clearer white lines between its jigsaw pattern of chestnut than other types of giraffe. The area has the Samburu people too, many still leading their traditional lives of herding and hunting. It is thought that at one time the Samburu were part of the Masai tribe, but they broke away. In many ways they still resemble the Masai however, particularly in their love of bright beads, ochre, scarlet cloaks and spears.

The Lodge was again full of Americans, and soon after arrival, the invitation was given to 'come and see the tribal dancing'. It was far more impressive than the Kikuyu performance; the dancers actually seemed to be enjoying it. The young warriors were jumping up and down, using their lungs as musical instruments, inhaling and exhaling, to produce a noise remarkably like an Australian dijeridoo. Young girls, weighed down with bead necklaces, also danced, a rather explicit, suggestive dance, almost certainly to do with fertility. Soon, the photographer was Blixenating again and getting the Samburu to plait her hair.

The inevitable game-drive followed. Four lions were bored by the proceedings. They had good cause to be, as they were surrounded by eight combies full of tourists each with a camera at the ready. A leopard up a tree was even better; eleven combies completely encircling the snoozing beast. Every time it yawned or scratched there was a great fusillade of camera shutters and cine action.

That evening we ate with a film-maker we had met, and Ginny showed a new-found passion for wildlife, as well as for the Lodge's stock of drink. I was amazed, not by her, but by the woman at the next table; she was obviously the missing member of the extraordinary negro tribe. She was huge, an American negro woman with bright ginger hair, scarlet lips, great white-framed glasses, dangling earrings, an equally large necklace, a tight-fitting silk dress that revealed every enormous bulge, and white, high-heeled shoes. Like the waiters, I stared at her with eyes agog. The waiter at the Safari Club had been right, she did come from a very 'funny tribe'.

Dawn arrived and Ginny was late for the game drive. She emerged for breakfast, looking bedraggled from the film-maker's luxury tent; Kenya's notorious three A's had struck again.

That evening we were in yet another lodge, Meru, watching elephants. Two seemed to be very good friends, until one suddenly and briefly mounted: 'Look at that,' Ginny laughed, 'a quickie with a lot of foreplay.' American is not a very beautiful or descriptive language and Ginny failed to say whether or not she was talking from experience. The Lodge was again full of her compatriots. 'Gee, it's bad news,' she gasped, 'I hate typical Americans'; it was strange – in my eyes, Ginny was a typical American.

* * * * * * *

Although the combie safari was on the well-worn tourist circuit, it had been a good trip. We had enjoyed perfect weather, fine views of Mount Kenya and we had seen every one of the 'big five' animals – the largest and most spectacular of Africa that every tourist wants to see – the elephant, leopard, lion, buffalo and rhinoceros. I think the 'big five' should be increased to seven, with the cheetah and hippo added for good measure; if so, we only failed to see the cheetah.

We had been to most of Kenya's famous wildlife parks, except the Masai Mara and Amboseli, and we had seen enormous numbers of birds and animals. But although the Americans had found it 'great', 'truly wonderful' and 'out of this world', I felt that I had experienced the real spirit of Africa only briefly, at Samburu. The spirit of new Kenya had been apparent in the stories of encroachment by cattle into several national parks, and by reports of rhino poaching, confirmed at Meru where five almost tame white rhinos were being guarded night and day by men with green uniforms and .303 rifles.

* * * * * * *

The streets of Nairobi were still full of traffic. The street names reflected Black Africa's search for an identity. Gone were the names of Empire; instead the roads were named after Kenyetta, Kimathi (a Mau Mau 'general'), Nkrumah, Kaunda and, surprisingly, in view of Ethiopia's recent history, Haille Selasse. As I passed the Thorn Tree café, a traditional meeting place for travellers, I saw Helen adorned with beads and bangles; her skin was tanned and her hair had absorbed sunlight to become even more blonde. 'Robin, this place is wonderful; I never want to go back to England.' The virus had struck her too. 'I've been to the desert, in the Turkana bus, it was brilliant.'

I was not impressed: 'I hate bus rides – I avoid them like the plague these days, even in England.'

'You will like this – it's different – it goes all the way to the Jade Sea.'

In Africa, nothing turns out to be what it is said to be and so it came as no surprise when the Turkana Bus turned out to be a lorry; the sea was no sea either, but a lake – Lake Turkana, formerly Lake Rudolph.

'You'll like this – it's different.' The words had a hollow ring as we left Nairobi. It seemed remarkably the same to me – the same as England; it was cold, grey and the rain teemed down – the 'spectacular' Rift Valley was lost in mist and I was actually shivering as we crossed the Equator. Suzie from Devon rolled her R's to say it reminded her of Dartmoor in winter: two Irishmen also felt at home in the mist. The rest of the passengers simply hoped for something better. The driver, Captain William, assured us that things would improve.

There was a white Kenyan, who at times seemed as if she wanted to be black; her arms were weighed down with assorted bangles – Samburu, Masai and Kikuyu. Fifty years ago she would have been writing poetry and communing with nature. In 1983 she was reading *Out of Africa* and visibly Blixenating. The cook, on the other hand, as black as the ace of spades, appeared to like all things white. Sporting a well-manicured British army-type moustache and a cravat, he appeared to be Kiplingating.

Captain William was right: things did get better. The rain stopped, the sun came out, and by the time we hit dirt roads we were travelling through real heat. The shambas (African gardens) gave way to bush – hot dry bush – exactly how I imagined virgin Africa to be.

From the lorry we saw Grevy's zebra, gazelle, hartebeest and, to my astonishment, camels. There were also Samburu tribesmen in scarlet cloaks, beads and smeared in ochre. At one stop I bought a bangle. It was soon a different world, virtually desert, and at night, as the land cooled, the sky turned velvet black, littered with a million stars.

In the morning, at a small town, I bought another bangle. Suzie had changed her mind: 'Good 'erre, innit – it's not like Dartmoor at all.' It was strange, most of the American travellers were in the medical service. A young 'macho' doctor from Hawaii, who had been doing voluntary work in Ethiopia; Lorraine, a medical student who had been working in Albert Schweitzer's old hospital in Gabon, and Gary, a sombre, patronising, middle-aged gynaecologist, with his equally sombre wife. Every night around the campfire, the Americans wanted to play games – especially a word association game. It was always the Americans who seemed to introduce the subject of sex. One night the inevitable happened: Gary somehow managed to follow 'existentialism' with 'sex'. His wife was sitting next to him and quick as a flash she responded with 'over-rated'. An old professor followed up with: 'I disagree'. He was penalised for using two words.

After their 'game', the medics began to talk shop. Gary proceeded to berate Lorraine for wanting to go into family practice and having no ambition. It seemed that his view of medicine was based on the cash register and not the hippocratic oath. He was one of those intolerant people who knew all the answers before he had even heard the questions. He found the Southern Cross – before it had risen; he always claimed to have found the best place to pitch his tent, and by his general manner he persuaded all those travelling not to go sick. Inevitably it was an Irishman who failed – managing to pour the boiling contents of a kettle over his foot. Then, to everybody's amazement, the great gynaecologist mellowed – he could have gone into family medicine after all.

One campsite was straight out of the journal of Livingstone, Baines or Selous – dry bush, backed by high mountains, with a river of pools, rapids and sun-dancing dragon flies. At dawn came the call of francolins and as the sun rose, babblers and doves joined them. The smell too was unforgettable: pungent, sweet and lingering.

In this setting the Samburu danced for us and posed for photographs, as long as a payment was made. I had a problem, I had run out of change and had only the equivalent of a £5 note. One well-endowed young woman, with many strings of beads, demonstrated with suggestive gestures how the change problem could be overcome in the bushes. I declined her invitation.

On we went, through an ancient, crumbling landscape of rocks, fragmented by heat. We collected firewood, as there were few trees, apart from palms, near the lake. Under a solitary thorn a gerenuk sought the shrinking area of shade, as the sun climbed higher. We stopped briefly to eat at an abandoned village, where the hot wind whistled through the thorns and the old huts were returning to dust; soon, fan-tailed ravens and a solitary kite were circling above. Already they associated the Turkana bus with food.

Trees and grasses disappeared and the landscape became almost lunar – littered with dark volcanic rocks. Shortly before mid-day on the third day Lake Turkana appeared, like an inland sea after all, jade-coloured, white-flecked and vast. We bought more bangles, swam in the lake, visited a fishing village and drank cold beer at exorbitant prices. The Kenyan girl began to write poetry and I started to read *Out of Africa*. Outside the campsite a group of youths were selling volcanic rocks, broken to reveal hollows and nuggets of astonishing crystal. One of the youths wore a 'Holy Father' T-shirt, commemorating the visit of Pope John Paul. Either the power of the Pope was very strong, or T-shirts were very scarce. As they tried to haggle over prices, a stunning Redille woman walked by. With their graceful lines and easy movement, the peoples of north-east Africa are among the most beautiful in the world.

All too soon the return journey began. There was more heat, rock, a camel train and Samburu tribesmen wearing beads and bangles. There had been heavy rain inland and the desert was beginning to green and flower. Some of the sand luggas contained streams of muddy water; one was too deep to cross, making us retrace our tracks to go another way.

We drove into the dry again, with the lorry creating a great trail of drifting dust. There were ridges and high kopjes and then a great sandy plain, where tribesmen had allowed their herds to overgraze. The sandy soil had been washed away leaving deep gullies and channels; it was a scarred, denuded landscape – a desert of the future. A few plots had been fenced off to keep animals out; there, grasses grew and their roots still held the thin layer of soil – they simply emphasised the scale of the problem.

In Nairobi I had spoken to an Englishman, David Hopcraft, who had advocated game farming. As I looked at the ruined land I remembered his words: 'Land degradation does not take place in areas where man has not ruined the ancient structure. Cattle and livestock are the things that make systems deteriorate. Instead of cattle, people should turn to wildlife. In Africa it is a vast natural resource, as important as oil, stretching from the Cape to Cairo. Managed correctly it could give the local people an interest in their land, and at the same time it could provide protein and revenue. It could stop the creation of deserts.' He was running a game ranch in the Athi Plains and meeting with some success.

We were all thinking how smoothly the trip had gone when the lorry's fan suddenly decided to make its way through the radiator. 'What do we do?' Dr Gary asked aggressively, 'I've got to get back to Nairobi, we've got a very tight schedule.' With comments and advice he then showed why an American gynaecologist does not necessarily make a good motor mechanic. The young 'macho' doctor was in his element, always in the forefront, undoing nuts and bolts, showing the same enthusiasm and bravado as American film-stars winning the war.

As the radiator was being taken out I noticed a metal plate showing the lorry's country of origin. 'Assembled in East London', it said, with the actual name of the country scratched out. I could not think of any Mercedes factory in East London, England. It seemed that somewhere a customs official had not been very good at geography, or he had been induced to turn a blind eye. Nearby too, I noticed a spent cartridge from a high velocity rifle, of the sort used by some sections of the Kenyan army. As we were close to the Samburu Game Reserve, it was not a good sign.

Captain William was not dismayed at the breakdown. He collected a great pile of plastic bags, melted them down and poured the molten plastic into the gaping holes. Apart from making everybody feel better it made little actual difference and we limped into Samburu still leaking like a sieve. That night, much to my amazement, and the even greater astonishment of Captain William, a replacement radiator was sent from Nairobi.

After a short game-drive in the rejuvenated lorry we were again heading south. It had been a remarkable trip, and the reappearance of tar roads was greeted with disappointment and despondency. At

Isiolo we demanded another stop. It was like an old frontier town – a mixture of Muslim and Christian, ancient and modern, nomad and settled resident. It was also the place where trousers, shirts and shoes replaced cloaks, ochre and bare feet. The young doctor exchanged two shirts and a pair of jeans for more bracelets; the Kenyan girl had no more room on her arms and bought a necklace and Suzie claimed to have lost all her lingering love for Devon.

The arrival back in Nairobi after a week away was bizarre. The passing Africans were wearing Western style suits, while the Europeans and Americans alighting from the 'bus' were in various stages of undress and African dress.

What happened to me in just seven days? My wrists were covered with bangles. 'When does the next Turkana Bus leave?' I asked. I have to confess that I too was Blixenating.

* * * * * * *

Rush hour in Nairobi soon brought me back to reality, with hooters blowing and drivers jostling for position. If the average traveller to Africa thinks danger is limited to hungry lions or charging elephants, he or she is wrong. In Kenya the most dangerous beast is the internal combustion engine in many guises. Lorries overflowing with people, and commercial lorries with bald tyres pounding along narrow roads, with little or no regard for oncoming cars, or the deep ruts at the roadside.

Buses too were overloaded as were the 'matatus' – small vans with exotic names such as 'The Orient Express', crammed with passengers, their possessions and livestock. As they hurtled along, many of the drivers seemed oblivious to any sort of highway code. The headline on the front page of the *Daily Nation* on the day of my return to Nairobi was not unusual: '13 Killed in Matatu Horror'.

For all those who view Kenya as one of independent Africa's successes, an inside story was also informative. Under the Headline 'KANU won't allow rivals', it read: 'The ruling Kenya African National Union (KANU) will never entertain attempts to establish an opposition party .... the Secretary General of KANU said that most opposition parties were fictitious and did not represent the interest of the majority.' Another headline, from England, made more amusing reading: 'Mrs Shakespeare's house ransacked – Thieves today broke into Anne Hathaway's cottage.'

By coincidence, Helen was again at the Thorn Tree, having just arrived back from visiting lakes Naivasha, Nakuru and Baringo; she had experienced Kenya's over-loaded traffic at first hand: 'I came back in an African service bus – it was amazing. I was the only white on board and even when I thought it was packed they still squeezed more in. I had to stand. It was so full that when I took my right foot off the ground to scratch my left ankle, I couldn't get it back on the floor again.' I did not believe her, but she insisted it was true.

* * * * * * *

Away from expensive hotels, such as the Hilton, the New Stanley and the famous Norfolk, Helen had found the 'Fairview' – a pleasant, but basic hotel with large gardens, just five minutes walk from Nairobi's city centre. I was surprised, for visits to Africa are normally considered expensive, but with 'bucket-shop' air tickets and hotels such as the Fairview, Africa suddenly becomes accessible to the ordinary traveller.

The rooms were comfortable. It was clean, secure and slightly colonial, and so the Fairview became my headquarters too. The cost was about the same as farmhouse bed and breakfast in a country area of Britain. It was busy with travellers waiting for connections of the more basic and adventurous type; there were many African officials and businessmen too, finding the Fairview's homely comfort more acceptable to their pockets than the four-star luxury elsewhere.

At breakfast on my first morning I was joined by an Ethiopian. He was well-spoken, almost refined. He claimed to be in Nairobi 'on business' for the Eritrean rebels, fighting the Marxist government of Ethiopia. He was a mild, gentle man with far-away eyes who loved to talk about his home. He was worried – a well-dressed Ethiopian man and woman had also arrived: 'I am sure they are Special Branch from Addis Ababa, out to watch me, or get me.' Consequently whenever I arrived in the dining room he always joined me: 'I must not be alone, I do not trust them.' They would always appear shortly afterwards, drinking discreetly at the bar or eating at a table tucked away in a corner. 'It is terrible what their Party has done to my country and my people; if every you want to see how we are fighting them I will take you. We can meet in Juba (in the Sudan) – it is time the world knew of our plight.'

I hoped I would not have to stay in Nairobi long – I wanted to get out into the bush once more, but not as part of an organised tour. What I really wanted was to go to the edge of the NFD again to visit George Adamson – an extraordinary old man, still living the life of an early pioneer on the banks of the Tana River miles from anywhere. The problem was how to reach him. If I drove, it would be over many miles of dirt tracks, through virgin bush, and the cost of hiring a four-wheel drive vehicle and the chances of getting lost on virtually unmarked tracks made it too much of a gamble. Instead I decided to fly.

Nairobi's Wilson Airport is said to be the busiest in Africa; it deals with small, private aircraft, practically all of them on internal flights. There are tourist flights to game reserves, the flying doctor, planes to spray crops and locusts and various other aircraft of farmers and people simply making money.

The Aero Club itself was remarkable; it could have been Wiltshire, or Hampshire, apart from the black waiters. The accents were golf-club British – the world of Biggles lived on. Somewhere through the atmosphere of World War Two, I heard a German accent – the Luftwaffe had infiltrated! It was Wolfgang, a tall gangling German, flying for an Austrian relief agency, taking supplies to remote schools, villages and mission stations. He regularly flew to George Adamson's camp: 'George is not a rich man and we often help him out with supplies; if you take him plenty of stores I will take you.' It left me with two days in Nairobi, but I accepted his offer eagerly.

Leaving the airport I got a lift straight away with an Englishman in a Mercedes. He was an engineer and seemed both nervous and hyperactive, which did not seem a good combination for driving. He had a fortnight to go before returning to England: 'I've had enough of this place; it's the one place in Africa that's said to be a success – I'd hate to see the failures. In three years I've had my house broken into three times and my car twice. Europe has nothing to fear from the developing countries; they will take at least 3,000 years to catch up. There are African pilots at Wilson's now. The other day one was trying to start his plane with the fuel gauge on E. When he was reminded that E stood for "Empty" he just said: "Oh, I though E was for "Enough" and F for "Finish".' I did not believe him, and it was a relief to get out of his car.

* * * * * * *

During my tour of the game parks many of the old white hunters, as well as the African game rangers, had expressed alarm at the amount of poaching still taking place – elephants for ivory and rhino for their horn. It was even suggested that in some National Parks the poaching was done from Game Department Land Rovers. At the East African Wildlife Society offices in the Hilton Hotel, there were various newspaper articles on view about poaching, as well as car stickers – 'My Horn is my Dilemma' and 'I love Rhinos'. The organisation was struggling to get the message across. Sadly most of its membership was white – living both in Kenya and overseas.

It is easy to be smug about conservation – running well-financed environmental campaigns from London or New York to save the rhino, gorilla, elephant and panda, in various parts of the 'ignorant' Third World. Yet Britain wiped out most of its large animals, particularly predators, many years ago, and any plans to reintroduce the wolf, or even the wild boar are greeted with expressions of shock and horror. In Europe and North America development, pollution and destruction not only continues to damage landscapes and put wildlife at risk, but they are now actually affecting the sea and the air we breath, thus threatening everything on which we depend. In the long term changing weather patterns and altered conditions of vegetation growth could put life as we know it in peril. The Third World can claim economic necessity for the damage it is causing – although the argument is false; in the First World, however, there are no excuses, only greed and stupidity. Next door to the Wildlife Society was an office of Bateleur Safaris. I was drawn to it because of its name – the Bateleur Eagle is one of Africa's most striking and remarkable birds of prey. The owner was inside, tanned, bearded and wearing a safari-suit that on him looked normal. Coming from Hull as a 17-year-old in 1952, Joe Cheffings had so loved the country that he had become a Kenyan citizen. Once he had been a big game hunter, but now most of his shooting was done with a camera. As the name of his company suggested, he travelled all over Kenya, and East Africa in general, when border disputes and lulls in wars permitted. His interest went far beyond the normal 'big five' and extended to the trees, flowers, birds and peoples of his adopted home. Normally he took wealthy American clients on luxury camping safaris, with plenty of ice; but with the next day free he offered to take me to the Rift Valley, watching birds and anything of interest.

* * * * * * *

Out in the street again I was approached by a smartly dressed young African. It depressed me – I obviously still looked like a tourist.
'You want to buy an elephant hair bracelet – only 50 shillings?'
'Is it genuine?' I enquired.
'Of course, only real elephant hair.'
'In that case I won't buy it. It's illegal and you shouldn't be selling them. If they had been creeper or plastic I would have bought one.'
He looked at me in blank astonishment, muttering how his bracelets were the best in Nairobi and completely genuine. Suddenly the penny dropped: 'Wait a minute – I also have a plastic one.'
'How do you tell the difference?'
'If you heat it with a match and it burns, it is real. If it does nothing, it is false.' It was the exact opposite to what I had been told in Rhodesia. I left him without a purchase.

I find that whole days spent in cities leave me exhausted. It is the noise, dirt and bustle, and the thought of people reduced to numbers, performing duties with the same sense of purpose as ants – termites building their castles in the air or soldier ants marching relentlessly forward. I went to the top of the Kenyetta Conference Centre, a high twentieth-century tower dominating the city skyline. It is sad how one of the priorities of developing countries is always a conference centre or a new sports stadium, or both, simply to impress their friends. The cost is usually millions, while at the same time they ask for aid to finance schools, clinics and agricultural projects.

From the top of the building the edges of Nairobi could be clearly seen; it was also possible to count the city's kites with more than a dozen in the air at any one time. Gradually day turned to night, showing as it did that Kenya's dusks are just as spectacular as its dawns. A young tanned 'ecologist' was also watching the sun set. He hated cities too, but somehow we both felt divorced from Nairobi, over twenty storeys below.

He was about to become a Kenyan citizen. He had worked in Tanzania, Uganda and Sudan: 'But do you know what my greatest ambition in life is? I want to go to St James's Park in London with bread crumbs and a tennis racket and whack the pigeons. I would pluck them and sell them, just to see the reaction of nice old ladies and animal-rights freaks. Over there they have no idea about real life any more – about ordinary people in Africa and how they live. Mind you the Africans amaze me too. Do you know that of all the tribes in Kenya, there is not one which has designed a saddle so that people can ride horses and donkeys properly? In fact their donkey saddles and harnesses for carrying things put all the weight on the donkey's neck – where you don't want it. Consequently it pushes them forwards going downhill and holds them back going uphill.'

The thought of living in a one-party state did not worry him: 'I just get on with my life; they let us, that's how I like it. In fact I get a lot of laughs out of their system. The news broadcasts are a tremendous hoot. They religiously record everything the President, sorry, His Excellency the President Daniel Arap Moi, does every day: "At 4.30 the President will be meeting the Chinese Foreign Minister; at 6.15 he will be attending a reception given in his honour and at 8.30 he will wash his hands and go to the toilet."'

* * * * * * *

The Assistant Director of the Wildlife Department was a smartly dressed, well-spoken man. He gave me the official view, that there was no conflict between wildlife, agriculture and Kenya's rapidly growing population. Poaching too was well under control; up to 1978 it had been out of hand, but since the government's ban on hunting it had reduced to just a few tribesmen hunting for the pot. He was pleasant and polite, but left me with the feeling that I had been listening to a government circular.

The Animal Orphanage next door also left me depressed. I could see the point of rescuing young wild animals that had been lost, injured or orphaned, but for a large, staring chimpanzee, the orphanage had become a prison. His name was Sebastion; at one time he had been owned by Brian and he could wash, dry himself and make tea. He was treated as part of the family. Then, through pressure of work, Brian had given him to a friend. One day Sebastion had been left alone in the house and in sheer frustration had smashed the place up; as a result he was sent to the animal orphanage. To me it seemed like a betrayal of the animal's trust. He just sat in his cage, overweight, sullen and empty.

* * * * * * *

Joe Cheffings and his wife Simonne picked me up in their Land Cruiser. Their choice of transport was another disappointment. It showed how a market once dominated by Land Rover had been almost entirely overtaken by the Japanese.

We headed out of Nairobi, past a small settlement and then up into grassland, approaching the summit of the Ngong Hills made famous by Karen Blixen. She loved the hills and wrote:

> In my day, the buffalo, the eland and the rhino lived in the Ngong Hills: the very old Natives remembered a time when there were elephants there, and I was sorry that the whole Ngong Mountain was not enclosed in the Game Reserve. Only a small part of it was game reserve, and the beacon on the southern peak marked the boundary of it. When the colony prospers and Nairobi, the capital, grows, into a big city, the Ngong Hills might have made a matchless park for it. But during my last years in Africa many young Nairobi shop-people ran out into the hills on Sundays, on their motor cycles, and shot at anything they saw, and I believe that the big game will have wandered away from the hills, through the thorn-thickets and the stony ground further south.

She had been almost right: 'There's still game there,' Joe informed me, 'but it suffers from disturbance – motorbikes and hang-gliders these days.'

We were almost into clouds as we reached the summit. Joe stopped. I was glad he did, as I was totally unprepared for the southern side of the Ngongs. There before us was a vast sweep of land – one of the most spectacular and ancient landscapes in the world – the Rift Valley. It was bathed in brilliant sunlight, a land of great folds and falls – golden grasses, bush and the smell of dust, cattle and people.

A small Masai settlement of shacks and shanties included a most unlikely 'New Hilton Hotel' and as we slowly descended Joe proved that he knew most of Kenya's 1,000 species of bird. In addition, from the narrow road, we saw gerenuk, reticulated giraffe and several dik-dik – a diminutive, graceful antelope barely 16 inches at the shoulder. An Egyptian vulture pulled at the intestines of a dead cat, like pieces of elastic; as soon as it flew off with its prize it was attacked by two martial eagles, but it managed to hold on to its snack. There were weaver birds, flocks of guinea fowl and large termite mounds. Masai tribesmen in traditional dress were herding their flocks, or simply walking to nowhere.

As the land fell away, the heat intensified. Old men sat under trees and dust devils whipped spirals of red dust several hundred feet upwards. Passing a traditional manyetta the air was infused with the smell of smoke, hide and animals. Lake Magadi was spectacular – a large lake of blue water and white soda, with platoons of pink flamingos and flotillas of pelicans. At the water's edge were small, chestnut-banded sand plovers, also known as Magadi plovers, and crossing a pan, seemingly oblivious to the heat, a group of wildebeeste.

On towards Tanzania, through more bush and dust devils and past Masai manyettas to the Ngare Ngiro swamp, where semi-desert suddenly gave way to marshland – reeds, rushes and open water. Lily-trotters fed as they walked on floating plants and a fish eagle called. Joe's knowledge was encyclopaedic – a squacco heron, glossy ibis, blacksmith plover, pink-backed pelican, spurwinged goose, purple heron, saddle-bill stork, purple galilule, an African marsh harrier and, appropriately, a bateleur eagle.

In the water, Jluos fishermen appeared, wading waste deep and inserting fish taps – the fish eagles had competition. In that remote place, with a man who loved the bush and understood, I received more from just one day, than I did from the whole black and white striped safari.

* * * * * * *

I was looking forward to visiting 'Kampi ya Simba' – Camp of the Lion – George Adamson's camp, more than 200 miles north-east of Nairobi. It would be back to almost virgin bush, to Kora, by the Tana River, deep in 'shifta' country, a large area of northern Kenya where Somali bandits with a mixture of old rifles and modern AK 47's roamed.

George Adamson's story had fascinated me for several years. Although his wife Joy had become internationally famous through her books about their lions, it had always seemed to me that George had made her writing possible. He had been the one to find Elsa, their first cub, and it was his knowledge of the African wildlife that had enabled Elsa to be returned to the wild. Yet it was Joy who received the recognition and the financial rewards that went with it. After the filming of *Born Free* it was George who gave the film lions their freedom. Finally he moved to Kora, and took some of his lions with him. There his lion work continued, and one day too, he hoped to be able to reintroduce leopards and rhinos – both poached into scarcity.

* * * * * * *

Boredom must be an occupational hazard for pilots, as Wolfgang appeared bored – loading the plane, checking his instruments and flying. Nairobi from the air was much larger than it seemed on the ground, and from the number of new houses, shacks and construction sites it was still growing fast. Around the Athi River it was ranch and shamba country, rising to wooded mountains and bare rock before returning to shamba. Gradually bush took over, until wilderness spread for as far as the eye could see, a wild land of sweltering, arid thorn scrub and sandy luggas [dry river beds].

Two or three rocky outcrops appeared, bringing Wolfgang to life: 'The largest is Kora rock – "Kampa ya Simba" is close to it.' The highlight of Wolfgang's day followed: he banked steeply and dived, to 'buzz' the camp. My stomach performed a somersault. In a clearing we could see a fenced compound, containing a number of thatched huts. An old white man walked out of the largest building and waved: it was George Adamson.

Wolfgang taxied along the dirt airstrip to stop by a tree with a sign 'Lion on the Road, stay in aircraft', and soon a Land Rover bounced up, driven by Clive, a young white helper. From the back of the ancient open vehicle the warm scents and sounds of the bush washed around us – dust, sage, cicadas in concert, doves cooing and a distant fish eagle.

The gates of the compound were opened and we drove in. With its high wire fence it was like entering a zoo in reverse, with the animals looking in and the human beings looking out. George strolled towards us wearing only green shorts and sandals made from an old car tyre. He had long flowing white hair, a matching beard, clear blue eyes and deeply weathered skin – he was a remarkable relic of Kenya's pioneer days, with the appearance of an Old Testament prophet. Like all prophets he had a vision – that the 500 square miles of the Kora National Reserve should be preserved as part of ancient Africa. His hope was that it would never be swamped with 'exclusive' tourists, or turned into desert by nomads, but left as virgin bush to the wildlife along the banks of the Tana River.

To George everything in nature had its niche, only man was out of place and had upset the balance. As we spoke beneath the palm-thatch of his open-fronted mess, his place in the bush was immediately clear – he was part of it, a modern-day pipe-smoking St Francis of Assisi. Wild weaver birds, yellow-throated sparrows, partridge-like francolin and vulturine guinea fowl all came into the hut for tit-bits. Two yellow-billed hornhills perched above him, to be thrown peanuts, which they caught eagerly and expertly. A ground squirrel climbed on to his lap, and two beautiful wide-eyed tree rats sat expectantly on a bookcase. He even had a large monitor lizard in the roof, which he fed periodically on raw meat. On the fence, two ravens, Croakey and Crikey, also hoped for food – he chuckled: 'They are an argumentative pair; they recently drove off their three young – I called them Mad, Bad and Worse.' Outside under thorns, maribou storks stood in the shade having their siesta. Later as the light faded, dik-dik approached the perimeter fence to receive peanuts, as George spoke to them gently. All these birds and animals had overcome fear, to share the company and food of this peaceful old man.

Several days followed of what can only be described as a primitive paradise – George had almost rejected the present and had managed to retain the best of the past. He lived at his camp with his brother Terence, Clive, the temporary young camp helper, and a group of African employees – a cook who had been with him for many years, a mechanic, a tracker and several workmen to help run the reserve and help Terence to cut rough roads. His other assistant, Tony Fitzjohn, was away; he was a wild Englishman – made wild, so it was said, by Kenya's three A's. Although he was wild, and was regularly chased out of Nairobi by an assortment of husbands and lovers, he had a natural affinity with the bush, and over the years had given George invaluable help. It was a case of two opposites fitting in well together – almost like Beauty and the Beast.

* * * * * * *

We lived in thatched huts with lizards and tree rats in the roof. The shower was a water container held aloft by a rope and pulley: it worked with a simple valve and a watering-can rose. The toilet was even more interesting – an extremely comfortable elephant's jaw bone above a trench.

Camp routine was simple: we got up with the sun to drive along the river bank looking for lions; after a light lunch it was time for a siesta; then more lion searching, or checking various parts of the reserve. 'Sundowner' time was special, sitting with George and Terence watching the evening rays catch Kora rock, and listening to the sounds of night, as they ousted those of the day. We would talk, or just listen until well after dark, then George would go to light his paraffin lamp. Dinner in the mess was the last activity of the day, with moths and other insects flying around the lamps and gheko lizards darting down the wall and on to the table to claim those moths that fell in dizziness.

George did not sleep in his hut: 'I only sleep inside when it rains and we haven't had any real rain for two years at least.' While he slept outside on a camp bed, under a mosquito net, a guinea fowl with a broken wing slept in his hut. Sleeping outside, George always had his rifle next to him, not for protection against lions, but against 'shifta'; a trench had been dug immediately next to his bed allowing him to roll to safety in the event of attack. Although the shifta had threatened George and Tony several times, they had kept well away from the camp.

I loved the night, talking to George in the darkness, beneath the stars, somehow brighter, closer and more numerous than in Britain. For long periods he would sit listening, interrupted by a bark – 'Hear that – the alarm call of a lesser kudi'; a distant roar – 'That's Black'n'Tan – a wild male lion. So he's back, he's been over the river and not fallen foul of the Somalis.

'You know, Robin, some people say I am mad; I have released 50 lions back into the wild. But I rejoice in my madness. It is tremendously pleasing to see animals from zoos brought here and watch them develop and live the lives for which they were created. Some have bred out in the bush – it's intensely rewarding. In Arabia, just because trained scientists are involved, they're falling over backwards to support a scheme to reintroduce the Arabian oryx.' He chuckled again: 'In Australia they've even managed to introduce the dung beetle with a considerable degree of success.' His chuckle was infectious, a cross between a giggle and a laugh.

'I don't know what the long-term future of Kora is because of these damned Somalis. North of the river the bush is full of them, with goats, cattle, camels and heaven knows what. Then, when their grazing runs out and there is drought, they stream into the reserve and I spend all my time chucking them out. Two years ago we had 50,000 head of Somali stock; if we had let them stay they would have turned this place into desert. That's exactly what's happening to the north, overgrazing – hacking down trees – it's tragic. My ambition for Kora is that in 20 years' time it will be exactly as it is today, with just more animals.'

Before I met George I had heard many stories about his relationship with Joy; how she had been domineering, temperamental and kept all the money from her books for herself. After her death George did benefit from her will, which made life easier for him, but he would never say a bad word about her. In fact quite the reverse: 'We had our differences, but we remained good friends – I simply wanted to get on with my work, and she wanted to get on with hers. We would get together every Christmas. She was a unique woman, and her contribution to conservation cannot be measured. Her pictures of Kenya's people are an invaluable record; her paintings of flowers and plants are remarkable – and then there are her books. They have been immensely important; they have caught the imagination of the public, and so the conservation message and the problems of Africa have been taken into millions of homes. We had some wonderful times together. Joy was a fine woman – she had her artistic ups and downs – but why not? She was sincere, genuine and had a lot of talent. She did a lot of good for Africa.'

Dawn on a normal day was hard to believe; at an age when many 'old people' are considered to be 'past it' and left shuffling around old people's homes, George, at nearly 80, was climbing into his Land Rover for the morning's activity: 'We'll go looking for Koretta – I haven't seen her for several days.' We drove 17 miles along the banks of the Tana, on my first morning. It was hard driving, bouncing over the narrow tracks of rocks and sand, down into luggas, through thick thorn scrub with wicked thorns: 'The one with the curved thorns is called the wait-a-bit thorn; when it sticks into your arm or leg you have to wait-a-bit, it's as simple as that.'

We followed the river – wide, deep blue, palm-fringed and ever changing – great spits and islands of fine sand; pools with hippos where fish eagles called; beds and folds of rock where the water was squeezed and forced into swirling pools and rapids. Periodically he would stop to look for lion 'spoor' (tracks) – talking to his tracker in Swahili. He would suddenly stop too – 'this shrub, the Africans use as a toothbrush – see – when you break it, the end is a mass of bristles.' 'Smell this sweet thorn flower – do you know what it is? Wild henna.' Most of the trees were leafless to conserve water – many with peeling bark. Most looked the same to my inexpert eye: 'Look at this, Robin,' he broke a twig and held it to my nose. It had a rich, oily aroma – 'It's wild frankincense, the same as that mentioned in the Bible.' We saw fleeting glimpses of dik-dik, waterbuck and lesser kudu, even more striking than their larger cousins, again with spiralled horns. I was astonished by two cheetahs: 'I though they were cats of the open plains,' I commented. 'Oh no – they do very well here – we've got several, and wild dogs too.' One of the cheetahs marked a tree, just like a domestic tom-cat.

There was a wide variety of birds: the African hoopoe, rollers, bee-eaters, the drongo with its distinctive forked tail, and vultures. One vulture's nest had black-headed weavers' nests hanging around it: 'They are quite safe. The vultures are so big, likely predators are frightened away.'

Across the river a Somali tribesman was watering his flock of goats: 'I hope he keeps them over there,' George muttered. 'Do you know the definition of a Jeddah virgin – a goat that can run faster than the Arabs.' Again he chuckled merrily.

We stopped under palms, a blacksmith plover called at the water's edge and a pied kingfisher hovered and dived unsuccessfully. George lit a fire: 'Coffee?'

I asked him if he had ever thought of working in any other country: 'Not really – I would have liked to introduce the tiger to Northern Australia – it is a vast area with few people. It also has thousands of wild buffaloes, camels and horses – none of them indigenous, so introducing the tiger would have been alright. It was the last wild area where the tiger could have been introduced, but the Australians are not interested in conservation; they are as individuals but not as a nation.'

Half way back to camp we found spoor and George walked into the bush and shouted 'Koretta – Koretta.' No lion came: 'I don't think it's her – it may well have been a wild lion travelling through.' It was approaching mid-day and the sun was beginning to burn: 'Is it all right if I swim?' I asked, by an inviting stretch of river.
'I expect it is,' he replied, 'if you're quick.' A quarter of a mile down stream we passed rocks and a dozen basking crocodiles. 'You have to be careful,' he chuckled again.

* * * * * * *

As the sun went down, all was quiet; a kudu barked, just one short, sharp cry of warning. The dik-dik looked up, but soon returned to their snacks. Minutes passed. Suddenly George stood up: 'Good heavens – there's a lion out there –'; the dik-dik wheezed in alarm. A beautiful lioness simply walked without warning out of the bush and stopped 20 yards short of the wire – George smiled in recognition and pleasure: 'Koretta come.' His cook brought him some camel meat and he passed through a small gate, out of the compound and walked to within ten yards of the lioness. He spoke to her quietly and threw her the meat. She was in magnificent condition, powerful yet gentle, and neither man nor lion showed any sign of fear, only affection and respect – words that most scientists would not recognise when describing the relationship between man and beast. From her size it seemed to George that Koretta had returned to Kora to give birth to a new litter of cubs. She was a third generation wild lion, but still 'Baba a Simba' – 'Father of the Lion' (the local name for George), had managed to keep contact with her. As he spoke, still welcoming the lioness, a young three-quarters grown cub moved in the background. Naja was an orphan, shy and looking as if she needed a good feed; he called for some more camel meat.

To me the sight of George with his lions was a moving experience, but there were some people in Kenya who doubted the wisdom of his work. Before moving to Kora he had worked with lions in Meru National Park, but some of those in authority considered that the animals posed a threat to people and so George moved on. Even at Kora a workman had been killed as he responded to a call of nature outside the compound. George shot the lion responsible; it had felt like shooting a friend.

Some of the Africans did not appreciate George's work either. The Somalis wanted the reserve's sparse grazing for themselves, and a few locals in a village downstream were capable of causing problems. One morning, Tony Fitzjohn managed to run his Land Rover into the only tree near the landing strip, the one with the Lion notice, throwing his three workmen from the back. They received superficial cuts and bruises. Shortly after dropping them off at the village two or three days later, George received the following letter from the local 'Assistant Chief':-

> Re. Casual Labourers' Injuries. – Thank you very much those people who were injured have arrived to me even though you have not done good. This is because these people were injured two days ago and you decided to store them there without taking them hospital for first aid. Also I have heard a report saying that your first intention was not to bring them for first aid because you are still bearing in your mind of Colonial era ie. they are black monkey therefore no need of wasting your fuel to take them fore early treatment.

And so it went on.

The last person who could ever be called a racist was George Adamson; the letter not only revealed the standard of administration in parts of Kenya, but also that racism is a two-way problem.

* * * * * * *

The following morning after our encounter with Koretta, George decided to go downstream in the Land Rover. It was against a trip of stunning views; elephants had passed by during the night and hippos were still returning to the river after a night of grazing. As we approached a lugga, a Somali went running into the bush. George sounded disappointed: 'I expect he's got his livestock in the reserve – I need more help to keep them out.'

We stopped where vultures were perching in the palms. George took his rifle from the Land Rover and we walked down into a lugga of loose, dry sand. More vultures were on the ground, feeding on a camel carcass: 'That's one less Somali camel I have to worry about,' George thought out loud, 'it's lions.' One vulture was so bloated that it could not fly.

A mane shook; the sudden movement gave away the position of two adult male lions, lying under a thorn tree. Again it was an example of instant recognition and pleasure; they were two lions George had not seen for many months, the brothers of Koretta: 'Hallo Shade – Hallo Daniel.' He was pleased. We approached to within 30 yards. They looked up, obviously recognizing a long lost friend; it was again touching to see the bond between the old white man and the wild lions. Noises in the bush behind us could have been caused by Somalis or the wind; it brought the lions to their feet in agitation and they started to come straight for us. My heart pounded, I suddenly felt vulnerable and the lions looked large. George unshouldered his rifle. At 10 yards they swerved around us and disappeared into the bush – away from the noise that had disturbed them.

* * * * * * *

Late that afternoon George broke his routine. Instead of going along the river, we headed inland, by a long rocky ridge, bronze in the sun, and down into a lugga. He drove towards a high kopje, then instead of going round it, he drove straight up the side, along a barely distinguishable track. It was so steep that at any moment I expected the Land Rover to topple over backwards. 'Look,' he said, from the top, 'this is Kora.' In all directions, for as far as the eye could see, it was bush, with just the dome of Kora Rock showing seven or eight miles away. He bent down to look at the quartz chippings: 'These are man-made – it shows that people have been coming to this rock for thousands of years.' It was quiet, almost holy and there was a timelessness and a vastness that were almost overwhelming: 'This is my home,' George whispered; there was far more to Kora than simply an old man playing sentimental games with wild animals.

* * * * * * *

George was worried for Naja and wanted to buy more camel meat from the village down river. Consequently Terence drove the spare Land Rover downstream and bought a slaughtered camel. Everything went smoothly until we crossed a lugga on our return journey, with the dead beast in a trailer on the back. Terence attempted to change gear, but nothing happened. We stopped – the gear lever was immovable. It was 11 am; George would not assume anything was wrong until our non-arrival at dusk. Instead of a long wait, I volunteered to walk back to the camp with Clive, and George's African tracker, Abdi. A distance of about 12 miles.

I was unprepared, with no sun hat or water bottle, and tried to shade my neck and shoulders with palm leaves. Three times our white skins had to be immersed in the river, while Abdi simply drank a few drops of water collected in his cupped hands. On the second time a fish bit my thigh as I was sitting waist deep in the refreshing, cool current; immediately I thought 'Croc' and literally flew out of the water.

Turning away from the river towards the camp seemed to increase the heat – lions scuttled into the bush. On foot and unarmed it did not seem a good idea; again my heart pounded. Abdi simply smiled: 'No problem,' and kept walking normally – the lions disappeared. I had estimated that the walk back would take about three hours; in the heat it took four and a half. On arrival George offered me a Coke – I could not drink it, I simply needed pint after pint of water.

* * * * * * *

My last evening at Kora was unforgettable. Thousands – hundreds of thousands of termites – filled the air, in astonishing numbers. It was like a blizzard of insects. George looked on impassively: 'Extraordinary, they only do this usually when there's rain about – to make the ground soft. It's their nuptial flight. After an hour their wings drop off and they start rogering. If the ground's soft they then try to burrow underground to start a new colony – they've probably been started off by rain upstream.'

By morning no rain had come and the termites could not burrow – the hornbills, guinea fowl, ground squirrels and even the maribou storks were having a feast on the wingless ants, as their shed wings blew in eddies over the sand.

Wolfgang flew in. He had piloted the plane using only one arm, as the other was in a sling after a parachuting accident. He had a muscle-bound American journalist with him who came with a collection of newspaper cuttings about George. He wanted to interview him about his life and work, in just one hour, before we took off again for Nairobi.

At the airstrip George shook hands: 'It's nice having you, Robin. You must come again one day.' He said it as if Kora was just 100 yards down the road. The American journalist had got his story and once airborne he confessed to being mystified: 'I don't understand how people can stay in a place like that. What do they do all day?'

9. Warnings of Drought

I returned again to Kenya in 1984 during the 'long rains', although no rain had fallen. Simply driving from the airport told the story; the whole countryside was dry and parched and I could smell the dust in the air. Kenya was locked in drought.

Nairobi was cool, but each time rain clouds built up, they melted away again, giving nothing. I stayed with Joe and Simmone who had become good friends. Their old-style bungalow, with a corrugated iron roof, looked out on to the Ngong Hills, with the five distinctive hilltops outlined against the southern sky. In the evenings we would watch great anvils of cloud form beyond them, over the Rift Valley, but still no rain fell.

The Rift Valley was in a desperate plight – hot, parched and thirsty. At times dust devils seemed almost too numerous to count and the atmosphere had a permanent haze from the pillars of red dust being sucked ever upwards. The ribs of the Masai cattle could be counted and the work of goats was ensuring that recovery would take time, even after rain. With Michael, Joe's eldest son, I stopped at Olorgesailie, where Louis Leakey had done much of his early work. In a dry lugga it was scorching and airless, with elephant tracks well outside a wildlife reserve, showing the animals' search for water. Higher, near the top of Olorgesailie Mountain, a temporary Masai manyatta betrayed the peoples' desperation for food. It was miles from water, but it provided the cattle and goats with sparse grazing among the thorn scrub. The cattle were beginning to waste away – a condition shared by the children too, their thin limbs and sunken eyes giving an uncharacteristic lethargy. Each morning the people were waking to another day of dust and unrelenting heat – a problem, it was said, that was spreading down from the Sahara. In England drought is a matter of brown lawns, brown bodies, fewer baths and a cessation of the Sunday morning ritual of washing the car; in Africa drought causes only resignation, despair and slow death.

* * * * * * *

The Masai Mara was slowly turning into a dust bowl in which the predators enjoyed easy pickings. Lions lazed under the bushes, tired and fat; in the heat of the day there was a peculiar feeling of waiting.

Our driver, Erastus from 'Scenic Safaris', seemed interested only in lions. When we saw a large bird on a small hillock he casually said 'vulture'; it was a bateleur eagle. I had heard that on the other side of the park great herds of wildebeest were in confusion at the start of their annual migration. Erastus was unconcerned; all he wanted to do was talk to his assistant and return to Fig Tree Camp.

Fortunately an African friend of Joe's was at the camp and he took me in his Land Cruiser close to the Tanzanian border. All the dried vegetation had been grazed away and around a sandy lugga, in a cloud of dust, was a great melee of wildebeest. Streams of animals were moving into Kenya at a canter, while another group were trying to move back into Tanzania. A long way back, towards the Serengeti, a huge black cloud was releasing sheets of rain; perhaps the returning animals could smell the downpour with its promise of new grazing. The rain clouds came no nearer to the Masai Mara and it stayed dry as a dust. A series of stagnant pools, once part of a flowing river were drying out; the remaining water was black and filthy and the hippos were facing a crisis.

At sunset the light faded from gold to bronze and the sky, from horizon to horizon, seemed streaked with blood. Without warning, three cheetahs were running within 30 yards of us, moving freely and easily in perfect symmetry, their dappled coats matching the light and shade of the last of the sun. I had never seen wild animals look so beautiful.

By contrast, at first light, I felt loathing. Coming from grassland were hyenas, bloated and soaked with fresh blood. One carried a chunk of torn flesh and their stomachs were visibly bulging. Their hunting ground had been charred black by a recent bush fire and it was littered with hundreds of bones, white against black and made brighter by the heat of the flames. I was looking over nature's killing fields – centuries of death. It hit me hard. For years I had said, and believed, that within nature there was no cruelty, but here was a vast natural grave yard where killing was endemic. When I looked at the hyenas, I gazed into the dark primitive eyes of ruthless killers, eyes that took me deep into Africa's distant past, still dripping blood in the present. It was sinister, almost evil, and for the first time I could see that nature has never had feeling. It is governed only by survival, instinct and darkness, whether hyena and zebra calf on the African plains or blackbird and worm on an English suburban lawn. Under the African sun I had seen horror amid beauty – death amid life – the true call of the wild.

* * * * * * *

Back at Joe's Langata verandah, as the sun set over the Ngong Hills, I spoke to him about the drought, bones and my loathing for hyenas: 'Robin, you should not react like this. You must never judge animals according to our standards. You must remember this from Henry Beston's *The Outermost House*:'

> For the animals shall not be measured by man. In a world older and more complete than ours they more finished and complete, gifted with extensions of the senses we have lost or never attained, living by voices we shall never hear. They are not brethren, they are not underlings; they are other nations caught with ourselves in the net of life and time, fellow prisoners of the splendour and travail of the earth.

* * * * * *

Just like Zaire, South Africa and Rhodesia, every African house and hut in Kenya seemed to be overflowing with children. It came as a pleasure to discover that Michaela Denis was a Vice-Chairman of the Kenyan Family Planning Association – the same Michaela Denis who, with her husband Armand, had awakened Western interest in Africa through their films for television. I was even more pleased when she agreed to meet me.

I arrived at Tchui [Leopard] Road in the usual battered taxi and she greeted me at the door. She must have been in her seventies, but looked much younger, with warm blue eyes and blonde hair: 'Oh, you caught me out, I'll only be a minute.' She soon returned wearing large false eyelashes; they gave her a more melancholy appearance – like the eyes of a giraffe.

The inside of her house came straight from the age of elegant English living – antique furniture, a grandfather clock, a marble statue, chandeliers and oil paintings. She was warm and friendly; locals had warned me that she was a 'little potty', but mildly eccentric would have been a more accurate description. Not only was she interested in Africa's population explosion, but she had also been a Vice-Chairman of Kenya's 'Men of the Trees': 'There are no Presidents or Vice-Presidents of organisations in Kenya, so as not to compete with the politicians.'

As we drank coffee she spoke of the drought: 'People want a great shock and fright. The real fear will come when they have years of drought. Drought should not surprise anyone. It has been moving down Africa and creating desert for years – at a frightening pace – that is why I am so interested in trees. But even if you plant trees it will take seven years before wind erosion is stopped.

'The President has banned the sale of charcoal abroad to save the trees, but it still takes place, quite openly, to the Arabs. The people say: "It can't happen to us," but it can and it will then be too late. I never go on safari now, because so much wildlife has disappeared and its habitat destroyed. The President has been very good and has tried – banning hunting – but poaching still goes on. Shooting is a despicable thing – just to prove manliness. The Arabs who shoot would be far more manly if they defied tradition and educated their people.'

Her reference to Arabs was not a surprise. While at the Masai Mara I had heard much indignation concerning an Arab Prince hunting quite openly a few days before, inside the National Park boundary. Hunting was rather an inappropriate word as he had simply been driving around in a Range Rover, shooting at anything that came within range. It seemed that money, or oil, had changed hands to give him his sport.

Despite her efforts for the Family Planning Association, Kenya's population growth was still over 4 per cent a year – the highest in the world: 'We haven't failed, but the message is a difficult one to get over when tradition urges a man to have a large family. The government is keen to raise the per capita income of its people, but a rising income is hard to maintain with a rising population. We are fighting a race between teaching people to control their families, or face famine and a degraded quality of life. It is based on choice, and the choice is clear – poverty, or a sensible future.'

To my surprise, Michaela's interests had developed beyond the physical world and into the spiritual. Each week she held a seance for her 'psychic circle', in which objects would move independently around the room and water would splash for no reason. Sometimes she would be taken over by an entity called Changa, who had lived in Zimbabwe more than 500 years before. All the seances were recorded and she played a tape to me of Changa: her voice was deep and unrecognisable; bells rang and there were audible gasps of astonishment from those present.

She claimed to be able to heal too: 'I am a physical medium. I have a definite power for healing – I feel like an electric light bulb with the power coming through me. Often my hands feel hot and go red. My gift is particularly good with depression, arthritis, twisted limbs and even slipped discs. I hold a clinic for ordinary people on Mondays and for doctors on Thursdays.'

Because of her 'gifts' she believed in life after death. She was also aware that all those with similar gifts could recognise each other: 'When we went on safari to the Congo in the Fifties I was invited to take part in a Sorceresses' dance by an old "muganga" [a good sorceress]. I believe I was the first European to witness it. I looked into the old lady's eyes and immediately I felt as if our personalities had merged. The sense of inter-penetration was almost physical. My mind was filled with the knowledge that we were no longer strangers. She said – "you are one of us and have been given special powers and strength".'

She dropped me back into the city centre. I had enjoyed meeting her, but it had been a peculiar feeling to be on the 'dark continent', renowned for witch doctors, spirit mediums and the 'evil eye', to hear of Europeans from 'civilised' backgrounds dabbling in the same shadowy world.

* * * * * * *

Even in the centre of Nairobi dust hung over the city, reminding me of the drought. Beyond a brand new football stadium on the road to Langata, an overcrowded shanty town by a lake must have been almost unbearable. 'Don't go in there,' I had been warned, 'you'll lose your wallet or get mugged.'

Close by was a large new building project, of terraced housing.

The houses had been built before the lack of water had been discovered. The new residents had all 'mod cons' – baths, flush-toilets and taps – but no water to go with them.

In the opposite direction the Nairobi National Park spread towards the Athi Plains. The drought had drawn in large herds of animals for the park's grazing. The grasses were dry and brown, but still plentiful. Elsewhere the cattle land had been over-grazed, with the result that there were large herds of cattle actually inside the park. 'What's happening?' I asked a ranger.

'We can do nothing,' he replied nervously, 'they are owned by a Colonel in the army.'

* * * * * * *

The main reason for my return to Kenya had been to go on a Wilderness Trail – not an orthodox safari, but a walk through the bush, to experience the feel of real wilderness. The idea had come originally from Ian Player in South Africa in 1957, with his multiracial Wilderness Leadership School based in Zululand. It had been so successful that Laurens van der Post had been keen to establish another, run from London, taking people from Britain and America out into the wild places of Africa.

His philosophy was quite simple: 'We are increasingly governed by people with a city mind – in fact it is the industrial city mind. They do not see the relevance of the seasons – growing, flowering and harvest, good years and bad – how things need time; they want immediate solutions. The country mind, on the other hand, has a sense of time and realises that there are no instant solutions. It is dealing with growth, the unpredictable, and it uses patience as a form of wisdom.'

I first met Laurens van der Post during my travels for *Journeys into Britain* (1982) and I was immediately attracted by his understanding, his aura of calm and his gentle sense of humour. Because he considered 'wilderness', and Western man's separation from it, as important, I was keen to go on a 'trail': 'You see Robin, modern man is sick at heart as a result of the slanted life he is compelled to lead in the increasingly urban context of a technological barbaric society. But let man go into wild places and his indifference is shattered. He is changed by what I can only describe as an elemental experience; he rediscovers his relationship with

Nature and is refreshed for transforming the arid patterns of the life of his time.'

* * * * * * *

Arid patterns of a more fundamental kind were obvious as the group of nine drove northwards. Along the Thika road now, strangely, pitted with deep pot-holes; the shambas and coffee plantations were desperate for rain. At Blue Posts the drought had transformed the 'waterfall' into a damp wall of dark rock.

We were a mixed group, ranging in age from Lorna, a 16-year-old schoolgirl from suburbia, with her mother, Barbara, to a 58-year-old GP from Chester with his wife Shirley; in between was an ex-Brigadier from the Falklands campaign, a young Old-Etonian, quickly known by all, black and white alike, as the 'Englishman', a schoolteacher, and Joe. All our medical needs were well cared for as the GP's wife was a physiotherapist, and Barbara was a radiographer.

Wilderness seemed far away as we ate lunch at the Aberdare Country Club, among an extraordinary bunch of old colonials. All of them had been in Kenya since its early days and viewed England as a distant, foreign land: 'What have you got in England – football hooligans, riots in your cities and union leaders who still think it's 1930. Kenya – you can't beat it.'

For some of the wilderness group it was their first visit to Africa. Consequently, before trekking through the bush, where game could be scarce, we stopped at the Ark, in the Aberdares, to give them easy and comfortable views of wildlife:–buffalo, elephant, wart hog, bushbuck, suni, colabus and Sykes monkeys and various others. The tall aboriginal forest was rich and luxuriant. It seemed that the Aberdare mountains was one of the few areas in Kenya to have received rain.

Like the earlier game lodges, the Ark was large, comfortable and full of Americans. Yet again, those who knew least made the most noise. Hence, when some buffaloes appeared at the water hole we had a running commentary: 'Hey, did you see that buffalo grinning?' After two buffaloes had a brief altercation it became: 'Boy, what a cow fight.' Another 'expert' went even further; when a wart hog appeared he described it as a 'rhino' and a hyena became a 'spotted pig'.

* * * * * * *

Further north, in the heat, the shambas of the Kikuyu were parched, containing only shrivelled maize and millet. Barley on a European farm had fared no better and would not even provide replacement seed. It was said that the drought further north was even worse; the prospects were bleak.

At Nyahruru, formerly Thompson's Falls, we met the trail leader Simon Evans. Simon was a third-generation Kenyan, a farmer's son, bronzed and powerfully built. He was trying to build-up his own safari business with camels, as well as spending seasons in Tanzania big game hunting. He had with him another third-generation Kenyan, Sharon Wreford-Smith who was to be cook. She was rapidly making a name for herself as a miniature bird sculptor – fashioning the birds from semi-precious stones. Both spoke fluent Swahili.

Simon was confident of a good trail, as we continued to head north on dirt roads. European ranches, although not overstocked, were eking out their almost worthless grazing, with silage. Most of the adjoining Samburu land had been grazed bare, the large herds of cattle having been driven further north in a forlorn attempt to find food.

Simon's camp was spectacular, overlooking the Uaso Nyiro. I was pleased to be back in the Northern Frontier District; it is a strangely beautiful and compelling place of heat and hostility – a huge land littered with thorn scrub, dried-out river beds, ancient shattered mountain ranges, vast plains, kopjes of resistant rock, sand and scorching sun. To me it was the real Africa – far preferable to the rolling plains of the Masai Mara, so loved by the tour operators.

The camp had the Samburu name for 'the place of the wild olive', overlooking 'crocodile jaws' where the water of the Uaso Nyiro was squeezed through a narrow gorge of high rocks in a torrent of white water – water rushing into the drought lands from the Aberdare mountains. There were rocks, thorns, twisted olives, euphorbias and calling birds. The birds were spectacular and included fish eagles, giant kingfishers, sunbirds, martial eagles and red-winged starlings.

As the sun began to sink, animals moved out to feed – impala, waterbuck and the small but agile klipspringer – an antelope that feels entirely at home among the boulders and cliffs of the kopjes. Suddenly there was more movement – flickering ears; briefly we saw the spectre of a young kudu bull.

We were to be accompanied by camels on our journey and one of the camel keepers found and killed a puff adder. Joe was hardly reassuring; to the question: 'What do you do if you get bitten?' He replied: 'Find a large tree to sit under, for the body decomposes so quickly in direct sunlight.'

The camp crew included Longori, a Turkana tracker and a young Samburu, Limileo. They prepared four riding camels for the first day – a gentle walk of four miles to a large kopje – Baboon Rock – to break us in gently. Simon led the way, carrying his rifle, followed by the schoolteacher and Lorna the 16-year-old. The doctor, with water bottle attached to his belt, looked the part, as did the Brigadier whose tidiness and camp routine betrayed his army background. The 'Englishman' was unruffled and unhurried too – no shorts for him, instead, precision creased trousers, cravat, and Old Etonian Panama hat; he could have been at the Cheltenham races. Joe brought up the rear with his rifle.

As we walked Simon explained the signs of the bush: a hole where the Samburu had dug down for honey; a baboon spider with its trap-door lair; a plant from which the Samburu extract poison for their arrows. At one point we were joined by a honey-guide, a bird that has a reputation for leading people to honey. Tradition has it that if the bird is not left any of the hive's goodness, next time it will lead the unwary to a rhino or a black mamba.

It was hard work climbing the kopje, but from the top we were given one of Africa's greatest gifts, a vast, almost endless view, fading into a haze of shimmering heat – great empty plains, ridges and far off mountain ranges – almost too much to absorb after the small horizons of over-crowded England. As we rested, Limileo wanted a cigarette, but he had no matches. Within two minutes he had made a fire by rubbing two sticks together; to him the bush was not hostile, it was home.

The walk back was hot and sticky. For some reason the schoolteacher had no hat and her neck and shoulders were bare. She began to sway as she walked. 'Are you all right?' I asked. 'Yes, fine,' she replied. Three seconds later she crashed to the ground. It took several minutes to revive her and a camel was brought up for her to ride. Once aloft she screamed, verging on hysteria: 'I can't ride this, I hate camels.' Her 'hate' seemed to be fear. Simon and Joe carried her back to camp, with the Brigadier taking over guard duty.

The main trail would take us 25 miles through inhospitable country, where the flying doctor could not land; the teacher was persuaded to stay at the camel camp, instead of going on the main trek.

* * * * * * *

At first light we followed the camels out of the camp; they were loaded with stores and equipment. I had always imagined camels to be awkward, dirty animals, from the tales I had heard, but Simon's seemed to be extremely good natured. He had purchased 118 camels at the Somali border and walked them the 360 miles back to his father's farm. It had been a three-week journey through some of the most difficult country in Kenya, almost ending in disaster through lack of water.

An ancient elephant track allowed us easy walking; it had been worn by generations of elephants, and already a small group had passed by that morning. The land was almost empty, although overgrazed, with great patches of exposed, compressed topsoil. If we had stayed on the track we would have seen the elephants by dusk; instead we veered away through the bush. The doctor continued to stride purposefully, while Shirley, Lorna and Barbara eased their feet with spells of riding the camels. The Brigadier was coping well, while the Englishman still appeared to be at the races. We passed Ndorobo huts as well as several manyattas of the Samburu; most of the men were away in the north with their cattle, trying to find new grazing. The women watched in amazement as the camels and strange, pink Europeans walked by.

We climbed into a rock-strewn valley, following an old mining track, where Europeans had once searched for gold and mica. Ridges and outcrops of rock were all around, with a desert rose giving a vivid splash of colour. Vultures and birds of prey circled above, thermalling in the hot dusty air. The track went on, and after a brief pause we continued through the heat of the day. Finally, in the bronze light of later afternoon, camp was set up in a dry lugga and the camels were allowed to browse briefly before being hobbled for the night. The Brigadier strung up a hammock, while I found the ground extremely comfortable. We had covered 17 miles in the day, further than usual, but with the camp fire bright, and supper cooking, it did not matter.

It was with a feeling of triumph that we hit the river again, where Samburu mothers were washing their children as their sheep and goats drank. Several goats had been taken by crocodiles over recent weeks and we waded across cautiously, with the Englishman at last revealing his legs. The campsite was reached by mid-morning; it was a bank beneath wild fig trees, close to rapids and a small waterfall where we could wash in safety.

Two days followed of what can only be described as an 'elemental experience' – living with the sights and sounds of old Africa that had remained virtually unchanged for a thousand years. Indeed, Simon considered that few Europeans, if any, had ever been to this section of the Uaso Nyiro before. Brilliant birds made it a bird-watcher's paradise – Hunter's sunbirds, little bee-eaters, fish eagles, a goliath heron and three types of kingfisher, the giant, pied and malachite. Marks in the sand showed where crocodiles had slithered into the water, and at night their eyes reflected back our torchlight. From black rocks, cut and polished by an age of rushing water, we caught catfish and barbel for supper – Lorna struggling with a fish of well over 20 pounds. Hippos surfaced close by, to stare, and vulturine guinea fowl scolded.

As we walked upstream through the shallows we found trailing plants with delicate flowers and heard the wind in the whistling thorns. Fresh leopard tracks led to a kill, a Samburu goat, and there were old signs of violence where lions had dragged down a buffalo. The northern lions are not the well-fed, heavily maned animals of the Masai Mara; they are short maned and easily angered.

During the day the camp crew sat around and repaired saddles, before rounding up the camels for the night. At intervals the local Samburu arrived to watch, with the 'murrani', young warriors, forever preening themselves in mutual admiration. They were as wild and free as the land in which they lived and I could not help wondering whether by offering them 'civilisation' we took more away from them than we gave in return.

On a hot morning we climbed through higher bush country to a towering kopje – Naltiodo – 'needle rock', where harrier hawks flew. From the top it was a scene of plains, peaks and a great castellated plateau, all viewed through the red haze of dust. Beyond was the Matthews Range, leading on to Lake Turkana and Sudan. As we sat in wonder, distant dust devils were sucking still more columns of swirling soil into the parched air.

The walk, the climb, the view, the harrier hawks and the power of the drought, summed up the whole ethos of wilderness and Man's continuing need for close communion with nature. To the average 'civilized' urban man, life is lived in a series of boxes – his home, his car, his office and his club or pub. They are small, insignificant worlds in which the individual feels important, yet the physical confinement restricts vision, constructs walls in the mind and destroys the spirit. It creates a constricted, distorted view of Man, his environment and his place in the scheme of things; but it is a condition affecting much of the Western world – from bank clerks to members of parliament. Yet from a wilderness of vast horizons, or a night sky of a million stars, the insignificance of man, and his folly, focuses into simple reality. It is through nature – the land we work, the air we breath, the water we drink, and the creatures with which we share creation – that hope lies and the spirit of Man lives. We ignore them, and destroy them, at our peril.

Shortly after the last dawn we walked out of the valley – a seven-mile trek through boulders and thorn scrub to the waiting vehicles. Lorna looked tired: 'When I leave school I want to come back to this place.' It was not just the voice of innocent youth, for Shirley at 55, had already decided to try for a year's Voluntary Service Overseas. The doctor, sun-tanned and fit, also wanted to return. Even the Brigadier was pleased: 'That was splendid – splendid; I can think of nothing better.' Only the Englishman seemed to have doubts. At last, looking dishevelled, he wanted to get to the coast to lounge by a swimming pool, clutching a gin and tonic.

A small Samburu town close by was full of people and cattle. The Kenyan government was taking action to try to combat the drought; food was being brought in and the local cattle were being bought-up for slaughter. The policy would, it was hoped, prevent the bush from becoming another graveyard.

* * * * * * *

There were more herds of cattle being driven to slaughter along the Mombasa Road, just outside Nairobi – the government preferring

Warnings of Drought

meat, to skeletons and death. Joe was happy to slow down: 'That's good to see. A few years ago that wouldn't have happened. It shows the government is getting its act together.'

After our trek Joe had wanted to go to the coast. Like many of the Europeans living in Kenya he had a holiday bungalow by the Indian Ocean, his being north of Mombasa, at Malindi. But he had another motive too; on the way he wanted to show me Tsavo National Park, or at least part of its 8,000 square miles.

Again the long straight road passed through parched land and unremitting heat. At the roadside a lorry was being filled with charcoal, showing that an edict of the President was being ignored. Strangely, some areas of Tsavo West had received rain and already they were like green oases surrounded by desert. With its backdrop of Mount Kilimanjaro it must be one of the most scenic National Parks in the world.

In Tsavo West Joe introduced me to a friend, Bill Woodley, a wildlife and conservation legend in East Africa who, in a long and active career had defied wild animals, poachers and even cancer. Two years before he had survived a pitched-battle with shifta in which he dive-bombed them in his fragile single-seater plane, throwing out grenades as he went. The whole gang was either killed or captured.

Bill was worried about the drought: 'If it continues much longer we will start losing animals – it's much worse in Tsavo East.' Although there was still plenty of game in Tsavo East, he was right, the drought was gradually taking its toll. The famous water hole at Mudanda Rocks was empty; it was a crazy-paving of hard dry mud, with cracks a foot wide and deeper than an arm could reach. White bones told of the victims that had already died.

At the Aruba Dam herds of animals were having to make a daily trek of many miles between food and water, with the approaches to the dam grazed bare. Already a solitary elephant was tottering towards death and a buffalo calf would soon join it. A large herd of buffaloes stampeded in spectacular fashion – hooves pounding, dust flying, and above the dust tick birds flying in disarray.

We stopped by a dried-out swamp, with no sign of water. Hartebeest, buffalo and impala grazed the sapless, bleached vegetation. I was sitting on the roof with Mike and in the front was a rather earnest English photographer. Suddenly I saw a flicker of movement. We scanned the bush until I began to imagine I had been seeing things. Then it moved again. It was a young male lion; he slowly stood up and walked towards another, under a small tree. Joe drove along the track towards them; in a dry gully was the carcass of an 18-month-old bull buffalo; its legs and stomach had been eaten – the rest was black with flies. They were two of the infamous Tsavo short-maned males, with their yellow eyes aflame with anger. Their top lips curled back as they snarled and their tails jerked from side to side. Suddenly they charged – one to the front and one to the back, spitting with rage. I fell through the sun hatch, not minding how I landed. Michael followed, on top of me. I had never before experienced such a sudden injection of adrenalin and our speed through the roof, if translated into a 100-yards sprint, would have broken all records. The photographer's reaction was astonishing: she was still taking pictures: 'Sit still – sit still – all you need to do is sit still.' Michael's response was quite simple too: 'Not bloody likely.'

'It's only a mock charge,' Joe said coolly, 'they are only doing it to impress us.' They had achieved their aim and we carefully backed away. For the lions, at least, the drought would be a time of plenty.

* * * * * * *

Towards Mombasa the road descended steadily and the humidity increased to create a sticky, prickly heat. The vegetation changed, with clusters of coconut palms and banana trees, beneath which the traditional African huts had become square instead of round. We dropped the photographer off in Mombasa, next to 'Our Hotel – Board and Lodging'. Its rival, the 'New Paradise', a few doors along, was offering 'Lodge and Boarding'.

The coast road was long, straight, flat and stifling, as it cut through palms, forest and traditional village. At Kalifi, an inlet of the sea, we had to join a queue for the ferry. The water was cobalt blue against brilliant white sand. As we waited a young, overweight Englishman approached, with a jaunty, confident stride. He was wearing an obviously new safari suit and the inevitable cravat: 'Hi chaps – what's the hold up – when are these guys going to get their act together.' His accent was unmistakable.

'What are you doing over here?' I asked.

'Oh man, I'm having a ball. I'm setting up the Tanzanian operation for one of Nairobi's biggest tour operators. A piece of cake, man, I had them eating out of my hand. I'm going to see the Malindi scene now, man – pull a few birds and see what business opportunities there are.' Almost inevitably he was called Rupert, but was obviously facing some sort of identity crisis, his language being a mixture of public school and what he understood to be the vocabulary of the 'with it' common man. He had a huge African with him: 'This is my driver Moses – he's a really cool guy. We are having a great time, aren't we Moses?' Moses nodded in agreement, with laughter in his eyes.

Joe's bungalow was set back from the sea – peaceful and surrounded by cashew trees. The drought was hitting Malindi's water supply hard – with just an occasional dribble during the night to be stored in the bath. The town's population seemed totally untroubled, however, for there was plenty of liquid available in bottles.

Life at the bungalow was quiet, but along the beach it was bizarre. At Lawford's Hotel, large overweight Germans were floundering about on sun-beds; rubbing themselves with oil, especially the bulging bits that spilled over from scanty bathing trunks and bikinis.

More Germans were going fishing, loading up with sun oil and crates of beer to fish for sharks and sail-fish. All morning they drank, smeared themselves and occasionally dashed to the 'fighting chair'. In the afternoon they returned to the jetty, burnt, half drunk, and happy, to be photographed with their victims. They were having a good time.

With darkness came the nightlife. At one hotel, the Driftwood, the disco was almost normal, apart from some of the 70-year-old locals dancing to the rock music as if they were still 17. At another hotel the disco was more like a cattle market. The huge bodies had dragged themselves from the beach and were dancing – gyrating and bouncing – together with younger tourists, mainly German, who seemed to appear only at night. 'Beach boys' were dancing with middle-aged German women; they seemed to be trying to imitate American negroes in both appearance and language. The prostitutes were doing good trade with the Germans too – many of them attractive girls, showing the endemic African feel for rhythm as they danced. 'Look at that,' a local European lusted, 'it's not worth it. Most of the exotic diseases round here don't respond to penicillin any more.'

Joe was staying on in Malindi, but I had to return home. On my final evening we were talking at the Beer Garden, belonging to 'Herman the German'. A group of hard-drinking English soldiers were eyeing up the local ladies – without a thought for drug-resistant diseases. We were talking to an American girl who had been teaching in a mission school. Like me she was amazed at Malindi: 'It's astonishing, isn't it? We come out here teaching what we consider to be the basics – reading and writing, diet, hygiene, family planning and a responsible attitude towards sex – and then plane loads of "responsible" Europeans come over and put a show on like this – the Africans will be sending missionaries to Britain and Germany before long.'

Rupert spotted us from the street, followed by the ever faithful, bemused Moses. His safari suit was still spotless and he even had creases in his shorts. On seeing Tracey he adjusted his cravat. 'Hail you guys – d'you mind if I join you for an ale?' Even the prostitutes nudged one another, smiling, as he flounced over. 'Man, what a place this is, good opportunities for making money here man. Hey Robin, where did you pick up this chick – me and Moses are on the look out for good crumpet.'

'I didn't pick her up,' I assured him, ' she's over here working – as a missionary.'

* * * * * * *

Getting out of Malindi posed a problem. An agent for a taxi offered me a ride to Mombasa for £1.50: 'We are leaving immediately sir.' His driver then opened the door and left. Another taxi offered the same terms – immediate departure to Mombasa for £1.50, with a driver, so I changed cars; a furious slanging match ensued between the two agents. The car left with me as the only passenger, but instead of heading for Mombasa we did a circular tour of Malindi's back streets, with the agent shouting and banging his door and the driver hooting and switching on his musical horn. Slowly we filled up with an old Indian man who appeared to be close to death and two Bajun women in black drapes. Back at the chaotic taxi-rank, more insults were exchanged and the old Indian was transferred to another car – if they did not leave soon he would need a hearse. Once more we failed to leave for Mombasa. This time instead of simply touting for passengers the driver kept being replaced at odd corners. An old African, a young African who seemed hardly old enough to drive, an Asian, and finally an African with wide staring eyes chewing miraa. An old Indian woman squeezed herself in, followed by an equally large African lady: 'Still room for more,' the agent informed us, two hours after his 'immediate departure.' Eventually he managed to round up a small Muslim man, complete with hat, and a black nun carrying a large suitcase and seven pineapples.

At last we were away and our driver, still chewing his drug, roared off – the ferry being the only obstruction to make him lift the accelerator from the floor boards. The nun was the first to be dropped off and she insisted that the arrangement had been to take her to the mission. We left the road and wound in and out of the palm trees. Suddenly the driver stopped: 'This is not Mombasa,' he said angrily, 'the agreement was Mombasa – get out.' Another argument followed between the nun and the driver. From their animated expressions I was glad it was in Swahili. At last the nun got out and we left her standing under a palm tree with her suitcase and seven pineapples, apparently miles from anywhere.

I got out with the Muslim at the station and paid the £1.50 as agreed; the Muslim paid the £1 he had agreed. The white man had indeed been taken for a ride.

* * * * * * *

I had always wanted to ride on the Mombasa to Nairobi train – first class – a slow 325-mile journey back into the colonial era. Even the station reminded of colonial times – clean, unhurried and full of memories of Empire, a complete contrast to Mombasa's roads. With my ticket chit I hurried backwards and forwards between two uniformed clerks before being presented with my ticket. Even the toilets at the station were in classes – First, Second and Third – the Third being holes in the ground.

The construction of the railway line had been a major achievement at the turn of the century, with the Indian workers being shot at by Wakamba tribesmen using poisoned arrows and some falling prey to the ferocious Tsavo lions. Twenty eight Indians and many Africans succumbed to the man-eaters in 1899, a story made famous by Lt. Col. J. H. Patterson's famous book *The Man-Eaters of Tsavo*.

Those aggressive, short-maned lions were far from my mind as I ate dinner, again in the best colonial tradition: a five-course meal, with silver cutlery and mauve curtains draped over the windows – all for £2.50.

Dawn brought low shafts of light illuminating the dew, and pools of mist hugged the contours like an elevated carpet. Through mist Thomson's gazelles, wildebeeste and giraffe were feeding; in the pioneer days it would have been an even more spectacular journey. As the sun climbed higher the mist melted away, the dew disappeared and it was back to the drought.

* * * * * * *

Close to Joe's home in Langata, a promising young sculptor, Tim Nicklin, lived with his wife Anne. Tim worked in bronze and cold-cast bronze and I liked his work – lions, elephants and cheetahs. I was particularly attracted to a cold-cast bronze of two dik-diks. On my father's visit to Africa he had admired the little antelopes and often talked about them on his return. I decided to buy the sculpture for his approaching 70th birthday.

Tim put the dik-diks in a wooden box with a string handle, so that I could keep the sculpture as hand luggage. That, according to Iberia Airlines, was 'no problem'. There was a problem, however: the plane from Johannesburg was over-booked and I was left in Nairobi.

I had better luck with Air France the next night and 'yes sir, it's quite all right to have your hand luggage and your box with you.'

The final channel leap was with British Airways. Their approach was different: 'Certainly not – one lot of hand baggage only sir.' The girl sounded bored: 'There can be no exceptions sir – it may be fragile, I can't help that. We have special arrangements for fragile luggage – we have handled it before,' she added with sarcasm.

At Heathrow I asked at a British Airways counter where my box would appear: 'Oh, it won't come with the ordinary luggage, it will come on a special trolley.' As he said that the box appeared – it spewed out of a hatch and rolled on to the ordinary conveyor belt along with all the other suitcases and baggage. The dik-diks were broken into a hundred pieces – British Airways was not my favourite airline.

* * * * * * *

On the train home, I still had the drought on my mind. I was sure that it would lead to catastrophe in the countries south and east of the Sahara. I opened a paper – *The Daily Telegraph*. I could believe my eyes; in the Correspondence Column were letters complaining of too much food, 'the European grain mountain'. Other indignant letter-writers were bemoaning the black smuts from a successful harvest landing on their curtains and cars. People complaining of too much food? It confirmed that we live in a world totally divorced from reality.

10. The Booze Cruise

One year later, in the summer of 1985, I returned to Africa, and 'the world' had at last begun to take notice of the drought. Unfortunately for those with no 'food mountains' at their disposal, the attention had only come after widespread starvation and death.

My destination was a new one – at least the country was new – Zimbabwe. Fortunately Zimbabwe had experienced a very good harvest and I was looking forward to seeing how white Rhodesia had been transformed into black Zimbabwe.

One of the changes came as we were about an hour's flight from Harare – formerly Salisbury. A Zimbabwean diplomat visited most of the members of the press group and asked each one to take two litre bottles of whisky through the customs for him. I obliged, as did my Swedish neighbour – he must have had a great thirst. Once safely landed, he approached another member of the group to change some sterling for him 'to save time'. I assumed it was because of Zimbabwe's tight currency controls.

I had landed in Zimbabwe with a group of 10 journalists on a visit organised by the Zimbabwean Tourist Development Corporation. The idea from the Zimbabwean view-point was to show us as much of Zimbabwe as possible, in the hope of favourable publicity; the purpose from our side varied. Some of us were genuinely keen to see and learn about the new country; others seemed to be on a free food and drink holiday. One appeared to be on a trip to spot any remaining traces of white racism and exploitation, and another was almost certainly on a political pilgrimage – to the shrine of African nationalism and liberation.

Guy was an editor of a glossy travel magazine, travelling with his Hungarian son-in-law who worked for the BBC World Service. Another, Jim, owned some weekly newspapers in the City of London and there was an extraordinary gaggle of assorted Irish writers and broadcasters: Mary ran a travel programme on Independent Irish Radio; Bob, a round, amiable Professor wrote about wildlife; and Sean, a Scots-Irishman or an Irish-Scot, was a political writer for British national newspapers. That left Anita, a Swede – a peculiar choice, as she wrote for a local newspaper in Southern Sweden with a circulation of only 11,000 – and Pamela who was 'into' photo-journalism for glossy magazines. Which magazines she worked for I never did hear; I was too busy waiting for the next disaster to befall her. When I first saw her at Gatwick she was wearing dangling earrings, bangles, a Chelsea jungle outfit and shoes with heels guaranteed to sprain her ankles. I thought she was destined for Majorca or the Canary Isles, not Africa. She was a vegetarian, a lover of homeopathic health foods and Eastern religions – whether Hindu or Buddhist, again I could not make out. She had a sticker on her case bearing the inscription:

> Thou art that that thou art.
> See God in each other.
> God dwells within you as you
> So'ham.
> (I am that).

Somehow it seemed to sum her up perfectly.

The final member of the party was Basil, a progressive militant socialist, anti-racist, anti-colonialist, anti-capitalist, anti-fascist – in fact an 'anti-body'. He was a South African Asian, living in London, who edited a free newspaper, apparently given away outside underground stations. He evidently saw Zimbabwe as a great socialist paradise where capitalism and Europeans had been given their comeuppance. He asked me whom I was writing for on the trip. 'Travel articles for *The Daily Telegraph*,' I told him. 'You fascist .....,' he replied. A tirade of abuse followed. I was impressed – an African-Asian 'liberal' living in London with a complete command of Anglo-Saxon obscenities.

It was immediately obvious that on the surface anyway, little had changed in Rhodesia – or Zimbabwe. Salisbury may have become Harare, but it was still a clean, pleasant city and certainly not in decline. Cecil Square contained a few more cigarette ends, but the fountains continued to play, the lawns were still well watered and cut, and the flag-pole commemorating the first Pioneeer Corps at Fort Salisbury was still in place.

Some things had been added however: an Independence Arch

spanned the main road from the airport. It had a permanent armed guard as it had already been blown up once. Jameson Avenue had become Samora Machel Avenue, and the statue of Cecil Rhodes had disappeared. Rhodes Avenue was also difficult to find – it had no name plates; they had been removed by 'Rhodie' souvenir hunters, not by the government wanting to remove all signs of the original great white 'oppressor'. Another change had meant that all the local citizenry had become 'comrades'. Even as we were welcomed by an official of the Ministry of Tourism he said: 'I could call you visitors to our country, or friends – but here we'll call you comrades.'

Naturally, on a trip to promote Zimbabwe's tourist industry, we were whisked about at great speed: 'We want you to see the best of our country.' First we had to see Harare's hotels. We stayed in one of the best, the Monomatapa, and were ushered round the others frenetically. At Meickles most of the party seemed to be 'racist' spotting: 'Did you see the white girl who took us round – the arrogance still in her eyes when she looked at the blacks.' Basil went even further: 'This place is full of racists.' It didn't stop him eating a good lunch however: 'Wine Sir?'
'Of course.'

I could not see anything unusual, but then I am not a practised racist spotter.

The girl seemed pleasant, showing us the hotel and telling us how the Meickles family had arrived in South Africa from Scotland in the 1860s. She also informed us that at one time the hotel had a dome with two lions on it: 'They are said to have roared every time a virgin walked by.' Consequently, true to the traditions of Africa, they were extremely quiet.

Pamela, with red-painted toenails and a different jungle suit, had spotted that not every room had a colour television and apparently these things were important to her. The answer was simple: 'Because of currency restrictions we can only get 17. The Holiday Inn, half government-owned, has colour TVs in every room and experienced no trouble in getting them.' The Animal Farm form of socialism was emerging, and already some animals were more equal than the others. Somehow the racist spotters failed to notice.

Pamela was desperate to see the 'executive bedrooms', a cry that became a repetititive plea – together with 'Where's my camera?' Already by lunch time she was feeling ill; she was very thin and I thought she could do with a good steak.

The Holiday Inn did indeed have a colour television in every room and Pamela had recovered sufficiently to ask: 'Can I see the executive bedrooms?' It is strange how hotel rooms the world over have become simply brochure look-alikes with no indication of national character or individuality. They are mass-produced and synthetic, catering for homogenised, inter-continental travelling man. The only way to match the hotel with the country is to look for the photograph behind the receptionist; in the case of the Holiday Inn it was of Robert Mugabe.

I was relieved that Harare's latest hotel had not been completed – the inevitable Sheraton Hotel and Conference Centre, a new 'prestigious' development being built at government expense with Yugoslavian help. To me it already looked liked a modern architectural atrocity, having all the charm and fine lines of a nuclear power-station. To the Zimbabwean Government it obviously represented growth, status and the arrival of Zimbabwe on the world scene; perhaps they had never seen a nuclear power-station.

Once out of the hotels a coach was waiting. Along Rotten Row I noticed at one house that business had not changed: 'Queen of Sheba, Health Studio. Open 24 hours dairly.' (sic) The top of the Harare Kopje gave a fine view of the city. It was at that Kopje on 12 September 1890 that the Pioneer Column arrived and stayed to build a fort that became the capital of the country – Fort Salisbury. There was a 'toposcope' on the kopje – bronze plaques giving the direction of various places where famous battles had taken place, particularly against the Matabele. Four of the plaques had been removed; presumably they commemorated victories against the Shona. Close by was the 'Flame of Independence and Struggle'; it was supposed to burn for ever, but it was out. Our guide explained: 'There is a gas shortage – we only light it for special occasions.' It was at the Kopje that the heels of Pamela's shoes complained at not being in Chelsea. An ankle turned over and she hit the ground hard, like a sack of organically-grown carrots. We picked her up, brushed her down and tested her ankle for breakages.

The need for accreditation meant that we had another whole day in Harare – a Sunday, the day of the Chibuku Trophy football final at the Rufaro Stadium. My Baptist background still makes me doubtful of visiting huge sporting occasions on Sundays, but as the President of Zimbabwe, the Reverend Canaan Banana, was also going, I thought it would be acceptable. George, a local African photographer, assured us that it would be a good game and promised to get both me and Sean into the stadium on his press pass. The match promised to have a slight political content as well, for it was between Arcadia, a coloured team from Harare, and Highlands from Bulawayo.

George's confidence in his Press pass was misplaced; the stadium was already full and even people with tickets were being turned away. Because of the throng we literally, quite by chance, bumped into a friend of George, a journalist who worked on an army magazine. She was plump, happy and as black as pitch, with the unlikely nickname of Blondie. We tried again where a large, burly, very black gateman was letting a few through. The crowd surged forward and to help stem the flow he waded in with his fists; fortunately I was carried past him by the general cascade of bodies.

I sat on the grass surrounding the pitch with Blondie. She was a happy, bubbling girl and we were relieved to be in. It was a huge crowd, totally integrated, red and white favours mixed with black and white, with no sign of trouble. The game itself was a revelation. The standard was probably the same as the English Third Division, the difference being that if there was a choice of doing something spectacular, or playing in the interests of the team, then the first option was always chosen. Consequently, I saw more overhead kicks, scissor kicks, backheels and forward rolls after tackles in one game than I would see in England during a whole season.

The game ended 1-0 to Arcadia, with a goal totally against the run of play. Their manager and coach, both Europeans, were obviously suffering from a universal footballing disease: they claimed that their team thoroughly deserved their win. The Highland players disagreed; at the final whistle eight of them collapsed to the ground crying with grief.

* * * * * * *

Our first flight to 'see the country' was to Masvingo. I had never heard of it before. It turned out to be Fort Victoria; like many of Zimbabwe's towns the name had been Africanised. Masvingo is not the easiest name to remember. As we left the hotel I told the lift man we were going to Fort Victoria: 'What's the new name? I can't remember,' I asked.

'I can't remember either – I prefer the old names.'

The old Viscounts were still being used for the internal flights, but I was relieved to see that they were no longer painted brown but were again shiny bright.

The aim of visiting Masvingo was to visit the Lake Kyle National Park and then to go on to the Zimbabwe Ruins. The National Park was a pleasant little place, designed to give easy viewing of game – common species such as impala, tsessebe, giraffe, secretary birds and dassie.

The park also had a flourishing population of introduced white rhino, originally brought into the country from South Africa. The highlight of the visit was again Pamela: she went sprawling as our open-backed Land Cruiser started again after pausing near impala. She was wearing loose open-toed sandals on this occasion, not the best footwear in which to visit a National Park, but they showed up her bright red toenails rather well.

The ruins of Great Zimbabwe were spectacular; their origin is still shrouded in mystery. As stone buildings are so rare in Africa, South of the Sahara, it was once said that the Africans were incapable of such achievement and the original walls and enclosures were built by Arabs, or other aliens. Now it is thought that the ruins could have been part of an old African Empire. The local Shona guide had no doubts at all: as far as he was concerned the ruins were the birth-place of the Shona people's superiority – showing how they were and still are Zimbabwe's top dogs. It was a remarkable and an inaccurate reappraisal of Zimbabwe's history.

A white tourist had tagged on to our group. I asked him if he thought the Shona people had built the original dry-stone walls. 'Certainly,' he replied. 'Anybody else, apart from the Irish, would have used cement.' As the guide went on, Pamela closed her eyes and lifted her face skywards: she was sunbathing standing up.

The tourist walked with a limp; he had received a bayonet thrust in the knee. 'We had been in a contact, and I was checking the dead when one lunged at me. Four or five of my mates filled him with about 200 bits of lead, but his momentum got me. We've got a few problems still – there are dissidents down here and there are people in top jobs who are virtually illiterate; they've been rewarded for their part in the war, when they are useless. Apart from that it's OK, and it's going to stay that way.' He paused and then added: 'I suppose you know we've got elections due at the end of the month.

Well, they've been postponed for a week or two – the results have been stolen.'

* * * * * * *

There is no doubt that Zimbabwean food and wine are excellent. The wine is not up to South African standard but steadily improving. At dinner Anita decided against Western cuisine – 'I'll have Sadza.' She was obviously trying to identify with the locals. She was served with a large white lump of maize meal and as she ate it she claimed to like it. I assumed she had lost her sense of taste. She did not have it again.

Although Anita had all the usual Swedish liberal-socialist clichés on tap, she was an easy-going, conscientious woman enjoying her trip but also making detailed notes for future use. It was only when she started talking politics that she became earnest, proving that she believed all she heard on Swedish radio. As she waded through her Sadza she was talking about the wonders of SADCC, the Southern African Development Co-Ordinating Committee – the economic union formed by the Front Line States. A well-dressed African businessman had obviously been wrongly programmed: 'SADCC is no good,' he said. 'The old federation was much better when Zambia, Rhodesia and Malawi all had the same currency and cost of living. Passports were not required to cross from one country to another. Federation was the best.'

The old Federation of Southern Rhodesia, Northern Rhodesia and Nyasaland was the pet-hate of Kenneth Kaunda and Malawi's Dr Banda. This unexpected praise halted Anita in her tracks, and Francis from the Zimbabwean Tourist Board was lost for words. Guy was never lost for words: 'Can we have another couple of bottles of white, please?' The extra alcoholic lubrication set Basil off on his usual course, but he went even further this time: 'It is a well-known fact that there were no tribal differences or antagonism in Africa before the white man came. It was the European who brought disease to this country.' Had he never heard of malaria, leprosy and river blindness, I wondered?

It was Wednesday 29th May 1985, and after the meal I decided to round off a good day by visiting the hotel's television room. It was nearly full with black, white and khaki, all eagerly anticipating the European Cup Final between Liverpool and Juventus. All we could see however were hordes of Liverpool football thugs rioting at the Heysel Stadium in Brussels. It was ironic. There I was in the middle of the 'dark continent', in a country that had just experienced years of civil war, watching British yobbo violence on television. The Africans were dumbfounded. I sank lower and lower into my chair. For the first time in my life I was ashamed to be British.

* * * * * * *

Next stop was Bulawayo and the pace seemed to be picking up. It was ironic that Bulawayo, the capital of Matabeleland, was now the centre of dissident activity; the dissidents were said to be members of Joshua Nkomo's wing of the Patriotic Front who objected to being ruled by their old enemy, the Shona. It seemed that Robert Mugabe now had an almost similar problem to the one that confronted Ian Smith. The very same Matabele who in 1979 were regarded as 'freedom fighters' and 'liberators' had become 'dissidents', 'bandits' and 'outlaws'. It was significant that the word 'terrorist' was never used. According to a white garage owner the reason for the army's lack of success was simple: 'The soldiers are not keen to follow the dissidents, for if they catch up with them, they would recognise one another as old friends and comrades.'

I had never been to Bulawayo before. It was a large, impressive city of 440,000, of whom 30,000 were still European. The roads were extremely wide – wide enough to allow a 16-span of oxen to turn round as a team. Near the city centre were two enormous signs – nothing to do with the election. One said, 'Jesus is Coming. Are you ready?' The other proclaimed, 'Saturday is the Sabbath – Keep it Holy.' Apparently Bulawayo has a large population of 7th Day Adventists.

The most interesting visit of the day was to the Matopos National Park or, as some people still call it, the Rhodes Matopos National Park, for at one time Rhodes owned much of the farmland around it and, after his death his company gave it to the nation.

It is an astonishingly beautiful place of domes, caves, boulders and castle kopjes, where leopards hunt, the wild fig tree grows and black eagles soar. Between the great ridges of rock there are miles of bush as well as pools of grassland, bleached by the sun, on which sable antelope graze. The whole area had a calm, almost mystical quality and it came as no surprise to find that it was in the Matopos that Rhodes chose to be buried. He wrote: 'I admire the grandeur and loneliness of the Matopos in Rhodesia, and therefore I desire to be buried in the Matopos on the hill which I used to visit and which I called the View of the World, in a square to be cut in the rock on the top of the hill, covered with a plain brass plate with these words thereon: "Here lie the remains of Cecil John Rhodes, 5 July 1853".' Nearby was another simple slab:

> Here Lies
> Leander
> Starr
> Jameson.

He was the man who led the ill-fated Jameson Raid into the Transvaal at the end of 1895; it was in effect the forerunner of the Boer War (1899-1902). There was another huge monument too, erected in memory of Major Alan Wilson and his men, killed in 1893 when pursuing the defeated Matabele King Lobengula.

It was a moving experience to be standing amid the memorials to the men who had given shape to so much of Southern Africa's recent history.

It really did seem like the View of the World. It gave an inner view too of how and why those first pioneers made their trek into the interior, including the Meickle brothers who trekked 700 miles from Durban in 1892 to open up what they saw as a new land. What a journey – by ox-wagon and horse through the Matopos, on northwards to Fort Salisbury. But that was only part of the European journey. Before them, men in tiny wooden sailing ships had arrived, increasing their frontiers of knowledge and experience, along the cold, hostile waste of Namibia's coastline, and on to the towering cliffs of Cape Point. Then came the great treks inland. Even for the pioneers it was an incredible journey, severing old roots to arrive in a huge new land of strange peoples, plants and animals.

There, sitting on granite warm from the sun, the story of the white man in Africa seemed remarkable. In its way just as incredible as man's current journeys into space. Too often, it seemed to me, those who simply condemned the European adventure in Africa, in terms of 'racism' and 'exploitation', failed to understand the simple sides of history and human nature. The European advance into Africa involved enquiry, discovery, bravery and for some a continuing physical and spiritual search. If Bartholomew Dias had not rounded the Cape and landed at Mossel Bay on 3rd February 1488; or if Rhodes had remained in Bishop's Stortford, and if there had been no settlers from Europe, what would have happened to Africa? I wondered what questions the Matopos posed in Basil's mind.

We climbed to another sight too, along a windy tree-lined path to a cave between two great slabs of granite. There on the walls were pictures painted by even earlier inhabitants, clearly recognisable – giraffe, impala, zebra and the bushmen hunters themselves. Pictures painted possibly 40,000 years before, with paints made from crushed rock, roots, fat, eggs, blood, urine and the latex from euphorbia plants. Just as the white man had ousted the Matabele, so during Africa's hidden past the Bushmen had been pushed down to the Kalahari desert. No language, no written word recorded their going and all they left behind was their art.

As we drove out of the hills the whole Western sky was aflame, with a great granite battlement etched in black against it. Again I thought of those early adventurers, under the stars after a day's trekking. Why would they ever have wanted to return to Britain?

Our return was slowed when the bus stalled and the battery refused to turn the engine. We all helped with a push-start – all, that is except Basil, who remained in his seat, apparently enjoying the feeling of being pushed by a group of 'racist' whites. His usual mealtime subjects of Hitler and racism actually covered new ground. 'Nelson Mandela was a bourgeois natonalist,' he informed us. It seemed a shame to have spent so long in prison simply to be written off in one sentence.

* * * * * * *

It was Saturday; it must be the Victoria Falls. We saw them, at least the spray and mist above them, long before we arrived, like a smoking bushfire. The pilot flew over the Zambian side to give us a better view of 'mosi-oa-tunya' – 'the smoke that thunders'. It even made Jim's Irish extraction surface; when he looked out the window his spontaneous response was simple: 'Jesus, Mary and Joseph, that's marvellous!' For somebody claiming no Christian affiliation, it was interesting.

The water was far higher than on my previous visit, but my

feelings were exactly the same – of wonder and of awe. I stood where the wide, gentle Zambezi, dotted with islands, was suddenly squeezed into a rushing torrent, plunging into a chasm of 350 feet deep. It roared, with the sheer natural force sending spray well over 1,000 feet into the air. In the sunlight a rainbow appeared in the mist, a perfect arch of brilliantly defined colour, and then above it another.

The statue of David Livingstone still stood watching. It seemed remarkable to me that he had been taken by canoe to an island on the very lip of the chasm; I would have reservations about such a venture even in a motor-boat. There is little doubt that despite his human flaws – his stubbornness and the way he dispatched his wife back to England – he was a truly great man, and it is indicative of the negative and unimaginative world in which we live that there are people today who try to belittle his achievements. The words beneath his statue decribe him completely and accurately: 'Missionary, Explorer, Liberator.'

For some reason Francis was not impressed: 'We were sitting around here and Livingstone came and discovered us. When will his nephew and grandson come and discover us? Then we can put their statues up too.' As a Shona he could not tell me whether his people had 'discovered' the Falls before Livingstone; if they had, they had kept very quiet about it. It is certain that most of those residents of old Africa more than two or three days' walk from the Falls had never heard of them.

Through the luxuriant rain forest the leaves dripped, and the creepers and trailing roots reminded me of Zaire. Close to the edge of the gorge, the descending spray was like a permanent tropical storm. Looking down through the mist to the base of the falls, with the water roaring like permanent thunder. Guy was not particularly impressed – 'All this water makes me feel like another beer' – while Pamela was almost in a state of shock. Dressed in a sari, she was soaked to the skin, the colours were running and she was shaking with cold and whimpering, 'I've left my star filter by the bridge.' Basil was not there; he had decided to have a cold and had gone to his hotel room.

The booze cruise was still in action, much to Guy's relief, this time with no armed escort. At intervals along the bank were large red notices:

Strictly No Entry
Danger
Unexploded Mines.

They were reminders of the war.

Along the bank were several Illala palms, the nuts of which are very hard and used for 'vegetable ivory', which is sometimes passed off as the real thing. Before they can germinate, they have to pass through the digestive system of an elephant. Then, if they are not eaten again, they take 20 years to mature.

For the whole cruise, I was riveted; next to me was an Australian group leader, with a gaggle of elderly Australian matrons, whose patter made the average American sound informed. I could hardly believe my ears.

'Look at that, ladies.' – 'What is it?' – 'It's a warthog.' (It was a hippo.)
'Look at those monkeys.' (Guinea fowl.)
'There's a duck.' (A bird in the moorhen family.)
'Look at that crocodile.' (A log.)
'I think that's a log.' (A crocodile.)
I began to think it was an outing for the short-sighted.

* * * * * * *

Still the Professor and I wanted to speak to conservationists and game rangers about the long-term prospects for Zimbabwe. Every time we approached Francis, he had a ready-made response: 'I have been trying to arrange interviews but have been unsuccessful.'

At the Victoria Falls Hotel I met old friends. Instead of talking wildlife, we went to see traditional dancing – spectacular and sometimes frenzied. When a warrior picked up a 70-pound iron bar with his teeth, the Professor had the answer: 'It's easy. He must have a magnet in the back of his head.' A dried-out Pamela had other things on her mind: 'I don't want to watch this. I want to see the executive suites, the à la carte menu and the nail sculptures.'

A 'Malawi Witchdoctor' was charging the astronomical price of three dollars a consultation. I paid up and sat in front of him. He was wearing a tunic of feathers and skins; when I looked up I could see his Western shirt and trousers carefully hanging behind various traditional artefacts on the wall of the mud hut. He used a variety of skills – a horn of a young impala in a calabash that somehow swayed and wobbled in the best traditions of the Magic Circle, and a variety of other aids: a tortoise shell, beads, feathers, seeds and even a hedgehog skin. He mumbled various incantations and rattled his wares, and then came a list of world-shattering predictions: 'Your lucky number is four. In 1986 you will have a car accident; a car will run into the back of yours, but you will be all right. You will have a bad leg from October the sixth which will last six days. Are you married? You will get married in September.' All his short-term predictions turned out to be wrong, which is not too encouraging for his long-range forecasts: 'You will be very happy, very rich and live until you are 82. Your eyes and ears will remain good, but you will get the shakes.' It all sounded very exciting. Jim was next. His three dollars gave him the same as me, minus the car accident and shakes, but plus an extra eight years of life.

* * * * * * *

Our final stopping-off point was Lake Kariba. It was strange to be back in peace-time, with the lake looking clear and blue, and the Cutty Sark Hotel busy with tourists, black and white. Exotic ornamental flowers were in full bloom, surrounded by clouds of butterflies looking similar to English Marbled Whites. It was a breathless schedule, and already it was time for a sunset cruise, the boat owned and captained by an ex-farmer. Despite surviving the war, his farm had been burnt down after Independence and his cattle stolen or ham-strung, so he sold out. He had been blown up by a landmine in 1976 and had spent eight years in a wheelchair; now miraculously he was almost completely fit.

If the Victoria Falls are one of the wonders of the world, then Kariba is a man-made wonder. There were more trees protruding from beneath the water – after three years of drought the level of the lake had fallen, although recent rains had brought relief. There were hippos, fish eagles and snake birds, and away from the shore the water was ideal for swimming.

Another enjoying the cruise was a young British scientist who had been working on new ways of eradicating the tsetse fly, but he was disillusioned: 'We've devised a superb method of controlling the tsetse fly, but we are now using it in the Zambezi valley. It's astonishing; the Zambezi valley is the last great African wilderness. If the tsetse fly goes, then the Africans will encroach with their cattle and this area will become an over-grazed wildlife desert, like most of the old Tribal Trust lands. In a place like this, the tsetse fly is Africa's greatest conservationist; it keeps men and cattle out. The techniques we have developed should only be used in areas where cattle have been traditionally kept – not here.' On my return to England I was astonished to see a BBC wildlife programme from Bristol about 'tsetse eradication' in the Zambezi valley, with no word of the likely consequences for conservation. I did not watch any more of the series.

The evening was a revelation. Basil, after missing the Victoria Falls, was getting stuck into free rum and Cokes. 'The Coke must be warm,' he barked at the waiter. I have trouble with waiters and porters, for my Baptist upbringing makes me uneasy at being 'served'. I feel obliged to offer a surfeit of 'thanks', and even carry my own rucksack whenever possible (it is far easier on long journeys than a suitcase). Basil, however, had no such problems; he never carried his own luggage and would ignore waiters totally when they removed his plate or refilled his glass. His was a view of socialism that I did not understand.

Francis committed a sin: he called Basil an Indian. The Indian was furious: 'I am not an Indian,' he stormed. 'I'm an African. I'm black.' He coughed and spat into a flower-pot containing a bougainvillaea. Francis looked sheepish and apologized. Not for the first time I was baffled, for Basil was an Asian not an African, and he was brown, not black. His behaviour reminded me of the old story attributed to Abraham Lincoln:- one day the President asked his advisors: 'How many legs does a sheep have, if we call the tail a leg?'

'Five,' they all answered.

'You are all wrong,' said Lincoln, 'calling a tail a leg doesn't make it one.'

Whether he liked it or not, Basil was an Asian. He might have been born in South Africa; he might have been a British citizen – but that did not change his race, however that word might have appalled him. Similarly, Europeans living in Zimbabwe could call themselves Zimbabwean citizens, but to call themselves 'Africans' was sheer nonsense. As far as I know only chameleons can change colour at will.

Anita was talking to me about elephants. By this time Basil was drunk and thought she was talking about him. 'Stop talking about me,' he shrieked in his music hall Indian accent. 'You fascist.' I learned something that evening; Swedish liberal-socialists do not like being called fascists. Poor Basil had not finished. Three quiet, harmless old men in safari-suits were sitting in the lounge. He approached them drunkenly. 'Are you Portuguese or Afrikaners?' he asked.
'Afrikaners,' came the reply.
'My brothers in the ANC will sort out you lot of racists.'

* * * * * * *

The final day dawned. There was just time for one last photograph of the group. Basil was again the odd man out: 'Oh no, I thought you wanted an all-white photograph. In any case I don't want to stand by any racist twits.'
In her charming combination of Swedish and English, Anita summed up her exasperation. 'He's shitsophrenic,' she sighed. I thought that word was far more suitable than the one she had actually been looking for.

* * * * * * *

For debriefing, back in Harare, most of the group had enjoyed their free trip with only one or two complaints. The Professor and I complained that we had wanted more wildlife and most people thought that the speed had been too break-neck. 'What about you, Basil?' asked Francis. It was a mistake: 'I wanted something different. I have not seen authentic African food. I had no chance to meet real Africans. My readers are de-colonised; they don't want to see waiters in white tunics. They want to see post-colonial Africa. They are a discerning audience between 18 and 35; they want to read about the newly-liberated Zimbabwe instead of boring wildlife and tourist places.' All this for a London free newspaper. As most of the party boarded the bus for the airport, I actually felt sorry for Basil. I even tried to like and understand him. I suppose he would have called me a patronising racist for my trouble.

11. Waiting For Madagafufu

I stayed on in Zimbabwe, for I wanted to visit some of the places I had seen during the war – before moving on to Zambia and Malawi. Following the whispers about rhino poaching in the Zambezi valley I was anxious to get to Mana Pools to see for myself exactly what was going on; Matabeleland was another possibility to find out more about the 'dissidents'. Sean and the Professor were staying on too; Sean also wanting to get into Matabeleland, while the Professor still yearned for wildlife.

Francis could not help with my requests. Instead he sent me to the Ministry of Information – to a huge smiling black woman, Eileen. 'Conservation – certainly, Mr Page, I will contact Mr Madagafufu in the Tourism and Wildlife Department. He is the man who can give you permission to go to the Zambezi.' She made a telephone call. 'He is busy right now. You must be patient and wait for a message from Mr Madagafufu.'

'Can I go down to Matabeleland while I am waiting?'

'Now Mr Page, you can only go where we tell you, you can go. You don't want to get into trouble or end up in prison, do you? You stay in Harare and wait for Mr Madagafufu.' She said it smiling, without threat or malice, a simple statement of fact.

The wait for Comrade Madagafufu did not pose a problem, as I have always been good at passing the time. I am interested in most things and I enjoy just sitting, watching the world go by. I also have the ability to go to sleep, when and where I like.

Browsing through the bookshops was a revelation – gone were all the books published by the Rhodesian Reprint Library, celebrating the achievements of the early pioneers and travellers such as Thomas Baines, Cecil Rhodes and Frederick Selous. In their place had come a variety of books from 'Progress Publishers', Moscow, all about struggle and liberation. One illuminating volume was entitled *Zimbabwe, A New History* – 'approved by the Ministry of Education and Culture'. It started with a quote from Patrice

Lumumba: 'History will have its say one day – not the history they teach in Brussels, Paris, Washington or the U.N., but the history taught in the countries set free from colonialism and its puppet rulers.' It seemed to be a plea for 'creative history', or even fictitious history, and it was clear from some of the books that their authors had succeeded completely. Another volume caught my eye: *How Europe Underdeveloped Africa*. It seemed a remarkable proposition to me, that people travelled miles from their home to 'underdevelop' a continent. The usual charge is that Africa was exploited by the white settlers. How can a country be 'exploited' and 'underdeveloped' at the same time?

The material at newsagents was in the same vein; revolution had become good weekly business. One magazine, *Dawn*, published by the ANC's military wing *Umkhonto we sizwe* [Spear of the Nation], came complete with instructions on how to make do-it-yourself detonators, with steel wool, a flash bulb, wire, batteries and cellotape. It was accompanied by the call: 'You too Countryman, can be a Freedom Fighter'. That same countryman, it seemed to me, could also be a Zimbabwean dissident, a bank robber, or simply a hooligan.

The Cathedral was more peaceful and the messages in the intercession book had changed:

> Please pray for me.
> Pray for the Scripture Union of Spain.
> Praise God for his Glory House of Praying where my needs were fulfilled.

By way of contrast, a British tourist had obviously been in, writing: 'Very delightful trip'.

New 'Stations of the Cross', featuring a brown Jesus and followers had been painted around the walls and the only reminder of violence was a poster about the approaching elections – 'Enough Blood – A time to vote not to fight – Blessed are the Peaceful'.

* * * * * * *

At last with the Professor, I went to see an African at the Wildlife Department, a meeting arranged by Eileen. It seemed to confirm the tale we had heard earlier of Africans being promoted for the sake of it, or as a reward: he was clearly out of his depth. We wanted to talk about conservation policies both inside and outside the reserves, yet all we could get out of him was: 'People should not destroy nature. They should stop using sleighs drawn by oxen to carry things. They should use wheels and lorries.' For 20 minutes, he gave variations of this one sentence. When we mentioned overgrazing, anti-poaching patrols or habitat management, we were met with a blank stare before we heard again, 'People should not destroy nature...'

Eileen had also arranged a meeting with a European Forestry Advisor. We told him of our earlier experience. 'That is the trouble; you obviously got the wrong man. Don't get the wrong idea though, there are some very good Africans. We have some excellent ones in the Forestry Department. The problem is, if you'll excuse the pun, dead wood manages to get top jobs too. If you get someone who is useless, it can clog up the whole system and it can also keep good Africans down, making them very disillusioned. The whites simply switch to the private sector or go down South.'

He had been in the old Rhodesia and the new Zimbabwe for more than 35 years. He was enthusiastic about his job and full of praise for Robert Mugabe: 'He's proved to be a winner. He's seen the dangers of de-afforestation, sheet-erosion and the importance of trees. If I'm honest he's got a better set-up than Smith; then the Forestry Commission was not responsible for the Tribal Trust Lands. Now it is in charge of the whole country. National Tree Day is held each year when something like four and a half million seedlings are planted and this is in addition to the normal commercial forestry.'

Despite his optimism, he could still see dangers: 'Although there are many good things it is not all roses; 85 per cent of the rural population depends on wood for its energy and so there is still tremendous pressure on trees. There are other major problems too. The country is still overgrazed and overstocked. It will continue for as long as a man's wealth is measured by the number of his stock and not the quality. At the moment 15 useless cattle, kept for prestige or used to buy wives, are considered to be better than five really good beasts kept commercially.

'The other problem is a tremendous one and could finish this country whether it is Marxist, capitalist or whatever: population. They have to take this threat seriously. Some of the politicians still claim that there is plenty of room in Zimbabwe – there is not if they want to feed their people. Half the population is under 15 and there are 850 children born every day. The economy must grow every year, simply for the country to stay where it is. The population now is eight million. The maximum population for a self-sufficient Zimbabwe is estimated to be 27 million. At today's rate the population will double by the year 2,000 and be at its maximum by 2,012. After that it will have to import food and would be in real trouble during a drought.'

They were sobering statistics. Francis who had accompanied the Press Trip for the Ministry of Tourism had been intelligent, likeable and articulate, yet one of his recurring themes had been Zimbabwe's promise for the future: 'There is plenty of room, we are nearly empty.' But in just over 20 years Zimbabwe could join the growing list of food consumers rather than producers. Twenty years in political terms is a very long time; in real, historical terms, it is the blink of an eye.

* * * * * * *

Still Mr Madagafufu did not phone, so I phoned his office. 'Mr Madagafufu's secretary here – Oh Mr Page, I see. I will see if Mr Madagafufu is in.' A hand was placed over the receiver and I could hear mumbling. 'Oh sorry Mr Page, Mr Madagafufu is at a meeting. Shall I ask him to call you back?'

I still waited and he did not phone. The next day his meeting had ended but he was 'very busy'. Then he had gone 'to see the Minister'. I was getting tired of waiting for Mr Madagafufu and hired a car to go to Karoi, to see if Peter was still at his farm.

It was good heading north again on my own, not being ushered in a group. I was looking forward to seeing Peter; at least I hoped he had survived. The European farms looked good after the rains and as usual I found the landscapes breathtaking after the cramped horizons of Britain: hundreds, even thousands of square miles of kopjes, bush, sun-scorched grass, green leaves and space – all simmering in the hot, clear air.

At some large grain silos, huge lorries were being filled with maize and within a few miles I caught up with a convoy heading north, carrying maize to Zambia. Initially I noticed nothing odd, but then I realised that the lorries had Northern Transvaal number-plates; they were South African, with black drivers. To avoid starvation in Zambia, South African lorries were being used, as neither Zimbabwe nor Zambia had enough vehicles. The lorries were arriving at Harare, where white drivers were exchanged for black. The South Africans then waited for the delivery to be made before returning with their lorries to the Transvaal. So Zambia, the great advocate of sanctions against South Africa, was depending on South African transport to survive and feed its people. I wondered why I had not heard about this in the British media.

After passing the Karoi Hotel I again drove on to dirt roads. What a contrast it seemed, driving along at speed with a great trail of dust in the air, without a worry about ambushes or landmines. A white farmer was sitting on his verandah surrounded by bougainvillaea and other flowering shrubs; the only visible change was that war had turned into peace.

As soon as I saw the kopje I remembered it, and the farmhouse close by. The once well-defended bungalow had changed completely; the gates of the security fence were wide open and the fence itself was falling apart and covered with creepers. The doors and windows of the house were open and I heard footsteps; a tall, military-looking man emerged, with half-moon glasses, followed by a bull terrier. He was the new owner – he had bought the farm with his son, from an agent. 'Peter? Never heard of him. I don't know anything about the previous owners.' I was surprised; when I had left Peter, I was convinced that he would survive and that he would stay on. I remembered his words clearly: 'I'm Rhodesian and I'm going to stay here. The only way they'll get me out is feet first.'

I walked along the farm track overlooking the area of the contact. A bee-eater flew and a drongo, with its distinctive forked tail, perched in a tree. It was difficult to imagine that such a place had ever suffered war.

Towards the old Urungwe Tribal Trust Land, the battle ground between 'terrs' and auxiliaries, it was the same: an atmosphere of rural peace. Africans in their kraals, white farms, cattle and old maize fields under the plough. I stopped at a farm; it was owned by a frail old couple who had been farming for many years. She had lived in Rhodesia all her life and he had arrived when he was 21, after working his passage as a carpenter. Strangely, although both had been politically opposed to the Smith Government and he had attended various independence conferences in London, to give an alternative white view, he was disappointed with the new Zimbabwe: 'I have always keenly supported the idea of a non-racial meritocracy, with an unimpeded journey to majority rule, so I was always on the side of the African, but I wanted a fair deal for the European too. In the end we were sold down the river by Britain – by a Conservative government.

'When I first arrived here, it was very backward. The men were in skins and the women were topless. But now look at them, and we get no credit. One of the problems is that the Africans want everything today; they don't realise that we had to go through an evolutionary process too.

'They have made some big mistakes since coming to power. In their enthusiasm to get more people to school, educational standards have dropped. Then they imposed a minimum wage which increased unemployment and fuelled inflation. Once I employed 70 men on my farm, but now I only have 50.'

In the hotel that evening I met a salesman with more confidence about the future, but he had one major reservation too: 'It's essential that Robert Mugabe wins the election. Forget all the rhetoric. Mugabe is a highly intelligent man and a pragmatist. He will not interfere with the economy too much. If he loses the election then we'll be on the first plane out.' It was a strange reversal, for they were saying the same about Mugabe as they had once said about Ian Smith.

Despite its good service, I was disappointed to be staying at the Karoi Hotel as I had expected to be staying with Peter, and nobody seemed to know what had happened to him. At last, in the morning I found a white farmer who remembered him: 'Oh Peter, yes, he went down South with his parents some time ago. Last thing I heard, he was running a quarry in the Transvaal or something.' I was surprised and sorry, for Peter had seemed to love the old Rhodesia and farming. After that I met several people who had known him, but when he left, he severed all his connections.

With time to spare, I went to the local 'Agritex' offices, the offices of the Agricultural Technical and Extension Services. As the European farmers had enjoyed such a good harvest, I wondered how the African farmers had fared. I was seen by a Mr Mutasa – an extension officer – a large, fat man who was forever smiling under his trilby hat. I was lucky, I had called as he was about to go visiting some African farmers and I was welcome to go with him. Extension officers, I learned were administrators who went out to the communal lands, the old Tribal Trust Lands, to advise the African farmers. Mr Mutasa had been doing this job for 20 years and was approaching retirement.

As we drove along the dusty roads, he pointed to tracks going off into the bush: 'He is a good farmer – very keen.' 'He is lazy and we have to give him much advice.' 'That is the co-operative farm. That has not been a success. There are 25 members and they spend all their time arguing – some of them do very little work. As soon as they form a committee with a chairman, a secretary and the rest, they decide that they are advisers and administrators and should not work – the rest then refuse to work under them and nothing gets done.'

The normal size 'farm' was just ten or twelve acres with hens, rabbits, cattle that grazed on common land, maize and tobacco. One farmer had a small brick bungalow, as well as traditional huts. Tobacco was drying in a shed and he was sorting cotton, at a leisurely pace, under a tree. Maize was heaped up to dry in the sun and he seemed happy. Another had 25 acres, two wives and ten children, as well as a huge tomb for a departed wife. He too had a large heap of maize harvested by hand and was waiting for a lorry. He was anxious for it to arrive quickly, in case it rained and spoilt his crop. Mr Mutasa assured him that he would hurry it up.

* * * * * * *

Back in Harare there was still no news from Mr Madagafufu, and his secretary claimed that he was at yet another meeting. To try to hurry him up I went to the Information Office. Eileen was not there; instead six African men and women were sitting around the table looking at a list of ZANU candidates. They were talking excitedly and at times heatedly. Some were smoking, an electric fire was blazing. The last thing they wanted to do, it seemed, was break up and talk to a white man. Hanging from the walls were various posters. One urged: 'Avert the threat of colonialism.'

To me it showed the schizophrenia of the late twentieth-century perfectly. The poster was screaming about colonialism, when the colonialists about whom it screamed, in most cases, had voluntarily withdrawn from their old colonies. As far as I was aware the only modern day empire was being built by the Soviet Union – with, ironically, the United States, Vietnam, Libya and Iran as the only other contenders, albeit on a much smaller scale.

I had not gone to the Information Department to ponder over modern political fashions – I had wanted practical help; it was clearly not going to come, so I left the civil servants, still presumably earning their salaries.

* * * * * * *

I called in at the National Archives in Harare. There I discovered the answer to one of my questions – for under some trees, was the statue of Cecil Rhodes. It seemed right that it had not been destroyed as there is little doubt that Cecil Rhodes was responsible for laying the foundations of the modern Zimbabwe. Rhodes was standing with his hands in his pockets, with a slightly bemused, disbelieving look. He had every justification, for a dove had scored a direct hit on his head and next to him was a large, god-like, naked gentleman on a bronze horse. Who or what he was, I had no idea.

Rhodes would have enjoyed the cucumber sandwiches and tea still available at Meickles, an appreciation that did not extend to Barry, a white lorry driver. Whereas Basil had thought Meickles was full of racists, Barry complained that it was full of 'kaffirs'. To me Meickles was still a very good hotel – with more whites obvious in its lounge during the day and more blacks during the evening.

Barry was just having a beer, and as we talked he kept calling me 'Rob'. He claimed to have been in the SAS and the Selous Scouts – with his service dating back to the bloodshed in the Congo, when he went in to rescue some nuns. More recently he had been on special missions in Zambia and Mozambique. He still seemed 'bush-happy' and bitter at the outcome of the war: 'I enjoyed the war Rob – sleeping out in the bush. Mozambique, what a scene – we were dressed as guerrillas and the terrs actually opened the gates of their camp and cheered as we arrived – then we started.'

He had no love for Afrikaners either. 'Those slopies are as bad as the munts – without them this place would have been all right – anybody with "van" in his name should be deported.' He broadened his accent into thick South African and made his eyebrows quiver – a supposed Afrikaner characteristic: 'Man, I tell you I reached grade six by the time I was nineteen. I'm so intelligent, you know.' Even when his impersonation was over, his eyes were wide and darting: 'I've got to stay here, I've got nowhere else to go – Britain stinks and South Africa – I'd rather have a munt for a neighbour than van der Merwe.'

* * * * * * *

The weekend came, with still no word from Mr Madagafufu. The Professor had returned home, leaving only Sean and me. Sean still desperately wanted to go to Matabeleland to write about ZAPU, the dissidents and the government's attitudes towards them, but like me he was stuck in Harare. All was not lost however, as he had seen a ZAPU rally advertised for Sunday afternoon, with Joshua Nkomo as the main speaker, at a local indoor stadium.

At last our taxi driver found the meeting. The taxi was stopped and searched by aggressive-looking individuals wearing 'Joshua Nkomo – Father of the Nation' T-shirts and we were frisked before being ushered to the 'Press bench'. Two or three thousand people packed the stadium but Joshua Nkomo was not one of them. Much of the speaking was in Shona or N'dbele, with brief bursts of English. Police were present in quite large numbers and one officer stood next to a tape-recorder placed conspicuously on the stage – a novel way of encouraging free speech.

The audience seemed to appreciate the speeches, even if the police did not, and there were frequent bursts of applause. At question time, the first had obviously been planted by ZANU: 'Why do you want democratic elections when you are murdering and intimidating innocent people?' A question that had not occurred to ZANU during the war. The speaker rather clumsily turned it around: 'I think you mean we are being intimidated, threatened and coerced – so I agree with you, we want to be left in peace to take part in a free, peaceful and democratic election.'

* * * * * * *

That evening I had another strange experience, visiting a Spiritualist Church with Peggy, a local European. Rather surprisingly, she had become a spiritualist after the death of her dog. The local medium had managed to receive a message from her faithful friend – he was happy and rolling on grass. I wondered if messages could be obtained from hamsters and gerbils too.

The service, if that was the right description, was held in a scout hut. A holy picture and a copper cross had replaced 'Be Prepared', and a blue bulb shone. By the platform was a tape-recorder.

The congregation numbered about 25, several of them disabled. Worship started in an orthodox way with the singing of 'Abide With Me' followed by a prayer: 'Dear Father God – the great white spirit,' with mentions of assorted spirits, 'our guides, friendly spirits and doorkeepers'. It ended with 'the Lord's Prayer – taught to us by our brother Jesus'.

The reading was not from the Bible, or even the Koran, but 'A Second Treasury of Kahlil Gibran'. They were not worshipping God, but 'connecting' with spirits. I felt as I had done when talking to Michaela Denis – how strange it was to be in the 'dark continent' witnessing white people 'connecting' with 'spirits and doorkeepers'! It did not seem far divorced from the ancestor worship of the Batonka around Kariba; they were upset when their ancestral homes were flooded to form the lake. I wondered if the small group of whites would be similarly upset if their scout hut were ever closed.

As we sang 'Just a closer walk with thee', Geoffrey, a one-legged, coloured medium, limped on to the low platform and gradually became 'connected'. As the congregation sang the last chorus, he slowly folded his arms. He stood still with his eyes closed. 'Greetings,' he said.

'Greetings,' they replied.

For the next 10 minutes he spoke to them slowly and fluently about the reasons for meeting and talking to the 'great spirit', who had lost part of his descriptive title – 'white'. Apparently, so Peggy told me, we were not listening to Geoffrey, but to a spirit. Finally the spirit had had enough. 'Farewell,' he said.

'Farewell,' they replied.

Geoffrey stood still, unfolded his arms, opened his eyes and shook his head. 'Thank you Geoffrey, and your Guide,' they said.

A rendering of 'Glory, Glory Hallelujah' followed. It was an Afrikaner translation which meant that the chorus fitted the tune, the verses did not, leading to total melodic confusion.

No sooner had the singing stopped, than Geoffrey was apparently taken over by his 'clairvoyant guide'. He hopped around the stage enthusiastically, telling members of the congregation things about their lives – what they should or should not do, what crises they were about to face and colours they should think about. At one stage he became so excited that he toppled over the edge of the podium causing his artificial leg to crash on to the floor. He told me various things I did not understand. With five minutes to go he checked his watch – his clairvoyant guide was not telling him the time.

I thought the whole performance was rather like a variety show. A message on the back of the hymn book seemed most inappropriate: 'From the Darkness of Past Ages a new light is dawning in the minds of men to free them from ignorance, fear and superstition'. The hymn book began with the Great Invocation – it would have been appreciated by Pamela – then the Seven Principles, which were little different from most Christian principles. It seemed odd to me that with these, and their use of the Bible, they were not straightforward Christians. But then the hymnbook contained wisdom from American Indians too – from Red Cloud:

> To honour God is to love your fellow men;
> To worship God is to serve them;
> To believe God is to succour them;
> And to see God is to bring Peace amongst the Nations.

My perusal of the hymnbook was brought to a sudden halt with the singing of the last hymn – or verse. It was nostalgic for me, as it was the verse we used to sing every evening at the end of school in my small country village:

> Lord keep us safe this night,
> Secure from all our fears.
> May angels guard us while we sleep,
> Till morning light appears.

The service was followed by tea. The medium asked me if his message had been relevant to me. He seemed disappointed when I told him that it had no link with me whatsoever.

* * * * * * *

My wait for Mr Madagafufu continued; by now it was obvious that I was not wanted in the Zambezi valley. Similarly Sean was having no luck with his efforts to get into Matabeleland. We had waited long enough and decided to head off in the opposite direction, to enable me to revisit Melsetter, which had become Chimanimani, and Sean to visit a remote mission on the way, which he believed was run by a number of Irish nuns. Just as we were about to leave, invitations arrived. Mine read:

> On the Occasion of the Birthday of Her Majesty Queen Elizabeth II, The British High Commissioner requests the pleasure of the company of Mr Robin Page at a Reception on Friday 14th June, 1985 from noon to 2:00 pm.

The chance of eating cucumber sandwiches on the lawn of the High Commission was too good to refuse.

One afternoon in Cecil Square, a white schoolgirl, about 12 years old, sat next to me. She wanted to know what England was like: 'I don't want to go, I was born here, but one day if Mr Mugabe gets beaten we might have to leave. A lot of blacks don't like us being here.' She attended a predominantly black school and some of the children did not like whites: 'One in particular says this is not my country and that I should get out. Sometimes one of the teachers joins in and agrees with her.' She thanked me politely for talking to her, put her satchel on her shoulder and walked away. For her it was an uncertain future.

A well-dressed African was much more confident about the truly multiracial society, but, I asked him, what would happen if Mugabe did try to implement some of his more revolutionary ideas?' The African laughed: 'He will not. I will tell you a story which I know is true, because I was there. Shortly after independence there was a meeting of the Frontline States in Maputo, with Samora Machel in the chair. He welcomed the Zimbabwe delegation; then, for no reason we could see, he asked the Tanzanians how long they had been independent – 20 years – and what have you done in that time? They looked embarrassed and confused, until he said "you've gone bankrupt." He then asked the Zambians what they had achieved with independence and gave them the same answer – "you've gone bankrupt." Then he asked himself a question – "and what Samora Machel have you done to Mozambique? You have destroyed it." He then turned to us: "Don't do what we've done – learn from our mistakes. You have the opportunity."' He was a fascinating, articulate man, but he would not tell me what he did or who he was. Two days later I saw his photograph in the paper – he was a Cabinet

Minister.

I wanted to meet Ted, the old farmer I had met at Inyanga on my first visit, and arranged to meet him at the Royal Harare Golf Club. Ted arrived, looking fit and well. He had always been a Rhodesian Front supporter and had agreed with UDI: 'But today we are trying to heal wounds and make the best of it.' He wanted me to see his farm and meet a neighbour. On the way we passed through new townships – acres of them still being built – no different from Soweto. Black government or white government, the need was the same – mass-produced, cheap housing of a reasonable quality, to cope with the exploding population as well as those still being drawn in from the countryside. Again, like parts of Soweto, instead of street lights there were tower lights; it was like a huge open prison. Where it differed from Soweto was in its facilities: the shops, clinics and sports grounds or, more accurately, the lack of them, bore no comparison. Ted was worried, not by the scale of building, but by its position: 'They are building in the Lake MacIlwaine catchment area, which could create massive water problems for Harare in the future. The townships are another problem too – if the economic improvement of our Africans is going to be as rapid as the politicians say it is, then these areas will be slums inside 15 years – by the year 2,000. It is an appalling prospect.'

Ted was proud of his farm – a bungalow, with a verandah and the inevitable bougainvillaea, plus 1,600 acres which he ran with his son, growing maize, soya beans and rearing cattle. He had the usual kraal for his workers: 'The workforce has decreased from 44 to 30 through natural wastage. With the minimum wage we couldn't afford to replace them – even so we have at least 400 living here, almost totally dependent on the farm for food and money.'

Two small hills rose from the grassland and on top of both were jumbles of stones that had obviously once been dry stone walls: 'I expect they were primitive defensive walls,' Ted said. 'It's tragic that this country seems to have always known death. I had a son-in-law, of just three and a half weeks, killed in the war – machine-gunned. I have never seen such a mess.'

I had a surprise; the friend he wanted me to meet was an 'old stager' – a man of legend and some notoriety, 'Boss' Lilford. He was a tall, thin widower, well into his seventies with tiredness in his eyes. In the drama of Rhodesia's UDI he had been a key figure. He played an important part in the formation and finance of the

Rhodesian Front, and in getting Ian Smith elected as leader. But despite being totally opposed to black rule, he had accepted it – he had no other alternative. He still farmed 22,000 acres near Harare with another 90,000 in the South East. In earlier days he had a reputation for being a hard taskmaster, yet he spoke in a soft, almost quiet voice: 'We lost what we were fighting for, but we must get on just the same. I'm not leaving – I had five relatives killed in the war – they did not die for nothing.' The two old men spoke about earlier times: 'Do you remember that, Ted? They were good days – but things have changed. It's not the same country.' Boss and Ted had remained as they had always been; events had simply overtaken them.

'Boss' showed me his farmyard, including a little cockerel: 'I call him Mugabe 2, he's a fierce little blighter. The cockerel is Mugabe's symbol, you know.' As we drove around his farm he showed me a herd of Blesbok: 'I brought five up from South Africa – now I have 200. We get poachers all the time. Blacks with snares – we've destroyed over 200 – and whites shooting with rifles from the road. Down in the South East we have sable, kudu and eland. We hung on to our sable during the drought.' As he spoke he briefly became angry: 'We were sold out by Soames and Carrington, the bastards – I hope this place doesn't go like Zambia – it's terrible. Kaunda had a scheme to give the natives draught oxen. As soon as they moved them on to the farms, they were eaten.' His anger and contempt soon lifted: 'You see that piece of natural woodland – I left that for the redwinged starlings. They love it in there and I love to see them.'

As we left him, he seemed a tired, lonely old man. Ted enjoyed his company: 'Robin – will you do me a favour? Will you send Boss your latest book so that he gets it just before Christmas.' I posted the book towards the middle of November – a fortnight later Boss Lilford was murdered. He was bound, beaten and shot in the head. The police never charged anybody with the murder.

I visited another from my first trip too – Ken Mew, the English Methodist, still active and independent and still criticising the goverment. Before he had been a thorn in the side of Ian Smith; now he was one of the few daring to criticise the new regime. Ken had moved from Ranche House college, but had founded an equally remarkable establishment – the Glen Forest Training Centre. It had been set up in the country and its purpose was simple. It was helping the Africans to help themselves, enabling them to return to their villages with straightforward, practical skills. At the blacksmith's forge, young Africans were being shown how to make tools and even how to make the forge itself with ingenious bellows worked by a bicycle wheel. His various schemes involved a solar cooker, solar-heated water, carpentry and keeping hens. Other developing work involved cultivation – a mixture of crops with quick-growing trees providing fuel,and shelter for the more vulnerable crops. It was the type of work that started, in more simple forms, with the first missionaries – they saw need and tried to answer it with medicine, nutrition and the Bible.

Ken was his usual blunt but amiable self: 'Mugabe is doing well, as I always knew he would. He's got a lot more up-top than some of those in Smith's old government. But they still talk a lot of rubbish about the white man in Africa. The real baddies are people like Kaunda, who have managed to create a poor, undernourished people from a rich country, and then they turn round and blame us.

'The biggest problem in this country is population – each woman has an average of 6.6 children, the equivalent of a new school everyday – yet family planning clinics were closed by the minister responsible, because they had been started by Europeans. That makes you realise just how lucky we are to have Mugabe in overall control. But he has problems – there are some real bad eggs in the shadows, but fortunately most of the people support him.'

* * * * * * *

At last the day dawned for the Queen's official birthday – well almost, the reception for some reason was being held the day before. The taxi was normal – a clapped-out Renault with a gap between the front door and body. However much I stared I could not work out how it stayed closed or why it did not rattle.

ZANU PF posters had sprung up during the night, featuring a cockerel and Robert Mugabe: 'Our authentic and consistent leader'; 'He gave us victory' and 'Power to the People'. Few posters appeared in the exclusive suburb containing the home of the British High Commissioner and we drove past roads still called Kensington, Grosvenor and Kew. It was an area of wealthy whites. By this time I had come to expect double-standards; many of those diplomats who worked at the High Commission spoke disparagingly of the local

'Rhodies'. Yet most of the scornful chose to live among the very people they claimed to despise.

Our taxi seemed most out of place among the limousines, but the High Commissioner and his Deputy welcomed us warmly. They did so with an easy-going charm, gained through years of climbing up the greasy diplomatic ladder.

There were white-clothed tables, sprinkled with cucumber sandwiches and Union Jacks, and people stood in clusters on the close-cropped lawn exchanging niceties. White-coated waiters served wine and champagne as a pipe band, of mixed hue, marched up and down with bagpipes, kilts and sporrans. 'Is that the British Army?' I asked the Military Attaché.

'Oh no – a local school, although looking at some of the faces it could be the Black Watch.'

The chairman of the Mashonaland Irish Society was doing what Irishmen the world over do best – filling his glass up at regular intervals. The chairman of the Mashonaland Welsh Society was trying to keep up with him. He was the first Welshman I had ever met who seemed to apologise for being Welsh: 'Don't judge us by Neil Kinnock – he's the biggest idiot God ever breathed life into. What an idiot – he makes you embarrassed to be Welsh.'

The language and alcoholic intake of the black Bishop of Mashonaland was more restrained. He was telling me about the important part the Church had played in the process of reconciliation in Zimbabwe – black with white and black with black. As he was speaking a young man in a dark suit approached, with the ill-mannered air of the British public school, which some people call self-confidence. He butted in as if I was a piece of grass on the lawn. The Bishop waved him away, 'I hear you – I hear you,' and continued our conversation. The dark-suited man was from the British Council and hovered around us, rather like the agitated 'White Rabbit' in *Alice in Wonderland*. He only wanted to introduce himself; he was one of those who, as he shook hands saying 'I'm Nigel Beddington-Smithers – I'm pleased to meet you,' was already looking over your shoulder for the next person to interrupt.

A girl from the High Commission rescued me: 'Oh Mr Page, there is somebody over here wants to meet you.' I was baffled; I did not know anybody. It was a secretary, again from the Commission: 'Mr Page, I'm glad you're here. You must go down to the Zambezi Valley before you leave and write about it when you get back to England. It's tragic – rhino poaching has started and it's being hushed up.'

'I'm trying to get there,' I informed her. 'I'm waiting for clearance from a Mr Magadafufu.'

'Ignore them and just go as a tourist,' she implored. 'You'll never get permission otherwise.' Her concern resulted from a holiday in the Mana Pools National Park: 'We saw two dead rhinos – poached for their horns. We were attracted by vultures – jackals and hyenas were also feeding off them. One was a pregnant female – it was disgusting. The poachers are coming over from Zambia. It is thought that they have taken 25 out so far – there is a North Korean connection and high-up Zambians are involved.' She was being posted back to Britain in the near future: 'So you must go there – I feel so helpless – I must do something before I leave.'

· The chatter stopped as the High Commissioner said a few words from the steps of his verandah. To the visitors from other embassies and the Zimbabweans it must have been confusing: 'Welcome to our little gathering to celebrate Her Majesty's special day. Of course Her Majesty's real birthday is in April, her official one is tomorrow, but we are celebrating today. Now a toast to Zimbabwe, Robert Mugabe and his Government.' Even I was confused.

The reply came from Zimbabwe's Foreign Minister; he again started by congratulating Britain on its 'special day'. I thought that only British civil servants regarded the Queen's second birthday as a special day – they all had yet another day off.

He then broke into a vitriolic anti-South Africa tirade. During the night the South Africans had attacked a 'refugee camp' in Botswana, killing 14. The South Africans had claimed that the victims were ANC members planning sabotage. The Foreign Minister did not agree: 'Which innocent neighbour will the brutal racist regime attack next?' he asked. While in Zimbabwe I had been reading a book about 'Zimbabwe's struggle for freedom'. Whenever the Rhodesians had attacked camps in Zambia and Mozambique, they had been described as 'refugee camps' in the world Press. The book, after victory, described them as 'guerrilla camps'. Consequently, I wondered about the real status of the Botswanan 'refugee camp'. The Foreign Minister had no such doubts and for 10 minutes regaled us with his anti-'racist' – 'colonialist' sentiments. He sat down to polite applause. I had another cucumber sandwich.

I was interested to meet Denis Norman, the Minister of

Agriculture and the only white member of Robert Mugabe's cabinet. He was friendly and talkative with an impressive grasp of his subject – a refreshing change from many British MPs I have had the misfortune to meet. He said that the 'commercial' (white) farmers had been at the forefront of the war: 'At least 200 were killed. In 1980 they were tired, disillusioned and suspicious because of all the rhetoric and what had gone before – but immediately on coming into office, the Prime Minister reassured them. He told them to get on with their work as usual. In 1976 there were 6,000 commercial farmers, in 1980 5,200 and in 1985 4,400; a few are still leaving, but most will stay – and we need them. Most have been very positive and they will have a good future here.

'Agriculture is a pivotal industry. If it does well, the country does well – if it does badly, the country does badly. With our population increasing, our production will have to increase. At the moment agriculture produces 54 per cent of our foreign exchange – mainly with maize and tobacco.'

Soon he had to fly to Europe to seal a beef agreement with the EEC worth between 50-70 million dollars. I could not understand why Europe wanted Zimbabwe's beef when it already had its own 'beef mountain'. 'It's part of the EEC's policy of helping the underdeveloped world. This deal is very important for Matabeleland where arable crops are not an option.'

Not only was he pleased with the progress of the commercial farmers, but also of the arable farms on communal land. 'Now we must turn our attention to cattle, introducing veldt management, fencing and cattle husbandry. We must convince people that they get a better return from selling their cattle after three years, rather than 13.'

Only on the subject of the tsetse fly did the true politician emerge: 'We have to eradicate it – we can't just keep it penned in the North East. We know that cattle can create dust bowls – we must make sure that it doesn't happen here. In Zaire 50,000 a year die through sleeping sickness from the tsetse – in Zimbabwe last year we had five.' I could not see the relevance of figures from shambolic Zaire for well-run Zimbabwe.

There was still no message from Mr Madagafufu. He had not been at the Queen's birthday party either and so with Sean I headed East along the Mutari Road – Umtali had become Mutari. Before reaching Mutari we turned off the tar to visit a Roman Catholic mission run by Irish nuns. In the past it had been under several orders – Jesuits, Carmelites and now Franciscans. In 1977 it had closed as it was caught in the middle between the 'boys' and the security forces.

For the last 10 miles we gave a lift to a young African hitch-hiker who was going home for the weekend. Thomas lived in Harare with an uncle and worked as a stonemason. He would have preferred to live in the village with his mother: 'I left in the war – it was too dangerous here – the boys [guerillas] made us attend "pungwes" [political indoctrination meetings]. If we didn't go, we were beaten up and the girls raped. There would be political speeches, singing and dancing; we had to listen to all their rubbish – it was rubbish. They abducted several people and made them go to Mozambique and told us to destroy all European things. My mother sent me off to Harare where it was safe.' He was equally forthright about the approaching elections: 'I am not going to vote; it is a waste of time. The "boys" have already said that if Mugabe loses, they will go back to the bush – the people don't want that again, so they will vote for him.'

* * * * * * *

The mission was a mixture of new white buildings and the original block, in weathered red brick. It was calm, hot and peaceful. An Irish nun, with rimless spectacles and soft brogue, was packing her case, about to return to Eire for a holiday. She invited us to return after a tour of the school for lunch.

The headmaster gave us a guided tour of his school – with sand underfoot and the classrooms looking out on to bush. Some of the roofs were being repaired: 'The buildings were all destroyed in the war – the tin was taken by criminals and sold in Harare. They started on the church too, but a man fell and was killed – the people were frightened and left it alone.' He too had been obliged to attend pungwes: 'We were in the middle here, between the boys and the security forces – it was the frontline. The boys killed a farm foreman (black) on a neighbouring farm and my daughter was injured in the leg during cross-fire. The old election result was one to stop the war.' On his desk was a book of poems with a picture of 'Heroes' Acre' on its cover – a monument to the 'heroes' of the war, being built just outside Harare, allegedly at a cost of £7 million. It was a book of poems about revolution and struggle.

After the mission had closed, the security forces had used the church as an interrogation centre and general billet. But since independence and the return of the missionaries nearly all the classrooms had re-opened: 'Things are very promising and the people are eager to learn.'

In the 'science laboratory', there were posters explaining and warning of malaria, tsetse, cholera, typhoid and bilharzia – while in an ordinary classroom a poster proclaimed:

Freedom does not mean licence.
Doing what *we want* without
caring about the *results* for
us and for *others*.

The nuns gave us lunch in their simple kitchen. It was simple food too, just tea, bread, marmalade, cheese and fruit. They were all Irish – quiet and gentle – in an atmosphere of total tranquillity and peace. On the third finger of their left hand they wore wedding rings – married to Christ. They made me feel very humble, for here were three good women devoting their whole lives to others – without publicity, recognition or self-promotion. They worked quietly, with dedication and anonymity. On the same day in London, 'Live Aid' was taking place in a blaze of publicity and media hysteria. Whereas the three Catholic women had heard the call for self-sacrifice years before London's pop stars and fashionable media men were announcing, with fanfares, that they had just discovered their brothers in Africa.

Sister Mary told how the mission closed in 1977 when it became too dangerous: 'The buildings were destroyed; the cattle-dip holed and large stones were even tipped into the bore hole. The clinics closed – everything European was attacked. We did not take sides – we could see the grievances on one side and the fears on the other and we were in the middle. We just wanted to care for our people but it became impossible and much too dangerous. But things have settled down and we hope and pray that the future will be good and peaceful – the people need it.'

She went on: 'Both Sister Catherine and I were in Uganda at Independence. That was a beautiful, well-run country and they were handed everything on a plate, with no violence or liberation struggle. They were given their independence and everything that went with it and we saw it just crumble. It was so sad, for the people were so pleasant and did not deserve it. I just hope it doesn't happen here – it seems all right so far.'

As we drove away I had mixed feelings – they were doing good work, but wouldn't it have been good too for the nuns to bring up children and families with their own outlook? Sean had an explanation: 'It's the Irish Catholics' way of ridding their gene pool of its most intelligent members. My brother was being lined up for the church, but then he preferred to lie within the legs of a woman than beneath the knees of God.' I wondered if he had made the right decision.

* * * * * * *

At Mutare we tried to get into Mozambique, at the Forbes Border Post. Despite the activities of 'Renamo', also known as the MNR – 'The Mozambique National Resistance' – we wanted to make a dash for Beira. Unfortunately to get out of Zimbabwe with a car we would have required a bank guarantee and an export licence from Harare: 'If you take that out and sell it, it would take us five years to get another one.'

It was quiet, and the Zimbabwean official let us walk over to the Mozambique side: 'At least you will have been to Mozambique.' As we were strolling in the warm sun, an army personnel carrier roared up from the Mozambique side and crossed into Zimbabwe. It was full of soldiers belonging to the Zimbabwe National Army, at combat readiness, in camouflage uniforms and heavily armed. It was said that 15,000 Zimbabwe troops were guarding the road and the oil pipeline running parallel to it.

The incident was ironic. When soldiers of the old Smith Government entered Mozambique at the request of the Portuguese, the world's Press and politicians howled their outrage. When Mugabe sent in troops to support a failed, crumbling government, it was called 'fraternal co-operation'. As far as I could see the language was different, but the situation was exactly the same.

* * * * * * *

Briefly too, we visited Vumba, to see if the lady farmer at the bottom of the valley had stayed, or 'gapped it' like Peter. I expected to find that she had gone, or been killed – but there she was, helping her men to worm sheep. The coffee harvest had been good and she was optimistic: 'My daughter and son-in-law are moving in to help soon. Most of my neighbours have stayed on as well – only two were murdered – we are Zimbabweans now and we must make it work. When my husband and me arrived, we had a dream. I want to see it completed.' It was said that her husband had been unable to settle after the war and had committed suicide. A neighbour shook his head sadly: 'It is strange – he was one of those who really liked the war.'

* * * * * * *

It was a pleasure to see Chimanimani [Melsetter] again, with its mountains spreading over the border into Mozambique. The village had altered – the fences had been removed from around the houses and there were no soldiers. But there had been a deeper, more significant change too, which at first I did not recognise.

We signed in at the hotel, where the white receptionist remembered me, before going for a stroll. Gradually reality dawned: whereas Harare, Bulawayo, the Victoria Falls, and even Mutare had remained essentially European, Chimanimani had become African. White faces had become few and far between and the whole village had developed a dishevelled appearance and atmosphere, one in which the smell of open wood fires was never far away.

An African market had been started at the village centre and a row of large trees had been chopped down and left where they had fallen. A feeble effort to cut them up and burn them had been abandoned. Just along the road the Moodie Memorial had been wrecked; it was said that the memorial had been attacked by members of the ZANU Youth Brigade. I wondered how long it took an artefact of colonialism – a symbol of oppression, to become a valuable historical monument or archaeological treasure.

When a European had tried to stop the vandalism he had been beaten up and hit in the face with a brick, causing him to lose the sight in one eye. He had already received permanent injuries from a landmine explosion and so had decided that Zimbabwe was not the place for him. The gun-toting milk-lady had also gone. One story claimed that she had travelled to Denmark to look after her aged mother. The other said that she had gone to South Africa with a lover. The butcher had returned to England, where he had become a London policeman.

Only the church remained roughly the same – St George-in-the-mountains – with more creepers growing over its tower. It was built to resemble the old church at Mylor in Cornwall, and with communion every other week and a small congregation, it seemed to be a matter of time before the creepers took over completely.

The village arboretum was a sad, silent place. It had several new trees planted, most of them in memory of local people killed in the war: 'In memory of Jim and Helen Syme tragically killed 13th September 1978.' In years to come the trees would be a constant reminder to those who paused, of a time of communal madness.

* * * * * * *

The hotel had several guests, a few of whom sat in front of a large log fire to combat the cool of the night. A heavy, over-made-up South African woman with legs like tree-trunks was talking to some white Zimbabweans. Suddenly she turned to me: 'And what are you here for – what do you do?'

'I'm a writer, from England.'

'Does that mean you are the usual sort of journalist writing biased articles about South Africa?' She then continued her conversation, ignoring me completely and giving me no need for bias: 'The cost of servants in South Africa is getting so high – it's becoming ridiculous, particularly in Jo'burg. You have to give them good accommodation these days and as much as 120 rand a month – it's only 70-80 rand outside. It's a shame – the Zulus are getting quite Bolshie too – real rotters – your houtes are super coons compared with ours.' When she left for bed, with her small, poodle-like husband, the other couple breathed sighs of relief.

It was a coincidence meeting John, as he ran a transport company and had actually serviced two of the South African maize lorries ferrying food to Zambia. He confirmed their place of origin and their destination.

His company had also arranged convoys to and from Mozambique: 'It's pretty hairy though, as Renamo are becoming more active, and I don't know if it's worth the risk.'

The world view of Renamo was that it was a movement financed and organised by South Africa. John's view was different: 'People would blame South Africa wouldn't they? The story I've heard is that at the end of the war a lot of the old Rhodesian African Rifles went over there. If you think about it – it must be right; they were a loyal lot and many of them hated Mugabe. There was certainly nothing for them here. If Mozambique does fall, then what's the betting about infiltration into Zimbabwe?'

* * * * * * *

Not everybody welcomed the transition to Mugabe's view of socialism. While walking through the village I recognised Henry; he had been one of the 'Dad's Army' veterans on the convoy, in charge of a Browning. He was in his seventies, which meant that he had been on active service even longer than Frederick Selous. But I was lucky to have caught him, for he was disillusioned and was returning to New Zealand to join his daughter, after 15 years in 'Melsetter': 'It's over for me; this place has become a kaffir town – it's full of them. We were sold out by Carrington and Soames – they were sell-outs – a couple of pommie bastards.'

'It was wonderful when I first came to this place. The mountains reminded me of New Zealand and I've been all over them – but now we've come to this. I was in action up to the end. I rode shotgun three times a week. The worst ambush was 6th December 1979. The army found 150 firing positions and my vehicle had 200 bullet holes. All I got was a bullet through my shoe – it just drew blood. Forty five Europeans got killed in this area; there are only about ten left in the village now and 30 in the area as a whole.'

'They blame South Africa for killing innocent people; these terrs shot at anything white – women, children or whatever. Our mistake was that we didn't shoot at everything black. I don't call him Robert Mugabe – but Mugarbage – that's much nearer the mark – he's got blood on his hands. I stayed on to give it a chance, but look at it – what a place. If you see any members of the British government, will you do me a favour – tell them to get stuffed.'

* * * * * * *

Bitterness was not an emotion experienced by a remarkable old doctor on the other side of the village. At 86 he still ran a clinic three times a week, but because of his failing eye-sight he could no longer make detailed examinations. The other problem was the shortage of drugs.

Dr Hendrick van Reenen-Mostert was born in 1899 – the same year as the start of the Boer War – in Johannesburg. He studied at Cape Town and Edinburgh universities and while at Edinburgh, not only did he get a Diploma in tropical medicine, but also a wife – several years younger than him, still with a pleasing Scottish accent.

They had no intention of leaving their bungalow, with its large well kept garden, the smell of pines and its view of the valley and mountains: 'We are going to stay, although there aren't really many people to talk to these days.'

For many years he was interested in the treatment and cure of leprosy and ran a leper hospital near Fort Victoria for over twenty years. When he arrived at the hospital there had been more than 400 patients; with new treatments that he developed and perfected there were only 47 when he left.

During the war he never carried a gun and their bungalow had no security fence. During that time too he continued to drive unarmed and unescorted to an African clinic several miles away, and he experienced no problems. Under the Smith government he was made an officer of the Legion of Merit, because of his work. When the change came, he continued to work normally.

I was struck by the unassuming dedication of the couple. It seemed unfair; here was a man who had spent his life simply doing good, and at the age of 86 still doing good. If he had been any nationality other than South African, or old Rhodesian, he would have had international honours heaped upon him for his life of selfless service. His service had not recognised colour, creed or political opinion; it seemed to me that he had been a victim of world apartheid.

* * * * * * *

Back in Harare I did not bother with Mr Madagafufu, I simply caught the next available plane to Kariba – in order to get into the Zambezi valley and the Mana Pools National Park.

It was relaxating by the pool at the Cutty Sark, without the threat of bombs or Basil. Coincidence is a strange, inexplicable force, and that evening I met a naturalist who had just left Mana Pools. He had visited the National Park because of his concern for the black rhino. He confirmed that poaching was being organised from the Zambian side, with the poachers crossing the river in canoes. 'They have to come into Zimbabwe as they have almost cleared the black rhino from their own country. It's not just casual poaching – corruption's so bad in Zambia it's commercial, and there are big wheels behind it. It is an open secret that a Zambian minister is heavily involved. Kaunda claims to be a conservationist but yet he does nothing to stop it.'

He had information that showed the Zimbabwe Government in bad light too. Recently two white game rangers had stopped North Korean diplomats from Lusaka. The diplomats had rhino horn and ivory in the boot of their car. Yet instead of being commended for their vigilance, the rangers were reprimanded for stopping the Koreans, although the diplomats were outside the country in which they were serving.

I was interested in the diplomatic link and asked why the North Koreans had not been arrested. 'They have done a lot of work here. They trained the notorious Fifth Brigade, which sorted out the Matabele, and they are building 'Heroes' Acre.' They have also just signed a big mining deal. You may depend on the fact that various people are owed favours.'

'There's a lot of stuff going out in diplomatic bags right now – it's disgusting – a total abuse. The North Koreans are not the only ones – the Taiwan and Indian embassies are heavily involved as well. The other way of getting tusks and horns out, is through Sudan and Zaire. Once out of Africa the cargo isn't opened until its final destination – so stuff leaving Zaire by air can then go anywhere in the world via Brussels, with no questions asked.'

* * * * * * *

To get into Mana Pools I had to join a walking safari. There were eight of us, to be taken to the river, where we would set up camp and go for a number of walks through the bush, with our armed leader. The group included one of Africa's rarest species – an ex-cabinet minister of Idi Amin who had survived to tell the tale. He had a local newspaper with him; its front page summed up black

Africa's attitudes and priorities well. The fact that Romania had given a Zimbabwe organisation 20 footballs was covered with a large headline and picture. An announcement of American aid worth $35 millions was tucked away in a corner.

* * * * * * *

Mana Pools lies between the Zambezi escarpment and the River Zambezi, in an area of well over 4,000 square miles. The descent is through scrub and mopane woodland, until the flood plain of the Zambezi gives a flat, wooded landscape, with pools, ancient woodland and small areas of open ground.

The trees were superb – mahogany, baobab, giant acacias, sausage trees and a few tamarind. The richness of Africa's wildlife is never ending, and there in the Zambezi valley, because of the hot, humid conditions, I was introduced to still more wonders of the bush – butterflies, including the blue pansy, common grass yellow, guinea fowl, brown commodore, African veined white and the oddly named common joker.

* * * * * * *

I was fortunate on the first morning: before the trek had started, a friend of the leader arrived who knew Mana Pools well: 'It's all happening,' he said, 'another poacher was shot dead yesterday and for good measure an elderly woman was rolled on by a buffalo. She survived, but it didn't do her a lot of good.' He was both knowledgeable and helpful: 'You want to know about rhino? Come with me.' I left the organised trip and went with Mervyn. He was a total backwoodsman and knew the bush and its signs like others would read a map. During the war he had been in the Selous Scouts, as well as a special training unit for Bishop Muzorewa's auxiliaries, and his reflexes in the bush still seemed to be balanced on a hair-trigger.

When a flock of argumentative red-billed hoopoes flew, he called them by their Zulu name of 'screaming women', and to him white-helmet shrikes were 'Granny Smiths' or 'sixes and sevens'. On seeing the long fruit of the aptly named sausage tree he said: 'Look at that – young African girls cut them in two and rub their breasts with them to make them grow. If mothers with babies do it – it helps the flow of milk. They treat cuts and bruises the same way. It's said that important medical research is taking place with the tree now. It seems the experts believe it may be more than a healing agent for cuts, and they are testing it on cancer.'

I asked Mervyn if he had ever had any frights when out in the bush: 'My worst came when I saw what I thought was an injured spurwinged goose in the shallows of one of these pools. I waded in to rescue it, when it was actually in the jaws of a crocodile – I've never moved so fast in all my life.'

He had a sneaking admiration for crocodiles and claimed to have seen one take a swallow as it skimmed over the water: 'Do you know, they can even take a dragon fly sitting on the end of their nose.' Although the Zambezi was full of crocodiles he sometimes went skin-diving in the river, with his ankle tied to a rope, secured to the bank, in case of crocodile trouble. I was wondering if he was telling the truth, when he screeched to a halt: 'Python', he said excitedly, 'look at this, it's magnificent.' It was more than ten feet long, slithering away from us. Mervyn wanted me to have a better look and pulled it back by its tail. The snake was not amused – it reared up, four feet high, and with its viciously fanged jaws wide open, it struck. It was a slow strike – as the python kills by constriction and it is not poisonous – and Mervyn simply let go of its tail. I was retreating rapidly, backwards, only to cartwheel over in a large, muddy elephant's footprint; perhaps he did skin-dive in the river after all.

A hornbill looked at my backward somersault in amazement. Mervyn's butterfly mind had already forgotten the snake: 'Aren't they great birds? The males have got the best idea. They cement their wives into their tree nests at incubation time – the females then lose all their feathers to prevent themselves from over-heating.' It sounded another tall story, but in fact it was partly true, for the female hornbill does cement herself into her nest-hole, with occasional help from her mate. Then, while incubating, she moults. A small vertical slit is left in the wall, through which the male passes food.

As we continued along the track he gave a running commentary. 'This is a rhino crossing' – 'A martial eagle's nest' – 'Fresh lion spoor'. We stopped by a thicket, where white bones were spread in the grass: 'The hyenas have scattered the bones a bit since I was here last,' he informed me. By the ribs was a pile of chewed thorns, from the dead animal's stomach, as thorns are the main food of the black rhino. Indeed bush-lore suggests that the black rhino's temper comes from its diet of thorns. The black rhino is in fact not black, nor is the white rhino white. In Afrikaans the white rhino was called 'witrenoster'; to the English ear it was 'white' and so the other variety of African rhino became 'black'.

Although Mervyn had seen the bones before, he was depressed: 'This place was the last great stronghold of the black rhinoceros in Africa, and now look. Until this year there were 2,000 in Zimbabwe, with most of them around here – 650 breeding females – what more could you ask for. The poachers have got 25 in six months and their visits are increasing; there's no way these animals can cope with that. Although the gestation period is 15 months – there is actually three years between calves. Do you know the little rhyme by Ogden Nash?

> The rhino is a homely beast,
> For human eyes he's not a feast,
> But you and I will never know
> Why nature chose to make him so.
> Farewell, farewell, you old rhinoceros,
> I'll stare at something less prepocerous!

The world is saying farewell to the rhinoceros right now.' He paused, looking at the bones: 'And do you know what they do with the horn – they sell it to the Arabs and the Far East for dagger handles and medicine. For piles they simply burn it and sit over the smoke – it's pathetic.'

* * * * * * *

Fortunately there were signs of hope. On the edge of the park was a camp where 'rhino capture' was in full progress. There were nine animals in strong wooden corrals, including two mothers and their calves; they had been darted to immobilise them, and taken to the camp. From there they would be carted by lorry to Hwange [Wankie], where they would be released – well away from the threat of Zambian poachers. By such a scheme it was hoped to establish another safe black rhino population – for the white rhino was also successfully re-introduced to Hwange.

The main problem with the scheme was that the equipment and

darts were home-made and sometimes fell out of the tough rhino hide. Exchange controls and an official refusal to deal with the South African wildlife service meant that even a conservation rescue programme was hampered by the politics and postures of apartheid. It was absurd – the South Africans would have been keen to help with the rescue of the black rhino – they had already been instrumental in saving the white.

As we were looking round the camp another bull rhino arrived on a trailer – its eyes covered to prevent injury. The African assistants rolled the drugged animal off and into the pen, where Clem Coetzee gave it an antidote in the ear and rump. Clem tapped him a couple of times on the backside and the rhino came-to and stood up. The warden hurriedly climbed to safety – another rhino had been saved.

* * * * * * *

In Harare I phoned the British High Commission about the North Koreans. An official confirmed that in the diplomatic world North Korea had a low reputation: 'Despite being an allegedly communist regime it has a policy of encouraging its embassies to become self-sufficient; consequently they become involved with businesses, both legal and illegal. In Sweden they have been involved in drugs and so involvement in smuggling rhino horn is not a surprise.' Diplomatic convention and protocol prevented any sort of public or positive action.

* * * * * * *

The North Korean influence in Zimbabwe could best be seen at Heroes' Acre – a tribute to the 'heroes' whose actions helped to create the new Zimbabwe from the old Rhodesia. In order to visit, I had to get a 'pass', and all the approaches were guarded by armed soldiers in camouflage uniforms. They were obviously trying to avoid the fate of the first Independence Arch.

The whole thing was set in an amphitheatre of rock, where work was still continuing, some being supervised by several white non-heroes. Wooden benches were being set down too, for the burial the next day of a recently departed 'hero' – the Deputy Minister of Labour.

The memorial itself consisted of three large heroes in stone, of caricature proportions – a man and a woman carried granite AK 47's and another hero had a rocket launcher. Behind them, steps climbed to what would be another eternal flame, provided gas supplies improved. On either side, the story of the struggle for independence was told in stone – a white policeman was allowing his dog to bite an innocent woman, while his black police collaborator was beating another local with a club. Next, in the village, the heroes were reading from a book – the holy book of Marx and Lenin, and giving out guns. Then came the climax – straight out of Red Square – the armed struggle and liberation, with grenades hurtling through the air, guns at the ready, flags flying at the front, and over them all the great Saviour – Robert Mugabe. It was a shrine to violence and the politics of the personality cult – with no mention of the loyal Africans burnt in their huts – their cattle hamstrung – the clinics, schools and cattle dips destroyed – old white farmers shot in cold blood – small children bayoneted, and two civilian aircraft shot down.

It was inexplicable: at the Zimbabwe Ruins, the message had been of Zimbabwe's unique and authentic past; at Heroes' Acre the culture was Eastern European, built by North Koreans, and it would not have been out of place in Moscow, Leningrad or Kiev.

The whole construction must have cost millions; it was ostentatious, pompous and misleading. The simplicity of the English Cenotaph was obviously not for a Third World country receiving regular donations of foreign aid. Heroes' Acre was an extravagant tribute – a tribute to the modern trait of self-deception.

As I walked back past the guards, feeling depressed, I was thinking of another great monument costing millions, further south. That too had an everlasting flame, and a story carved in stone – the Voortrekkers Monument. If it had not been so tragic it would have been funny: two great man-made monuments – Shona and Afrikaner; black and white, hate and self-love. Not for the first time it seemed to me that in reality black and white nationalism were almost mirror images of each other.

12. Arrival in Wonderland.

I had enjoyed Zimbabwe. I had been genuinely surprised by its mood of reconciliation and cautious optimism, and if realism continued to dominate rhetoric, and its birth rate could be controlled, then its chances of a resonable future seemed fair.

Zambia was a different prospect. I did not really know what to expect. In theory, having suffered from no 'armed conflict', and with rich reserves of copper to augment a flourishing agriculture, it should have been one of independent Africa's successes. Yet in Zimbabwe, black and white alike had spoken of Zambia in disparaging terms, verging on contempt.

At Lusaka airport I was immediately filled with confusion: there on the tarmac was a plane belonging to South African Airways. 'What's that doing here?', I asked an Indian.
'Oh that is the regular service from Johannesburg. It arrives twice a week.'

It was the first in a long sequence of oddities that left me feeling like Alice, arriving in Wonderland. The second was the 'Health Check' counter in the airport building. They wanted yellow-fever certificates; the bored clerk looked at my cholera card and waved me through.

The usual taxi fiasco followed. I climbed into a Fiat – the window was stuck half open, the seat seemed unattached to the floor, managing to rock and swivel at the same time, and it rattled – all while stationary. For good measure, the windscreen was cracked: 'I did it,' Joshua explained, 'there are so many car thieves in Lusaka that I cracked it, so that I can find it more easily.'

He turned the starter – nothing happened – he turned it again; there was still no sign of combustible life. Other taxi drivers homed in, like vultures wanting to pluck me from the carcass. Fearing my defection he push-started the wreck into action. It rattled, knocked and swayed as it travelled with the speedometer in a state of permanent flux from 20-60k.

The airport car park was huge – large enough for hundreds of cars; it contained two cars and a van – a slight miscalculation somewhere. Then came the 'Independence Arch'; a far-sighted entrepeneur must have made a fortune from mass-produced independence archways for Africa in the Sixties.

Joshua, was not one for polite conversation, 'Have you changed your sterling into kwacha?', he asked.

'Yes.'

'Oh no – I would have given you 7 kwacha to the pound.' The official rate was only 3.33; Indians would have paid up to ten.

'Isn't it illegal?'

'Sure, but everybody does it, even ministers and the police. It's so expensive here, we need foreign money. I hope the Europeans are staying in Zimbabwe; if the British go, nothing works. Nothing works in Zambia, we have made so many mistakes.' The Fiat was not the only vehicle on the road. Three African driven Mercedes cruised by almost in convoy; they were members of the Mbenzi tribe – Mbenzi as in Mercedes Benzi. Nobody stopped for a road-block that was almost non-existent – just a few pieces of wood on the road and two uniformed men and one large whale-like woman, with a single .303 rifle between them. 'It is because there is a secret meeting of the ANC taking place,' Joshua informed. 'It is at Kabwe.'

The outskirts of Lusaka had a seedy run-down look. The old colonial city was not simply fading at the edges, like Nairobi, it was crumbling – with dust, dirt and banana skins adding to the air of decay. Shacks in a township had roofs held down with rocks and old bedsteads, and several did not even have a door.

I got out in the centre of Lusaka. Joshua whispered: 'I'll take sterling.' He asked for £15 and settled happily for £6.

Daphne, a loud European, was surprised at my arrival, although I had spoken to her on the phone from Harare. Zambian-style efficiency was apparently endemic to all races. 'I can't do anything yet, I'm busy,' she almost shouted. Her loudness appeared to be a substitute for order. I had contacted the firm as it ran 'big-game hunting' safaris; I thought it would be interesting to see if the old style big game hunting still took place. Although Kenya had banned hunting, in Zimbabwe, South Africa and Tanzania it was enjoying something of a revival. Its economic value had been recognised, as had the fact that it was a 'renewable resource': it could provide a

Arrival in Wonderland

long-term supply of both money and meat, if managed sensibly.

While Daphne organised herself, I went for a walk. Lusaka city centre was busy – but at the same time disintegrating. Broken paving stones had not been replaced and a grass strip between the two carriageways of the main road had been allowed to turn to bare soil. Outside a chaotic building site a thin ragged woman with sunken, unseeing eyes and a baby at her breast sat begging in the dust. A large poster proclaimed: 'KK Liberator of the People', and another: 'UNIP means National Reconstruction'. Reconstruction from what, or why, the United National Independence Party, Zambia's one and only party, did not say.

A bookshop had little stock, but the books were well spread out to make it look like a large selection. 'Progress Publishers, Moscow' were again in evidence, as were the assorted works of Kenneth Kaunda. One called *Fundamentals of Zambian Humanism* quoted the President as saying: 'The Party must strive to relentlessly establish in Zambia a true Socialist State.' I wondered how the blind beggar woman and the new Mercedes fitted into this scheme of things.

The shops were reasonably well stocked – including plenty of South African wine, tinned meat and fish. There was a large pile of light bulbs too. This surprised me as there had been a shortage in Zimbabwe. The explanation was simple: most of the light sockets in Lusaka were of the bayonet type; the light bulbs were all screw-in.

Another shop caught my eye, the 'City Free'; it was a 'Duty Free' shop in the middle of Lusaka. The locals were not able to shop in it of course, only the wealthy and foreign passport holders with their country's currency. It was another extraordinary interpretation of socialism. It traded in luxury goods – 29 brands of genuine Scotch whisky, Stilton cheese from Nottinghamshire and plenty of superior South African wines and South African chocolates. It was busy, serving white ex-patriots and assorted diplomats; a Tanzanian diplomat departed with a box of South African wines and Scotch whisky.

By mid-afternoon Daphne was ready for me: 'Come,' she said imperiously as she walked towards her brand new Mitsubishi Shogun, paid for in foreign currency with 150 per cent duty. 'My friend Roy will put you up for the night.' The well-manicured driveway turned off the Livingstone road, through a field of irrigated maize, to a large, new, two-storey house. 'With all this

maize Roy is going to make sure that he does not go hungry like the rest of the country. Wendy and Roy both work for a company involved with relief work and development projects – they are making lots of money. Jonathan founded the whole thing, he should be flying in from Johannesburg in their private jet at any time.'
'Johannesburg?'
'Of course,' Daphne laughed, 'without South African help, Kaunda would have been out on his neck years ago.'

Our arrival was unannounced and unexpected. Wendy emerged from a bedroom; Roy was having a mid-afternoon drink, smoking English cigarettes; his afternoon siesta was drifting into sun-downer time. 'An English voice and an English face,' Roy said in welcome. 'I've just come back from England. I can't afford to stay there; they won't let you earn any money.' He was a tax exile; his wife and family lived in a large farmhouse in Essex and he visited them just three months a year.

His company was currently involved in a number of relief operations. 'I was in at the start of the company,' he enthused, 'we work closely with a lot of agencies. We work as agricultural advisers for development schemes, and we are on hand to deal with disasters – starvation and distress – we love them, they make us very rich. Our clients include governments, the World Bank and a variety of charities and relief agencies. We prefer "World Vision", they pat with their money quickest, in large amounts, and with few checks.' I did not know whether this was drink talking or the truth, although he seemed to believe what he was saying. 'Then comes Oxfam; think of it – they collect money from all those British do-gooders and then give it straight to us – they pay very well.' He laughed, as did Wendy; she was prospering too. She had arrived in Zambia from the London suburbs, with a degree in estate management. She rarely returned to England and at 26 already had a villa in the Algarve, overlooking the sea.

Roy's father had once farmed in Zambia, but he had never been interested in farming: 'It's too much like hard work. For the last few years I've simply followed the aid around – Malawi, Zambia, Chad, Nigeria, and don't forget Ethiopia, the world has just discovered it. That has been a good bonus.'

I asked Wendy if she felt guilty about taking money from gifts made by people, often with little money themselves, to help the Third World. 'Of course not,' she replied contemptuously. 'Do you know the definition of foreign aid? It's what the poor people of rich countries pay to the rich people of poor countries – and we are rich people in a poor country. Zambia could be very rich if it liked, but not while these motoes keep getting hand-outs. They are talking about getting agriculture off the ground again here, but Germany has just given another 8 million dollars worth of maize. That's the quickest way to kill it. It's no use giving aid with the infrastructure like it is. They want to get the roads sorted out and stop the shortages, then things can go. Its the inefficiency and infrastructure falling apart that's making the whole of Black Africa go backwards, and hand-outs encourage it. So if all this money's being wasted, why shouldn't we get as much of it as we can.'

Roy was pleased with what she had said: 'The Japanese have just given seven lorries with generators and videos as mobile demonstration units; one puncture and they're finished and the generator will end up in the driver's village; what a waste. That kind of aid's not wanted.'

But although they both thought Zambia was going down hill, they liked it better than Zimbabwe. Roy explained: 'Zimbabwe's too much like Surrey in the sun, south of the Sahara. There are still too many Europeans down there and things still work. If you want to run a business in Zimbabwe it's all regulations and forms. Here the system folded years ago – they have no idea what's going on, so we can get on with our business with no hassle.'

He must have thought me very naive: 'If Zambia is so chaotic,' I asked, 'how do you distribute aid from it?'

'We don't,' he replied, pouring himself another whisky, 'if there's a famine, with starvation and television cameras, we simply organise. For example, last year America gave five million dollars worth of aid to Mozambique for maize. Now that country is in such a mess we simply found surplus maize in northern Mozambique, when people were starving in southern Mozambique. We bought it cheap – moved it a short distance and received the dollars out of the country. If there's a problem you don't go to the food mountains of Europe or America to solve the problem – that's too expensive. You find the nearest country that's had aid, when it's not using it or doesn't need it – buy it and ship it. The smaller the distance you move it, the more money you make, and the donor country, or charity, never asks you where it comes from.'

'There are other ways of making easy money too,' Wendy butted in.

'Already we have been asked about ostriches, tobacco, citrus fruits and coffee. As soon as you have something you don't know anything about, you read it up in two days and become an expert. I'm now an expert on ostriches. I just got a little book on ostriches and read. The Zambians could have done the same thing, but they chose to pay us lots of money instead.'

Roy was not to be outdone: 'We don't just make money on obscure things – ostriches, or Mozambique. We made a lot of money out of the Ethiopian drought. We both went, and Jonathan. It was terrible, you could hardly get into the Addis Hilton for all the aid agencies, do-gooders and camera crews. The Swedish air force took over a whole floor, but we all lived well – steak, chocolate gateaux, strawberries and cream, wine – whatever we wanted, with a few trips north to look at the starving for good measure. The good thing about it all is that we don't get our money from just one rich old lady, but from hundreds of rich old ladies whose cash is conveniently collected together for us.' The telephone rang; Jonathan had arrived at the airport and Roy had to go and pick him up in the Mercedes: 'It's nice meeting you,' Roy beamed as he offered me his limp hand: 'I'll be in town tonight at Jonathan's place – more money to make – but next time you are in church and they announce a collection for the Third World, give generously and think of me.'

* * * * * * *

Wendy had drunk a lot, but still wanted more: 'Shall we go to the Flying Club?' It was more a statement of intent than a question. Flying appeared to have nothing to do with membership of the Flying Club. It was a strange place. The public bar was full of black and brown faces, the lounge bar was almost exclusively white – yet there were no rules to make it so. 'We all like it like this,' a farmer told me, in a broad Yorkshire accent. Most of the accents were regionless, BBC, quite unlike the average gathering of Europeans in Zimbabwe.

'The only odd accents you are likely to hear are from the Scandawegians, doing their liberal bit among the natives,' a swimming pool engineeer from Tonbridge told me. He liked Zambia: 'It's a wonderful place, much better than Zimbabwe, simply because the entire country has run down such a long way.

Things are not available; people don't arrive on time and so the whole pace of life slows.'

'The Brits and the Afs get on well – it's the Ities and Porks who keep their distance. The "Grindians" are the worst – the Greeks and Indians – they keep their distance until they want something, then they go grinning and fawning and offering gifts – only we call them bribes. The Africans still respect us, for they know that we will deal with them straight – the Indians are more crafty than monkeys in business – they are not liked. But if you want some advice, come and live in Zambia. If you can't get anything, that's no problem – you expect it. Living in a country that's running down is so relaxing. Have another beer.'

I mentioned that I was staying the night with Roy and Wendy. Another farmer laughed: 'We don't need them, South Africa is our relief agency. Without South African help Kaunda would have been out on his neck years ago. He thanks them with abuse. They've just given us eleven million litres of diesel fuel. Without it there would have been no harvest.'

'If you had a harvest why are South African lorries delivering maize from Zimbabwe?' I asked, astonished.

'Now you are getting complicated. You see every year the harvest takes the Zambians completely by surprise. This year, out in the bush, they had a good harvest, but the government had forgotten to order the sacks – so the crops can't be collected. So, while the maize spoils in heaps in the villages, we have hand-outs from South African lorries in the cities. Then all the wheat flour in at the moment is South African, and so it goes on. Any genuine Zambian maize you see, has been grown by a European.'

'If you farm like I do, it's not easy. I reckon a third of my production is lost or stolen and I can't get spare parts for my machinery. Things are going backwards. In the Sixties, under wicked white rule, one in a hundred black children died. Now 40 per cent of children under five die. The country used to export food, now it only grows 50 per cent of what it needs – yet it has a comparatively small population and good land.'

'Things are getting more violent as well. Two years ago my wife was held-up by armed robbers. When the Rhodesian war was on, it was chaos – gun law – the guerillas did just as they liked. If South Africa gets warmed up – then I expect the ANC will do as they like here, just like the last time.'

He was a third-generation Zambian and was pessimistic about the future: 'I love it here, but it is not the place for my children. We are aliens, with an alien culture. It was brought home to me while on holiday in England – in Bath – all those beautiful buildings and baths with piped hot water, so that the Romans could enjoy their baths. It was 2,000 years before people enjoyed hot baths in England again. The same will happen here, it must, this is Africa. We will all go and what we have built up will go. Whether the same will happen in Zimbabwe and South Africa, I do not know.'

Heroes Day and Unity Day were approaching so I asked who the Zambian heroes were. The Yorkshire farmer was interested: 'Zambian heroes? Well we gave them independence didn't we? They didn't have to fight for it – just the odd riot and the occasional dog bite – no I don't know of any Zambian heroes.'

The swimming pool engineer was no help either: 'I did hear that someone had his foot run-over by a Land Rover once – perhaps he's the hero. Is it one hero or several heroes?'

The Yorkshireman found a more realistic answer: 'In the old days we had Rhodes Day and Founders Day – they've not changed the dates, just the names. It's simply an excuse for a holiday – we are all heroes for still living here if you ask me. They ought to have Political Prisoner Day. I suppose you've never heard of Simon Kapwebwe. When he was going to stand at the elections for President, Kaunda changed the constitution to stop him. He was a former Vice-President and Prime Minister. He was Kaunda's right-hand man when they were agitating for independence. He died in prison.* You don't hear Kaunda talking about that. He wants one man one vote in South Africa. In Zambia we all have one vote – we have to vote for him.'

Wendy wanted a bottle of brandy to take back with her, but the rules did not allow it. The Yorkshireman again had the answer. He turned to the barman: 'Johnnie, 21 brandies please and keep them in the bottle.'

* * * * * * *

---

* In fact, he died on release from prison.

Arrival in Wonderland

By mid-morning Wendy still had not emerged from her room. The houseboy Patrick was cleaning up. He only looked about 25, but claimed to have nine children already. After much thought he had been persuaded to sign papers for his wife to go on the pill: 'But the clinic it has run out – it is very difficult and she is pregnant again already.'

* * * * * * *

I had not enjoyed the philosophy of my hosts and returned to central Lusaka, to the Lusaka Hotel. Inevitably payment had to be made in sterling, in advance, and my room had no soap, toilet paper or hot water. I doubted whether the dining room would have any food, so I visited the nearby 'Zamby Snack Bar', which had an additional name of 'Mr Rooster'. Half the items on the menu were not available and there were no sweets whatsoever.

Daphne at last had the dates of my hunting trip, which left me with six free days. It gave me time to go to the Luangwa Valley – an area I had always wanted to visit because of its rich flora and fauna. At one time it had possessed Africa's most flourishing black rhino population. Booking the plane for the next day was not easy. According to Zambia Airways the flight was full; according to a travel agent it was virtually empty. I bought a ticket and took my chance.

The old colonial names of the roads had nearly all been changed. Livingstone had become Chachacha; Stanley had been reincarnated as Freedom and George V1 had become Independence Avenue. Typically, the one road with the most obvious colonial link had been left with its original name – Cairo Road – running north-south through central Lusaka. Cecil Rhodes had wanted to take the British influence in Africa from the Cape to Cairo; Cairo Road had been part of the route and had evidently remained so. Apparently the strange horse and rider next to the statue of Cecil Rhodes in Harare had once stood in Lusaka. It was called 'Physical Energy' and depicted the energy required by the Europeans to reach Cairo.

The origin of the name 'Chachacha' was also significant. Before independence Kenneth Kaunda had promised to make the Europeans dance to the Africans' tune. The chant Chachacha had grown from it.

Off Independence Avenue was a huge building site with acres of new construction taking place. At first I thought it was a new hospital or university. I asked a passer-by: 'It is the new Party Headquarters of UNIP.' So Zambia's one and only party was spending millions of pounds on itself, while accepting free maize from Zimbabwe.

At the entrance was a large statue of an African in shorts breaking his chains; it was the 'Monument Dedicated to Freedom Fighters – In Memory of all those who lost their lives for Zambia'. Around the base were pictures of Africans waving banners: 'Africa is our motherland for ever – we trust Kaunda of UNIP'; 'Kaunda Means Freedom for Zambia', and 'Forward Ever – Backward Never'. It seemed to me that the words of the last slogan were in the wrong order. Shortly after the monument had been unveiled in 1974 a hand-written message had been placed conspicuously underneath. It read 'Trust a kaffir to break these'.

* * * * * * *

The cathedral stood at the end of Independence Avenue. The Zambians could not be blamed for that – the foundation stone was laid in 1957 by the Queen Mother. From the outside, it had all the charm of a cross between a grain silo and an amusement arcade, of British design and construction. Inside it was slightly different, with windows of gaudy glass – mauve, purple, orange, yellow, red and a number of sickly greens – it could have passed as a discotheque or a bingo hall. Its only redeeming features were a beautiful sculpture of a negro nailed to a tree, and a cross of nails sent from Coventry.

As I was looking round and pondering, a white cleric approached me and asked me what I thought of the cathedral. I told him, as politely as I could. I expected him to tell me the error of my ways. Instead he said: 'I know how you feel. I feel like that sometimes. The trouble is the people are slow and suffer from the Z factor.'
'The Z factor?'
'Yes – we have to be polite. The ordinary Africans are super, lovable people, but they are slow. Nothing happens when it is supposed to; things are late or don't get done at all. They get everything wrong. They talk about the oppression of colonial times – but they've got oppression now; it's not overt nastiness, it's just life. There seems to be no hope and no way out – there's no leadership. I don't think there will be a coup, they just haven't got

the energy or the interest. The last ones that tried even got that wrong - they have been sentenced to death. It makes them feel worse when they hear about money being wasted. The President has just got a brand new Mercedes costing thousands of kwacha. But he knows how they feel, and for the first time it's bullet-proof. There have been riots recently in the copper belt and the police stopped them with clubs and guns. I bet you didn't see that on British television.

'The living compounds on the outskirts of Lusaka are terrible, with no hope for jobs or improvements and it's steadily getting worse. Half the poulation is reckoned to be under twelve and of the working population a third are government bureaucrats – all good Party men with their fingers in the pie. You can't run a country like that. I stay here because of the people, they are lovely and gentle and deserve better.

'If you go to Malawi you will see the difference – yet in the old days Nyasaland [Malawi] was always the poor relation. There, the fields are neat and cared for, and they are self-sufficient in food. Dr Banda has built up the essentials – yet he is abused for being a dictator – apparently Kaunda is not. It is just because Banda deals openly and unashamedly with South Africa. He simply says he needs to, for the good of Malawi. Sometime ago his entourage was driving along past an unkempt farm. Dr Banda stopped and told the farmer that if the farm was not worked properly in six months time it would be confiscated by the state. He actually returned himself in six months – but the work had been done.'

* * * * * * *

Back towards the Lusaka Hotel a small sign had been erected giving both an alternative to the cathedral and to Heroes Day:-

> Heroes '85 Retreat
> Your bad luck, sickness, sin,
> marriage problems will vanish as
> you meet the hero of heroes Jesus Christ.

Inside the hotel a large crowd of Africans was watching the News in the 'television lounge' – a television placed on an open landing with chairs around it. The news reader was saying how Mugabe had won the Zimbabwe election easily, but because Ian Smith's party had won a majority of the white seats Robert Mugabe had promised to abolish them at the earliest opportunity. The watchers were excited and obviously had no time for Mugabe: 'Ah, Mugabe is cheating as usual'; 'Mugabe never stops cheating', and 'I expect Nkomo will soon have to flee to Britain again.'

It was also reported that Denis Norman, the only white in Mugabe's cabinet, had been sacked. It was in response to the white support of Ian Smith. In reality it was a remarkable act of racial spite, especially in view of Denis Norman's fine record as a minister. The sacking was made even more petty by the fact that only one in four of the Europeans had voted for Smith. Most had not bothered to vote for they accepted that the white seats were of no relevance in a black Zimbabwe; they were happy with what was going on and they had no wish to vote. Robert Mugabe saw things differently.

* * * * * * *

At breakfast the waiter was very civil and friendly: 'Continental breakfast or English, master?'
'Continental, please.'

I was joined by an air conditioning engineer from Peterborough. He looked tired and grey. 'I'll have a Continental too.'

He was depressed: 'I've had enough – I've been here five years but I simply can't take it anymore. I used to get on with these blacks, but I hate them now. They're so stupid and dishonest. I get people wanting work with great sheets of paper – certificates and qualifications. Yet when you leave them on their own they can't put a light switch on straight, or change a plug. And then there's the violence. Last year I got forced off the road by armed bandits. They took my car, my watch, my money and told me to run off into the bush before they shot me. I ran off into the bush. I expect my car was in Zaire before the day was out.'

The waiter brought two cups of tea. 'But we ordered Continental breakfasts.'

'This is the Continental breakfast master – there is no bread today – we have tried, but there is none – perhaps it will come tomorrow. There is plenty more tea.'

'Don't say anything, it's not worth it,' the engineer sighed, 'it's useless. Even the money you earn here is useless; it gets less valuable every day. You can't believe anything they say or anything you read. The oil pipeline is supposed to be out of action, but according to the paper a ship was pumping diesel into it. I'm going to Saudi where you get real money without hassles.'

After another cup of tea the waiter brought the bill, for a Continental breakfast: 'But I only had tea,' I complained.
'I am sorry, it is a set price, master, for the Continental breakfast.'
'Pay,' the engineer sighed again, ' it's not worth quibbling.' He walked off, with a slight stoop; his soiled grey suit looked as run down as he was.

* * * * * * *

If Luangwa Valley had been my first visit to a National Park in Africa I would have enjoyed it; instead I was disappointed. It was a pleasure to be out in the wild again, after Lusaka, but the absence of black rhinos cast a shadow. Our ranger pulled no punches: 'Poaching is virtually out of control here. Forget the rhino – it's had it. If things go on as they are elephants will be lucky to survive too. Any ivory is taken – large and small, good and bad – and do you know what's done about it – sweet fanny adams.'

* * * * * * *

Mfuwe Lodge had simple comforts, made simpler by the usual lack of towels and soap, but much to my total astonishment it had warm water in the evenings. I queried the absence of soap and towels, and next time I visited my room half a bar of green soap had appeared; it looked as if it had been sliced in two by a panga.

If American and German tourists have faults, then at Mafue, an English woman took a lot of beating. She was with her bald, harassed-looking husband, spending a few days at the Game Lodge after visiting her son in the Copper Belt. She was a social worker from London with a broad cockney accent and a voice like a foghorn: 'I don't know why you brought me here Gilbert. I don't know why we didn't go straight home after we had seen Cyril.' The wretched Gilbert nodded, for some peace. 'I'd give anything to get out of this place – how long are we here for – the twelfth – 10 more days? Think, we could be in Cornwall right now. It's so boring with nothing to do – I'm not used to doing nothing. When I'm at the chalet I can take the dogs out, then get dinner and wash up – there's never a moment and it's so beautiful down there.' Whenever the coast was clear Gilbert would slink off to take photographs, furtively. As his wife slept he made a confession: 'I like it here.'

* * * * * * *

My main reason for staying at Mfuwe Lodge was to see Norman Carr, another pioneer of African conservation, in his late seventies. He became Northern Rhodesia's first game warden in 1939 and was working in the Game Department until the early sixties. He was also the man to start walking safaris in Africa, as an alternative to the black and white striped combies and the bar-propping game lodges. 'I started my safaris for the nostalgia of my early days as a game ranger – to recapture the whole atmosphere – living in the bush and being part of it. I hate the "infernal" combustion engine and wanted to get away from it – they are so noisy, dirty and always breaking down – I wanted something completely different. We are all running away from life and sticking our heads in the sand – but these days you can have a foot in both camps – it's the noise and bustle we try to avoid.'

He was another of those remarkable old white men in Africa, at peace with the world. He had found what few people seem to find in the late twentieth-century – contentment. But although happy, he was not complacent: 'Poaching is still rife; it must be stopped. The position regarding the black rhino in Zambia has become critical – but they still have a chance. It is a fire-engine exercise with the fire almost out of control and with little equipment with which to fight it.'

'Part of the problem is that poaching is still only considered to be a "misdemeanour". A much tougher line should be taken: poachers should be declared enemies of the state, for they are involved in smuggling, and corruption. They infringe the foreign currency regulations and they represent a security risk. The authorities know who they are, and even what guns they've got, they must take action.'

Some 'Scandawegians' had been appointed to spend three of four years on a 'Noraid' project in Luangwa investigating 'how to utilise the natural resource.' They had arrived directly from a project involving polar bears; one day a thesis should be written on how researchers manage to find the various research grants available and migrate to them. They feared that the Luangwa rhino population was already down to 35 animals, almost entirely restricted to the central area. They were being enclosed by a large fence, as the only possible way to save them. Norman Carr drove us around part of the reserve – showing me features of general interest, and passing on information that would be of use to the researchers. I hoped they had not arrived too late.

* * * * * * *

The plane for the return journey was a small turbo-prop, less than half full. The Indian in front of me sat transfixed, staring intently out of the window. He was watching a little stream of liquid flowing from the engine, trickling down the wing and dripping to the tarmac. I too sat transfixed. As we taxied and took-off the stream continued: 'What is it?' I asked the Indian.
'It must be aviation fuel,' he replied with tension in his voice.
 For the whole flight I sat waiting for the explosion, as the trickle continued. Even on landing the dripping continued. 'Do you normally have liquid flowing from the engine and down the wing,' I asked a stewardess.
Her eyes bulged: 'Oh, I'll get the Captain.'
The African Captain arrived, jacket off and smiling: 'Oh that – it is only oil – they always over fill it.'

* * * * * * *

Lusaka was in a state of excitement; during the night a small bomb had exploded outside the ANC headquarters. It had been followed by automatic fire and there were rumours of South Africans being killed and captured. Dave, an English lorry driver, was getting used to explosions – he had been in Namibia at the time of the South African raid: 'Last night it was different. I was watching television with some coloureds when we heard the bang. They weren't bothered at all, all they said was – "it's only the ANC being blown up, it serves the swines right – they're getting some of their own medicine for a change."'
'Didn't they support the ANC?'
'They didn't appear to. A friend of theirs was close by when the bomb went off – he says all the talk about killing South Africans is

nonsense. The guards had been asleep, they just rushed out shooting in all directions in panic. They don't like terrorists, they said that when Nkomo's lot were in town all they got was hassle. Sam was stopped and threatened by them at a road-block one day, and local blacks and whites were murdered by them. Now they've been lumbered with the ANC.'

Dave had driven his lorry overland from London to Johannesburg. He was now delivering it to the hunting safari company arranging my trip. He would be arriving at the camp in northern Zambia two days after me. He was a likeable, easy-going mechanic, who had just fancied a few months of adventure before settling back into work in England. I accepted his invitation to sleep in the back of his lorry – it seemed a better prospect than the Lusaka Hotel, and at least I would get a proper breakfast.

* * * * * * *

Visiting the Lusaka 'Save the Rhino' campaign was depressing. A new African co-ordinator had been appointed. He was wearing an elephant-hair bracelet, which hardly seemed appropriate, and most of what he had to say blamed 'colonialism' for Africa's problems, including the Rhino poaching: 'Surely,' I interrupted, 'from what I have seen Zambia's problems have been caused by independence coming too early?'
'Oh no, you are wrong – there were no problems in Africa before the whiteman came. There was no tribal trouble – we all lived in peace. Colonialism said divide and rule – tribe against tribe.'
'But what about the Bushmen, they had been driven from this part of Africa, long before a white foot stood at the Cape.'

He was silent for several seconds, before changing the subject. Already he believed the new history of Africa. Progress Publishers could take a pride in their achievement.

The African Executive-Director of the Wildlife Conservation Society of Zambia was more reassuring, but he was depressed: 'We have over 2,000 members, but most of those are white. Not many Zambians are members – the average Zambian simply does not go to national parks, he is too busy making ends meet.'

'We are fighting an uphill battle against poaching – the market is there and getting bigger. We must re-examine our policies – we should be employing and involving the local communities. They must realise the benefits, then they will look at conservation in a different light. The money from conservation goes to central government at the moment, it should go to the local area.'

As I left he was preparing a conservation pamphlet, quoting the words of Henry David Thoreau: 'A town is saved not more by righteous men in it than by the woods and swamps that surround it.' Lusaka had no woods or swamps surrounding it.

* * * * * * *

That evening I again visited the Flying Club, this time mingling with the black and coloured faces, as Dave had gone to say goodbye to his friends before driving north. Sam was a large and jolly coloured bus driver – he laughed, pointing at the white faces in the lounge bar: 'We call that little Pretoria,' he said, completely without malice. He then started on a whole series of van der Merwe jokes in which Van appeared, as usual, to be stupid, crude and violent. Even jokes that would have been frowned on as 'racist' and 'anti-black' in some white liberal circles, he told with a mixture of gusto and mirth, and his friends, black and brown, all laughed heartily. 'Van goes to Salisbury sees an African working: "Hey kaffir," he says, "if this is Rhodesia, which way to Salisbury?"
The African replies: "It is not Rhodesia, it is Zimbabwe. It is not Salisbury, it is Harare. I am not a kaffir, I'm a comrade."
"What's a comrade?"
"It's Russian for kaffir."' They laughed so loudly that Little Pretoria stared in to see what was happening.

On the television behind the bar some school children were discussing 'The Liberation of South Africa'. The conversation was sprinkled liberally with the usual words and phrases: 'racists', 'the armed struggle' and 'the evil apartheid régime'.

'Jesus Christ,' Sam muttered in blasphemous exasperation, 'what do those kids know about it? Why don't they discuss why we have to queue for mealies or where we can get diesel?'

Another white face joined us – three in the public bar – it must have been approaching a record. He was another studying the use of wildlife and 'conservation resources'; 'ecology' seemed to be something of a growth industry – if only they could produce concrete results, instead of written reports. He had already been working in the country for six months and realised the size of his task: 'Zambia is a strange place. The locals are empty, and just stand about, staring at you, or studying outer space. I reckon this country is made up of all the slowest tribes – they've simply been pushed here by the more go ahead peoples surrounding them. For Africans, cities simply do not work.

'Mind you, the Europeans here are no better. They are weird – totally different from the whites elsewhere in Africa. I think it's because they're separated from their culture and traditions. In the evenings they sit around listening to Beethoven and reading Walter Scott, because that's how they think people in England still live. Here they've got power, money and prestige – back home a lot of them wouldn't even make good bank clerks.' Looking at the assembled group in Little Pretoria, I agreed.

I left with Dave to sleep in his lorry. We would both be leaving for the Bangweulu swamps in the morning.

* * * * * * *

I was picked up at dawn, by Richard, the white-hunter. He looked the part, wearing a smart safari-suit, but there was also an air about him that suggested he could cope with most situations. He lived half the year in Kent, and the other half he hunted with clients in Africa. He was English, but had gone through the Rhodesian war. He just liked Africa more than England and had no particular desire to settle down. His insurance was his house, which he could always return to.

The British Caledonian flight was on time when Richard went to pick up his client from the airport. I had expected him to meet an aristocrat, a failed aristocrat, or a business man with a hyphenated name. Instead he arrived back at the Land Cruiser with Eddie, a short chubby man from Derbyshire who sold motorcycle spare parts and spoke with a broad Derbyshire accent. To arrive in Zambia to shoot big game he must have sold many spare parts.

As Eddie was the client, he sat in the front; I was the observer, so I was given the open back. The start had been almost too good – and I was not surprised when just five miles out of Lusaka we were waved to a halt. It was a military police roadblock, and there, Lance-Corporal Max Mushiba decided to stop us. He was wearing a red beret, camouflage jacket and trousers, white gloves and bright blue socks – he looked very fetching. His AK 47 was aimed at us and he smelt strongly of drink. He spoke to Richard: 'Where are you going? What are you doing? You are a hunter? You are armed you bugger? You have a gun you shit pull off the road.'

I was not sure what to do. Was he a bandit? Or was he a real soldier? It was the blue socks that confused me. If we ran – soldier or bandit – we would be shot. If we tried to tackle him we would be all right if he was a bandit. If he was a soldier we would be in real trouble.

He made all three of us get out, and asked Richard to identify his bags. As he inspected the contents he became increasingly excited and his gun swung freely around his neck. It seemed to me that he might even manage to shoot himself. I decided to bide my time; at the slightest hint of trouble I would hit him, or run off into the bush. He went on, his voice getting higher: 'Where is your vehicle from? Zimbabwe? You are from that shit Mugabe.' He came across a heavy duty-pullover: 'You bugger – you have more military equipment.' He turned to me: 'Come here you shit, which is your bag?'; he seemed to be searching for items worth stealing. He took out a black rubber torch and my heavy khaki jumper: 'You have military equipment you ....'. He knew Anglo-Saxon too.

Eddie was clearly anxious. How could I tell him not to worry? I could see that Richard was weighing up the situation as I was. Eddie's bags were a treasure-trove of 'military equipment' – jumpers, army boots, hunting knife, torch, as well as his rifle and shot-gun.' Each time Richard tried to show him the various certificates and licences he waved them away: 'They mean nothing.' Eddie looked pale and ill: 'I'm only a tourist – I've never been to Africa before – I've only just got here – I've only just left England,' and then in desperation and bewilderment: 'I paid a lot of money for this trip.'

The Lance-Corporal called another soldier from the bushes who had been cooking breakfast: 'I have caught mercenaries the buggers.' The new soldier was polite and sober. He looked at the gun licences: 'There is nothing wrong.' He shrugged his shoulders apologetically and went back to his fire; he could not intervene, he was only a private.

'You are mercenaries,' the Lance Corporal shouted, 'you are shits and buggers, you are going to Lusaka.'

We retraced our steps, with Comrade Max sitting in the back with me, his gun still swinging loosely around his neck: 'You are in big

trouble now,' I told him, 'you wait until your officers hear of this. They will make you leave the army.'
'They can't do that I have been fighting for Zambia for 20 years.'
'Where?'
'In Zimbabwe, Mozambique and Angola.' Had the Zambian army really been fighting abroad? I didn't believe him. It took an hour for an officer, of impeccable accent and manners, to decide that Richard and Eddie really were hunters, and we were again ready to begin our journey, two hours late. Lance-Corporal Max Mushiba asked for a lift back to the roadblock. Richard left him standing at the gate.

It was a good journey north; the Zambian countryside was not particularly beautiful, but it was almost empty and we travelled miles without seeing another vehicle. Mountains appeared, just over the border, in Zaire, which led to more roadblocks: 'We are looking for bandits from Zaire.' The soldiers were in complete contrast to Comrade Max – polite and smiling; one even asked: 'Excuse me, have you any diesel to spare, we have not enough to get home?' Unfortunately we could not help.

The road north was long, straight and apparently never-ending, going on to Tanzania and up into Kenya. At a white stone by the wayside we turned off tar to hit dirt and every time we slowed I was engulfed by dust. We travelled through bush, forest, and even a national park – the Lavushi Mandu National Park, established in 1949 as a rhino sanctuary – now totally devoid of rhino.

On, through wayside villages of mud huts, where dogs barked, hens ran in a state of hysteria and ragged, barefoot children shouted and waved. The men in trousers and shirts watched while women, some bare-breasted and others in long cotton wraps, cooked or pounded maize. Surrounding the settlements it was slash-and-burn agriculture of manioc and maize. In such a remote place I thought about the people; how did they learn? What future did they have away from the centres which dictate policies and produce slogans? And how are rural areas developed without creating the universal urban ailments of envy, materialism and greed?

* * * * * * *

I enjoyed the hunt; both Richard and Eddie were good company. The camp was perfect, with thatched huts and excellent food,

Arrival in Wonderland

cooked on a wood fire, and the landscape was totally new. The area's historical connections added to its interest, for it was first explored by David Livingstone in 1868 and it was in the southern part of the swamps that he died on 1st May 1873. It was a remarkably remote, lonely and hostile place in which to die. He was looking for the headwaters of the Nile – he had in fact found the beginning of the River Congo [now Zaire].

Eddie had come to Zambia to shoot a buffalo, with various other options for antelope, if and when he got his main prize. In England he stalked deer and rough-shot in the Midlands: 'But I've always wanted to come to Africa. I got interested in wildlife through watching programmes on the telly – I've wanted to shoot a buffalo for years.'

The routine was the same every day. We would rise just before dawn and drive to the edge of swamps. The great plain over which we passed looked like a vast lake, but there was no water or even a mirage, just countless dew-soaked cobwebs catching the first rays of the morning sun. As reeds replaced grass we would stop to walk through thick papyrus and sharp mutete reeds. Birds would warn the wary of our advance – a black egret, sacred ibis, a spurwinged plover and spurwinged geese. Other animals could betray our presence too, black lechwe, bushpig and there were also signs of leopard and lion.

Once the hunt was over, with the herd stampeding prematurely away at our scent or sounds, we would return to camp. As the sun warmed, so the plain filled up with thousands, of grazing black lechwe – probably as many as 20,000, making an unforgettable sight. Kori bustards and ground hornbills were others to love the open grassland and they moved among the antelope quite unconcerned. After lunch and a siesta we would go in the opposite direction, through grassland containing even more termite mounds than the lechwe. Among them we would catch glimpses of reedbuck, tsessebe and oribi. The tsessebe is another animal that looks as if it was put together with the spare parts left over at creation, yet despite its ungainly appearance it is said to be Africa's fastest antelope. The evening hunt would again be in the swamp, after buffalo, finishing with the sun blood red, and nightjars hawking over the reed tops.

There were several near misses. Once we were almost on top of the buffalo in thick papyrus before we realised it. We heard them galloping away, with cattle egrets and oxpeckers flying above the reeds to avoid the chaos. Another day, with the sun well up, Eddie was about to shoot when the herd caught his scent. Instead of running away, they panicked. From 30 yards away, where I was watching, it looked as if both Richard and Eddie would be flattened, after their long and laborious approach , creeping and crawling over the ground. Richard stood up waving his arms and was on the verge of shooting in front of them, when they veered away. On yet another occasion we followed spoor through shallow water, where temporary shelters on the banks showed where fishermen lived during the wet season. The tracks went on into drier country where large old termite mounds were covered with trees. At last we caught up with the herd; this time the buffalo made off just as Eddie and Richard fired – both missed the animal they had chosen. Eddie was philosophical: 'Oh well, I got the termite mound – I'd better have it stuffed and sent home.' They were long and arduous hunts and it began to look as if Eddie would not get his animal.

Back at the camp one morning, after the buffalo had disappeared early, an American hunter from Luangwa Valley drove by with his Afrikaner 'white-hunter'. He had flown into a nearby camp and still looked as if he should be accompanying a wagon-train; it was the Davey Crockett/John Wayne syndrome. I was astonished, in only an hour he was back, with both a shot lechwe and a tsessebe balanced in the back of his vehicle. He stopped to exchange news and views: 'Boy that was a wonderful hunt.' I did not see how it could have been, as he must have shot both animals from the vehicle in such a short time. At least Eddie was hunting properly, on foot, involving stamina, skill, and sometimes courage. Riding about in four-wheel drive vehicles bristling with guns, shooting whatever fresh species came into view, seemed a singularly pointless pastime.

He had been in South Africa, Zimbabwe and Zambia for six weeks: 'It's been a great trip – I've got lion, leopard, hippo, crocodile, two hartebeests and a white rhinoceros (in South Africa). I'm having the trophies sent home ahead of me. The lion was a great hunt. It fed at the bait, lied down, got up to wander around and then bang. With the croc and hippo it was just death out of a barrel – tremendous.' He had not called for a chat after all. He had stopped to sing his own unedifying praises. I was glad to see him leave.

My time was running out, as I had to return to Lusaka, in order to catch a flight to Malawi and I left, before Eddie had shot a buffalo. He eventually managed to shoot one on his 10th day. He and Richard crawled almost into the herd. After much deliberation they decided to shoot a young bull. It turned out to be an old cow and her head now hangs on a wall in Derbyshire.

13. The Great Dictator

My plan seemed simple: leave the Bangweulu swamps in the hunting camp's Land Cruiser, drive to Lusaka and catch the plane to Malawi. The one thing I had overlooked in such a straightforward plan, however, was that I was still in Zambia. Half way back to Lusaka we needed petrol and stopped at the only petrol pumps for 150 miles. We arrived at the same time as the pump maintainence man, who was to service the generator that drove the pumps. The attendant was polite: 'I am afraid you will just have to wait a quarter of an hour.' An hour and a half later the maintainence man had transformed the smooth running motor to a coughing, spluttering wreck, belching out black smoke and incapable of running the pumps.

Dave went into the engine room to see what was happening and returned almost immediately: 'I don't believe it. They've cocked the whole thing up – everything that should be screwed up just enough, they've tightened solid, and everything that should be tight is loose. We won't get out of here today. Do you know – I came out here full of nice multi-racial ideals – in just seven months I've been turned into a total racist. They are just stupid – what they've done to that generator is unbelievable – they're unbelievable. The only place where anything works is South Africa – this place is just a tip, and believe it or not there are even worse ones in West Africa.'

Briefly the generator coughed and spluttered with more vigour. It speeded up, slowed down, coughed, died, sparked into life again, all while filling our tank. We paid with relief, pleased to get away, and sure that those following us would have to wait for days to get their petrol.

By the time we reached Kabwe it was cold and dark. Only a third of the street lights were working; at least the large and impressive offices of the Pan African Institute for Development had something to develop.

My final night in Zambia was not spent in the Lusaka Hotel as planned; we arrived back so late that we slept in the vehicle. But even then it was not easy to get out of the country. While checking-in at the airport, I found that the departure time on my ticket was 13.45; an American girl, working for 'Africaid', had 11.00 for the same flight. It did not matter – in fact the plane's engines were in pieces on the tarmac, and it still had to undertake a number of local flights. Dave went with me to the bar, for a farewell drink – there was no barman.

The plane eventually left; but still the passengers had no idea what was happening. The airport's public address system was not working, and neither were the telephones. Eventually the message came: 'Departure would be 16.00', then it became '17.30', then '18.20'. The only people to get away were a large group of African youths on an Aeroflot flight to Moscow, via Luanda. Whether they were ANC volunteers, or students, nobody claimed to know. Suddenly, an hour before the new time of departure, an airline official told me in casual conversation that the flight was about to leave – no customs officials were on duty and the passport control officers were crammed into an office eating cake, laughing and joking, quite uninterested in passports – one was practising writing his name in pencil on a piece of polystyrene.

I was relieved to be on the plane, even if it was the same type that brought me back from Mfuwe – I was past caring. The American girl was relieved too, although she had one slight worry: 'You know what they call Zambia Airways?' she said seriously. 'Zambia Scareways.'

'That's nothing,' I told her, 'Air Malawi is known as Air Where-are-we.'

* * * * * * *

The airport at Malawi's new capital, Lilongwe, was impressive – there was even a batman to guide the plane to its parking position, something unknown in Zambia. The officials were smartly dressed and efficient; it was difficult to believe I was on the same continent.

Any doubts quickly left – the passport control officer was too efficient. In my passport I was described as a 'writer'. As soon as he looked at it, his expression changed and I thought – 'trouble': 'You are a writer? What are you going to write about? – We allow no writers into Malawi – You are a journalist? – Have you got permission to come to Malawi? - You will not be allowed to stay – why haven't you got a return ticket? – You must leave on the next plane tonight – go and change your money and buy a return ticket.' The bank was shut; the Air Malawi office was shut, and still he insisted that I purchased a ticket and left immediately. He made two phone calls. 'Wait here, I must find out what to do with you until you catch the plane.' He was serious: 'We don't like journalists here – you can stay the night at the Capital Hotel in Lilongwe, and you will leave the country tomorrow.' I had to relinquish my passport, and my flight ticket home, from Harare. I then received another shock: I rode in a taxi that did not rattle.

* * * * * * *

As soon as it opened in the morning I visited the British High Commission: 'Can't you do anything?' I asked. 'I want to stay.' The passport officer was pleasant and friendly and gave me a cup of coffee, but all he could say was: 'You've got no chance whatsoever. You'll be away today and there's nothing we can do about it. If it's any consolation you are not the first and you certainly won't be the last.'
'Couldn't I simply ignore them, and go back and collect my passport and ticket when I want to leave?' I asked.
'If you want to see the inside of a prison you can. They have a good plain clothes police force and the prisons are not a pretty sight – 40 to a cell – it comes as quite a shock to the European system. So it's up to you. I wouldn't advise it.'
I walked sadly back to the hotel, past the South African Embassy – said to be the only such embassy on the entire continent. I had set my heart on ending this particular journey by travelling up the lake, and again traversing the ancient footsteps of Livingstone; but I decided that I did not really want to share a small prison cell with 39 others.

From the taxi heading back to the airport, the countryside looked beautiful. Bush, small villages of mud huts and distant mountains – seen through clear, hot air – what a shame to be leaving so soon. The immigration officer ushered me into an office; he looked severe – it reminded me of when I was sacked from the civil service, 15 years before: 'Mr Page,' his tone was ominous,' it has been decided that you can stay.' It was difficult to believe – so the High

Commission had been wrong. The condition was simple: before leaving the airport building I had to buy a ticket to Harare, and they were allowing me up to 13 days in the country. The Air Malawi ticket office was supposed to open at noon, but the ticket-seller did not arrive until 1.30 – I did not mind. I treated myself to a beer and a packet of Smarties to celebrate – the Smartie packet was written in Afrikanes. As I waited, a private South African executive jet landed. The occupants were met by some Chinese, or Japanese; after two hours they were flying south again. At last the ticket-seller arrived. I showed my purchase to the immigration officer – he returned my passport, wished me a good stay and actually smiled.

The British Deputy High Commissioner was astonished to find me still in the country. To celebrate, he invited me back to his house for tea on the terrace. He was a large, jolly man, fascinated by wildlife. His large bungalow was liberally decorated with his own photographs, for wildlife photography was his main pastime and he was actually a director of a wildlife picture agency in Britain. Ironically, shortly before being posted to Malawi he had been asked to write a book on the terns of the world. The project was being held in abeyance, as Malawi had a grand total of only two species of tern. He actually kept a list of all the birds he had seen – which suggested that he might even be a 'twitcher', a birdwatcher obsessed by spotting new species and keeping a list of all new sightings, however fleeting the glimpse. At the time of my visit his 'life-list' was 1,938. His immediate target was 2,000 – then he would have seen a quarter of the world's birds; quite an achievement.

* * * * * * *

Lilongwe was a remarkable place – like a giant Milton Keynes, but hotter, not so ugly and without the concrete cows. The buildings were widely spaced; there were large gum plantations within the city boundary to provide fuel, and there was a wildlife reserve to remind the citizens and visitors of the country's natural heritage. The shops were full and even contraceptives were on open sale. To Malawians 'family planning' was a dirty, unacceptable phrase, the words in favour and being urged on the entire population were 'family spacing'; there was a subtle difference somewhere.

At the side of a wide road, a small, simple memorial had been constructed – not to unknown 'heroes', but to Malawi's dead in two

World Wars. The inscription was just 'Lest We Forget', in memory of fallen members of the King's African Rifles – it was quite a surprise, for even in independent Malawi's new capital, part of their colonial past was being remembered.

The reason for the new city was simple. Blantyre, the old capital and economic centre, was at the southern end of the long thin country. By building Lilongwe in the bush it pushed economic activity and development towards the middle, leaving just the north feeling neglected.

After weeks of travelling it was pleasant to relax by the pool of the new Central Hotel. As I went inside for a coffee I dropped my pen. A passing Malawian swooped down and picked it up, saying 'Oh sorry'. They all seemed extremely warm and friendly. A Scot in a safari-suit had witnessed the incident. 'We are so lucky here,' he said in a broad Highland accent, 'Malawi's Africans are the best. Do you know they are so pleasant, that if you hit one over the head with a cricket bat, he would thank you and say sorry to the bat.'

He was a cynical, happy man, who loved Malawi: 'I've been here 15 years and thrown in my lot with this place. I used to have a home in England, as a safety net, but I've sold up everything – all I own is here.' He was developing and trying to sell solar energy: 'There's a better market for it here than in Scotland', and considered the future potential for it to be enormous: 'Solar energy would save them so much money – it would be cheaper and more sensible, with no pollution. It would reduce their dependence on the West; presumably that is why the developed world doesn't seem all that interested.'

He was a great admirer of Dr Banda too: 'He looks a laugh, with his three-piece suit, his homburg hat, fly whisk and maroon, convertible Rolls Royce – but look what he's achieved here. When you get out of the towns it's still primitive and Third World – but it's now self-sufficient in food, and if any civil servant slacks, or falls down on his job, he is out on his ear; where else does that happen in black Africa?'

'He was educated in South Africa, the USA and Britain. When he came to power he said: "I lived among white people for much of my life. In England the majority of my patients were white. How, then, could I hate Europeans? My quarrel was not against the white people but against a system of government that allowed a tiny minority of foreigners to rule a huge majority of indigenous people."'

Even Dr Banda's policy of keeping out journalists met with Alistair's approval: 'He must be right. What would the foreign press do here? They would not describe the old boy's achievements – they would go on about him being autocratic and his links with South Africa. You must admit the Western Press is entirely negative these days. Most journalists wouldn't recognise the truth if they tripped over it.' Sadly I had to agree with him.

'It's quite a laugh though – read the paper and half the words are "His Excellency the Life President did this" and "His Excellency the Life President did that" – not bad for a one-time small town GP in the North of England. He's an original – a one-off.'

'Most of Black Africa is on about "educating the masses". The President has set up the Kamuzu Academy – based on Eton, with white teachers and creaming off the brightest children. His argument is – get the intelligent qualified for the important jobs needed to lead Malawi into the 21st century and the rest will follow. Just the other day seven Malawian prep schoolboys went to Germany to take part in a classical Latin speaking competition. They actually sang the Malawian national anthem in Latin.

'The President's best joke was on his recent state visit to Britain; did you see him arrive in the Air Malawi jumbo? Air Malawi doesn't have a jumbo. It was a South African Airways plane, painted in Malawi's colours. Believe it or not the pilot was called van der Merwe, and all the South African crew were given Malawi passports especially for the occasion.'

* * * * * * *

Alistair had some business to attend to in Blantyre and was then going to Lake Malawi for a few days. 'If you are at a loose end drop into Club Makokola. I'm due for a break, anything you want to do I'll try to help you.' He asked me what I had planned.

'Not a lot, but a friend in Kenya told me that the boat trip up Lake Malawi is the greatest journey left in Africa today. The boat is captained by a drunken Australian; once he was in charge of ocean liners, but he has gradually worked his way down. By the time a sea captain has reached Lake Malawi there is nowhere else to go.'

* * * * * * *

It was a good idea – the lake was beautiful and the drive to it showed why Malawi is called 'the warm heart of Africa'. The landscapes were huge – almost lunar, with great plugs of volcanic rock protruding from bush with shambas and traditional villages. It was as if life away from the towns was as old as the landscape itself. Then came the lake, like a huge inland sea, with more mountains beyond, in Mozambique.

At Monkey Bay's booking office it was not so good; the sea captain was a Scot, and sober, and the boat was full, except for third class. Having seen third class before, on the Zairian river boats, I decided it was not for me; it made the average cattle truck seem spacious, clean and comfortable. If I wanted to travel first class, I had to book three months in advance.

Instead I hitched a lift to Cape Maclear, a large promontory within the Lake Malawi National Park, and there I swam, slept on the sand and walked by the water. The lake was vivid blue, the sand was white and by mid-day it was so hot that even the birds were quiet. At a village of palm thatch, among baobab trees, Stephen's Rest House gave a roof, food and shelter, almost on the beach for just £5 a night. My room was basic – a bed, a small table and four walls, with not even a light – I did not need one in such a place.

An offshore rocky island had a profusion of baobab trees growing, and from them came the haunting, evocative calls of the fish eagles – cries that once heard are never forgotten and are always associated with Africa. After dark, fishermen caught tiny silver fish in nets, putting them out in the sun to dry during the day. Then the fishermen changed: pied kingfishers, hovering and diving close to the shore.

The lake was like a vast inland sea, with its northern shores way beyond the horizon. In fact Lake Malawi is a huge expanse of water. It is the ninth largest lake in the world (the third largest in Africa), covering 11,430 square miles. It is 2,310 feet deep and at its deepest point it falls to 447 feet below sea level. The days and weeks in a year give its length and breadth; for it is about 365 miles long and 52 miles wide, which makes it half as big as Wales and means that if placed into England, its southern end would be in London, while its northern tip would reach the Firth of Forth.

It has numerous species of fish, the number varying according to which 'experts' are consulted. It is said that it has more types than any other lake in the world and new species are still being found.

The lowest figure given is 400, while some scientists believe that there could be as many as 1,000 different types. The lake is so deep that the fish cannot cross the open water, consequently, it is argued, many of the fish communities around the lake have been isolated, allowing them to evolve slightly differently from their neighbours. Among the fish are several varieties of 'mouth-brooders'; the female mouth-brooder actually hatches the eggs and keeps the young fish in the safety of her mouth. There can be up to a hundred young fish, and they will flee to the safety of their mother's jaws until two months old.

While snorkeling in the warm water I was astonished. I had expected great forests of trailing weed. Instead there was nothing, just boulders, crevasses and cliffs of rock, around which hundreds of fish, blue and black striped, mauve, yellow, light blue, brown, black and many more, fed on algae.

Almost inevitably, I was snorkeling with a group of American 'ecologists', who were studying the fish of the lake. They caught some fish, injected one with air and whistled as they threw it back into the water. As the fish floated helplessly on the surface a fish eagle swooped several hundred feet to take it with its talons. It was a stunning sight, but as 'scientists' they seemed to have no regard for the suffering of the inflated fish.

In typical American fashion they were equipped for the necessities of life in Africa: a refrigerator packed with Coca Cola, a computer and cassette recorder, an inflatable dingy with outboard motor and water-skis. They spoke to their houseboy as if he were aged three. Duane was reading a book called *Livingstone's Lake*; he did not like it because of the 'author's colonial attitude.' He did not like the local Europeans either because of their lives of 'privilege, affluence and arrogance'. I considered his comments more appropriate to their own life-styles. The average American attitude towards 'colonialism' is peculiar; they seem to equate the situation in Africa with the American war of independence. They forget that they were the real colonialists in America, and like the Australians, they ruthlessly killed and swept aside their country's indigenous peoples when it suited them; that did not occur in many parts of Africa.

* * * * * * *

Club Makokola was as I expected – like a luxurious part of the Mediterranean shore, deposited on the side of an African lake, but less crowded. That it reminded me of the Mediterranean was not surprising, as it was designed and owned by an Italian building contractor. Every room was air conditioned; the food was good, there was water-skiing, wind surfing and paddle boating. And then if the lake was not good enough there was a swimming pool. With sun-loungers and thatched roofs it was possible to stay on the beach all day. A new conference centre was also in the process of being completed – in its foyer a number of old framed prints were being hung. One was painted by Thomas Baines and dated 1st May 1852 entitled: 'Kaffirs leaving the colony for their native seat, with all their acquired property.'

Alistair was on the beach, and as I had not been able to get on the boat he had a suggestion. 'Why don't we go up the lake in my old Land Rover – I could do with a few days at Nyika Plateau.' It sounded like a good idea.

That evening as the sun died, we sat with a French doctor and his wife. They were due to return to France within a fortnight, after two years of work both in Blantyre and in the bush. For only the second time in Africa I heard the word 'Aids' mentioned. 'What is the truth about it here?' Alistair asked. 'Nobody seems to know, apart from the fact that most of the Europeans have nominated their friends, to give blood if ever they should need it.'

The doctor's wife, Barbara, was a nurse and she had the answer: 'That is very wise. When I was in Blantyre we started testing blood for Aids. Out of 16 pints, 12 had the virus – we were told to stop testing after that – it costs the equivalent of just over one of your pounds for each test, whereas only 15 pence, on average, are spent per head on health in Malawi. They just pump any blood into people now – Aids is out of control.'

While at Stephen's Rest House an unpleasant Canadian social worker announced that it was possible to contract Aids from mosquito bites. 'Quite untrue,' the Doctor insisted, 'that has not been proved anywhere. I should say it is quite impossible. But you want to avoid mosquitoes anyway – there is a potent variety of cerebral malaria about in Malawi and Tanzania that is resistant to drugs – we had a young voluntary worker from England die of it recently. It killed him within 24 hours and he had only been here three weeks.'

'You should be like me,' Alistair laughed. 'I have a natural immunity – I haven't taken malaria tablets for years.'

'What are the hospitals like here?' I asked.

'The ones in Blantyre and Lilongwe are OK,' Barbara replied, 'but the clinics in the bush have the problems of Africa – too many children – a lot of endemic disease and not enough drugs and equipment. Even in Blantyre there are problems, for slowly the hospital is being Africanised. There are good Africans – but some can not cope. One African doctor runs his haulage business from the hospital – how can he perform his duties properly like that?'

'Barbara has a theory about all this,' Jaques informed us, 'and I think she has a point.'

'I love the Africans and want to help them; we may even come back. But if you take the average European intelligence as 100, then the average African is 80. This is the average. There are very good Africans and they can be as good, even better than other nationalities – I am sure you have met some. Now people get offended by that. But the average for the oriental is 120 – now I am not offended by that, it is obvious. On the other side of the coin the stupid European is no different from the ignorant African. Until this is accepted, then the problem cannot be dealt with, the main issue has been evaded. It is not genetic, or environmental, but a mixture of both.'

'How do you mean?' I asked.

'Well at the simplest level, Africans have a bad start. They do not have toys as we do and so they don't play in the same way. In addition they don't learn early as we do the differences in texture and performance between metals, fabrics and plastics, and so they have to learn the hard way, later on. In *Out of Africa*, Karen Blixen has more to say – you must read it later. She loved Africa and the Africans, and wrote from the heart. Because she is dead her book is called a classic, quite rightly. If she had written it today she would have been labelled a racist.'

On returning to my room with Barbara's copy of *Out of Africa*, I read the quote: 'The dark nations of Africa, strikingly precocious as young children, seemed to come to a standstill in their mental growth at different ages. The Kikuyu, Kawirondo and Wakamba, the people who worked for me on the farm, in early childhood were far ahead of white children of the same age, but they stopped quite suddenly at a stage corresponding to that of a European child of nine. The Somali had got further and had all the mentality of boys of our own race at the age of 13 to 17.'

* * * * * * *

The following day Alistair greeted me with enthusiasm: 'Come on hurry, we are going up the lake now.' I could not see his Land Rover. 'No, not by road, air.' He was friendly with the Italian owner, whose small four-seater plane had arrived to take some equipment to Likoma Island, where his company was building a new secondary school. The club manager, Jonathan, went with us, a very bright Malawian, as intelligent as any European – in fact more intelligent than most. He spoke perfect English and had been to college in both Kenya and Switzerland to learn hotel management; he had even been to South Africa, on business: 'I got on all right, it was not as bad as I expected.'

From the narrow dirt runway we flew 150 miles up the lake to land on the small island of Likoma, which although only five miles from the Mozambique shore was Malawian. It was like everyone's dream of a tropical paradise: a small undulating island of boulders, baobabs, mango trees and native huts, with the fresh water sea an even deeper blue than the sky. It was dusty; goats seemed to roam at will and small plots of manioc were squeezed in wherever soil could be found among the rocks.

We travelled to the school in the only vehicle on the island, and that was owned by the building company. Only a third of the 420 labourers helping to build the school were local; most of the islanders quite sensibly preferred to fish. Before the arrival of the school, and outside workers, nearly all the business transactions had been carried out by barter. The weekly wage packets had introduced something new – money.

Close to the school site the contractors were also repairing St Michael's church, made out of red bricks and tin. Ants were eating the roof timbers, and one leg of the crucifix had disappeared. It was strange seeing a one-legged Jesus. Around the altar was a curtain and strange wooden icons, which together with the bats hanging in the roof gave a strange feeling of voodoo.

The feeling was not entirely misplaced, for in the centre of the island was an even more remarkable church – in fact a cathedral – the Cathedral Church of St Peter, Likoma Island, built close to a place where witches were once burnt. Considering its remote site, it was the most inspiring building I had ever seen: a huge church, built in local red brick, as large as Winchester Cathedral, with magnificent archways, portals and pillars, like the great ecclesiastical buildings of Europe. Here, on a remote African island was a building whose architecture praised God and whose construction was an expression of the deepest love for Africa, its people and the Almighty. Incredibly it was built by just one European architect, a European carpenter, and the local islanders.

Brass plates on the wall reminded of its history and of the sacrifices of the early missionaries: 'Chauny Maples – Bishop of Nyasaland drowned 12.9.1895 – When thou passeth through the waters I will be with thee – From shadows and images unto truth – R.I.P.' and 'Charles Frederick Mackenzie 1st Missionary Bishop to the Tribes in the Neighbourhood of Lake Nyasa and the River Shire – Born 10/4/1825. Died of Fever near Chiromo 31/1/1862.'

The ivory of the cathedral staff was presented by the Angoni chief whose people had, a few years before, speared to death the Reverend George Atlay on 26th August 1895. He had gone to the mainland opposite for hunting and rest. He was found lying face down, by a stream, after meeting an Angoni war party; his loaded gun was by his side – he had always insisted he would never use a gun against the local people, regardless of circumstances.

There were many features showing how the cathedral had once been encouraged by the wider church abroad. The figure on the rood was carved at Oberammagau; earth from Jerusalem was under one of the altars; the wood of the crucifix over the pulpit had been cut from the tree under which Livingstone's heart was buried, and a plaque in the south transept was carved from a stone taken from Canterbury Cathedral and placed at Likoma in the 1930s. The Stations of the Cross depicted an old-style Jesus, complete with halo; there was a beautiful stone altar seat, and all the time a little man in shorts, shirt and a tie was polishing the altar stalls – the whole place was spotless.

But there was an air of sadness, despondency and decay too. For the cathedral was running down; gradually it was being reclaimed by Africa. Some of the stained-glass windows were broken; great cracks had appeared in the stonework, and one of the high towers had been lowered because its top had become dangerous. The Cathedral was dying, withering and falling, crumbling on its own foundations. The chapter house and library were in a similar state of decay and its once fine collection of books had gone – destroyed by the ravages of ants and time. An old cover lay in the dust: *Our Colonies and India. How we got them and why we keep them*, by Cyril Ransome M A Oxen.

Among tall trees were small crosses for those who had died. It was all very moving, a tribute to the faith of men in earlier, less cynical times. Alistair sighed: 'It's dust to dust. The Cathedral is doomed – it is gradually returning to dust. There are other fine buidings on the mainland – some have already caved in. The whole of Africa is doomed – the European presence and influence is only transient – one day it will be as if we had never been here and this will really be the dark continent again.' Already there were stories suggesting that the people were crumbling spiritually too, for witchcraft was again said to be practised on the island.

* * * * * * *

Walking back to the plane we came across a flock of goats, each with an ear cut off as an aid to identification, another of Africa's unfeeling acts of cruelty. The pilot also had two large scars, across his cheek, stopping just short of an eye. He had caught a six-foot python and had put it down to enable a friend to photograph it: 'It struck and I wasn't quick enough. I had 13 stitches – its teeth were like razors.'

* * * * * * *

The day of my departure north with Alistair was hot and cloudless. Unusually there were at least 30 fish eagles flying, calling and fishing together, just off shore. The Italian owner claimed that the wind and the current had pushed all the fish into one place. Then as the heat increased the eagles thermalled upwards, like vultures.

The journey north was like re-entering the world of Livingstone. Soon we hit dirt roads. It was the Africa of an earlier age; there was dust, forest, fishing villages and always the lake, with clouds of lake flies rising from it like smoke.

That evening as night fell Alistair was sweating and looked ill. We stopped at a lakeside hotel. Once the staff had emerged from the bar, Alistair went straight to his room. It was a magnificent African night; crickets and cicadas chirring, and moonlight reflecting in the 'lake of stars'.

By morning Alistair had recovered and we drove inland, climbing steadily. We climbed into forest where rose-coloured proteas grew and vervet monkeys moved along arboreal highways. The dirt road went higher, trees grew fewer, until we found ourselves in rolling grassland, almost downland. Where rocks broke the surface the wildflowers and plants were so rich it was like passing through a giant rock garden. Simply driving at dusk we saw a cerval cat, reed buck, eland, duicker, zebra, a blue monkey, klipspringer, a roan antelope and a leopard.

We stayed in a visitors camp among pine trees, in a log cabin complete with open fire and an African to cook and clean.

Nyika is an astonishing place: a vast plateau of high open land with an average altitude of about 7,000 feet. To be seeing its almost deserted beauty, in the comparative comfort of an old Land Rover, made a complete contrast to the epic journey made by Laurens van der Post 35 years before and described in his memorable book *Venture to the Interior*.

The abundant wildflowers would have given the most ignorant traveller an interest in botany, as would the few areas of ancient aboriginal forest. There were birds and butterflies, and in three days I saw three mature leopards. One day, we crossed briefly over the unmarked border to Zambia, to get morning coffee at a Guest House; boards were over the windows and the doors were locked. Zambian lethargy had spread even as far as its remote Nyika border.

The Plateau was a place that demanded time, for contemplation as well as observation, but Alistair, now fully recovered, was anxious to return to the Lake to get to Livingstonia. From the edge of Nyika the vast views covered hundreds of miles – across land and lake and into Mozambique. One high point fell away vertically to a huge virgin valley, of rocks, flowers and bush: 'Do you know,' Alistair mused, 'that is one of the few areas of Malawi without people. It is like a lost world and only last year a hitherto unknown herd of elephants was found down there.'

The only depressing thing about Nyika was Bill, in the next log cabin; he was on a last pilgrimage to the place he loved most. He was leaving Africa for good, after a friend had been given a week to leave the country for some minor misdemeanour. He was a sad, disillusioned man: 'I never thought I would get like this. I came here loving Africa. Now I never want to see another black face making a decision again. Africa is finished. In 50 years time it will all be over for the national parks; conservation in Africa is only saving Africa from the Africans.

'Even this place is doomed. When Dr Banda dies Malawi will go like all the rest – it will go backwards. Even now, without him decisions are never taken and nothing is done. They take, but never give anything back. If it wasn't for the British there would still be slavery here.'

'What about the influence of the local Christians?' I asked.

'The Africans only have a thin veneer of Christianity – at their first encounter with the Devil they will dip their hands in the till or take another wife; but they see nothing wrong and remain good Christians. And then there is the way they treat animals – it's disgusting; we have a saying here – if you leave Malawi, don't give your dog to an American or a Malawian.'

'Why not?'

'Because if you give it to an American, he will give it to a Malawian. They don't feed them; they mistreat them – it's pathetic. But, I've had enough – my wife can't leave fast enough either – she even thinks Nyika has a bad feeling; Africa has won.'

* * * * * * *

As we descended into the heat Alistair again began to sweat. By the time we had hit the lakeside he had asked me to drive. The light of the lake was like a painting – bright and dark – misty and clear – mountains and water. 'I need shade,' he moaned, holding his head in his hands. He grew worse, and soon he was delirious with fever: 'Dear God, I don't want to die.' It was the first time I had seen anybody delirious except in party political broadcasts.

At the top of the 24 hairpin bends to Livingstonia, the view was spectacular; Alistair gave only the occasional groan. I wondered about cerebral malaria. There were bungalows with tin roofs and we were directed to the old manse, where I helped Alistair to a bed.

Livingstonia is still a mission, supported by the Church of Scotland, and I was quickly directed to a clinic, for the under-fives, to find a nurse. It was full of mothers and babies and little sisters with even smaller sisters on their backs. It reminded me of Zaire with the smell of Africa and Africans, and a black assistant giving tablets for malaria and anaemia; both were serious scourges, causing the local people to trudge up the steep escarpment from the lake-shore, because of their need. Miss McKeown was looking at the more serious cases; she was a small, pale Scottish nurse from Fife. She smiled, and said she would get to the Old Manse as soon as possible. She was maintaining Scotland's long links with the people of Malawi.

The village was quiet and peaceful. I walked to the church; it was simple, holy and unfinished. Inside there were beams, pews and an atmosphere of holiness, and there, facing the light above the entrance, was a beautiful stained-glass window of David Livingstone. He was holding out his hand. Again I was astonished – to find such a building and window in such a remote place.

An American joined me. He too had walked up the steep escarpment from the lake, where he was working on a boat carrying out a geological survey, looking for oil: 'If we find any there will be trouble. Most of the lake is owned by Malawi, but there are some sections claimed by everybody – Malawi, Tanzania and Mozambique.' Despite being in one of the most far-flung reaches of Africa, he was worried by the problems of the world: 'It's terrible – have you heard the news. America has bombed Libya – it will have a terrible affect on world opinion.'

'World opinion' has always seemed an exaggerated force to me. Malawi's Third World opinion did not seem too concerned what the USA and Libya were getting up to. The bombing incident was dealt with in a single sentence towards the end of the news. Priority items concerned 'the Party'; Dutch aid to Mozambique; cycle racing; and briefly, the bombing.

* * * * * * *

The drugs pumped into Alistair by Nurse McKeown seemed to work, and when she checked him in the morning he had almost recovered. Despite appearances, however, it was thought wise for us to begin the two-day drive back to Blantyre straight away, in case of problems. As we left we stopped at the mission's graveyard, among the patches of maize; there we saw the price the early missionaries had paid for their calling. The names on the stones were mainly Scottish – Fraser, Finlayson and McGregor; several had been cut off in their primes through fever and one stone simply read 'Jesus called a little child unto him'.

For the rest of the day Alistair was fine, and by the afternoon, he was driving again. At a small village a Kamikaze chicken ran under our wheels: 'I daren't stop,' he said, 'if I do, then that will be the most valuable fowl ever to have been hatched in Malawi. I stopped once, never again – it was a two hour haggle before I got away.' It was there too that I first noticed the dogs – a puppy, with every rib clearly showing and an older dog that was so emaciated it could hardly walk.

Within minutes of leaving a lakeside hotel in the morning, Alistair started sweating again. I drove fast, as he seemed even worse: 'Oh dear God – get me to a doctor,' he groaned. At Salima I stopped at the small local hospital; it was seething with people – whole families, inside and out – in the beds and under. 'Get me away from here – I need medicine and white people.' The hotel had no quinine and so I made for Club Makokola again, with my foot on the floorboards. It was with relief that I hit tar and Alistair groaned at the jolt. I remembered the words of wisdom once told to me by a member of a mountain rescue team: 'If they groan they are all right – it's when they make no noise you want to worry.' The French doctor and his wife were still at the Club, and Alistair was again filled with drugs. He was topped up again for the final leg to Blantyre, and as soon as we arrived his wife summoned the doctor – it turned out to be a quinine-resistant strain of malaria – fortunately he recovered.

* * * * * * *

Despite my arrival at Blantyre being both premature and unexpected, I was pleased to see the old capital. With the use of Alistair's Land Rover I drove down to the great block of Mulanje, made famous in *Venture to the Interior*. Then along roads littered with sugar-cane debris, I followed the spectacular Shire valley, another area celebrated in the story of Livingstone and his opposition to the slave trade. On to Lengwe National Park where I encountered the beautiful nyala antelope. But at Lengwe I saw something far more important than antelope, for it was the first time in all my trips to Africa, that I had seen a family of Africans in a car – a husband, wife and two children – watching wildlife. I had seen Indians in the National Parks of India, but they were the first

African 'tourists' I had met, complete with binoculars. It was important; for without the long-term development of a genuine African interest in conservation for its own sake, the spectacular wildlife and landscapes of Africa are doomed.

* * * * * * *

Blantyre still had an old colonial feeling, with its verandahs and corrugated-iron roofs. Ryall's Hotel provided a good old-fashioned English breakfast, and in the town centre there was even a Regency Tea Room, complete with chocolate eclairs and fresh cream teas. There was an old mission too, inevitably started by Scots. Although now called the Church of Central Africa Presbyterian, it was still receiving much help from the Church of Scotland to run its schools, workshops and church.

The Church of St Michael and all Angels was another astonishing building – it was like a mixture of mosque, Scottish castle and Abbey shrunk into one jumbled building. It was built by the Reverend David Clement Scott between 1888-1891. Simply looking at it, it was clear that neither he, nor his African helpers, had received any training in architecture or construction. They had made their own bricks – 81 varieties of them, and the Reverend Scott's architectural philosophy was summed up by his most famous observation: 'Symmetry means poverty of ideas.'

I wanted to continue in Malawi, but thought it wise not to overstay my 13 days, promising myself another visit, before completing this book. Whereas Zambia had left me with feelings of despair and contempt – Malawi had lived up to its own advertising slogan – it really was 'the warm heart of Africa.'

* * * * * * *

Back in Britain's summer, 'Live Aid' was still in full swing and pop stars and 'personalities' were tripping over themselves to demonstrate their public generosity and saintliness. There were even suggestions that pop-culture's leading light, Bob Geldof, should be nominated for the Nobel Peace Prize. His achievements had been enormous, but I thought of the nuns in Zimbabwe, and of Nurse McKeown working above Lake Malawi; they were not giving money but their lives to Africa, with no public recognition.

14. The New King

In Malawi there appeared to be no natural successor to Dr Banda, and with advancing years it was apparently a subject that the old man was not keen to discuss. Swaziland was slightly different, for when the King, Sobhuza 2nd, died in 1982, after a reign of 61 years, he left 100 wives, and a huge array of children – estimates varying between 400 and 600.

After the old king's demise various intrigues occurred until Queen Ntombi became the 'Queen Regent'; she was also known as 'Indlovukazi', or the 'Great She-Elephant'. It was her son who was chosen to become the new King and whose coronation, or Swazi equivalent, was planned for 25th April 1986. The ceremony would be quite a shock to Crown Prince Makhosetive, for he was not a diplomat, or a member of Swaziland's complex system of traditional government. He was a 17-year-old schoolboy, studying for his O-Level examinations at Sherborne School, Dorest, one of Britain's better public schools.

Not only would the Prince become a King, but he would also be expected to take a wife. 'Would he be expected to take as many wives as his father?' I asked, 'after all Sherborne taught moderation in all things, including wives.' A European who had made Swaziland his home had no doubt of the answer: 'If he doesn't take a new wife every year he will be out on his ear. He'll be expected to keep the birth rate rocketing.'

Like the rest of Africa Swaziland's rising population was frightening, especially as the country already depended on South Africa for much of its food. In 1900 there were just 50,000 Swazis. By 1980 the population had risen to 600,000. The projected figure for the year 2,000 was 1,200,000, and by 2,025 was expected to be 3,000,000. For Swaziland it could create a crisis of hunger, overcrowding and pollution. When it is realised that Swaziland is typical of virtually the whole of Africa it becomes frightening, and many agriculturalists and ecologists expect the year 2,020 to be the new Doomsday.

The attitude of the Swazis was summed up for me by Finneus, an articulate and educated member of the Tourism Department. He had four children and was about to take another wife: 'My father he keeps telling me I am slow. My younger brothers have taken more wives already.' But at the same time he was convinced that family planning was being a great success: 'Why some people are now only taking one wife and having seven children.'

I arrived in Swaziland to meet Finneus a few days before the coronation ceremony was due to take place. The country is bounded on three sides by South Africa, with Mozambique on the East. It was given its independence by Britain in 1968. As it is the traditional home of the Swazis, the South Africans claim it was Southern Africa's first 'homeland'. Many Afrikaners defend their present homeland policies by saying: 'Well Britain did it with Swaziland and it was all right then.'

It is a small mountain kingdom – Swaziland covers just 6,704 square miles, slightly smaller than Wales. It was rather like entering a hot Wales, with mountains, wide valleys, clear mountain streams, and something I have seldom seen in Wales, a heat haze.

To early travellers it would have seemed that the natives were restless, for already Swazis in traditional dress, or more accurately 'undress', were making for the royal kraal. There were men in skins, beads and feathers, carrying shields and sticks, some walking, others crammed into vans and lorries, and even a few driving Mercedes. One old man with his impala skin loin cloth flapping was walking with the help of a strong staff – his highly polished shoes were hanging around his neck, to keep them clean for the big day.

* * * * * * *

The Swazi Inn gave old colonial style comfort, including black and white television. The early evening news was read by a half-naked gentleman in traditional dress, while the 9.30 news was astonishing. It was ITN's News from London, a week late – complete with maps of Britain, unemployment figures and interviews with little known politicians and union leaders. What the local Swazis made of it I could not guess.

I asked Finneus about the strange News broadcast: 'Oh yes. It was taken off once. There were so many complaints they put it back again.' The main stories in the local newspaper were also a surprise. Various Swazi football teams were being criticised for relying on 'muti' instead of playing to win by their own efforts, and there was a story of someone missing – believed to be a victim of witchcraft. Apparently witchcraft was still rife in the kingdom, and to be a success, various organs had to be removed from a still living victim.

Finneus was supposed to show me Swaziland's tourist attractions – he took me to the Malolotja Nature Reserve; it was not unlike a lower, smaller Nyika, yet. Finneus was almost apologetic: 'It has not many animals.'
'But it's got flowers,' I said.
He was not impressed; he seemed to assume that lions and elephants were essential for a national park to be attractive to tourists.
'It has a waterfall,' he informed me.
'Can we see it?'
'Oh no, you would have to walk – Europeans like to ride on safari.'

* * * * * * *

To Finneus, Mlilwane Wildlife Sanctuary was a complete success – it had animals, having been created by a European worried at Swaziland's loss of wildlife through agriculture and hunting. Consequently he was trying to re-introduce a wide variety of the country's indigenous animals. Midway through the afternoon the visit was made worthwhile for Finneus – cow-nuts were sprinkled at the edge of a pool and three semi-tame hippos came out of the water to feed. One, Winnie, had been born at London Zoo, and transported to Africa by South African Airways.

A 'free day' followed, as Finneus had to prepare for the expected rush of foreign journalists. I was glad, it meant that I could return to the Malolotja reserve, to do what Finneus had been most anxious not to do – walk. It was a large area of deep valleys, rolling grassland and highland, with waterfalls and mountain streams. It was like a vast wild garden containing a host of wildflowers with common names such as wild sorrel, doll's powder puff, morning glory, purple pea and tumbleweed. There were several varieties of orchid and wild gladioli too, making it a botanist's paradise. The view of the falls was worth the walk: the river narrowed into a series of falls and shoots until it finally plunged spectacularly over 300 feet into a forested gorge.

Upstream another gorge with large pools had one of the last nesting sites of the bald ibis – it was good to see the large dark bird with a bright red bill and bald head. I swam in the river to cool off before the climb back; to me it was a place of peace, tranquillity and beauty, in its way just as attractive as many of the larger and better-known national parks of Africa.

* * * * * * *

For the arrival of the Press I moved to the other side of Mbabane, to the Ezulwini Sun, a more modern hotel geared to the needs of Swaziland's most numerous tourists – those looking for casinos, swimming pools, bars, and women. Many of the pleasure seekers were Afrikaners, denied such dubious delights in the Transvaal and the Orange Free State.

The journalists were divided in two main groups – those who were enjoying the hospitality of Swaziland's tourist department and who wined and dined well, before looking for 'stories'; and those visiting the coronation at the expense of their newspapers; who scurried about trying to produce 'scoops', to justify their expenses, regardless of whether there was anything of substance to write about. Consequently 'stories were filed' and readers in Britain were confronted by a number of totally fabricated accounts; some concerned the Coronation ceremony itself, and others were about Princess Michael of Kent who, with her husband, was representing the Queen. The philosophy seemed to be, 'if you can't get a story, make it up, phone it in and I'll see you at the bar.'

I was with a small group enjoying a 'freebie' – two representing the 'diary' columns of competing tabloids; a feature writer from a 'heavy' daily and another from a news agency. On their first night their main aim seemed to be to find the seediest part of Mbabane.

They found what they wanted. One of the diarists tried to take a coloured girl back to the hotel with him, only to be refused entry at the door. Back home, Roland would probably have referred to the pastime by its slang name of 'golly dipping', as he wrote about the misjudgements, misfortunes and improprieties of others – all for the edification of his readers. Yet in Mbabane he seemed quite proud of

The New King

his achievement.

* * * * * * *

The evening before the big event Swazis were streaming into town in their traditional dress. Markets were busy selling food to the travellers, and feeding and sleeping centres had been set up. There was a feeling of excitement and expectancy. On an area of open grass spontaneous dancing broke out with the throbbing rhythms of drums and stamping feet vibrating the air. Returning to the hotel I crossed the river – naked men and women were washing in the river; some of the men appeared to be wearing bright yellow cod-pieces, or had even painted their private parts. It seemed rather an exotic fashion for a coronation.

* * * * * * *

The actual details of the Coronation ceremony were still a mystery. Some said the ceremony took place on the Friday; others knew it took place on the Saturday. In the first instance not even the Swazis had known, requiring them to call in an 'expert' from London.

The news-hounds were in a quandry; a rumour had been started that both President Botha and the ANC leader Oliver Tambo had been invited, and were expected to meet at the airport; but that might mean the 'scoop-seekers' would miss the coronation itself. They were totally uninterested in the other airport drama, in which a delegation from Kenya landed. As soon as they were told of the impending arrival of President Botha, they reboarded their plane and flew back to Nairobi. It seemed to be a rather expensive performance, entirely for home consumption, as the Kenyans had known of the South African invitation before setting out for Swaziland. However there had been student riots in Nairobi and so a great 'moral gesture' was made, in order to divert attention away from the problems at home.

The place where the new king was to be presented to his people was curious. Some officials described it as the Royal Kraal, others as the Royal Cattle Byre. Whatever it was, it was surrounded by thousands of visitors, including a regiment of chanting Zulus with shields and 'knobkerries'. The Swazis just stared and said 'Zulus', in a mixture of admiration and apprehension. Wearing leopard skins and lion skins they looked formidable, and were led by a medicine man; their rhythms were almost intoxicating and I felt sorry for those unfortunate men at Rorke's Drift in 1879.

By the time the new king was presented to his people inside the kraal it was packed with Swazi warriors, wizened old medicine men, bare-breasted maidens and elderly matrons, all obliterating the view from the assembled world dignitaries. The members of the Press did not help either, as they ignored all instructions and wandered at will, in large numbers, to get their 'piccies' and 'stories.' It was almost as if they regarded the Coronation as an event put on especially for them.

The VIP's were a contrasting collection – the Prince and Princess Michael of Kent; P.W.Botha, the President of South Africa; Samora Machel, the President of Mozambique; President Kaunda; Paramount Chief Nkosi Yamakosi Ngomane 3rd of Malawi; King Zwelithimi of Kwazulu; and Maureen Reagan (President Reagan's daughter) who from her dress and ebullience seemed to be representing Hollywood.

As the dignitaries climbed out of their limousines and walked to the kraal, the greatest cheer and ululations were reserved for Samora Machel, who seemed to have both charisma and a large popular support. The second loudest cheer went up for President Botha.

When the king appeared – completely hidden from the main guests – he was wearing a leopard-skin loin cloth, and feathers in his hair. The regiments of warriors danced, women ululated, and old men watched with pride and admiration. The new King actually looked like a shy young schoolboy having time off from his homework. The scene was watched too, by an old black man in a trilby, plus-fours and gaiters. He sported a small grey moustache, and apart from his colour he looked like a retired British major from Worthing.

There were veterans of the King's African Rifles, proudly wearing their tattered old uniforms and World War Two medals, won in the desert campaign and Italy. One old man, resplendent in kilt and sporran (the Monroe tartan), claimed that his father had been a Scot. Amid all the noise and celebration, a cattle lorry, with several cattle on board was driven to the rear of the kraal. Ritual killings were apparently next on the schedule.

The New King

* * * * * * *

The following day the proceedings moved to the national stadium, where 60,000 people were packed and perched around the arena to greet their King. Even the dignitaries could see at last; it was amusing, with President Botha seated next to Kenneth Kaunda, and an over made-up Mrs Botha, looking rather like European mutton done up as lamb, seated next to the King of Zululand – a wild looking, half-naked gentleman adorned with skins.

This time the journalists were penned in and warned of their conduct – with just a few given opportunities for photographs and told to pool them with their colleagues; such a plan was not popular in the world of dog eat dog. It was the British journalists who seemed to object most: 'What a way to organise an event'; 'Don't they know who we are?'; 'You must know we came here to publicise your country for your own benefit'; 'We don't get treated like this in England'; and best of all: 'You realise we can do a lot of harm to your country if you don't co-operate.' An Australian was not impressed: 'What a whingeing bunch of pommies – don't they make you sick? Do you know how we tell when a plane load of poms has landed in Australia? – The plane keeps whining even after the engines have stopped.'

The celebrations were an enjoyable but unusual mixture of old and new: trooping the colour, as superbly disciplined troops marched to tunes such as the British Grenadier, accompanied by the screams of a white sergeant major; poetry; and massed choirs singing parts of the Messiah, including 'the King shall live for ever'.

The master of ceremonies became impatient, cutting off both a poet and the choir before they had finished their performances. He obviously wanted to see the next item – 3,000 scantily dressed 'maidens' singing and dancing their way into the arena.

Then came old matrons in long robes, including the survivors of the late king's numerous wives, before the thousands of warriors showed their loyalty and respect. They included a handful of American Peace Corps members adorned in animal skins, the ultimate Blixenation. They looked as out of place and absurd as would a group of Swazi warriors morris dancing in Norfolk.

President Kaunda thanked the new king – Mswati 3rd – and wished him well on behalf of the assembled guests. Unfortunately,

the sight of a microphone had a potent effect on Kenneth Kaunda, for his 'thank you' developed into a lecture on racism and leadership. The crowd became restless, and my immediate neighbour, a Swazi who had climbed in to the press enclosure, was not impressed: 'Why doesn't he shut up and sit down.'
It was a spectacular and good humoured occasion – at last a happy story emerging from Africa.

As I was driving back towards Johannesburg across Northern Transvaal, thousands of European swifts were heading north – some, I hoped, flying to an English summer. I thought of the new King and how he would cope returning to Sherborne to continue his studies. How would he answer the questions of his friends: 'What did you do during your holidays Mak?'
'Oh nothing really. I was crowned King, helped to pummel a bull to death with my bare hands and inspected 3,000 naked maidens.'

* * * * * * *

Despite expressing the wish, before his Coronation, to return to England to take his A-Level examinations and go to Sandhurst, the young King did not return to England. Since then, various members of the large Swazi Royal Family have been tried for corruption and treason, and some have been sent to prison.

15. The Last Laager

With all my intended journeys complete, I was still not entirely happy. On television, radio and in the press, it seemed as if South Africa was about to burst into a bush fire of flames and bloodshed. Briefly I had touched down in Johannesburg while visiting Zimbabwe, Malawi and Swaziland – but had the temperature really increased since my earlier visits? I was not sure. After all, the same message had been given by some prophets of doom since the early fifties, The difference being, that now they were accompanied by pictures portraying a country close to revolution. I decided that I had just one more journey to make, in case circumstances in South Africa had moved on.

I wanted simply to gauge the mood of the country, to see if the images of riot, oppression and impending civil war, daily beamed into my house on television and radio, were correct. I also wanted to see more of South Africa's wildlife, for in all the arguments about government, power and people, the surviving remnants of original South Africa – with longer roots than the Europeans, Zulus or Xhosas – rarely received any consideration.

* * * * * * *

On landing, after the latest BBC news bulletin had shown riots, smoke and stones, accompanied by the monotone incantations of impending disaster, I wondered if I had arrived in the right country. I had – it was the Jan Smuts International Airport, complete with polite airport officials and a few policemen, white and black, some of them armed.

Driving to Pretoria I was immediately struck by another baffling phenomenon. Again, before leaving for South Africa I had become used to hearing assorted pundits and experts in the British media talking about the South African economy being in a state of recession; how the policy of disinvestment by large multinational companies was having an effect; and how all that was needed was economic sanctions – they would be the final push, and white South Africa's resolve would crumble. Instead, what I saw was an economy that appeared to be booming. It is true that the value of the rand had fallen – making a visitor with sterling in his pocket feel wealthy - but there were new roads and houses, for black and white, as well as huge new office blocks and factories, with work still continuing. Blacks and whites were in the streets and on the road, and from the number of new cars, there seemed to be neither a shortage of fuel, nor money.

Lieb met me and took me to his father's home for dinner. He was despondent. He explained in terms of an economist why the 'boom' I had seen was misleading. His position continued to be unusual for an Afrikaner as he still thought economic sanctions were urgent: 'White South Africa can maintain the status quo for the next 50 years if it likes, quite easily. Even sanctions could be resisted – there is enough oil stored down disused mine shafts to last three years already. Why I want sanctions is so that it concentrates the minds of the whites in this country on the real problems and issues. Too many of them still live in a comfortable dream world. They must be brought back to reality, and that is quite simple – the world has changed and the black people must have justice.'

'Does that mean you now believe in one man one vote?' I asked him.

'One man one vote yes – but not in an election like you have in Britain. There has got to be a federal system in South Africa, so that each group and area is not dominated by another – that is the only way for peace and progress. There must be fairness to all nationalities, and the reality is that unless solid guarantees are given, the Afrikaners will never relinquish power.'

Again, I had learnt more in one hour, than from a dozen of the usual 'in depth' analyses in the British media. Lieb was trying to make his own contribution to change: 'We have to start regarding Africans as our equals in all aspects of life, to give them dignity. That is why Jane and myself never refer to Africans as "boys".'

He had a long way to go; a few minutes later his father arrived home: 'Lieb, have you seen the garden boy anywhere?'

I returned to see the Voortrekker Monument. Like the Vatican there was no admittance for those in shorts, bare feet or T-shirts and the 'Stations of the Cross' had been replaced by the story of the Afrikaners' hardships and final victory. Afrikaner Nationalism had ceased to be a movement of self-determination and political hope: it had become a religion.

A queue of school children were waiting to see Paul Kruger's house. 'Where is he buried?' I asked an official.

'Heroes' Acre,' he replied.

The economist's non-existent economic boom seemed to be taking place in the heart of Pretoria itself. There was a huge new, recently completed bank, outside which was a superb group of bronze horses. A large bust of J.G. Strijdom (Prime Minister between 1954-58) had also appeared, while on the pavement of the main street were three beautiful bronze giraffes, almost full size – an astonishing and exceptional work of art. That was another peculiarity – where else in the world would such an attractive and expensive piece of sculpture have been placed on the pavement? In Britain it would have been vandalised almost immediately, with graffiti, and 'yobbos' swinging on the giraffes' tails and necks.

* * * * * * *

Just outside Pretoria is the De Wildt Cheetah Research Centre, which has pioneered the successful breeding of cheetahs in captivity. Finding it was difficult, and even with a navigator I ended up in the homeland of Bophuthatswana – one of South Africa's most absurd fantasies. It is called a 'homeland', but is made up of many fragmented parts.

In a matter of a few hundred yards the First World had become the Third, and although the 'independent' country had no border posts or passport control, it was clear we had travelled into deepest Black Africa: dirt roads, overgrazing, old men sitting under trees; wandering cattle; haphazard farming; traditional huts and shacks with corrugated-iron roofs; wayside stores and Toyota pick-up vans overloaded with people.

The homeland had the usual problems of Black Africa: half the population was under 15; numbers were rising by 3.6 per cent a year and urbanisation was growing at 2.51 per cent a year. For even in the homelands the towns were thought to have streets paved with gold.

While in Pretoria, Lieb had introduced me to an agriculturalist who did not share the political worries of his compatriots: 'The biggest threat to South Africa is food shortages. If you take South Africa as a whole, only 12 per cent is suitable for arable agriculture, and of this, only 10 per cent can be regarded as good. Ignore what you are told in England – 50 per cent of the good land is in the homelands. If farmed properly it could produce 25 per cent of South Africa's total agricultural production. At the moment it is producing less than 5 per cent – partly because of African traditions. Then they own 40 per cent of South Africa's cattle – but contribute only 3.5 per cent of the beef market. I can't see things changing.' Driving through Bophuthatswana, I could see why he was so worried.

We crossed back into South Africa, and at last found the Research Centre. It was run by Ann Van Dyke, who had become interested in cheetahs after being given two cubs by her husband several years before. Because she had no permit, the animals were confiscated by the authorities. But by that time it was too late – Ann had fallen in love with cheetahs. She and her husband complied with the various pieces of red-tape, the cubs were returned and her cheetah work started. In the beginning, her efforts were subsidised by her husband's poultry farm, but she was so successful that her projects multiplied and the centre became linked with Pretoria's Zoo.

Initially she wanted to breed cheetahs, as she believed them to be an endangered species. Now, not only have some of her captive-bred animals been released into the wild, but she also breeds animals for zoos all over the world, so taking some of the pressure away from the wild stock. Her animals are wanted in South Africa too, and at the time of my visit Natal required 20 for restocking.

There were 65 cheetahs at the centre, in large enclosures, some with cubs; several were quite tame and could be stroked like large domestic cats. These days many people, not fully aware of the numerous environmental threats to wildlife, condemn the keeping of captive animals. Yet in the future, animals in captivity, whether in zoos or breeding centres, will be vital to the survival of many species, and already, throughout the world, once threatened animals have been successfully returned to the wild.

After her success with cheetahs Ann had expanded to include several more of South Africa's threatened wildlife, including some of the most maligned, which she claimed did not deserve their bad reputations. She had breeding enclosures for wild dogs, caracals, brown hyenas and the aardwolf. She had just started a new project for the attractive little suni antelope and hoped to move on to ground-hornbills in the near future.

She had one more successful breeding programme operating, involving the Cape vulture – an attractive bird, for a vulture, and also one of the most threatened. The problem was simple: as a carrion eater there was not enough carrion available to the vultures, either from wild animals or domestic stock. Bone fragments are also important to the birds, as in natural surroundings pieces of bone would be picked up, especially where hyenas had fed. Because of this, young wild Cape vultures often suffered from acute calcium deficiency, which even prevented their wings from developing properly, leaving them grounded.

At De Wildt, a breeding cliff had been created, bone chippings were fed as a normal part of the diet, and a vulture restaurant had been started, which was attracting wild vultures. Farmers phoned in when one of their stock died, and the body was taken to a rocky area and left for the birds, complete with bone chippings to ensure a complete diet. With young, healthy vultures already flourishing, it was highly likely that the Cheetah Centre could have another success.

I enjoyed meeting Ann Van Dyke – for hers was a positive, encouraging story – of the type not normally associated with South Africa. It was also reassuring to find someone who believed that others had a right to life, in addition to Man.

* * * * * * *

Like Pretoria, Johannesburg also appeared to be in a state of economic boom, and I was put up at a huge new hotel, complete with a shopping complex on several levels. The Sandton Sun was like a futuristic nightmare from George Orwell's 1984; I assumed it had won numerous architectural awards, for within an hour of my stay it had given me a headache. On one side of the huge entrance hall was a great slab of marble with water falling from it; while on the other, wall lifts, like space modules of glass, whisked guests from floor to floor. It was the great impersonal dream, of glass and glitter, of affluent, homogenised twentieth-century man. It was another monument – to wealth, cash-flow and status. I wondered how a small boy plucked from a kraal in Zululand would cope with such a place; it was certainly too much for a middle-aged farmer's son from rural Cambridgeshire.

When Peter McIlroy picked me up, it was like being released from prison. He was still in good spirits: 'Trouble? What trouble? I'll tell you what Robin, there have been changes – job reservation, Pass Laws, all those have gone and if you fall in love with another race you can marry them. To the Afrikaners they were big deals – but all the West did was criticise – "not enough" – "too little, too late", and all that sort of stuff. If they had helped and encouraged it would have worked, and they would have gone further. People abroad just don't understand the Afrikaner, and they don't want to. It's almost as if they want bloodshed here – you know, they've been talking about it so long, they want to make it happen. But I still feel totally secure. I've got guns at home like I've always had – but I never carry one around with me. I never feel threatened. It's the same with my friends. I'm no admirer of the Afrikaners or the system, but in Britain you are fed a lot of rubbish about this place.'

'There's another thing you will notice – people are openly discussing all the options and you even hear jokes about the government – that wouldn't have happened a few years ago. For instance P. W. Botha was walking down the street the other day with a hen under his arm, when a bloke approached:"Hey, what are you doing with a pig under your arm?"

"It's not a pig, it's a hen," the State President replied.

"I wasn't talking to you," the man said, "I was talking to the hen."

That was told to me by a member of the National Party. Yet a few years ago the President was treated like God – they've at last discovered he's mortal.'

* * * * * * *

For some reason one of the officials at the Tourist Board seemed very ill at ease with women. I asked one of his colleagues if it was my imagination. I was amazed at the answer: 'I don't know – all I can tell you is that he's happily married to someone of the same gender.' I had thought by this time that there was nothing left in Africa to surprise me; but it did. I simply had not expected to find this particular sexual deviation in white South Africa. Because of my surprise I was shown a whole new sub-culture, hidden beneath the surface of white orthodoxy. There were street markets and 'arty-crafty' shops in which hippies, Hell's Angels and Progressive Party voters mixed in a loose association, together with Africans, Asians and coloureds. At one market there was even an African in dark glasses, platform shoes and a kilt – I wondered how he was classified, racially.

Another market could almost have been taken for London's Portobello Road, with stalls of second-hand books, home-made jewellery, cheap clothing, records, and assorted old household junk, given value through alternative fashion. Spontaneous singing and dancing broke out with guitars, tambourine and a harmonica. Black and white were dancing while joss sticks smouldered. Was this really South Africa?

* * * * * * *

At Cape Town, storm force winds were blowing – actually sweeping an elderly white woman from her feet. She began crawling along the pavement until a passer-by went to her aid. The east wind, known as the 'Cape Doctor', is said to blow all the dirt and diseases out of Cape Town; consequently some people actually welcome the wind. High cirrus clouds stretched over the vast South Atlantic sky; it signified, so a local informed me, that the Cape Doctor would be visiting for several days.

Cape Town itself seemed normal and relaxed. The building boom had reached the extreme south too, with great new housing estates for coloureds and Africans. From a hilltop once loved by Cecil Rhodes, his bust looked out approvingly. It was an impressive monument, set in pine trees and designed by Francis Masey and Sir Herbert Baker. The great man gazed out from a building like an imitation Greek temple, below which were steps with four large bronze lions on each side. At the bottom, was that man again – the original naked gentleman on his horse – 'Physical Energy', looking north. This time he was in his original position, and not just a pigeon perch hidden from view. Beneath the bust were words of Rudyard Kipling on the death of Rhodes: 'The immense and brooding spirit still shall quicken and control. Living he was the land and dead his soul shall be her soul.' Rhodes lived from 1853 to 1902; it seems remarkable that a man whose life was so short should have aroused such admiration and pride, as well as hatred and loathing.

Near the memorial two footprints had been drawn on the tarmac. Inside one was written: 'March to Freedom', and in the other 'Stamp out Apartheid'. There were political posters too, of red blood, a skull and a helmet, with the words: 'Apartheid Emergency – Conscripted to Kill – End Conscription Campaign.' Not for the first time in South Africa, I was amazed at the contradictions, for although portrayed as a 'police state' in the West, with no freedom of expression, many articles and letters in the South African press expressed the same views as the graffiti. Yet in black Africa I saw and read no words of opposition, either as graffiti or in the newspapers.

* * * * * *

When I visited the Cape of Good Hope Nature Reserve, the wind was still blowing hard. The previous day three people had been killed by falling objects, another fact missed by the British Press. Three with sprained ankles from riots would have been a major news story. Approaching the reserve, workmen were having to clear the roads of drifting sand – a job that always accompanied the 'Cape Doctor'.

A wildlife ranger showed me around the nature reserve – a wasteland of plants, tortoises and wind. The area is especially famous for its aloes, orchids and heathers. Some of the aloes had developed strange and specialist features, and one had evolved to be pollinated by rodents. In a small white bungalow around which the sand and surf blew horizontally, English bird watchers were studying the birds of the area. As we spoke, immature sandwich terns were flying over the boiling surf – miles away from the likely English colonies of their beginning. British arctic and common terns had all been recovered from the area, as well as storm petrels – a remarkable journey for those almost fragile wanderers of the open seas.

Cape Point was a maelstrom of wind and tossing ocean – a vast area where the Atlantic and Indian Oceans meet. Cormorants hurtled by, with wings and feet out to act as air-brakes, and one was buffeted into a somersault and for several yards was travelling upside-down. High up on the rocks at such a place I could not help but think of those early European explorers and settlers again;

simply reaching the Cape and surviving the physical elements seemed remarkable in itself.

Driving back to Cape Town along the coastal road great sheets of water were being whipped up from the sea and funnels of white spray, like liquid dust devils, were being sucked two and three hundred feet into the air. It was one of the most spectacular sea-scapes I had ever seen.

* * * * * * *

North of Cape Town was one of South Africa's newest and most interesting Nature Reserves, taking in Langebaan Lagoon, ten miles long and one and a half miles wide, one of the most important wetland areas in southern Africa for birds, both local and wintering from the northern hemisphere. I had been promised a boat trip. Unfortunately the sea was too rough for the wildlife warden's own boat, but fortunately the South African navy had a rescue boat about to go on a training trip, and so we hitched a lift. It had a top speed of 35-40 knots, and with its wooden hull, it was similar to an old Motor Torpedo Boat. It cut through the heavy seas with ease and it was possible to feel the power of its engines. A small island was covered with cormorants and their guano – an old-fashioned local cure for clearing a 'hangover' was to sniff guano. As we proceeded I wondered whether I would need a cure for sea-sickness. The reason for the trip was revealed on a larger island – a close-up view of jackass penguins – at last.

The following day there were still more jackass penguins, at very close quarters, on Marcus Island, linked to the mainland by a causeway. The island was run by the Percy FitzPatrick Institute – named after the author of the South African animal classic *Jock of the Bushveld*. Some penguins were swimming, others were in regimental order, and a few were incubating eggs. When they called, they sounded just like donkeys braying. In addition there were gulls, turnstones and cormorants – some with red eyes, and others with green. The oystercatchers sounded just like those on the shores of Britain, but they were jet-black, apart from their red eyes, legs and beak.

* * * * * * *

Although seeing the penguins had fulfilled a long-held ambition, a visit to the South African National Federation for the Conservation of Coastal Birds – SANCCOB – on the outskirts of Cape Town was both depressing and reassuring. Because of the treacherous waters around the Cape, there are numerous shipping accidents, causing oil spills and leaks, which in turn lead to many oiling incidents with gannets and penguins.

The centre is run by an English woman, married to an Afrikaner, who has managed to retain her Chelsea accent after years of living in South Africa. She was wearing oilskins and bandages, as her hands are frequently cut by the penguins' powerful beaks. Every day the cleaned birds have to be fed with pilchards and vitamin tablets, and clean water has to be put in their pools. It is hard dedicated work, and when an oil spill occurs she and her volunteers sacrifice day and night to clean the birds with detergent. The penguins then have to be kept until their feathers have regained their natural waterproofing.

In 1983 SANCCOB dealt with 600 penguins following an incident involving a Spanish super tanker, and then 800 when a Greek cargoe ship ran aground. The worst case was off Langebaan, when a tanker split in two and 1,400 gannets dived into the oil, thinking it was fish. She gets help from the Sea Fisheries Department, and the Air Force to get the oiled birds, and the Prison Department helps in the release by taking the restored birds to the safety and isolation of Robben Island. It was strange to hear of actual releases on Robben Island. The success rate was between 60 and 90 per cent. All the treated birds are ringed; one bird cleaned and returned to the wild in 1971, was taken in again for re-cleaning in 1985.

She was not too interested in politics: 'You know what they call Cape Town? The Insular Peninsula. All I know is that we don't want sanctions. Not for ourselves, but we work entirely from voluntary donations. If sanctions come and money gets tight – then our money will be the first to suffer – that's wrong – the penguins will be the first to suffer.'

One of the helpers was a young Welsh scientist – he described himself as a 'bomb-maker' – he worked at the nearby 'top-secret' South African atomic plant.

'Bomb-maker,' I asked, 'what bombs – have you got nuclear bombs?'

'All I can say is that nuclear bombs are old hat. We've moved on since then.'

'Moved on – what do you mean?'

'Well we haven't got it yet – but it's not far away – the neutron bomb.'

He sounded sincere, but I did not know whether or not to believe him. South Africa with the neutron bomb would certainly give many people food for thought.

Although embargoes on weapons and technology had been operating against South Africa for years, from general conversation it seemed clear that the links between South Africa, Israel, Taiwan and South Korea – the world's outcasts, or near outcasts – were very close. It was also clear that if modern equipment was obtained by one, whether for warfare or industry, the technology involved would also get to the others. With South Africa's reserves of gold, diamonds, coal and iron ore, payment was simple. Indeed, while travelling out of Langebaan Lagoon to see the penguins, our boat had passed a huge ore carrier from Taiwan being filled with iron ore.

* * * * * * *

It was on my way out of Cape Town that I saw my only trouble. The dual carriageway passing the airport was busy, but a troop carrier had stopped on the central reservation to watch small boys from the nearby township throwing stones at cars.

A businessman returning to Johannesburg was not worried: 'Oh that's no problem. But notice how it's the older ones sheltering behind the youngsters. If you've been to South Africa before you will have noticed something – reports of the "totsis" have disappeared. They call themselves "comrades" now. The ANC have just given the hooligans another outlet. Half the trouble in the townships has been caused by hooligans – the political agitators are just giving them the opportunity to throw their weight about.' He then began to tell jokes about the 'troubles', and not for the first time I wondered about the place of humour in life, for 'sick jokes' often accompany problems and tragedy, as if to lessen the impact of the unacceptable: 'Hey you know these Soweto necklaces – these rubber tyres they set on fire around the necks of "sell-outs" – well how many Soweto necklaces can you make out of one car tyre? 365 if it's a Goodyear!'

* * * * * * *

If the large cities did not seem in a state of imminent revolution, neither did the wilderness. I drove from the small town of Uppington, on the Orange River, through almost deserted semi-desert to the Kalahari Gemsbok National Park, which shares boundaries with Botswana and Namibia. In such a remote place there were no soldiers, no warnings of land-mines in dirt roads, and the few ranches had no security fences. Everything seemed at peace, even lethargic in the heat. In 220 miles I passed just two lorries, two pick-up trucks, a car, a mule cart and a man on a bike.

Without a doubt the Kalahari Gemsbok Park was one of the highlights of all my journeys. It covers a huge area – 2 million acres in South Africa, with another eight million acres in Botswana. It is the true Kalahari desert of dunes, sun-bleached grasses, pans and dust. Once it had Bushmen too, but slowly they moved out.

The main entrance camp is at Twee Rivieren [Two Rivers], where the Auob and Nossob meet. Few people have ever seen them with water; they are two winding, sandy river beds that may carry water once every century. I decided to drive a hundred miles north along the sand road to Nossob.

The track wound through ridges of red dunes, white pans and thorn scrub – a thirsty land, relieved only by the occasional artificial water hole. In such a setting it was astonishing to see so much wildlife. Martial eagles, the pale chanting goshawk and the sociable weaver bird with its huge communal nests. Eland, wildebeest and springbok were all quite plentiful too, although there were many carcasses of eland and wildebeeste where weak animals had died of thirst during a local migration.

While watching springbok, as I drove, I let the revs of the car fall too low and stalled in the sand. It was impossible to get out. The front-wheel drive vehicle simply dug itself deeper into the sand. Even with wood and grass under the wheels I could make no headway, so I sat contentedly under a thorn tree for seven hours, sleeping, and watching the life of the desert. I lit a fire and had sausages cooking when rescue finally came. It was the local game ranger, a young, blue-eyed Afrikaner, with his Bushman/Hottentot tracker – Yapi. It was reassuring to find such good organisation at such a far away place. Every day information concerning each vehicle heading north was radioed through, so that all could be accounted for at the end of the day.

As we stood by the fire eating sausages, Jan told a tale: 'You've done better than an American,' he said, 'he totally freaked out about getting stuck in darkest Africa. He wrote his last will and testament, as well as a letter to his mother, and then wandered off into the bush. His footprints showed that he walked close to three lions under a shepherds tree, without noticing them. We found him half-way up a windpump – burnt and dehydrated – he had heard a ram springbok getting fruity and thought he was about to get attacked. He must be the first person in Africa's history to have been terrorised by a springbok.'

* * * * * * *

Jan was enthusiastic about his section of the park and at dawn, until the heat of the day, he took me through miles of wilderness. All we saw was desert and its wildlife – gemsbok, springbok and eland as well as colonies of one of Africa's most attractive small animals, the suricate or meerkat. Suricates are the little people of the desert, colonies of them, like small mongooses, living in holes, and sitting upright to scratch and watch the world go by. Their expressions are almost human, and from their puzzled looks they evidently find human activity difficult to comprehend. It is good to think that after the bomb drops, wearing little bowler hats, the suricates could take over the world from their desert fall-out shelters.

Yapi's eye-sight was totally attuned to the desert; out of sand and grasses he saw a leopard from a range of at least half a mile – a large male moving easily and low, with what to my unfamiliar European eyes seemed to be perfect camouflage.

We were lucky too, for a normally nocturnal honey badger was hunting, with a pale-chanting goshawk in attendance. Honey badgers are rather like large snub-nosed, short-tailed ferrets – renowned for their courage and ferocity when roused. They have been known to put up good rearguard actions against lions, and there are records of them killing animals many times larger than themselves, including a wildebeest and a waterbuck. In such an encounter their method of attack is not very gentlemanly – they go for the scrotum. They have been seen to take on large pythons, quite deliberately, and one was even recorded killing a black mamba in the Kruger National Park.

Another interesting aspect of the honey badger's life is that it is said to follow the honey-guide, because of its liking for honey. As it goes, it is often also followed by the pale-chanting goshawk, for when a honey badger finds a good termites' nest, it digs out the grubs, which it regards as a great delicacy, while the goshawk sets about the excavated termites.

After our good luck we searched for the famous Kalahari lions, without success. What we did see, were more dead animals – their mouths fixed in an exaggerated grin of death, their skin stretched tight, and their eyes sunken. Jan was not dismayed: 'It all works wonderfully – it all makes up a finely tuned balance.' But the balance depended on death – 'finely tuned', inevitable and without feeling.

Back at Twee Riveren, an Afrikaner ranger, who could hardly speak English, found lions, beautiful specimens, dark, sleek and powerful. Two were mating – every 20 minutes for hours on end – some say they do so for two days – quite a feat in itself. They looked at us with disdain and arrogance. Before getting stuck in the sand I had seen much lion spoor, but no lions. Being unable to leave the track in the under-powered car, I had stopped and walked into the bush, looking for lions. I had not seen them; but I wondered if they had seen me. What would I have done if any of these large Kalahari lions had taken an exception to my human presence? Not for the first time in my life I was amazed at my own stupidity.

Before leaving the Kalahari I saw more death. Thirteen jackals picking the bones of a wildebeest – a deserted lion kill. Hyenas too, a group of them under bushes, including a mother and her cub. Again I was struck by their look of ancient evil – alive and well and given sharper focus when the mother shifted an old carcass of hide and bone, dribbling great threads of saliva as she did so.

* * * * * * *

I witnessed the harshness of nature again at the Okavango Swamps in Botswana. I had wanted to break my South African journey into two halves, by going off to Malawi in between. For months I had tried to arrange a proper, official visit, to avoid a repetition of the 'You are a writer'saga. But despite letters, telephone calls and a plea from an official tourist organisation, no approval arrived, and I was advised not to try to get in again.

Okavango was the alternative; it was a revelation – a wildlife oasis of water and islands in an almost lifeless desert. It was a world of lily-pads, kingfishers, papyrus – a haven for hippo, crocodile and otter. There were frogs, large fish and lechwe in the reeds. There were lagoons and channels of clear water, where dragonflies flew and fish eagles called.

In a canoe trip towards a fishing village, a hippo suddenly came at us, its enormous mouth open and a bow-wave of water rushing in front. It stopped, thirty yards short – just as I was going to evacuate and make for the nearest tree. A photographer in front of me – a taxidermist county-girl from Suffolk was actually trembling with fear. Our guide stayed cool, banging his punting pole on the side of the canoe and making a large, slow detour. Once clear he smiled: 'No problem.' I had to disagree.

In addition to water there were large islands and pans, with lechwe, hartebeest and lions – many lions. A large pride rested in the shade overlooking grassland, where many wildebeeste had new calves. One calf stood alone, and the lions watched. It was lost, or its mother had died. Two hours later the calf had moved closer to the lions – the herd had gone and it was entirely alone. I asked if we could leave the grassland and not return.

* * * * * * *

At one of the camps two South African girls had arrived with me. They had travelled on the same plane via the small desert town of Maun, and were two more of those remarkable sub-urban South Africans who lived in a world of hair-lacquer, nail varnish and the cost of servants. One had been so 'freaked-out' by sitting next to a black man she had said: 'Did you see who I sat next to on the plane? It was Oliver Tambo' [leader of the ANC]. The one person it had not been was Oliver Tambo; he had simply been a smartly dressed African businessman or official.

The girls professed to love Okavango, but they seemed to be in a state of constant anxiety – each new noise caused alarm, and they looked as if they were getting no sleep. After two days of their five-day stay they returned to Johannesburg.

The camp manager was just as strange, but in a different way. He was 'Rhodesian' and proud of it. Throughout my stay he would try

to corner me; while at the same time his wife would attempt to interrupt or lead him away: 'Please don't talk to him about Zimbabwe – we don't want to get into any trouble – we must forget it and start a new life.' I pointed out as politely as possible that I was not talking to him, he kept way-laying me. He claimed to have been third in command of the Selous Scouts and he could not accept that Mugabe had won the war: 'The war proper hasn't started,' he told me. 'You know Nkomo is Kaunda's brother-in-law? Well in northern Zambia ZAPU are still in training camps, with new Russian weapons, and in Northern Transvaal there are camps of Muzorewa's auxiliaries. When Renamo win in Mozambique, it's going to be a whole new ball game. If you write about all this in an English newspaper, I'll tell you all you want to know.'
'Come away George – think of something else, it's time to forget.'

* * * * * * *

There were other things to worry about in the Okavango Swamps. It is one of the most important and spectacular wildlife reservoirs in the world, yet there are threats on the horizon. Europeans wanting wealthy clients have started using speedboats, which could destroy the area's peace and character, as well as erode the banks of the waterways and physically injure wildlife. Botswana is also Africa's only genuine democracy, with universal suffrage and a choice of political parties and candidates. Knowing that some herdsmen are casting a covetous eye towards Okavango's water and grazing, some politicians, wanting electoral advantage, are suggesting that cattle be allowed into the swamps, and that some of the water should be used for mining and new industries. Within months of such developments Okavango would die – it too would become part of the Kalahari desert – over-grazed and dead.

* * * * * * *

Durban had no worries about desert or rain – I arrived in a deluge. It had experienced township troubles – but on the surface it seemed quiet. A European safari guide had seen riots and was shocked by them: 'It was mob-rule man – it was the Zulus – they didn't bother about us, they turned on the Asians. My brother is in the army, he saw a little Asian boy, only about two or three, caught by the mob –

he was swung by his feet so that his head was smashed against a wall. He was just dropped – like a discarded doll – quite dead. There is one thing people in the West forget: if the Europeans packed up and went tomorrow, there would be mayhem here – black against black, and black against brown. The British can stay in Northern Ireland to keep the peace – but we are wrong to maintain standards and keep the peace here. You want one man one vote for us – when did you hear anybody in Britain advocating one man one vote for a united Ireland? You've got a federated, divided Ireland – that is the only answer for South Africa in the long term.'

Ian Player, an ex-game ranger, who had long been a voice for a multi-racial South Africa, seemed to agree: 'One man one vote is not the immediate answer, and despite the troubles South Africa is not falling apart. It has too many minerals to fall apart – and everybody wants them, even the Russians. If Russia gets them, then as far as the rest of the world is concerned it will be check-mate.'

'You can't apportion blame for the troubles. All sides have behaved badly – The Nats [President Botha's party] and the troublemakers in the townships. The West too has behaved badly – it seems to be encouraging violence and terrorism, and by so doing it is encouraging a right-wing backlash – we don't want that – that is even more dangerous.

'Chief Buthelezi is a good man and should have been part of the government years ago. The Zulus hate the Boers and the Boers hate the Zulus – but they both realise that they need each other.'

Near to Durban, we called in at a Zulu tracker's kraal; it was genuine black Africa once more. He was directly responsible for maintaining 24 children, both his own and those belonging to various other relatives. Another, who had been a tracker, friend and helper to Ian Player for many years had three wives and 20 children. Again it seemed to me that I had come to South Africa for the wrong reasons, to see the wrong problems. Because of the images portrayed in the English media, I had arrived expecting to find the Afrikaners with their backs to the wall, both entrenched, and surrounded. Consequently I had already named this final chapter 'The Last Laager'. Yet the situation was far different – a successful revolution did not seem imminent, the Afrikaners were still in full control, and population pressures were South Africa's most obvious threat; the chapter should have been called 'The Overcrowded Kraal'.

* * * * * * *

For my final few days in Africa I wanted to return to the Kruger National Park. I did so via one of the private game parks on its edge - Londolozi. 140,000 acres of bush – the dream of two brothers who wanted to create a wildlife paradise. They were working on 'habitat management' to create the maximum number of ideal conditions for wildlife, to ensure a wide range of birds, creatures, and flowers – from elephants and rhinos, to dung beetles and tree orchids. They were doing well with tourists:'There are still plenty of British coming, but the Americans have slowed down. That is one of the problems – if the economy does break down, or sanctions are put on – then we will be one of the first places to be put under pressure.'

If places like Londolozi were to suffer through outside influences or interference it would be tragic. Its wildlife was rich – including weaver birds, pygmy kingfishers and the rare side-striped jackal. We saw a female cheetah too, with five quarter-grown young, following their mother through the dappled light of bush – perfectly camouflaged.

Night drives were also undertaken in Londolozi in open vehicles, to see the bush at night. As we followed a male lion, periodically roaring, it suddenly rushed up a termite mound and started scooping out great paw-fulls of sand from a wart hog's hole. He worked with amazing speed and power, every now and then putting his head well down the hole for a better view, or a smell. It soon gave up however – the wart hogs must have been shaking with fright.

Finally I moved on to the Kruger proper. I had changed since my first visit years before. I remembered the disappointment of missing the lioness rushing at impala, and my wish to see a kill. As I was leaving on an overcast day, lions were in the final stage of a hunt, with lionesses accelerating after a wildebeest. I drove straight on – I did not want to see a death. To me the scene summed up Africa – death and conflict were endemic; I could never see the dust settling on the dark continent. I stopped and scribbled a few words on my notebook:

The Last Laager

Muscles, sinews – tense, taut.
Power – springing, running, leaping.
Claws – clutching, tearing, holding.
Frenzy – dragging, falling, dying.
Feeding – growling, purring, sleeping.
The wind whistles in the thorns.

I called them 'African Death'.

Reflections

After visiting Africa each year for nearly ten years, sometimes twice a year, I have not returned for well over a year. But if I sit quietly in my study and think of my journeys I can hear the cooing of the emerald spotted wood doves in the heat of the day, and the call of the francolin with the dew still on the grass. I see smiling faces, black and white – vast plains and deserts and sunsets colouring the entire sky. I see death too: shattered limbs and broken bodies lying in the sun, and smell the stench of animals beaten by thirst. I think of George Adamson too, that wonderful old man, gunned down quite needlessly by Shifta at his African paradise, on 20th August 1989. The realities of Africa have not changed for hundreds of years and there seems little likelihood that its course or destiny will change in the immediate future.

As I started *Dust in a Dark Continent*, the spectre of South Africa cast a lengthening shadow. It still does today, yet 'the world' seems intent on driving that vast and complex country into a corner where violence is the only answer. A healthy and prosperous South Africa would benefit most of the black African states who cry for its blood, but peace seems unwanted. Indeed to some, the image of South Africa is a godsend. It diverts attention away from the damage they have done and are still doing to their own countries, and if sanctions came, it would mean that they could increase the size of their international begging bowls.

When I was a boy I was told that one of the Christian commandments was to love your neighbour. Now I hear of Christians joining the advocates of hatred and even violence towards South Africa. It is strange, in the case of Russia we are told we should have more contacts, offer the hand of friendship – 'we will understand each other better then, and the more contacts we have, the easier it will be to influence and change the rigid Soviet system.' Over recent years that policy appears to have worked, although Estonia, my sister-in-law's home, is still an occupied country. In our attitudes towards South Africa, however, we are urged to take an opposite view.

The part played by the church in this is important. Jesus lived in a country in which he was denied certain rights, because of his race, and in which his people were dominated by an occupying, alien force. There was a strong nationalist movement, advocating violence against the Romans. Yet Jesus proclaimed peace and that people should live on a higher plane, based on love. When the Pharisees tried to trap him into a more political stance (St Matthew ch. 22 vv. 17-21), he was both amusing and contemptuous in his reply. The parallels between New Testament Israel and South Africa are unavoidable: as the death of Jesus approached, the people were offered the man of peace, or the release of Barrabas, the nationalist leader who advocated violence. If that scene had been re-enacted in South Africa recently, the cry would have been for the release of Nelson Mandela the nationalist leader, with many churchmen, including bishops, at the front of the mob.

Yet common sense dictates that South Africa needs help. Physical help for its rocketing Third World population and guarantees and safeguards for its minorities. Help and understanding are what it needs, threats and abuse are what it gets – making reaction and intransigence a certainty.

This back-to-front approach seems to reflect the thinking of our age. African nationalism is described as 'black consciousness', yet the white nationalism of the Afrikaners is called 'racism'. One-party despotic rule in black Africa is regarded as 'democracy'; any infringement of 'rights' by the South Africans, however small, is said to indicate a Police State. The South African government has done many senseless things and could have created a multiracial state years ago, but why should it be the one African country singled out for criticism and vitriol? It is also significant that in many Black African states the process of law has simply become an arm of government, the Party, or some passing despot. In South Africa its legal system and judiciary still offer a degree of protection for the ordinary citizen and put real limits on the powers of politicians and the police force.

In both Britain and America there is much smugness peddled about 'democracy.' We have certain 'freedoms', but the democracy of Britain leaves much to be desired. For instance, who picks British political candidates? Small unrepresentative cliques behind closed

Reflections 341

doors. Our democracy gives us the right to vote but for people we do not necessarily support or respect; they have already been chosen for us. 'Government by the people, for the people' is virtually unknown. Is this distorted system really one of which we should be proud? It is marginally better than the American way of government; that appears to be a self-indulgent game played by people with money – and a great deal of it.

In 1979 I was a political candidate at the British General Election. As the election drew near I had the temerity to speak out publicly about the way in which candidates were selected. Because of this, although in theory we are a country proud of our traditions of free speech, Conservative Central Office tried to get me 'de-selected'. They failed, but it was a strange manifestation of 'freedom'.

Once too, I worked as a civil servant and felt obliged to make public certain everyday matters of a non-security nature, as two senior politicians appeared to be misleading the country. I got sacked and threatened with prosecution for my trouble, for telling the truth as I saw it. The politicians were outraged; one of them has since departed this world – the other has been enobled. On the subject of freedom and democracy we can see the substantial mote in the South African eye, but we cannot see the beam in our own.

Many of the misconceptions we have in the West concerning Africa are due to the media coverage of the continent. Press, radio and television no longer report straightforward facts as 'news', they are too easily influenced by fashion, and whether the story has 'colour', and will it help boost circulation or viewing figures? Some people claim that this is 'political bias' – it is not, it is simply bad or dishonest reporting. It is surely time that offending newspapers and journalists were fined, or suspended, until journalistic integrity returns.

In 1986 the Chairman of the Conservative Party accused the BBC of political bias in its news bulletins; on the same day there was an item on the Corporation's 6pm News about South Africa. It reported that the South African government had produced a propaganda 'pop' record encouraging racial harmony. Two people were then interviewed: a record shop manager who was refusing to sell the record, and a coloured singer who refused to take part in the recording. There were many coloured singers who had taken part and many shops that had sold the record – viewers were not given the chance to hear their opinion. That was not political bias – simply bad, unbalanced reporting, which is accepted today as normal; consequently, by some people it is not even recognised.

During the last few years South Africa has made headlines at regular intervals – often over quite trivial incidents. During the same time other events have been virtually ignored; when the Bangladesh government closed down an opposition newspaper, one British paper covered it in just 18 words; the BBC seemed to miss it altogether. On the BBC, a report of 20 Brazilian miners being shot dead by police was mentioned in one sentence; not even a single sentence appeared in most English newspapers. The great issues and events of our age do not necessarily qualify as 'news'; their fate depends on what those with the editorial power think makes a good 'story'.

* * * * * * *

On leaving Kenya in 1984 at the start of the drought I tried to inform various people, including the BBC, of the approaching disaster. Only the *Daily Telegraph* showed the slightest interest. A year later, a year of hunger, the BBC showed film of the dead and dying. Why? Did death, suffering and grief make better television than warnings of drought? If I, as a country boy cum farmer cum do-it-yourself writer cum traveller, with limited money, could foresee starvation, why could not the BBC with its resources and its permanent staff abroad? Yet despite arriving a year late at the drought, the BBC then performed paroxysms of public self-congratulation for its alleged good work.

* * * * * * *

Since my journeys several changes have occurred. Not only was George Adamson murdered at Kora but, Koretta and her pride were poisoned by Somalis, and throughout Kenya elephant poaching has become out of control. In Zimbabwe the march towards a one-party state has continued and nobody was ever arrested for the murder of 'Boss' Lilford. More riots have occurred in Zambia, with none appearing on British television, as usual, and its economic plight has become even worse.

* * * * * * *

Reflections

But what of Africa? What will become of it, its peoples, its wildlife and its landscapes. Sadly, if current trends continue, I see little hope. I remember sitting, looking over Lake Malawi with Alistair, who said: 'Robin, you are lucky, you have seen Africa just before it is too late. I have seen it change. The truth is that West Africa should have been given its independence about now. East Africa should be getting it at the turn of the century, and Central and Southern Africa about the year 2,010, then it would have had a chance.'

Having seen the shambles of Zaire and Zambia; the tragedies of Zimbabwe and South Africa; and heard of the hardships in Mozambique, Tanzania, Uganda – and the rest – he could be right. I simply hope for a miracle.

Final Thoughts

After three weeks in Africa you want to write a book. After three months you want to write an article. After three years you realise how little you know, and you want to write nothing at all.
                                                                    Anon

To save the lives of babies and mitigate the suffering of mothers must be seen as a great and Christian Good. Death by starvation of tens of thousands, eventually millions, of people, and especially of children, can be seen only as a great Evil. Yet the first creates the second.
                                    Elspeth Huxley – *Out in the Midday Sun*

There is not another people in the history of the world which has been less corrupted by great power than the British, in spite of the poor view they themselves take of their own imperial past.
                                    Laurens van der Post – *The Heart of the Hunter*

I believe that the wildlife sanctuaries of Southern Africa as we know them now have got absolutely no future beyond the end of this century.
   There is every reason to believe that before the year 2010 South Africa itself will be facing the same problems as India and Bangladesh, namely an inability for much of the population to feed itself from land that has deteriorated almost beyond redemption.
                                    Dr John Hanks – Natal Parks Board 1976

It is ironical that the 'Apartheid' Government, so much under fire for racial discrimination in the Union of South Africa, has done far more to protect the Bushman in their part of the Kalahari in South West Africa than the British Government has done in its own.
                                    Laurens van der Post – *The Heart of the Hunter*

Acknowledgements

Without the help of many people and organisations this book would have been impossible. I am grateful to them – for all the assistance they provided, sometimes at personal cost and inconvenience – yet willingly and usually with a smile. A bed and a safari around rural Cambridgeshire will always be open to them.

The journeys themselves were only possible through the co-operation and assistance of my family – my parents for looking after my house and dog and my brother John for running the farm single-handed as usual. Then thanks are due to my mother, sister Rachael and sister-in-law Ellen, for reading the script and to Vicky Carlisle for editing the final draft and for coming to terms with my unique and bizarre form of spelling.

To many people in Africa my unreserved thanks are due – Mr John Matthews and his excellent airline South African Airways; Air Zimbabwe, the Royal Swazi National Airline, Egypt Air and Air Zimbabwe (British Airways is not included). The Zimbabwe Tourist Development Corporation, the Southern Africa Regional Tourism Council and the South African Tourism Council, Safari Interlink (Harare), Bateleur Safaris and Safari Camp Services (Nairobi), and Ecosafaris U.K. Ltd., 146 Gloucester Road, London, SW7 4SZ. An assortment of fine hotels showed great generosity; in Nairobi The Fairview and the Norfolk; in Zimbabwe – Meickles, the Karoi and the Cutty Sark (at Kariba); in Malawi – the Capital (Lilongwe), Ryall's (Blantyre) and Club Makokola; in Botswana – the Xaxaba Camp and the Tsaro Safari Lodge (Okavango Swamps – please call them swamps, tourist organisations, not 'Delta' – swamps are excellent places) – the list could go on – full details of all these places can be easily obtained from regional and national tourist offices around the world.

Many individuals have frequently made Africa seem like a second home. I have valued their company and their friendship – Africa is lucky to have them: Joe and Simonne Cheffings, Simon Evans, Ken

Mew, George Adamson, Frank Johnston, Brenda Bodde, Reg Nardi, Tim and Anne Nicklin and many more. Because of the uncertainties and sensitivities of Africa there are many others to whom my gratitude is due, but I will not name – I thank them most sincerely. They have all helped to make Africa a warm part of my memory.

* * * * * * *

For those wanting to help Africa's wildlife the following addresses will be useful:
The South African National Federation for the Conservation of Coastal Birds (SANCCOB), PO Box 17, Cape Province, South Africa.
The East African Wild Life Society, PO Box 20110, Nairobi, Kenya.
The Wildlife Conservation Society of Zambia, PO Box 30255, Lusaka, Zambia.